Politics in the Andes

Pitt Latin American Series

George Reid Andrews, General Editor

Politics in the Andes
Identity, Conflict, Reform

Edited by Jo-Marie Burt and Philip Mauceri

University of Pittsburgh Press

Published by the University of Pittsburgh Press, Pittsburgh, Pa., 15260

Copyright © 2004, University of Pittsburgh Press

Manufactured in the United States of America

Printed on acid-free paper

10 9 8 7 6 5 4 3 2 1

LIBRARY OF CONGRESS CATALOGING-IN-PUBLICATION DATA

Politics in the Andes : identity, conflict, reform / edited by Jo-Marie
   Burt and Philip Mauceri.
      p.   cm. – (Pitt Latin American series)
   Includes bibliographical references and index.
   ISBN 0-8229-4225-9 (cloth : alk. paper) – ISBN 0-8229-5828-7
   (pbk. : alk. paper)
      1. Andes Region–Politics and government–20th century.
   2. Democracy–Andes Region   3. Indians of South America–Andes
   Region–Ethnic identity.   4. Social change–Andes Region–History.
   5. Violence–Andes Region–History.   6. Drug traffic–Andes Region.
   I. Burt, Jo-Marie.   II. Mauceri, Philip.   III. Series.
   F2212 .P615 2004
   980.03'3–dc22

Contents

Tables and Figures

Acknowledgments

We began discussing this project at the Latin American Studies Association meeting in Chicago in 1998, where we were struck by the fact that while there was much intellectual ferment and innovative research occurring among scholars of the Andean region, there was little in the way of comparative analysis of the countries of the region. Our frustration extended beyond the arena of research to the classroom, where in teaching our classes on Latin American and comparative politics, we both struggled in finding useful and up-to-date works that addressed the problems of the Andean countries in a comparative perspective. As we discussed these issues with scholars and policy analysts, both in the United States and Latin America, we became convinced that a theoretically informed comparative volume on the countries of the Andean region would fill a major gap in the literature on Latin American politics. We hope that this book will meet that objective.

The editors would like to thank the many people who have helped us in producing this volume. Above all we wish to thank the contributors for their efforts and their patience as we coordinated the multiple rounds of comments and revisions across the hemisphere. Our efforts could not have succeeded without their spirit of scholarly commitment and community. We would also like to thank Cynthia McClintock and the anonymous reviewers for their insightful observations and comments on the manuscript. Our thanks also to William Nelson, who crafted the map of the Andean region, and to Tina Chwat, who did the research for the table in the introduction. Finally, we want to express our deep appreciation to Nathan MacBrien and the staff at the University of Pittsburgh Press for their professional advice, their sharp editorial judgment, and, above all, their good humor.

Each of us has incurred debts of our own as well. Philip Mauceri would like to thank the Graduate College of the University of Northern Iowa for providing a sabbatical during which much of the writing and coordinating of this project took place. In addition, the Fulbright Commission funded his stay in Colombia during the spring 2001 semester, a period that contributed to the sort of comparative thinking that was essential in helping to put this volume together.

Jo-Marie Burt would like to thank the College of Arts and Sciences at George Mason University for providing a sabbatical through the Mathy Fellowship Award, which provided the crucial time necessary to complete this project. The Department of Public and International Affairs at George Mason University also provided support and encouragement during this period. In addition, she would like to thank the Social Science Research Council, and in particular Latin America Program Officer Eric Hershberg, whose ongoing special project on the Andes has offered a stimulating environment for thinking about the region in comparative perspective.

As editors we worked collaboratively, and our names appear in alphabetical order. Although bringing this work to fruition has involved much work and time, we have both found it intellectually rewarding. We would finally like to thank our spouses, César Espejo and Miryam Antúnez de Mayolo, for providing us with the support and understanding that allowed us to sit for long hours in front of our computers and books and to do the field research without which scholarship is impossible.

Politics in the Andes

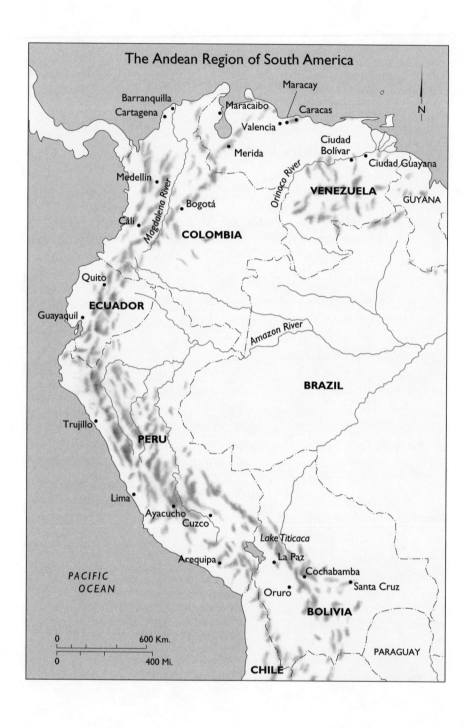

The Andean Region of South America

Jo-Marie Burt and Philip Mauceri

Introduction

ᗦᗩ Since the early 1990s, the Andean region of Latin America has been the most unstable and violent area in the hemisphere. The intensification of guerrilla, paramilitary, and drug violence in Colombia has raised the specter of the regionalization of a conflict that has persisted for decades. The weakness of political parties has strengthened the hand of the military elsewhere in the Andes, most notably in Peru, where democratic institutions were systematically undermined during the Fujimori administration. In Venezuela, President Hugo Chávez's caudillo-style government used executive powers to curtail and control the power of other governmental institutions, while in Ecuador the chronic inability to forge and maintain a governing coalition has resulted in weak governments, a presidential impeachment, and Latin America's first successful coup d'état in over a decade. The turmoil and violence that has affected the region have been accompanied by important social changes, particularly the emergence of previously excluded sectors as important political actors. New indigenous and women's organizations have challenged traditional relationships as they assert and redefine the nature of citizenship in their countries.

Although part of the Andean region's instability results from the continued difficulties in resolving ongoing political conflicts and institutionalizing democratic procedures and norms, persistent economic crises have also taken their toll. Over the last two decades, economic crises have taken different forms in the region, and policy responses have also varied. Although this makes it difficult to apply broad generalizations to the entire region, it also underscores how policy makers have responded in different ways to the opportunities and challenges confronting them. While neoliberal economics is often depicted as having triumphed throughout Latin America, the record of the Andean region in the last two decades suggests a more complex scenario. In Venezuela and Ecuador, resistance to International Monetary Fund (IMF) austerity packages by sectors of political and civil society has forestalled neoliberalism, while in Colombia, until the early 1990s, a record of steady economic growth—and the absence of populism—allowed the country to avoid the high debt levels and external pressures that were a prelude to neoliberal structural reforms elsewhere in the region. By contrast, external vulnerabilities in Peru and Bolivia led to significant neoliberal restructuring of their economies, although even here paths diverged, with Peru's unsuccessful "heterodox" experiment in the late 1980s leading the country into its worst crisis since the Great Depression before neoliberalism was imposed in the 1990s.

There is clearly a need for renewed attention to the nations of the Andes. Although comparative studies of the large countries of Latin America (Mexico, Brazil, Argentina) and the smaller countries of Central America and the Caribbean are common, there are few systematic book-length studies of the middle-sized countries of the Andes.[1] Building on a detailed comparative analysis, the current volume focuses on the key factors that have influenced political patterns in the region. A comparative analysis of the region is justified not only by the fact that the countries have faced a similar set of challenges during the last decades but by the fact that in many ways the problems the Andean region faces have diverged significantly from those confronting the other subregions of Latin America. In facing the challenges of neoliberalism and globalization, the medium-sized countries of the Andes lack the economic diversity and large internal markets of Brazil and Mexico, although they are also clearly in a more advantageous position than the largely monoculture economies of the Caribbean and Central America. Democratization in the Andes faces some of the same problems as elsewhere in Latin America, but the task of institutionalizing democratic norms and procedures in the region is made more complicated by the more intense, though varying, combinations of drug trafficking, corruption, violence and human rights abuses, fragmented party systems, weak national identity, and autocratic executives that seem to have plagued the Andean region. Here too there are important subregional differences that merit greater attention: while elites in Colombia and Venezuela engaged in pact-making in the 1950s in order to institutionalize relatively stable democratic governments, Ecuador, Peru, and Bolivia were classic praetorian societies suffering seemingly endless cycles of alternation between civilian and military rule. Recently, however, the challenges facing democratic governance in both Colombia and Venezuela have raised important questions about the viability of these institutions in an increasingly globalized world—questions that a comparative analysis of the region might help to inform.

Both state development and social organization in the Andes have been shaped by historically persistent factors shared by the five Andean countries. Yet political actors have responded in different ways to the challenges and opportunities these forces have presented. The purpose here is to flesh out the common historical forces that have shaped the region and the conditions created by the different choices, policies, and priorities of its actors. The book is organized around three specific themes: the struggle for identity; conflict, violence, and drug trafficking; and political change and democracy.

The Struggle for Identity

Ethnic and regional diversity in the Andes has been a significant source of political and social conflict since the creation of nation-states in the region. Indigenous rebellions, civil wars, border conflicts, caudillismo, and guerrilla insurgency are all manifestations of this diversity. The pattern of colonial settlement and later political and economic development accentuated social and regional cleavages and made the formation of national identity a difficult and to some extent an incomplete process, especially in the central Andean republics of Peru, Bolivia, and Ecuador (see table 0.1). Cleavages in each of the countries are the unique product of a particular national history, and not surprisingly, the specific path taken depends on the choices and opportunities of different national actors.

Ethnic cleavages exist throughout the Andes, and inclusionary reforms have been undertaken, with varying success, in almost every country. The 1991 constitution in Colombia guaranteed new political autonomy for indigenous groups and greater control of natural resources in their territories, as did the new constitution approved by a wide majority in a referendum in Venezuela in 1999. Ethnic-based identities are strongest in the central Andean countries of Ecuador, Peru, and Bolivia, with their larger indigenous populations, yet there is considerable variation in their salience. Bolivia, the only Andean nation to have experienced a social revolution, has seen the greatest integration of indigenous identity into national symbols and a substantial legitimation of Aymara culture. On the other hand, Peru's political elites, intellectuals, and indigenous leaders opted for a discourse that was overtly "classist" rather than ethnic/cultural. This led to an absence of significant indigenous organizations and a denigration of indigenous culture among elites. Still, Peru is the first Andean nation to elect a mestizo/cholo president (Alejandro Toledo, elected in 2001). Ecuador offers a third model of ethnic identity in the region, based on the gradual emergence of indigenous identity from below and a long and at times difficult effort to legitimize the political, cultural, and economic demands of the indigenous population and integrate them into the national agenda.

Sometimes overlapping with ethnicity, regional cleavages have exercised an important influence on the politics and economies of the Andes. Patterns of colonial settlement were reinforced by the structure of the emerging primary-product export economy to create highly unequal distributions of wealth and power within countries. The emergence of megacities like Caracas, Lima, and La Paz, with their multiple concentrations of populations, industry, and political power, has exacerbated these inequalities. Even Ecuador and Colombia, with their long histories of competing and conflicting regional elites, have not escaped this pattern.

The tradition of unitary government has historically been used to suppress regional autonomy, but this has not meant that strong central control has been established. Despite repeated efforts, central states throughout the region have had difficulty maintaining and establishing effective control in much of the countryside. Weak national identity and political unity have combined with geographical barriers to impede the exercise of strong state control outside of key population centers. Indirect rule through the power of local notables, caudillos, or landowners has thus been common, a situation that has exacerbated economic and political inequalities and limited the possibilities of reforms, particularly in the countryside. These trends have been accentuated in more recent decades by neoliberal economic policies, which have tended to further centralize economic decision-making in the hands of a centralized executive, often at the expense of regional and local government.

Ethnic and regional diversity presents a number of challenges to efforts at democratization. In addition to being a source of conflict and inequality, the lack of an integrated national identity has made the forging of notions of democratic citizenship and effective representation difficult. Recent trends in the region, particularly decentralization, including the democratic election of mayors and local officials previously appointed by the central government, offer some hope. Combined with the growing organization of indigenous groups and gender-based associations, these efforts may present effective challenges to the barriers that have impeded full national integration. It is important, however, to also assess whether decentralizing reforms contribute to democratization or further reinforce age-old practices of clientelism and corruption, and the degree to which social movements are engaged in practices that challenge established orders as opposed to defensive mobilizations that are easily co-opted by local and national elites.

Conflict, Violence, and Drug Trafficking

The Andean region has been the focal point of numerous internal conflicts during the twentieth century: rebellion and social revolution in Bolivia; guerrilla insurgencies in Peru; rebellions and military coups in Ecuador; civil wars and insurgency in Colombia; and military coups and rebellions in Venezuela. The human toll of these conflicts has been enormous, not to mention the social and economic dislocation caused by the virulence of the violence unleashed. Although the origins and course of all of these conflicts are unique to the countries involved, they have all tended to result in similar distortions at both the state and civil society levels. Political violence has resulted in the armed forces taking on increased control of the state apparatus, in certain situations coming close to militarizing the state in the name of "protecting" it. Militarization has been exacerbated in some cases, notably Colombia and Peru, by the emergence of paramilitary groups that are at least tacitly endorsed by state actors and by the U.S. funding of a "war on drugs" that has enhanced the power of the military even as civilians attempt to establish control over it. Social and political polarization has intensified dramatically with concomitant declines in institutional legitimacy and the ability to forge a programmatic consensus. Finally, egregious human rights records reflect a pattern of abuse that political actors and the population at large increasingly accept as tolerable, thus making the establishment of democratic norms and procedures more difficult.

The continued power of state security forces, especially the armed forces, which have maintained traditional prerogatives and thus limited democratic accountability, remains a significant obstacle to deepening democracy. Historically, one of the few national institutions with legitimacy and effective organizational capacity was the armed forces, which took on a dominating political role in the aftermath of independence. A clear exception to this pattern was Colombia, which has had few experiences with direct military rule. The historic dominance of the two traditional Colombian parties (Liberal and Conservative) has been an important factor in limiting the development of a strong institutional identity within the military. Elsewhere in the region, however, the lack of early party-system consolidation created a political vacuum usually filled by the armed forces. Long-standing traditions of military autonomy on such issues as budgets, missions, and training have had a pernicious effect on civil-military relations by restricting civilian oversight and control of the armed forces. Moreover, civilian leaders and institutions have often turned to the armed forces for political support or to help carry out policies: witness the use of the military to suppress labor, peasant, and student protests by Colombian administrations in the 1970s and 1980s; the reliance of the Fujimori government on the military for support of its "self-coup" in 1992; the alliance between sectors of the indigenous movement and the military in ousting a sitting president in Ecuador in 2000; and the failed coup of April 2002 in Venezuela, which was closely coordinated between the military high command and business leaders. This situation has been worsened by cycles of political violence in which the military has engaged in human rights abuses with impunity. Massacres, torture, forced disappearances, and extrajudicial executions are an unfortunate part of the reality of those countries that have experienced internal conflicts.

Violence in the region has been exacerbated since the early 1980s by the dramatic growth in narco-trafficking. Exploding demand for cocaine in the

United States and Europe laid the basis for the emergence of powerful organized criminal syndicates willing and able to use violence to achieve their ends. The "narco-terrorism" that Colombia experienced in the early 1990s, which led to the assassination of four presidential candidates and a wave of terrorist attacks, stands as a reminder of the political distortions created by the narcotics trade. The breakup of the large Colombian cartels in the early 1990s, initially seen as a victory in the war on drugs, has only led to the emergence of smaller, although still powerful, groups throughout the region. Money from the drug trade has become an important source of funding for guerrillas and paramilitary groups in Colombia and has corrupted political parties, government officials, militaries, and civil society actors throughout the Andes.

Narco-trafficking has also brought renewed pressures on the region from the United States. The decertification of Colombia during the Samper administration (1994–98) was a reminder of the continued dependence of the region on U.S. economic and military assistance. The launching of Plan Colombia in 1998, and its later expansion into the Andean Regional Initiative, has deepened U.S. involvement in a region that historically has been tangential to U.S. interests. It has also distorted U.S. priorities. The United States supported the authoritarian government of Alberto Fujimori during the 1990s in part because of Peru's commitment to Washington's supply-side antidrug strategy and its adoption of extreme tactics, such as the shooting down of civilian planes. Although many of these problems were restricted to Colombia, Peru, and Bolivia, they have now spread throughout the region and present a significant challenge to the consolidation of democracy as well as social and economic stability in the region.

Political Change and Democracy

All of the countries of the Andes have had a tentative and incomplete experience with liberal democratic institutions. Through much of the nineteenth and twentieth centuries, military dictatorships and/or oligarchic democracies effectively limited political participation and rights for the majority of the population in the region. After World War II efforts to establish democratic institutions accelerated but were hampered by inequality, political violence, weak civil societies, and the continued power of the armed forces. Venezuela and Colombia were the most successful countries in the region in creating liberal democratic institutions, including strong political parties, a marked contrast to the central Andean republics, which despite the existence of historic parties such as the Nationalist Revolutionary Movement (MNR) in Bolivia and the American Popular Revolutionary Alliance (APRA) in Peru, failed to consolidate viable party systems. At the same time, however, the functioning of Venezuelan and Colombian democracy relied heavily on both explicit and implicit restrictions on participation and the possibility of reform. The 1990s witnessed significant efforts at institutional reform in the region, but this has not indicated a clear pattern toward greater institutional democratization. While constitutional reforms in Colombia (1991) and Bolivia (1994) were aimed at providing greater local government autonomy and new rights for indigenous peoples, clearly opening the political field to new contenders, in some cases they have also provided governing elites with new opportunities for clientelistic forms of co-optation and control. The new constitutions adopted in Peru (1993) and Venezuela (1998), while including some interesting innovations (such as an ombudsman's office in the Peruvian case), primarily strengthened the powers of presidents at the cost of local governments and legislatures.

Particularly in the central Andean republics, political parties have grown even weaker, giving rise to an alarming personalization of politics that presents a serious challenge to the consolidation of democracy in the region. In Ecuador, Peru, and Bolivia, party systems have become increasingly fragmented, with electoral competition focusing on "independents" and ever-changing lists of notables. With little internal structure, national organization, or programmatic interests, these "parties" are short-lived and have accelerated the tendency toward the personalization of electoral politics. The lack of a structured political society has increased the level of unpredictability in electoral politics and blurred the political spectrum, allowing politicians to base their campaigns on contradictory promises or to simply abandon their promises once elected. The ever-changing acronyms that dominate political society confuse voters and allow politicians to switch allies and programs without concern for party loyalty or organizational accountability, contributing to a growing cynicism about the electoral process.

Venezuela and Colombia, which managed to preserve a modicum of electoral democracy from the 1960s onward, have not been exempt from the disintegration of political society in the region. In both cases, the inability of political society to adapt to social and economic changes, corruption, and fierce factionalization has led to the decline of traditional political parties. The stunning election of President Hugo Chávez in Venezuela and the virtual electoral disappearance of the two traditional parties—Democratic Action and COPEI (Partido Social Cristiano de Venezuela)—reconfigured the country's electoral map. In Colombia, the gradual emergence of independents, particularly at the local level, the disappearance of significant differences between Liberals and Conservatives, the rapid growth of multiple electoral lists by the two parties, declining state resources to support traditional clientelism, and growing levels of extrasystemic violence have all represented a significant challenge to two-party dominance. While the traditional party systems in both countries were fraught with corruption and clientelism and were far from fully representative of their diverse societies, it should also be emphasized that the decline of these parties without an adequate reordering of political society could result in new dangers, from military coups and caudillismo to outright civil wars. In both cases, the final outcome of many of these changes remains to be seen, although electoral instability in the coming years is almost a given.

Throughout the region, clientelism has endured as a way to link parties with their supporters and the state with society. Even where traditional parties have decayed, politicians such as Alberto Fujimori have created clientelist networks upon which they base their support. With their unequal power relations, clientelist networks have contributed to the persistent corruption and authoritarian practices of the region's political elites. The inability of political society to develop more open and accountable forms of relating with citizens represents a continuing challenge for the region. Internal democratization of the parties, new laws that regulate campaign financing and media access, and limitations on the political usages of governmental bureaucracies are among the reforms that remain to be considered in much of the region.

Weak civil societies have proved fertile ground for the persistence of clientelist practices. Violence, state repression, ethnic and regional cleavages, and high rates of poverty and inequality have all conspired to limit the possibility of developing civil society organizations. Although the 1980s and 1990s witnessed a growth of autonomous social organizations throughout the Andes, for the most part, they remain weak and vulnerable to economic pressure and outside manipulation. Still, there are clear differences in civil society organization throughout the region that are likely to shape future developments. One notable pattern is the link between these organizations and parties. Where civil society organizations in Venezuela and Bolivia had close relations with the traditional parties (with labor unions as virtual creations of the dominant reformist parties), those in Ecuador and Peru had greater autonomy, but not necessarily more political influence. The growing personalization and fragmentation of the party system in the region may thus provide civil society organizations an opportunity to gain both greater autonomy and greater influence, as appears to be the case with the indigenous movement in Ecuador. The role of Peru's civil society groups in challenging the Fujimori regime's fraudulent 2000 reelection suggests a more active if still limited role for these organizations.

Clientelism, corruption, and the difficulty in establishing citizen representation are to a large extent the result of persistent social and economic inequalities in the region. The lack of a sustainable development model that effectively reduces poverty and inequality remains a significant problem for the deepening of democracy in the region. Economic development throughout the Andean region in the nineteenth and early twentieth centuries was based on a primary-product export model that linked these countries with Europe and North America. Tin, petroleum, copper, coffee, bananas, and sugar were and continue to be the region's main sources of income. While all of the countries in the postwar period adopted some variation of state-led development to deal with the difficulties posed by external dependence, there was considerable variation in the types of policies adopted and their implementation.

The central Andean countries of Ecuador, Peru, and Bolivia fared worst. Sharp swings in policy directions, poor implementation, and uneven export income produced persistently weak currencies, high external debts, balance of payments crises, and bouts of hyperinflation. Continued high rates of poverty and income inequality have resulted in persistently low standards of living for the vast majority of the population. Macroeconomic instability also contributed to an accentuation of external dependence. International financial actors, particularly private banks and lending agencies such as the IMF and the World Bank, acquired an increased role in determining policy priorities. Economic crises prompted governments to put forward a series of IMF austerity packages, the burden of which have fallen most heavily on the lower classes. Not surprisingly, such measures provoked sustained opposition, including strikes, demonstrations, electoral backlashes against governing parties, and even military rebellions, though resistance to austerity and the neoliberal restructuring of the economy has varied. The strongest opposition has been evident in Ecuador, where successive mobilizations by civil society helped overturn or stall neoliberal measures, with the least effective resistance in Bolivia (until recently, as witnessed by an explosion of protests against neoliberal measures, such as the 2000 protests against the privatization of public utilities). In Venezuela, Hugo Chávez came to power on the heels of anti-neoliberal protests. Meanwhile, in Peru, the turn to "heterodoxy" under President Alan García in the 1985–89 period, in defiance of international financial actors, was quickly followed by the more orthodox policies of the 1990s under the Fujimori administration.

By contrast, Venezuela and Colombia offer two distinctly different patterns from those found in the central Andes. From the 1960s through the mid-1980s both countries were more consistent than their central Andean counterparts in economic policy-making, and both enjoyed substantial growth and even poverty reduction. (The resulting improved living standards are evident in the socioeconomic indicators listed in table 0.1.) In Venezuela, the petroleum export boom provided the state with the wherewithal to fund distributive policies, build infrastructure, and avoid high external debts or currency crises. Colombia kept its exchange levels at reasonable levels, stimulated the economy through modest expenditures, and successfully diversified its export base beyond coffee into other profitable products, including manufactures. Yet by the 1990s both of these countries were facing economic slowdowns. Declines in the price of petroleum between the late 1980s and late 1990s led to a crisis in Venezuela reminiscent of prior crises in the central Andean nations. The political repercussions were felt almost immediately, starting with the 1989 Caracazo protests that left hundreds dead. Continued protests of neoliberal austerity throughout the early 1990s finally culminated in the rise of President Hugo Chávez, elected in 1998 on an explicit promise to reduce poverty and end policies that result in economic inequalities. The economic consequences in Colombia of economic restructuring have also been severe. The gradual adoption of neoliberal policies during the Gaviria administration led to a decade-long slowdown and by 2000 the highest unemployment rate (20 percent) in Latin America. Politically, the gradual erosion of the traditional parties and perhaps most importantly the exponential growth of the Revolutionary Armed Forces of Colombia (FARC) in the 1990s attest to the long-term challenges confronting the country.

The lack of sustainable development models in the region, combined with internal market distortions and external vulnerabilities, has been a major source of concentration of wealth, income inequality, and persistent poverty. Governmental policies have failed to meet the basic needs of citizens, and this is as true for "populist" governments as it is for more conservative governments. The sizable proportion of people engaged in the informal economy has not only distorted the economy and state development in tangible ways—that is, by limiting tax revenues—but has made it more difficult to design policies capable of breaking cycles of poverty. Meanwhile, corruption, drug trafficking, high rates of military spending, and mounting foreign debt continue to siphon off resources that could be used to meet basic needs.

Organization of the Book

Part 1 of *Politics in the Andes* examines the issue of social identity in the Andes and the ways identity has shaped political conflict and representation in the region. Chapter 1, by Xavier Albó, provides a historical overview of the role of indigenous organizations in the central Andean countries, focusing special attention on the factors that have led to an indigenous "awakening" over the last three decades. Jennifer Collins's chapter focuses on Ecuador, a crucial case study of indigenous mobilization, where ethnic-based organizations have become important social and political players. Collins argues that the indigenous movement has had a positive impact on democratization by channeling the demands and participation of a previously excluded sector of the population. Amy Lind rounds out the discussion by analyzing the changes in women's political practices in the context of neoliberal economic and social policies in Ecuador and Bolivia. The rise of new women's organizations such as communal kitchens in the context of economic and political restructuring has brought both fortune and misfortune to women. While they have gained increased political space both within governmental institutions and in the nongovernmental arena, women's organizations have remained fragmented and often vulnerable to clientelist manipulation by political parties or state organizations.

Part 2 focuses on explaining the high level of violence, human rights abuses, and drug trafficking in the region. Fernando Coronil and Julie Skurski analyze the semantics of political violence in Venezuela. Focusing on violent confrontations in the late 1980s in a nation that at the time was held out as a model democracy, Coronil and Skurski argue that violence played an important role in defining and reordering politics in the country and relate that violence, by no means unique to Venezuela, to new forms of social relations that have begun to emerge in the globalized era. Examining the case of Colombia, Ricardo Vargas emphasizes the importance of regional dynamics in the drug trade. Arguing that the link between drugs, violence, and politics begins at the local level, Vargas reminds the reader that simply destroying coca fields can often exacerbate political problems and violence. Coletta A. Youngers focuses specifically on how the U.S.-sponsored "war on drugs" has distorted regional priorities. Comparing the situations in Colombia, Peru, and Bolivia, Youngers argues that U.S. involvement in the region has led to unholy alliances with militaries that have deplorable human rights records and are often involved in the drug trade themselves, with serious negative consequences for nascent democratic institutions. Philip Mauceri offers some comparisons between violence in Colombia and Peru, arguing that national and local elites and their relation with the state are significant in explaining how states respond to violence. Mauceri suggests that Colombia's historic preference for a "privatization and abdication" model and Peru's adoption of an "authoritarian reengineering" model of counterinsurgency in the 1990s have less to do with state weakness and more to do with state-elite relations. Finally, Mark Ungar examines the issue of human rights in the Andes, focusing his attention on the development of new state institutions, such as ombudsman offices, to defend human rights and hold states accountable. Although they are promising, Ungar finds that such institutions are often subject to the sort of political attacks and bureaucratic inefficiency that undermine many state institutions in the Andes.

In Part 3, the authors focus on evaluating challenges facing democracy in the region. In her analysis of Ecuador, Liisa L. North examines the dynamic between a dependent economy and rising social demands, arguing that the

TABLE 0.1 Human Development, Demographics, Poverty, and Inequality in the Andes

	Bolivia	Colombia	Ecuador	Peru	Venezuela
Human Development Index (HDI)					
HDI rank	104	62	84	73	61
Life expectancy at birth (years)	62.0	70.9	69.8	68.5	72.7
Gross domestic product					
(GDP)/capita (US$)	2,355	5,749	2,994	4,622	6,495
GDP growth (annual %), year 2000[a]	3	3	2	4	3
Total debt/GDP, year 2000[b]	83	44	105	53	31
Demographic Trends					
Total population (millions)					
Year 1975	4.8	25.4	6.9	15.2	12.7
Year 1999	8.1	41.4	12.4	25.2	23.7
Year 2015	11.2	52.6	15.9	31.9	30.9
Annual population growth rate (%)					
Years 1975–99	2.2	2.0	2.4	2.1	2.6
Years 1999–2015	2.0	1.5	1.6	1.5	1.7
Urban population (% of total)					
Year 1975	41.5	60.7	42.4	61.5	75.7
Year 1999	61.9	73.5	64.3	72.4	86.6
Year 2015	70.1	79.1	75.8	77.9	90
Population under age 15 (% of total)					
Year 1999	39.8	33.1	34.3	33.9	34.5
Year 2015	33.7	27.0	27.1	26.7	27.6
Ethnic composition of population (% of total)[e]					
Indigenous	55	1	25	45	2
Mestizo	30	58	65[f]	37	65
White	15	20		15	20
Black		4	3		10
Other		17	7	3[g]	3
Poverty and Income Distribution					
Adult illiteracy rate (% above age 15)	15.0	8.5	9.0	10.4	7.7
Population below national poverty line (%)					
1984–99[c]	n/a	17.7	35.0	49.0	31.3
Population living on less than $1 a day (%)					
(1993 US$) 1983–99[c]	29.4	11.0	20.2	15.5	18.7
Survival					
Life expectancy at birth (years)					
Years 1970–75	46.7	61.6	58.8	55.4	65.7
Years 1995–2000	61.4	70.4	69.5	68.0	72.4
Infant mortality rate (per 1,000 live births)					
Year 1970	144	70	87	115	47
Year 1999	64	26	27	42	20
Under-5 mortality rate (per 1,000 live births)					
Year 1970	243	113	140	178	61
Year 1999	83	31	35	52	23
Maternal mortality/100,000 live births,					
year 1990	373	107	150	280	200
Maternal mortality/100,000 live births					
1980–99[c]	170	80	160	270	60

TABLE 0.1 *(Continued)*

	Bolivia	Colombia	Ecuador	Peru	Venezuela
Inequality in Income or Consumption					
Survey year	1997	1996	1995	1996	1997
Share of income or consumption (%)					
Poorest 10%	0.5	1.1	2.2	1.6	1.6
Poorest 20%	1.9	3.0	5.4	4.4	4.1
Richest 20%	61.8	60.9	49.7	51.2	53.7
Richest 10%	45.7	46.1	33.8	35.4	37.6
Inequality measures					
Richest 10% to poorest 10%	91.4	42.7	15.4	22.3	24.3
Richest 20% to poorest 20%	32.0	20.3	9.2	11.7	13.0
Gini Index[d]	58.9	57.1	43.7	46.2	48.8

SOURCE: All data is from the UNDP 2001 Human Development Report, unless noted.
NOTES: All years other than 1999 are noted.
a. Data from World Bank. Available at <http://www.devdata.worldbank.org>.
b. Data from USAID. Available at <http://qesdb.cdie.org/lac/index.html>.
c. Results are averages of the years noted.
d. The Gini Index is a common statistical indicator of inequality, with 0 representing perfect equality and 100 perfect inequality.
e. Ethnic composition statistics for Bolivia, Columbia, Ecuador, and Peru are from *The Columbia Encyclopedia*. 6th edition. (New York: Columbia University Press, 2003). For Venezuela, *The World Factbook*. (Washington, D.C.: Central Intelligence Agency, 2002).
f. Includes "white" as category
g. Includes Peruvians of African, Japanese, and Chinese descent.

country's economic model has been catastrophic for both social and political stability. Engaging in a broad historical analysis, North concludes that Ecuador's economic elite and its political allies have at critical moments blocked the possibility of significant redistributive reforms or alternative development strategies, a strategy that in turn has provoked financial crises and political instability. In their chapter on Venezuela, Margarita López Maya and Luis E. Lander evaluate the implications of Hugo Chávez's rapid rise to power for Venezuelan democracy. The authors suggest that Venezuela is undergoing a "recomposition of hegemony" that is radically transforming the country and creating an unprecedented level of indeterminacy in the political system. Examining Colombia's evolving political system, Francisco Gutiérrez Sanin and Luisa Ramírez Rueda undertake one of the few analyses that tie changing electoral and party dynamics to the political violence that affects the country. The authors raise an important question: How to characterize a political system that incorporates electoral competition and is relatively open to participation and at the same time has low levels of protection for political actors as well as ordinary citizens? Finally, Jo-Marie Burt examines the process of state breakdown in Peru in the 1980s, arguing that this is a key variable in understanding the rise of an extremely personalistic and authoritarian regime in the

1990s. The process of rebuilding state institutions under the Fujimori regime, she argues, became inimical to the imperative of building democracy and offers important lessons for other countries, such as Colombia, that have similarly experienced significant state breakdown.

In the conclusion, Jo-Marie Burt and Philip Mauceri return to these themes and attempt to place them in the context of wider-ranging trends in Latin America as well as within the current scholarly debate regarding democratization, economic reform, and social identity. The objective of *Politics in the Andes* is to highlight some of the unique contexts and processes occurring in the Andean region but also to provoke theoretical and comparative analyses with other regions of Latin America and the world that face some of the same challenges. We hope this book will provide the necessary context to understand the unfolding and often dramatic events in the Andes and allow the interested reader to see beyond the sensational news of the moment and link events to broader historical, political, economic, and social trends.

I The Struggle for Identity

Xavier Albó

1 Ethnic Identity and Politics in the Central Andes

The Cases of Bolivia, Ecuador, and Peru

As part of the Viceroyalty of Peru during Spanish colonial rule, the three states of the central Andes—Bolivia, Ecuador, and Peru—shared a relatively similar history. In the pre-Columbian period this area was part of the Inca Empire, which extended from southern Colombia to northern Chile. It was in the aftermath of the independence wars of the nineteenth century that the current separate states emerged, creating divisions that have led to wars and left behind a legacy of resentments. Within these states there live approximately thirteen million indigenous people belonging to numerous nations, each with their own particular identity.[1] The borders of the present states, which were created without their consent, have divided many of these nations. The largest group—the Quechua or Quichua, with more than ten million people and some thirty dialects—can be found from southern Colombia through northern Argentina. The second-largest group, with approximately two million people, is the Aymara, who since the War of the Pacific (1879–80) between Chile, Peru, and Bolivia have lived divided among these three states. Most of the remaining nations live dispersed in the vast Amazonian basin, divided into forty ethno-linguistic groups in Peru, over thirty in Bolivia, and nine in Ecuador and totaling over seven hundred thousand people. How have these ethnic identities interacted with national identities? In order to answer this question, I will examine their development across time, emphasizing in particular the organization and identity found among indigenous peoples rather than government policy toward the indigenous.

History and Identity

The Inca Empire, known as Tawantisuyu or "the four united districts," incorporated a large territory and numerous groups through conquest. However, its existence was short-lived, lasting barely a century. Could Tawantisuyu have created a common identity among the various nations it encompassed? In the pre-Columbian period, it is difficult to speak of clear

"Quechua" or "Aymara" identities. The people of the central Andes most likely identified with their immediate surroundings, *ayllus* (kinship-based indigenous communities), or a federation of local *ayllus*. It is not known exactly what role language and dialects had in establishing identity in this period, and we cannot say with any certainty that the linguistic groups in the pre-Columbian era corresponded to current divisions (Bouysse-Cassagne 1987, 2). It is more likely that language divisions corresponded with ecological zones rather than political districts. The identification of Quechuas and Aymaras as homogenous groups, each with its own language, was largely the result of changes that occurred during the colonial period. These changes included the relocation of *ayllus* and indigenous communities to newly created towns, for purposes of tax collection and religious evangelization. This process gradually reduced the links between ethnic identity and *ayllus*. By the eighteenth century, the association of ethnic identity with *ayllus* or local dialectics had been transformed into an identity linked with one of two language groups—Quechua and Aymara—that were tied to specific geographic regions.

At the end of the eighteenth century the rebellions of Tupac Amaru (in Cuzco, Viceroyalty of Peru) and the Katari brothers (in Charcas, Viceroyalty of La Plata) occurred. Tupac Amaru's rebellion took place largely in Quechua-speaking zones, while the Katari rebellion occurred in Aymara zones. When the leaders of both rebellions met at the siege of La Paz in 1781, there was some tension due to the linguistic and geographic differences between them. Despite these differences, however, there was a surprising degree of unity between the two groups. In order to repress these rebellions, forces from outside the region were required.[2] The experience of these rebellions and their suppression suggest that loyalties and identities were not easily shifted, despite continued jurisdictional changes throughout the colonial period. These changes were especially common toward the end of the colonial period. For example, in the south, the adjustment of frontiers between Peru and La Plata divided the Aymara population, with largely Aymara-speaking Puno passing into Peru's jurisdiction; in the north, Maynas's jurisdiction shifted from Nueva Granada to Peru, dividing the Jibaro (Shuar) population.

The New Republics

The creation of new states in the aftermath of independence further divided indigenous peoples. Upper and lower Peru became the modern states of Bolivia (1825) and Peru (1821), effectively dividing the Aymara population. The Audiencia of Quito, which had been part of Peru and then Nueva Granada, initially became part of the new state of Gran Colombia. With the breakup of this state, the new state of Ecuador was created in 1830 from what had largely been the old Audiencia. Needless to say, indigenous identities and loyalties were not taken into account during the formation of these new states. The new oligarchic republics controlled by Creole elites intent on imitating European styles viewed the indigenous mostly as cannon fodder during the wars of independence and later conflicts and as sources of cheap labor and revenue, collected through special indigenous taxes. When the expansion of primary-product exports later in the nineteenth century provided new sources for state taxes, the tributes of communal lands were no longer needed, and encroachment on these lands increased to create new haciendas, especially if these could provide new export commodities, such as alpaca wool, or provide access to the new railroads. For the indigenous populations of the central Andes, "independence" was a cruel misnomer.

Competition for access to raw materials was behind numerous interstate conflicts in the region during the nineteenth and twentieth centuries and had important implications for indigenous peoples. The War of the Pacific (1879–82) between Peru, Bolivia, and Chile, fought largely over access to rich nitrate mines, resulted in Chile's conquest of Aymara-speaking parts of Peru and Bolivia, further dividing the Aymaras. Increased demand for quinine and rubber led to the loss of Bolivia's Acre region to Brazil, while the Chaco War of 1932–35 led to Bolivia's loss of oil-rich lands to Paraguay. Continued border conflicts between Ecuador and Peru, begun in the War of 1942, revolved around access to the Amazon River. This latter conflict appeared to end only in 1998, with a final agreement between both sides marking the established border in the Amazonian region.

These conflicts all occurred in areas where the indigenous population was numerous. Although not involved in the issues being fought over, indigenous peoples suffered the consequences of these wars, including being targets of attack by the "enemy state" and displacement and loss of land. During the Chaco War, the Guaraní Chiriguano were considered traitorous by both sides and were often forcibly removed from their lands. The traditional leader of this group, the *mburuvicha,* was shot by Bolivian troops, and the Guaraní Chiriguano had their lands expropriated by the expanding cattle ranching of the region. As a result of the Peru-Ecuador conflict, four indigenous groups were divided and forced to pledge their loyalty to one of the states. The Shuar in Ecuador and the Aguaruna in Peru, along with the Guambisa and Achuar, who were divided across the frontier, were recruited by the rival armies and— appealing to their warrior traditions—taught to view their indigenous brothers on the other side of the border as enemies to be fought. Overnight, the indigenous were transformed from savages into brave defenders of the threatened fatherland (Endara 1998, 107–9).

The encroachment of haciendas on traditional indigenous communities during the nineteenth and early twentieth centuries continued a process that had begun during the colonial period. Paradoxically, the liberal rhetoric of "progress" fostered a racist ideology and feudal labor relations such as *huasipungo* in Ecuador, *yanaconaje* in Peru, and *pongueaje* in Bolivia. The ideology and practice of the dominant social classes adeptly combined the colonial social caste system with the ideas of racial superiority found in social Darwinism and the private property rights of economic liberalism. These ideas and the repression that accompanied them did not go unchallenged. Indigenous resistance could be found in the hundreds of rebellions that occurred, many of which ended in bloody massacres. Among the most notable were those of Fernando Daquilema, known as the "last guaminga," and the legendary Dolores Cacuango in Ecuador; Zarate Vilca, Santos Marca Tola, and others of the Cacical movement in Bolivia; and the mestizo military officer Teodoro Gutiérrez in Peru, who declared himself Rumi Maki and led thousands of followers against the Peruvian state.

In the aftermath of the Mexican and Russian Revolutions, indigenous organizations and rebellions became increasingly linked to political parties of the left with a classist discourse and a focus on land reform. As agrarian reforms were implemented, they began to weaken the traditional feudal hacienda system that had been in place since colonialism. The first reform, and the most revolutionary and participatory one, occurred in Bolivia in 1953. In Ecuador and Peru, the reforms were slower in coming and implemented in a vertical fashion: in 1964 and 1972 in Ecuador and in 1964 and 1969 in Peru. The Peruvian reform, which occurred during the radical military government of Juan Velasco Alvarado (1968–75), promoted large agrarian cooperatives but largely ignored traditional indigenous communities. As the reform process continued, particularly in Peru and Bolivia, the issue of ethnicity became blurred, as the term "campesino" began to replace "indio" to describe the indigenous inhabitants of the Andean region. The term "indígena" was increasingly used only to describe the peoples of the Amazonian rain forest. This shift in discourse, which was used both by the political left and right, appeared to put an end to the divide between ethnic identity and nation-state identity. But as we shall see, this situation was only a temporary pause in an ongoing negotiation between identities that is linked to historical context and the deliberate strategies of social actors (Baud et al. 1996).

From Campesinos to Ethnic Nations

The campesino identities fostered by nation-states and political actors and adopted by many agrarian interests could not sweep away the rich culture of the indigenous, which was still alive in the organizations, celebrations, and everyday aspects of communal life. The continued defense of communal space by indigenous communities during and since the colonial period is an indication of their ability to preserve their culture and local political practices. As the Aymara intellectual Víctor Hugo Cárdenas has noted, the indigenous community in many ways represents a "mini-state."

Nonindigenous Politicians and Intellectuals

Anthropological studies and literary and artistic representations of indigenous communities proliferated at the start of the twentieth century. The indigenous were a source of inspiration for artists and intellectuals, who also denounced their poor social conditions. By the 1950s many intellectuals had adopted the idea that emerged from the Mexican Revolution, that nation-states should define themselves as "mestizo." As President Lazaro Cárdenas noted at the first Inter-American Indigenist Congress in Patzacuaro (1940), "Our 'indigenismo' does not Indianize Mexico, but Mexicanizes the Indian."[3] This became the approach of the National Revolutionary Movement (MNR) in Bolivia in the wake of the 1952 revolution. In Ecuador, the National Culture Law of 1972 noted that "all Ecuadorians are part indigenous," implying that those who are completely indigenous cannot be Ecuadorians.[4] In Peru, the Velasco government opened up the issue of national identity even further, making Quechua a recognized national language (something Bolivia's MNR never considered), publishing a Quechua-language newspaper—*Cronicawan*—and giving Tupac Amaru a new place in the history of the country. All of the above clearly served the reformist and nationalist goals of the military government (Morin 1983, 212–39).

The main nonindigenous intellectual of this period who developed a truly "Indian" proposal was the Bolivian Fausto Reinaga (1969), who as a result was marginalized by most of his colleagues. There are no equivalent intellectuals in Ecuador, although a lively debate between indigenists and classists took place, mostly on the political left. In Peru the sociologist Aníbal Quijano began a discussion not about the "Indian" issue but on the emergence of "cholos," a name that is given by the nonindigenous to those Indians who attempt to become mestizos, mostly migrants to the cities. Significantly, Quijano did not publish his text, written originally in 1964, until 1979, largely for lack of an adequate conceptual and sociopolitical atmosphere in his country. The term "cholo" has now gained common currency in Peru and to a lesser extent in Bolivia.[5] In contrast, in Ecuador the ethnic categories used are either indigenous or mestizo-white.

The Indigenous Awakening

By the early 1970s, the assimilationist model began to decline, replaced by the growth of indigenous organizations and discourses that emphasized an autonomous indigenous identity. The first expression of this awakening did not occur in the Andean highlands but in the Amazonian basin of Ecuador, specifically among the Shuar. Starting in the early 1960s, Salesian missionaries helped organize the first Shuar Centers to promote economic and social development, which later evolved into the Federation of Shuar Centers. This spurred the formation of other indigenous organizations in the Amazonian region, particularly after 1972, when the presence of oil companies dramatically increased. This organizational process culminated in 1980 with the formation of the Confederation of the Indigenous Nationalities of the Ecuadorian Amazon (CONFENIAE), which was the first group to use the term "nationality" to identify itself, an element that would become key in all later movements. In this way, the indigenous movement helped rescue the concept of "nationality" and separate it from the notion of nation-state.

In the Peruvian Amazonian region a similar organizational process started with the meeting of an Amuesha Congress in 1968, followed by the formation of an Aguaruna and Huambisa (close relatives of the Shuar) Council and eventually by the creation of the Shipibo Native Community Defense Front. Between 1977 and 1980 the three organizations formed the Interethnic Development Association of the Peruvian Rainforest (AIDESEP), which has gradually become the principal voice for Amazonian peoples in Peru. In Bolivia, inspired by AIDESEP, indigenous groups in the forest lowlands created the Confederation of Indigenous Peoples of Lowland Bolivia (CIDOB). Initially a hierarchical organization, it was gradually joined by other grassroots organizations such as the Assembly of Guaraní Peoples (APG), founded in 1982.

The first organizational efforts among the highland indigenous of the Andes occurred in Bolivia in the late 1960s with the formation of the Katarista Movement, named after Tupaj Katari, an Aymara leader of the 1780–81 rebellions. Concentrated among the Aymara of La Paz and Oruro, the movement grew rapidly, by 1971 taking over the principal campesino organizations, which until then had been associated with the MNR. After General Hugo Banzer's coup (1971), the group organized clandestinely until 1977, when it reemerged to again take a leading role in campesino organizations. In 1979 the Katarista Movement joined with other social movements to form the Confederation of Peasant Workers Trade Unions of Bolivia (CSUTCB), a name that does not reflect the ethnic origins of the Kataristas. At the end of the 1980s the National Council of Ayllus and Markas of Qullasuyu (CONAMAQ) was created, specifically rejecting all references to "peasant syndicates." The group has a base of support among intellectuals and urbanized Aymara, but its relation with peasant communities has been weak, even in those areas where *ayllus* remain strong, partly because of CONAMAQ's resistance to a closer association with CSUTCB.

In the Quichua highlands of Ecuador, efforts similar to those of the Kataristas developed in 1972 with the formation of Ecuador Indians Awaken (ECUARUNARI), building on local groups that had been closely tied to the Catholic Church. During the 1970s the organization grew rapidly and in 1980 formed a coordinating council with CONFENIAE, an effort that finally resulted in the formation of a unifying federation for all indigenous in Ecuador in 1986: the Confederation of Indigenous Nations of Ecuador (CONAIE). The most significant confrontation with Ecuador's society and politics occurred with the massive rebellion—dubbed the "indigenous earthquake"—in 1990 that shook the political establishment. This was followed in 1992 by the March of Five Hundred Kilometers, in protest of the celebrations commemorating the five hundredth anniversary of Columbus's arrival in the New World. In 1994, a series of protests and strikes forced the government to back down from enacting a neoliberal agricultural law, which would have opened up communal lands to the agricultural land market.[6] Given the new profile of the indigenous movement, the older classist organizations have had to adapt. The National Ecuadorian Federation of Campesino Organizations (FENOC) in the 1990s added an "I" to its acronym, standing for indigenous, and began to work more closely with the CONAIE. The new power of indigenous organizations became most obvious in early 2000, when a massive indigenous mobilization against the neoliberal policies of President Jamil Mahuad sparked actions by other social actors, including the military, ultimately resulting in the overthrow of the president (see chapters 2 and 9).

The highland area of Peru is the only one that has not experienced a dramatic growth of ethnic consciousness and organization. Despite initial efforts, particularly during the Velasco regime, the failure of the military government's agrarian reform opened up greater opportunities for the political left in the countryside. Leftist parties, with a traditional class-based discourse, viewed efforts to organize the indigenous along ethnic lines as racist deviations. An additional factor that stifled indigenous organization in Peru during the 1980s and 1990s was the presence of Shining Path insurgents, and to a lesser extent the Tupac Amaru Revolutionary Movement (MRTA), which, along with the growing presence of the Peruvian military, contributed to a vicious twelve-year war in the Peruvian highlands. Existing campesino organizations, such as the Campesino Confederation of Peru (CCP) became the targets of one or more of the armed groups operating in the highlands. Political and social organization became a dangerous activity, and as a result few new efforts were undertaken. After the Shining Path leadership was captured and violence decreased, the only region that witnessed significant growth in indigenous organization was the Amazon.

All this organizational development has not been confined to just the territory of each country. As we mentioned earlier, many ethnic groups span national borders established without their consent. Moreover, many of the new organizations realize that they have common problems as well as common allies beyond their own borders and have tried to develop links among themselves. This dynamic has been stronger among groups from the Amazonian regions than from the Andean highlands, in part because the latter groups have centuries-long links to the state that now keep their political and ideological focus mainly within this framework. Two contrasting examples of this international dynamic in the region are the Indian Council of South America (CISA) and the Indigenous Coordinator of the Amazonian Basin (COICA).

CISA was first organized at a meeting of indigenous from Peru and Bolivia at the Inca ruins of Ollantaytambo (Cuzco), Peru, in 1980. Initially CISA reached out to indigenous peoples from northern Colombia and Venezuela to southern Chile and Argentina. Within a short period it became associated with the World Council of Indigenous Peoples and was formally recognized by the United Nations in Geneva, where it participated in the effort to promote a Universal Declaration on the Rights of Indigenous Peoples. But soon after, at its second congress, held in Tiwanaku, Bolivia, in 1983, leadership divisions emerged, and the founding group of Peruvian and Bolivian intellectuals gained control. They had urban and even international links but lacked close ties with grassroots communities in their respective countries. CISA established its offices in Lima and began publication of a journal, *Pueblo Indio.* Picking up on the ideas of the Bolivian Fausto Reinaga, CISA emphasized the common anticolonial political approach of the region's indigenous peoples rather than the cultural pluralism of so many different native peoples. This approach and the lack of close ties to indigenous communities, along with leadership conflicts, led to a rapid decline of CISA's influence by the early 1990s. A group of Aymaras from the Lake Titicaca region sought to reinvigorate the movement, organizing Aymara parliaments in the border region between Chile, Peru, and Bolivia that they refer to as Taypi Qala, the Center Rock. Nonetheless, this initiative remained isolated even from the main grassroots Aymara organizations in these three countries.

The CISA experience suggests a problem common among indigenous organizations, namely their weak representation of indigenous communities. Many times a new organization starts on the basis of the insight and inspiration of a few. But if after several years it fails to penetrate into the grassroots, something has gone wrong. Almost all of these organizations have had difficulties integrating their leadership with their purported constituents, for a variety of reasons, including internal leadership conflicts, the lack of sustained financing, and the difficulty of moving from personal or direct forms of democracy to a more distant representative democracy. CISA's difficulties illustrate these problems inasmuch as the leadership focused on acquiring resources from international sources and pursuing an international profile in general but was not as concerned with developing and deepening ties to indigenous communities throughout the region. Although CISA had developed good ideas and projects, without a strong connection to indigenous communities, it increasingly appeared to be made up of a sort of "Indian jet-set."

Another regional indigenous organization that acquired importance in the lowlands region was COICA, which took the opposite path from CISA. COICA was created in 1984 by the principal Amazonian indigenous organizations of the region: CONFENIAE in Ecuador, AIDESEP in Peru, and CIDOB in Bolivia. Unlike CISA, the founding organizations played a primary role in defining the mission of and leading COICA. The leadership of COICA has rotated among the heads of the constituent organizations, with a multinational coordinating committee that emphasizes the local identity of the member organizations as well as the need to develop cooperative efforts to solve common problems. One interesting aspect of COICA is that it was formed at a moment when the member organizations had still not consolidated a national profile within their respective countries and had just begun to develop solid ties with indigenous communities. COICA has expanded to include lowland indigenous from nine countries throughout South America, covering the whole Amazonian basin as well as the Orinoco river basin and the Guyanas. It has played an important role in the demarcation of indigenous territories, promoting indigenous participation in environmental programs and helping defend indigenous interests against the encroachments of oil and more recently pharmaceutical companies. With its headquarters in Quito, Ecuador, COICA has also been at the forefront of promoting the peaceful development of the Peru-Ecuador border, putting forward proposals to create a binational park in a region that is still largely indigenous territory (Brysk 2000).

Political Reactions

It is important to emphasize that the growing indigenous movement in these three countries did not occur as a result of government actions, but usually in spite of government efforts to impede indigenous organization. Given the growing political power of the indigenous and the acceptance of pluralism at the international level, governments have had to recognize indigenous rights and identity as a new factor in the national polity. In Bolivia, government attitudes shifted slowly away from open hostility, particularly after the country's return to democracy in 1982. The first significant changes occurred during the government of Jaime Paz Zamora (1989–93), which was one of the first in Latin America to ratify Convention 169 of the International Labor

Organization (ILO) in favor of indigenous peoples (created in 1989), but only after the indigenous marches for "land and dignity" in 1990. The MNR government of President Gonzalo Sánchez de Lozada (1993–97) continued this trend. Attempting to win votes from rival populist parties, Sánchez de Lozada made the Aymara Katarista Víctor Hugo Cárdenas his vice-president. The new government also endorsed changes in the constitution that recognized the "multiethnic and pluricultural" nature of Bolivia and the right of indigenous peoples to maintain their resources and traditions, including their language, organization, and system of justice. Among the results of these changes have been the promotion of bilingual education and the granting of land titles to indigenous communities that are now considered inalienable and indivisible. Finally, the 1990s saw the election of at least five hundred indigenous to municipal councils, while nearly one hundred indigenous have become mayors (Albó 1999c, 2002).

In Ecuador, shifts in governmental attitudes toward the indigenous took place largely after the 1990 uprising. The attempt by President Sixto Durán Ballén to force through neoliberal agricultural reforms despite widespread public opposition led to the 1994 uprising. Shortly thereafter, CONAIE created a political organization called Pachakutic to participate in the 1996 elections (see chapter 2). With several members of Pachakutic in the newly elected Constituent Assembly, the 1998 constitution incorporated several proposals important to the indigenous. Article 1 of the constitution recognizes the "pluricultural and multiethnic" character of Ecuador, while an entire section is dedicated to the "collective rights" of indigenous peoples who "define themselves as a nation." The constitution also declares the indivisibility of communal lands, promotes bilingual education, and ends with the Inca injunction that rings with symbolic weight throughout the Andes: "Ama quilla, Ama llulla, Ama shua" (Don't be lazy, don't lie, don't steal). How many could have believed these changes possible within a mere decade?

Although in Peru there was no similar organized pressure from indigenous groups, the 1993 constitution included some significant changes, including recognition of the ethnic and cultural pluralism of the nation and official recognition of Quechua, Aymara, and "other aboriginal languages in areas where they are predominant." Unlike the constitutions of Ecuador and Bolivia, and even the 1979 Peruvian constitution, the neoliberal 1993 constitution does not prohibit communal lands from being bought and sold among landowners, demonstrating that not all changes that have occurred are the result of pressures from below (Aroca 1996). There are clearly international factors that, while emphasizing the importance of multiethnicity, also insist on the need for open markets. Recognizing the multicultural character of a nation is an important step in the right direction, but unless they are backed up by social and economic policies that improve the conditions of indigenous peoples, such measures can constitute little more than empty rhetorical gestures.

The reticence of governments to recognize the legitimacy of ethnic identities is based in part on the suspicion of political parties, both right and left, of ethnicity. Even the trade union movements of the region were slow to recognize the importance of ethnic identity in mobilizing lower-class sectors. Bolivia was the first country where political parties began to consider ethnic identity important. With the return to democracy, a number of parties began paying attention to ethnicity, although without much direct participation of the indigenous themselves. It was the Kataristas who began an effort to enter the national party scene. Within a short time, however, a division occurred between those who wanted an exclusive "Indian" identity and others who wanted to begin a dialogue with parties of the left. Although neither current had immediate success, the growing indigenous presence in political life bore fruit with the revisions in the constitution discussed earlier and the inclusion of Katarista Víctor Hugo Cárdenas on the national ticket of the MNR. By the 1990s, the earlier Katarista parties had practically disappeared. However, the ethnic dimension is now represented within almost all established parties.

In Ecuador, political parties had little interest in ethnic questions until the 1990 uprising. As in Bolivia, after an initial interest in the political arena, an indigenous party becomes the focus of organizational activities, in this case the Pachakutic party. Nonetheless, indigenous groups have allied themselves with various politicians, such as President Abdalá Bucaram, and with military rebels, as in the January 2000 coup, who have not advanced the strategic interests of indigenous peoples within the democratic system. In Peru, agrarian peasant unions such as the CCP and the CNA systematically blocked the emergence of ethnic dimensions in their political rhetoric and practice. Neither the Unified Mariateguista Party (PUM), one of the most organized leftist parties among Andean peasant communities, nor the insurgent group Shining Path could overcome their narrow classist discourse to include an ethnic dimension.

Collective ethnic identities are not fixed in time and space. In the three countries under review, indigenous peoples and their leaders and intellectuals appeal to the past to strengthen their identities and even create utopias. But this vision of the past is constantly being reconfigured according to the immediate challenges faced by the indigenous. This process can sometimes include denying historical realities. For example, the indigenous often appeal to that part of the past that most closely corresponds to current realities: in Bolivia, the indigenous and their leaders refer to Collasuyu, which was only the southern part of the Inca Empire; Ecuadorian indigenous if anything refer to the Reign of Quito (Kitu), or the northern part of the empire. Only the Peruvians refer to Tawantisuyu, whose center was in Cuzco.

Explaining the Indigenous Awakening

Although this analysis is limited to the central Andean region, it is clear that a dramatic growth in indigenous organization is taking place across Latin America, from Chiapas, Mexico, to the Mapuche in Chile. This suggests that there has been a confluence of similar factors, apart from specific local conditions. In both Bolivia and Ecuador, local conditions combined with external factors led to indigenous awakenings. Peru, however, has been the exception to these trends.

Local Conditions

The March toward the Amazon. A significant increase in colonization by peasants, oil exploration, and the lumber, cattle, and agricultural industries occurred in the late 1940s as a result of rapid population growth and economic development. This increased activity led the indigenous peoples of the area to mobilize and cooperate across ethnic lines, a situation that resulted in the indigenous adapting their traditional forms of organization to new challenges. These movements, in contrast to highland groups, were able to organize more effectively around ethnicity rather than ideological or partisan identities. Due to their distinct social and cultural context, which includes hunting and gathering, these groups had a more extensive understanding of land usage than their highland counterparts, whose interest in land to cultivate crops created a focus on access to agricultural land and land-reform efforts. It was therefore much more difficult to mobilize indigenous peoples of the Amazonian region around the identity of "campesinos," as occurred in the Andean highlands.

The Failure of Development Models. The scarce benefits in the highlands of the assimilationist/integration model imposed on the region by successive governments created increased disenchantment and a search for new models. The turn toward historic memory often results in a search for a utopian past that can be the basis for a future society, an alternative to Western culture and society. Criticizing these efforts as an impossible return to the past or for their lack of historic accuracy misses the point: idealizing the past is a powerful strategy in the search for alternatives. This can be an important mobilizing factor in the struggles of indigenous peoples.

Urban Migration. Many indigenous who migrated to cities and were exposed to the political and social practices of urban society have come to play important roles as intermediaries, innovators, and "organic intellectuals" of the indigenous movement. Among many indigenous, the move to cities leads to a loss of ethnic identity or the construction of an alternative identity. Among an influential minority, however, the migration experience awakens a greater ethnic consciousness. The effect of this process and its contribution to the indigenous movement should not be discounted. Those movements that began in the 1970s would most likely not have been as widespread or as easily organized without the expansion of migration and the acceleration of education and communication that was a part of this development process.

Nonindigenous Allies. Almost all indigenous groups began their organizational efforts with outside assistance. Three actors in particular are worth noting. First, among some in the Catholic Church, the emergence of Liberation Theology in the aftermath of Vatican II and the Medellín Conference prompted an emphasis on the need to liberate the poor. This has had a profound impact, as church leaders such as Bishop Leonidas Proaño of Riobamba, Ecuador, helped the indigenous organize and insisted on the need to place indigenous issues on the political agenda. Also important to the growth of the indigenous movement are the various nongovernmental organizations (NGOs) operating in the Andes. A vast gamut of NGOs operate in the region, helping the indigenous in such diverse areas as human rights, agricultural development, and technology. One of the first and most important programs was the promotion of indigenous-language radio stations. A final key group is the academic community. By studying and promoting indigenous languages and cultures, academics have created increased consciousness among the indigenous. As consultants to governments and private foundations or as governmental functionaries, academics have taken up the cause of promoting indigenous rights and culture.

The impact of the indigenous on these supportive groups has also been profound, helping them share experiences and overcome legacies of personalism, paternalism, and divisions. The most important test of their change of attitude comes when indigenous organizations, after a period of time, "cut the umbilical cord" tying them to a particular group. The most notable case is that of the CONAIE in Ecuador, whose members gradually distanced themselves from the Catholic Church while maintaining and making their own the practices and discourses that had developed when they were closely tied to the church.

External Factors

The penetration of the Amazonian region would most likely not have been as rapid and intense without transnational interests in the rubber, quinine, petroleum, and cocaine markets. Likewise, significant assistance for the indigenous came from beyond the borders of their nation-states, both within and beyond Latin America. Regional and international meetings of indigenous peoples, several of them sponsored by the United Nations or the World Bank in distant nations such as Canada or Australia, have been critical in providing information and organizational experience. As mentioned, the changing role of the Catholic Church also was an important factor. Finally, the proliferation of academics and NGOs is likewise linked to transnational forces, given that many are financed by foreign governments and foundations. During the 1990s, however, there were more specific international changes that helped shift attitudes among parties and governments in the Andes toward the indigenous, creating a more auspicious climate for the development of indigenous identity and culture.

The Collapse of Communism. The fall of the Berlin Wall and the end of communism in Eastern Europe and the former Soviet Union created a crisis among much of the traditional left in the Andean region. As the classic Marxist approach, with its emphasis on the development of class consciousness and struggle as fundamental to all social change, became less attractive, the struggles and programs of indigenous peoples gained attention among those interested in social change. Moreover, the ethnic conflicts that emerged in the 1990s in former communist states appeared to underline the fact that despite decades of communist rule, the ethnic and cultural dimensions of society had not been eliminated. The weakening of the traditional ideology of the left as a result of these international changes led leftist parties to modify their discourse toward the indigenous and to make political alliances with the indigenous more frequent. Although some critics continue to argue that a focus on ethnicity in the region could lay the basis for a future "balkanization" of the Andes, the reality of indigenous peoples throughout the region is that the repression of social, cultural, economic, and political rights of indigenous peoples is more likely to lead to conflicts, as has been the case in the past.

The Imposition of Neoliberal Economic Models. The 1980s and 1990s saw the implementation of austerity packages and neoliberal economic restructuring in the central Andes, usually as a result of "recommendations" from international financial organizations. This process, which involved mass firings and the introduction of "labor flexibilization," helped reduce the strategic role of the working class in both the economy and the society. In Bolivia, such programs were implemented in 1985 and followed by all subsequent governments, concerned about the need to maintain investor confidence in the country. In Peru, they were largely implemented after the 1990 election of President Alberto Fujimori. In Ecuador, they have been implemented sporadically by diverse governments over the last two decades. As salaried employees and workers increasingly became "informal workers," political parties that had relied on the working and middle classes were forced to search for a new social base. In this context, the indigenous and their struggles became attractive to politicians looking to cobble together a winning electoral coalition. While the changes wrought by neoliberalism have often been catastrophic for indigenous peoples, particularly in the opening up of land markets and the new activities of international corporations in indigenous areas, the social changes introduced have also opened up opportunities for indigenous political organizations to develop new allies.

Democratization, Human Rights, and Concern for the Environment. A very positive development for indigenous peoples has been the increased concern for democracy, human rights, and the environment in the international arena. Each of these concerns has developed a particular "synergy" with indigenous movements. Human rights organizations have focused their interest on the rights of indigenous peoples, given the fact that they are among the poorest and most marginalized and repressed groups in the region. Democratization throughout Latin America and a renewed attention on the part of international organizations, NGOs, and the industrialized powers toward the promotion and consolidation of democratic norms and institutions have also benefited the indigenous. On the one hand, governments can no longer repress indigenous peoples as easily as in the past, given this new international scrutiny. On the other hand, the installation of democracies in the region, as imperfect as they may be, opens up political spaces within which the indigenous can organize and advance their rights in a context that makes it difficult for judiciaries and security forces to deny citizens rights guaranteed under both domestic constitutions and international conventions.

The international ecological movement has found in the indigenous, particularly in the Amazon basin, a group that shares many of its values concerning the need to respect and live in harmony with nature. This coincidence of interests may lead to improved social and economic conditions for indigenous peoples as efforts to protect the biodiversity of the region and protect the plant life that provides much of the world's oxygen lead to the protection of these areas or their development in an ecologically friendly manner, such as the fostering of ecotourism.

Comparing Peru with Bolivia and Ecuador

Despite the common historical trajectories of Bolivia, Ecuador, and Peru, as well as the similar conditions in which the indigenous peoples of the Andes and the Amazon subsist, each country has unique characteristics that must be analyzed. In this sense, ethnic awakening takes on distinct hues in each country. Peru, in particular, represents a unique trajectory in terms of indigenous organization.

Ecuador's ethnic movement shows a higher level of coherence, mobilizing all its ethnic groups at once in the Andes and in the Amazonian lowlands. This can be explained partly by that country's higher demographic density, its easier geographical linkage, and the smaller number of ethnic groups involved. On the other hand, the abiding antagonism between the highlands (Quito) and the coast (Guayaquil) forces Andean Quichua migrants in Guayaquil and other coastal locations to become culturally "invisible" and to disconnect from the movement. This trend is even stronger among highlanders (*serranos*) in coastal Peru, even though they may maintain regular links with their highland communities, and among Andeans who migrate to eastern Bolivia. The 1952 Bolivian Revolution marked the specific characteristics of the ethnic awakening in the Andean region of this country and remains tightly connected with the CSUTCB, whose origins and characteristics are rooted in the popular mobilizations of the 1950s. This explains why in Bolivia there is less polarization between the "peasant/class" and the "indigenous/ethnic" approaches. By contrast, in Ecuador, this polarity was found in each Andean community, with some people belonging to a "class" organization and others belonging to an ethnic group (with the latter finally winning out).

A comparative analysis of indigenous movements in the central Andean countries would be incomplete without an explanation of the weakness of Peru's indigenous movement. As renewed emphasis on ethnic identity swept across the Andes, there were certainly some echoes to be found in Peru, such as the influence of Bolivian Katarismo among Peru's Aymara or the experience of CISA. Nonetheless, these influences were limited, and ethnic identity and indigenous organizations remained largely restricted to the smaller groups of the Amazonian region, scarce among the more numerous highland Quechua and Aymara, whose organizations continued to emphasize their "campesino" identity over ethnicity. As noted earlier, the difficulties in organizing indigenous movements in the 1980s were clearly related to the political violence that wracked the countryside during the 1980s and early 1990s. But with the end of conflict, there still had not developed a significant indigenous movement in this area, as has occurred from Chiapas, Mexico, to southern Chile. What can explain this situation?

Few Peruvian social scientists have focused on this question, suggesting that the issue of indigenous movements is irrelevant in the Peruvian context. One of the few efforts in Peru to explain this situation was undertaken by Carlos Iván Degregori (1998), in his comparative analysis of Peru and Bolivia. Although there are a number of similarities in the historic development of both nations, including the adoption in the 1950s and 1960s of assimilationist policies, the expansion of internal markets and communications, and the adoption of capitalist development models, these similarities did not lead to similar outcomes. Degregori suggests two main differences that may help explain this.

First is the massive migration experienced in Peru, involving the movement of people from the highlands to the capital city of Lima. In 1988, anthropologist José Matos Mar (1986) estimated that there were eighteen hundred *barriadas* (urban squatter settlements) in Lima and other coastal cities in which some eleven million highland migrants lived—double the number of people remaining in the 4,885 campesino communities in all the highlands. For Matos, this migration represented a "popular overflow" that would change the face of Peru. Carlos Franco (1991) agrees that "migration constitutes the most important common experience of a majority of Peruvians" but adds that its main protagonists are no longer indigenous but "urban plebeians" who are shaping a new and ever-changing identity for themselves. In my opinion this pattern represents the major structural difference between Peru and its Andean neighbors. Although migrations occur in Bolivia and Ecuador, migrants from the Peruvian highlands enter an urban coastal environment that is much more hostile to them than that encountered by the Quichuas in Quito or Aymaras and Quechuas in La Paz or Cochabamba. Not only is Lima a much larger metropolis, with some eight million inhabitants, but it is also a city with significant social and cultural mixtures, and in contrast with the main highland cities in the other two countries, it is physically distant from the points of migration. In order to survive in this new environment, highland migrants adopt a low-profile strategy, which in the long term erodes previous identities and subsumes them in a gamut of new identities that Guillermo Nugent (1992) has termed "the labyrinth of *choledad*" to refer to the complex identities represented by the category "cholo," or urbanized Indian. If in Bolivia or Ecuador highland migrants had settled only in Santa Cruz or Guayaquil, then a situation comparable to the Peruvian one might have developed. But in Bolivia the majority of migrants arrived in the La Paz/El Alto compound, which is not only the administrative center of the country but also Chukiyawu, the natural center of the Aymara world. Similarly, Quito remains at the same time the Creole and the indigenous capital of the country, where many thousands of Quichuas go to work but maintain their households and social obligations in nearby communities. Although the impact of the "cholo" in Lima has transformed the once oligarchic capital, the transformations have been even more dramatic in Quito and La Paz/Chukiyawu. In the latter city, nearly half the population speaks either Aymara or Quechua (over 65 percent do in El Alto), and there are numerous indigenous institutions, events, and feasts (Albó 1991a).

The second factor suggested by Degregori to explain the contrast between Peru and the other countries is more symbolic. As he notes, in Peru the Creoles and later the mestizos expropriated from the Indians a good part of the symbolic capital from which they could construct an Indian "we." In the first half of the twentieth century, in order to compete with the Creole elite who sprinkled their Hispanic identity with references to the glorious Inca Empire, mestizo sectors appropriated in a more direct manner the Inca heritage as well as the indigenous communitarian tradition. This tradition was highly valued by early Peruvian indigenism and socialism and became part of the symbolic discourse of the state long before the Velasco era.

This reasoning is certainly attractive. Peruvian historian Jorge Basadre has noted that "perhaps the most important phenomenon in Peruvian culture during the twentieth century has been the increased consciousness regarding the Indian on the part of writers, artists, scientists, and politicians" (Tamayo Herrera 1980, 15). This appropriation of indigenous issues by nonindigenous, reminiscent of Mexico's indigenism, led to the inclusion of certain indigenous elements in the discourse on Peruvian identity adopted by nonindigenous. Tupac Amaru, for example, was transformed into a hero of the independence struggle, after having been identified as a leader of an indigenous rebellion against established Creole and Spanish power. According to Degregori, this symbolic appropriation left highland Andean peoples without their own cultural referents. Their only remaining identity was campesino. The ways in which mestizos and Creoles appropriate Andean culture in Peru is indeed clearly different than in Bolivia or Ecuador. One study examines the ways in which the urban Cuzco elite reinforced their regional identity vis-à-vis Lima and Arequipa, which had become economically and politically important, by appealing to the "Inca" legacy (de la Cadena 1995). This elite, rather than the rural Quechua, is responsible for mounting the annual Inti Raymi festival that celebrates the Sun, sponsoring a Quechua-language academy, adopting the *huipala* as the regional Cuzco flag, and filling the streets and plazas of Cuzco with monuments to Inca rulers. As Jorge Flores Ochoa notes, this new regional identity is a form of "neo-Incan identity."[7] In the words of Cecilia Méndez (1995), it appears to be based on the slogan, "Incas yes, Indians no."

Although this symbolic explanation appears to have some weight, it does not sufficiently explain the lack of an identity-based indigenous movement. Peruvian highland communities have kept alive their culture, celebrations, and languages, differentiating themselves from urban mestizo culture, without any need to recur to their glorious past. If they wanted to, it would be very easy for them to make their current cultural identity fully explicit, as Ecuadorian and Bolivian organizations have done. The cultural influence of relatives who have migrated to Lima and the coast, and who already feel ashamed of identifying themselves as Indians, is great among those who remain in the highlands. But this does not fully explain why the latter still resist expressing a cultural identity that remains profound and alive in the Peruvian highlands.

Perhaps part of the explanation for this situation in the postviolence period has less to do with historical symbolism than with the politics and society of Peru during the Fujimori administration (1990–2000). Although indigenous identity developed during a variety of regimes in Ecuador and Bolivia, its dramatic growth occurred largely after the transition to a civilian democratic government. Beyond the rhetorical emphasis the new governments in these two countries have placed on indigenous rights, social and institutional changes have fostered the notions of participation, dialogue, and negotiation among all sectors of society. In contrast, the Fujimori regime was characterized by an authoritarian approach to civil society that manipulated local identities (by wearing a poncho and *chullo*) while building up clientelistic networks in rural areas. But Fujimori was not open to ideas regarding cultural pluralism and free expression. In this way his approach to the indigenous of the Andean highlands was similar to that of General René Barrientos in Bolivia during the late 1960s—namely a mix of clientelist programs, populist rhetoric, and empty symbolic gestures combined with strict authoritarian control by local political and military figures (Albó 1999b, 470). The governing model adopted by Fujimori was not propitious for the development of a pluralist democracy able to take into account the cultural heterogeneity of the country.

The end of Peru's authoritarian regime thus opened up new opportunities for constructing an identity-based movement among Peru's indigenous. The new president, Alejandro Toledo, has created the self-image of a cholo born in a poor highland community who migrated to a popular *barriada* on the coast and then went on to study in the United States, receiving a Ph.D. in economics from Stanford and serving in a variety of international financial institutions. After marrying a foreign professional (an anthropologist), he returned as a successful cholo, eventually running for president and using extensive references to the Inca roots of the country. From offerings to ancestral gods and references to Pachakutic, to a massive "March of the Four Suyos" against the Fujimori regime, to his final triumphant presidential inauguration at the ruins of Machu Picchu dressed in full highland regalia, Toledo has employed a range of indigenous symbols that are unmatched in Peru's recent history. Does this signal that Peru has finally caught up with other countries in the region? In many ways this is reminiscent of Aníbal Quijano's (1980) "emergence of the *cholos*," but only of that cholo who has prospered abroad. Significantly, Toledo does not speak Quechua, although his Belgian-born wife does. His ethnic approach may more closely resemble that of the Cuzco mestizos: Inca yes, Indian no. Clearly, the return to ethnically minded grassroots Andean indigenous organizations in contemporary political Peru is still pending.

Projections for the Future

Comparing what was happening in the mid–twentieth century with what is occurring today, there is no doubt that the ethnic factor and ethnic consciousness have grown substantially in these three countries, Peru included. Will this revival be short-lived, giving way eventually to a new wave of homogenization? Or is it the beginning of a new understanding and respect for ethnic diversity? Is Peru the last runner in this race to the future, or is it the forerunner toward a new future? Any answers to these questions must take into account the meaning and dimensions of current globalization processes and their impact on the indigenous movement.

Whether the forces of globalization will sweep away all efforts to build on cultural pluralism both in Peru and elsewhere in the Andes remains to be seen. The rise of ethnic consciousness and the rapid growth in indigenous organizations since the 1970s do not represent a return to the past, but a phenomenon that is directly linked to globalization, a process that has created new opportunities and induced negative reactions, both of which have helped foster the rise of ethnic identity. In an earlier work (Albó 1991b), I discussed the "boomerang effect" of a homogenizing model of development, which insists on neoliberal structural adjustments and Western cultural hegemony, in the Andean region. By excluding a significant part of the population, particularly the indigenous, from the economic growth that occurs under neoliberal economic policies and increasing the concentration of economic power in the hands of a few, one would expect a counterreaction to occur. In the case of Ecuador at the start of the new millennium, we have already seen the boomerang effect: a mass rebellion led by the indigenous against official economic policies brought down a government.

Efforts to correct some of the nefarious effects of these policies have also been undertaken. Many Bolivians remember the case of Sánchez de Lozada, who in 1985, along with Jeffrey Sachs of Harvard, was the architect of neoliberal shock policies that resulted in severe social dislocations. As president during 1993–97, however, Sánchez de Lozada, working with his Aymara vice-president Víctor Hugo Cárdenas, introduced corrective measures to alleviate some of the negative pressures and advanced a number of new legal rights for the indigenous. Whether such corrections and adjustments work only to distract the population from the ongoing neoliberal reforms of the economy, or can help alleviate social problems in the long term, remains to be seen.

The impact of globalization in its broadest sense, beyond the free movement of capital, creates both new opportunities and dangers for the indigenous. The expansion of communications via computers, satellites, and the Internet may help connect previously isolated groups with peoples from around the globe and preserve rich cultural traditions. On the other hand, if communication technologies become dominated by a small group of multinational corporations whose products and services are culturally homogenized for everyone across the globe, the impact on native cultures could be the gradual loss of identity. As in the past, much will depend on how indigenous peoples adapt to and appropriate these changes for their own purposes. Although difficult, this is possible. And it is certainly needed.

2   Linking Movement and Electoral Politics

Ecuador's Indigenous Movement and the Rise of Pachakutik

On January 21, 2000, a dramatic takeover of Ecuador's National Congress by thousands of primarily indigenous protesters, joined by a couple hundred disaffected army officers, resulted in the ousting of President Jamil Mahuad. The protesters and their military allies declared the formation of a three-member Junta of National Salvation that included a representative of the rebellious army colonels, the then-president of the most important national indigenous organization, and a former Supreme Court judge, representing the coast. The self-declared junta did not succeed in holding onto power and was disbanded in less than twenty-four hours, after it became clear that the high command of the armed forces was not going to accept this new government. While these protest actions did not result in a revolutionary change in government or even a reversal of the neoliberal macroeconomic program, they did succeed, although through unconstitutional means, in sparking the downfall of a highly unpopular and corruption-tainted president, without a drop of blood shed.

Exactly four months after the controversial January 21 takeover the indigenous movement made its mark yet again on Ecuador's political stage, but this time via elections. On May 21 the independent political movement Pachakutik made impressive gains in local elections, emerging as a powerful new electoral force in the country's highland and Amazonian regions.[1] The Movement of Plurinational Unity—Pachakutik (MUPP)—is the political wing of the Confederation of Indigenous Nations of Ecuador (CONAIE), the country's most important indigenous organization, and the Social Movement Coordinator (CMS), a national umbrella organization uniting many of Ecuador's nonindigenous social movements and unions. The multiethnic Pachakutik, which got its start in 1996, won five of the nation's twenty-two prefectures, more than any other single party, and over 12 percent of mayoralties and provincial council seats in the 2000 elections. In a highly fragmented party system like Ecuador's, these percentages are significant and qualified Pachakutik as one of the country's six most important parties in terms of seats won. While indigenous participation is a central part of this movement, Pachakutik is not strictly an indigenous party. MUPP's ethnic mix is evident in the candidates elected in 2000: one of the five Pachakutik prefects was indigenous, as were eleven of the twenty-seven mayors; the rest were mestizos, most of whom had been involved in progressive social movements.[2]

The events of both January 21 and May 21, 2000, attest to the unprecedented political power that the indigenous movement has built at the national level, as well as to the remarkable changes that have taken place within indigenous communities over the last thirty to forty years. At the same time, the contrast between the two strategies employed, the first involving an explicit challenge to and even rejection of constitutionality and the second consisting of conventional participation within the country's formal political institutions, is striking. It points to an important tension within the movement over strategies for pursuing social change.

The Indigenous Movement and the Origins of Pachakutik

Representing somewhere between 10 and 40 percent of the population, Ecuador's indigenous peoples are very culturally diverse.[3] The vast majority, probably about 75 percent live in the highland region, much of which was conquered first by the Inca Empire and then, less than fifty years later, by the Spanish in the early sixteenth century. Five hundred years of conquest and rule by non-natives resulted in an extended process of ethnic blurring, including the loss of most of these groups' original languages.[4]

Ecuador's tropical lowlands have the second-largest number of indigenous people, somewhere between eighty and one hundred thousand (CONAIE 1989). By contrast, in this region, extended and intense contact with the outside world did not occur until the second half of the twentieth century. As a result, Amazonian groups there have retained their own distinct cultural identities and languages to a far greater extent than those in the highlands.[5] Indigenous peoples make up only 3.4 percent of Ecuador's rural coastal population (SIISE 2000b). These smaller, more isolated groups have not been as politically active or visible as their counterparts in the highland and Amazonian regions.

Historically, indigenous people have been among the most marginalized in Ecuadorian society. In the highlands a long history of oppressive land-tenure systems kept many Indians in situations of servitude well into the second half of the twentieth century.[6] According to 1950 census figures, the illiteracy rate among Quichua speakers, who would have represented the bulk of the indigenous population at the time, was 92 percent, compared with 36 percent for Spanish speakers (Ministerio de Economía 1960, table 27). It is safe to assume that these figures would have changed little until the 1970s, when access to education was expanded under a reformist military government. Given this

extremely high illiteracy rate, the literacy restriction on voting, which remained in place until 1984, served as an effective means of disenfranchising
indigenous people. Racial discrimination further entrenched their unequal
status and severely limited their opportunities for social mobility. Conversely,
geographic isolation allowed Amazonian Indians to remain highly autonomous and effectively outside the reach of the state until the 1960s, and
consequently they took no part in national politics. It is quite remarkable
then that by the close of the twentieth century, indigenous people in Ecuador
had forged the country's most powerful social movement and transformed
themselves into one of the most important collective actors on the national
stage, becoming a force with which every administration has had to reckon.

While a social movement cannot be conflated with a single organization,
the vast majority of indigenous advocacy and activism is led and/or coordinated by a single national-level body, CONAIE, or by one of its member organizations.[7] CONAIE was founded in 1986 and claims to represent 70 percent of the country's indigenous population. Its organizational membership
includes federations representing all thirteen of the country's indigenous nationality groups from all three regions (CONAIE 1989, 37).

While the movement carries out many programs autonomously within and
among indigenous communities, the central target of indigenous political organizing has been the state. CONAIE succeeded in getting the state to create
a nationwide bilingual education program that assures that indigenous students can study in their native languages as well as in Spanish. Movement
representatives participating in the 1997–98 National Constituent Assembly
were able to make important changes to the 1998 constitution, including official recognition of Ecuador as a multiethnic and pluricultural nation and
provisions recognizing indigenous collective rights.[8]

In addition to cultural and identity issues, another central concern of
CONAIE and its constituents is land rights and aid to small farmers and
campesinos. One of the most dramatic victories in this area was achieved in
1992 by the Organization of Indigenous Peoples of Pastaza (OPIP), an Amazonian member organization of CONAIE. After a two-week march from the
Amazon to the nation's capital, indigenous leaders negotiated the establishment by the government of nineteen territorial blocs, encompassing over 2.75
million acres, to be given to 138 indigenous communities (Yashar 1999). In
1994 a major nationwide indigenous uprising forced the government to back-
track on an agrarian law that had been pushed through Congress without input from small farmers and peasants, eventually establishing a commission
that included indigenous organizations and other affected sectors to draft an
alternative bill more favorable to campesino interests.

Until the mid-1990s protest actions and civil disobedience were the chief tactics employed by CONAIE to pressure the state to address its demands. In the organization's early years, during the late 1980s, the strategic position that gradually emerged was one of opposition to the government in power, autonomy from political parties, and nonparticipation in formal politics. This was based on a radical critique of the Ecuadorian state, which CONAIE's political manifesto describes as "exclusionary, hegemonic, antidemocratic and repressive" (CONAIE 1994, 7). Likewise, prior experiences of indigenous collaboration with mestizo unions, social movements, and parties had often ended in frustration, as these organizations were happy to avail themselves of indigenous organizational strength but were unwilling to take on their political agenda.

Despite the risk of friction between an oppositional stance and political participation, with its corresponding fear of co-optation, support for complete withdrawal from electoral politics had never been unanimous within the movement.[9] For those in the movement who argued for the advantages of electoral participation, winning political office offered the possibility of greater access to resources to meet the concrete material needs and demands of their communities. At CONAIE's 1993 congress a compromise position was reached that seemed to resolve the corruption and autonomy problems while allowing for electoral participation. It was decided that members would be allowed to run in local and provincial elections, but only once Ecuadorian law was changed so as to allow participation by independent candidates. Not long thereafter, voters overwhelmingly approved a public referendum allowing the participation of independents, opening the door for CONAIE to enter the electoral fray. In January 1996 CONAIE joined an independent multiethnic alliance, the Movimiento de Unidad Pluri-nacional Pachakutik–Nuevo País (MUPP-NP), which was poised to run candidates for national as well as local offices. MUPP-NP ran its own presidential candidate, television journalist Freddy Ehlers, and placed CONAIE president Luis Macas in the top spot of its congressional ticket. The formation of MUPP-NP represented a significant shift in indigenous movement strategy, both because participation was no longer limited to the local level and because the electoral initiative was undertaken jointly with nonindigenous groups.[10]

Since 1996, Pachakutik has become the most successful movement-based party in the Andean region and one of a handful of such parties that have sprung up in different parts of Latin America, notable examples being the Brazilian Worker's Party (PT), the Party of the Democratic Revolution (PRD) in Mexico, and Frente Pais Solidario (FREPASO) in Argentina. In determining when social movement parties might emerge and their probabilities for success in developing countries, there are two sets of factors that must be taken into account: those external and those internal to the social movements themselves. External factors include the type of political institutions in place in each country and the political opportunity structure at any given time. Internal factors include the movement's organizational strength and structure, as well as its ideology and outlook. While external factors are important, they alone do not determine whether or not a movement party will emerge; permissive external conditions must be coupled with the existence of a strong, independent social movement.

Ecuador's formal political institutions are not markedly more permissive than those in Peru or Bolivia, and all three of these countries have experienced ongoing political crises that have eroded the legitimacy of traditional political elites and thereby opened a space for new competitors. However, no social or indigenous movement–related party has emerged in Peru, and in Bolivia, despite the fact that Indians represent a much larger portion of the population, indigenous parties have not been nearly as successful as Pachakutik. While making inroads at the local and regional levels, Bolivian social movement parties have seen their national-level efforts hindered by internal divisions and intraorganizational competition.

As a general rule, the more proportional the electoral system, the more favorable it is to minorities and small parties. It stands to reason that resource-poor, nontraditional parties like Pachakutik would have more advantages in more proportional systems. However, of the three central Andean nations, Ecuador's system is the least proportional. Since 1995, Peru has used a single nationwide district to elect all 120 legislators, making it extremely proportional. Bolivian legislators are elected from nine provincial districts with an average district magnitude (DM) of 14.44.[11] In contrast, Ecuador has a two-tier system, with 16 percent of its representatives elected from a single national district and the rest from twenty-two provincial districts. Its average DM, including both the national and provincial districts, was about 3.5 until 1998 and 5.5 thereafter, making it the least proportional of the three.

However, other aspects of Ecuador's electoral system have proved advantageous for the indigenous movement, in particular the way districts are apportioned. Since the provinces serve as congressional districts and have varying-size populations, the number of representatives elected from each district is determined by a formula based in part on population size. However, because the variations in population from province to province are so extreme, the formula still tends to overrepresent small, sparsely populated provinces. The vast majority of sparsely populated provinces are located in the Amazon and the highlands, where the indigenous movement has its organized base. Thus the provinces where the indigenous movement is strongest have more representatives per capita.

Another factor favoring indigenous electoral participation in Ecuador is the fact that local elections have been part of the political landscape since 1978. Local seats in areas where the indigenous are in the majority or represent a significant minority are often easier to win than national-level posts, and these offices provide good opportunities for political and administrative training for movement leaders. Likewise, local government can offer greater possibilities for implementing desired programs and policies than is often possible in Congress, especially for a minority party. The nature of congressional policy-making in a multiparty system like Ecuador's requires a great deal of negotiation and compromise with other parties.

The other relevant external factor is the overall political context and the level of legitimacy of traditional political parties. The political and economic crises that all the Andean and many other Latin American countries experienced during the 1980s and 1990s are extremely important in explaining the tremendous flux that the region's party systems have experienced since the return to democracy. As these crises undermined the legitimacy of the traditional political leadership, space opened up for new competitors. However, in many cases these spaces were filled by charismatic leaders with little or no social base; it was less common to find social movements with the capacity or willingness to take advantage of these openings. In Peru, for example, over a decade of civil war debilitated and inhibited the growth of the country's social and indigenous movements. Alberto Fujimori, initially a dark-horse candidate with no social base, stepped into this void in the 1990s, and of this writing no movement-related party has emerged in Peru. Bolivia has also gone through a long series of crises since the early 1980s, and many new parties have emerged, including some with organic ties to social and indigenous movements. But again, the electoral impact of Bolivia's social and indigenous movements has remained weak compared to that of Ecuador, due primarily to debilitating infighting among movement leaders and their organizations.

Like its neighbors, Ecuador experienced a series of political and economic crises during the 1980s and 1990s. When Pachakutik was founded in 1996, the administration was reeling from corruption scandals. Public opinion was extremely negative not only toward the president but also toward Congress and political parties. Social movements took advantage of the public disgust with the administration and traditional political elites to fight the president's proposals for privatization and structural adjustment. They argued that privatization was simply a means of siphoning off the state's wealth to benefit a few and would harm the country as a whole. The left's growing popular support became evident in 1995 when a broad-based campaign led by labor unions and social movement organizations, including CONAIE, succeeded in defeating a presidential referendum on a package of neoliberal economic policies. Despite polling predictions to the contrary, all eleven referendum questions were decisively defeated. This victory, despite the government's far superior access to media and advertising, indicated to progressive sectors that they possessed greater potential at the ballot box than they had thought.

In the wake of the success of the "no" vote on President Sixto Durán Ballén's referendum, the mestizo left sought to convince the indigenous movement to move beyond fielding independent candidates only at the local level and instead to assume a leadership role within a broad anti-neoliberal electoral coalition fielding candidates at all levels. The fact that CONAIE agreed to participate in such a coalition is significant given its concerns about autonomy and its reservations about the nonindigenous left.

What had changed by 1996 and made possible this multiethnic coalition? Between 1986 and 1996 a notable power shift had occurred between the indigenous movement and the other labor and social movements: the former had grown significantly in stature and mobilizing capacity relative to the nonindigenous sectors of the left. Thus by 1996 indigenous organizations could enter into alliances with these other groups from a position of strength. Given the indigenous movement's impressive mobilizing capacity, mestizo left-wing organizations could no longer ignore or marginalize this movement's perspectives or risk its withdrawal from the broader coalition.

Thus, a combination of conditions and changes both external and internal to the indigenous movement made possible Pachakutik's emergence. Most important was the movement's own sense of confidence and power, which came after decades of organizing. The relatively permissive external political environment became fertile ground for a powerful indigenous movement to test the waters of electoral participation.

Just as the strength of the indigenous movement was important to Pachakutik's emergence, it has also been vitally important to its electoral success. If it had not been for the previously consolidated structure of the indigenous organizations, Pachakutik might have been just a one-time experiment.

Indigenous Movement Key Resources

Pachakutik's electoral success since 1996 has not been due solely to the indigenous vote, and indeed there are questions about the extent to which the movement has been able to capture as much of that vote as would be expected.[12] Nevertheless, it is clear that Pachakutik has consistently won an important share of the vote, often more than any other party, in many poor rural indigenous communities.[13] This is surprising in light of historical patterns in the region, as well as social science theory.

Peasants have never figured as agents of democratization; social science theory has attributed this role alternatively to the middle or the urban working classes. Instead, peasants have been portrayed as backward and resistant to

change. In attempting to account for why rural democratization is such a jug-
gernaut, Jonathan Fox points to the continued power and presence in the
countryside of rural elites and archaic political and economic structures that
perpetuate patterns of clientelism. The persistence of these old patterns of social control, he explains, "limit the extent to which mass-based social and economic protests translate into party identifications and issue-based voting behavior" (Fox 1990, 7–8). Other impediments he mentions include limited
access to information and flawed electoral systems that make it difficult for
change to be achieved through electoral competition.

Pachakutik's ability to overcome many of these obstacles and achieve a degree of support among rural indigenous voters is due, I argue, to its close connection to the indigenous movement. My argument focuses on the importance of three key resources, which are the result of over forty years of
indigenous organizing: (1) the cultivation of a strong and positive indigenous
identity; (2) the provision of programs and projects that play a visible role in
local development; and (3) the development of a thick, fundamentally democratic organizational structure.

Identity

The development of a positive "indigenous" identity that encompasses culturally and historically distinct ethnic groups is one of the fruits and, at the
same time, a main resource of the modern indigenous movement in Ecuador.
"Indigenous" identity in today's Ecuador unifies all native peoples without
homogenizing them: the principle of unity in diversity. Quichua speakers in
the highlands and Shuar Indians in the Amazon recognize an affinity as "indigenous" even as they assert and reaffirm their own separate and distinct ethnic identities vis-à-vis each other and the nonindigenous.

The history of native peoples in Ecuador, and in particular in the highlands, illustrates the fluidity of the concept of self- or group identity. At the
time of the Spanish Conquest there were numerous ethnic groups in present-
day Ecuador with distinct languages, cultures, and economic practices. Three
hundred years later, by the time of Ecuador's independence from Spain in
1830, highland indigenous society had become highly homogenized and internally leveled. Spanish rule resulted in the emergence of a generic "Indian"
identity that was largely negative (Zamosc 1994). Colonial policies like *repar-
timiento,* which entailed the forced reorganization of Indian communities,
served to undermine Indian social structure and eliminate unique differences
among ethnic groups.[14] Evidence of the blurring of ethnic lines is the fact
that the only indigenous language that survived among highland peoples is
Quichua, the language of the Inca conquerors.

Independence from Spain in 1830 did not bring about an improvement in indigenous status; in some ways conditions for Indians actually worsened as Spanish protections of indigenous communal lands were eliminated. According to Gerardo Fuentealba (1983), these communal lands were spaces of relative autonomy in which indigenous communities were able to construct and maintain their own modes of production, forms of organization, and systems of representation. These autonomous spaces aided in the conservation and reproduction of fundamental aspects of indigenous identity. The usurpation of indigenous communal lands accelerated under the Liberal Regime (1895–1920), as the government sought to free up land for agro-export production and to integrate indigenous peasants into the burgeoning national capitalist economy. (Iturrable 1995).

The changes that began with independence and intensified under the Liberal Regime had a complex impact on the evolution of indigenous identity in the highlands. On the one hand, the breakup of communal lands had a deleterious impact on indigenous peoples' independent base of subsistence and threatened the survival of their communities and cultures. At the same time, these policies reduced their cultural, social, and political isolation (Iturrable 1995). As Indians were forced off their lands and into the capitalist labor force, the lines dividing communities became more and more blurred. Greater mobility, combined with a common experience of racial discrimination, eventually served to foster the emergence of a generic "indigenous" identity in the highlands.

From the 1930s through the 1960s organizing among highland Indians was led by non-Indian left-wing organizers and focused on campesino demands for better wages and agrarian reform.[15] An ethnic agenda and consciousness began to emerge during the late 1970s and were consolidated in the 1980s. A crucial antecedent to the emergence of autonomous indigenous organizing and eventually to the development of a new ethnic consciousness was the implementation of agrarian reform in 1964, which succeeded in dismantling the *huasipungo* system and freeing indigenous people from debt bondage. While this transformation in the relations of production in the countryside was very significant, the extent of the reform itself was meager in terms of the amount of land confiscated and redistributed.

The history of ethnogenesis and the emergence of an "indigenous" identity in the Amazon is radically different and much more compressed than in the highlands. Previous to the 1960s, contact with the outside world was very limited, but in that decade the discovery of oil and the beginning of a massive government-sponsored colonization of the Amazon by landless peasants from the highlands put an end to the region's isolation. Because extended contact with the West occurred so much later than in the highlands, no comparable process of ethnic blending occurred among these groups, and Amazonian groups continue to maintain their distinct tribal identities and languages. Traditionally Amazonian tribes did not interact with one another, and when they did intertribal relations tended to be conflictive and warlike, but the common experience of threats to their cultures and their lands by nonindigenous outsiders, including the government and Catholic and Protestant missions, has helped unite these previously autonomous peoples. Because they were never conquered by the Spanish the way highland indigenous people were, Amazonian groups have not had to overcome the psychological baggage of five hundred years of oppression and subjugation. On the other hand, the challenge to assimilate and react to the threats facing them in such a compressed historical period is a truly formidable one.

The full flowering of a positive indigenous identity that is shared among lowland, highland, and coastal groups began to take shape in the 1980s, crystallizing in the dramatic 1990 national indigenous uprising that paralyzed the country for a week as indigenous people engaged in nonviolent protests, blocking roads and keeping food from getting to market.[16] The 1990 uprising is viewed as the watershed moment when indigenous people demanded their place as an integral and valued part of the Ecuadorian nation. Indigenous demands for inclusion are not strictly for integration, but for recognition and acceptance as "different citizens" (León 1994).

While Pachakutik is not an "indigenous" party, it has adopted many of the principles and symbols of the indigenous movement. The party's main symbol is the rainbow-colored flag, known as the *huipala,* which is also the movement's chief emblem. The Quichua commandments "Ama quilla, ama llulla, ama shua" (Don't be lazy, don't lie, don't steal) were adopted as the political movement's bedrock principles. The practice within the indigenous movement of unity in diversity is being expanded to include not just indigenous peoples but all those who share the party's political vision of a culturally plural, more economically just society. While Pachakutik is a multicultural organization, ethnic demands fit into its broad plural agenda because unlike the old left, it explicitly recognizes the importance of culture and ethnicity. It is also the only party to have indigenous people in positions of power at all organizational levels.

Finally, identity has played an important role in voter choices, especially among young, better-educated Indians. In a fascinating study of indigenous voting patterns carried out at the time of the 1996 elections, the Centro de Planificacion y Estudios Sociales (CEPLAES) found that the most common response of those polled to the question of why they voted for a given candidate was that the candidate was indigenous. This indicates that indigenous people are identifying with indigenous candidates and that they want to see their own people in positions of power. This is especially significant given that most indigenous candidates do not have the economic resources that most other candidates bring to a campaign.

Indigenous participation in electoral politics is not only affecting the attitudes and behavior of indigenous people. In those places where indigenous elected officials have run efficient and transparent local administrations, and especially when they have been able to attract international money to their cities or provinces, the attitudes of mestizos also show signs of change. This was evident in indigenous mayor Auki Tituaña's reelection campaign. Tituaña's administration of the Cotacachi municipality (1996–2000) was exemplary in its effectiveness and transparency (Guerrero 1999). As a result mestizo support for his 2000 reelection bid and participation in the campaign were very high. In a canton that is 40 percent indigenous, Tituaña was reelected with an unprecedented 80 percent of the popular vote.

Important dents then are being made in the armor of racism that is still so prevalent in Ecuador. And Pachakutik's multicultural political platform celebrating difference while championing broad causes such as transparency and participation in government both fosters and capitalizes on these changes in attitude.

Material Resources

While it is clear that fundamental changes have occurred in indigenous consciousness and pride over the last thirty years, the majority of the population is still extremely poor and educational levels remain low, especially in rural areas. Poor, uneducated voters are least likely to vote on programmatic grounds and are also the most susceptible to vote buying and other types of political manipulation. How is it then that the resource-poor Pachakutik has been able to garner an important share of the rural indigenous vote? I will argue that there is a material component to the party's success. As a result of its activism, the indigenous movement has helped to secure resources and programs from governmental as well as nongovernmental sources at the national and international levels. To the extent that Pachakutik is closely tied to these indigenous organizations, voters associate the political movement with the provision of these resources. In other words, support for Pachakutik, especially among poor rural voters, is not based solely on voter affinity with the party's political philosophy but also fundamentally on the belief that its candidates will be effective suppliers of local-level resources. While this may sound like a new version of clientelistic politics, there are important differences.

Traditional patron-client relationships and the more complex notion of "political clientelism" involve relationships of dependency and unequal power. They are based on reciprocity, but the exchange is unequal and serves to maintain the status quo power relationship, in which the client is subordinate to and dependent upon the patron or political broker. Typically "political clientelism" refers to situations of vote buying and the delivery of small public-works projects and/or patronage by the political broker or politician in exchange for votes. These political practices may offer limited help to individuals, but they are often associated with corruption and as such impede the attainment of collective goods. Likewise, when voting is based upon this type of an exchange, voters have little ability or incentive to hold the politician accountable for implementing policies that serve their collective interests, because their votes were cast on the basis of the delivery of some particularistic good. Finally, the relationship is one of dependency, in which the "clients" or voters are dependent on the broker as opposed to empowered to develop solutions to their own problems.

Pachakutik politicians and indigenous movement organizations have worked to bring development and education projects to their communities, but their philosophy rejects the clientelistic model and seeks instead to create a political practice that empowers local communities by involving them in developing solutions to their own problems. Many Pachakutik elected mayors and prefects on taking office have organized assemblies of local residents for the purpose of collectively planning the work to be undertaken in the canton or province. Likewise, Pachakutik elected officials have made an effort to ensure a higher degree of outside oversight of their administrations and their leadership. This is not to say that all MUPP elected officials have successfully implemented this philosophy; there certainly are cases of MUPP authorities who have resorted to tactics similar to those of traditional political practices. Nevertheless, in cases where an MUPP politician has violated these principles, he or she has been thrown out of the party.

Social movements, especially those representing the poor, need to secure material resources for their constituencies. Very often this forces them into a compromised position as the state has so often been the primary source of such resources. The indigenous movement in Ecuador has been better able than most popular movements in the region to avoid co-optation by the government for a combination of reasons. In the first place, it faces a weak state and a divided political and economic elite. Second, the movement emerged during a period of prolonged economic crisis, which has diminished the state's capacity to address social needs. Equally important has been the movement's capacity to attract international resources. Not being solely dependent on the state has granted the indigenous movement a greater degree of latitude in its dealings with and stance toward the government. Finally, the movement's mobilizing capacity and its national reach also contribute to its power. Consequently, the indigenous movement has been able to extract programs from the state largely on its own terms, thus creating institutional structures that do not undermine the movement. Historically in Latin America, when a central state has funds at its disposal to undertake significant social welfare programs, they have frequently been used to undermine and divide autonomous social movements.

Access to international resources can play an important role in the ability of social movements in the Third World to remain autonomous and free of dependence on the state. Alison Brysk's (2000) study of indigenous movements around the world suggests that increased international interest in indigenous peoples and their issues during the 1980s and 1990s helps account for the ability of indigenous groups to advance their cause and win important concessions from national governments despite their small numbers and limited access to financial resources.

Finally, with regard to internal cohesion, one factor that distinguishes Ecuador's indigenous movement from those in other Latin American countries is its national scope. In Bolivia, by contrast, internal divisions kept indigenous and peasant movements weak and fragmented, allowing successive governments to play one group off against another. This is precisely how the government dealt with the major social upheaval in September 2000. Campesino organizations in the Altiplano and the coca-growing region of the Chapare spearheaded protests that were joined by myriad groups throughout the country. Demanding changes in government policy toward coca production as well as greater access to land and more support for smallholder production, these organizations blocked major highways and paralyzed interprovincial commerce for a whole month. The government brought an end to the standoff by acceding to virtually all the Altiplano group's demands, while completely sidelining groups from the Chapare (Collins 2000a).

Even bilingual education, one of the clearest examples of the indigenous movement's cultural-identity agenda, has an important material dimension. The creation in 1988 of the bilingual education program (DINEIB), which is run out of the Ministry of Education, resulted in professional employment for many indigenous people. Opening up the system to indigenous educators has gone a long way to changing the distribution of power within rural communities. As Melina Selverston-Scher explains, "The schoolteacher is often one of the most important influences in an indigenous community, and also one of the few steady jobs in the countryside." (1997, 181). This new structure effectively removed a powerful tool for political patronage from the politicians and put it in the hands of the indigenous organizations, thereby undermining traditional patterns of political clientelism.

An important factor in indigenous mayor Auki Tituaña's highly successful 2000 reelection bid in Cotacachi, where he won by more than 80 percent, was his ability to secure funding from international nongovernmental organizations (NGOs) for a variety of municipal projects. According to Tituaña, the nongovernmental funds secured during his administration more than doubled the municipal budget.[17] In addition to the benefits of this budget increase, the presence especially of international NGOs, which are known to have rigorous oversight practices, helped make credible the municipality's claims of transparency.

Thus Pachakutik is not a programmatic party in the mold of Western European parties; it would not have succeeded electorally if it had concerned itself solely with advancing a national ideological platform. Instead, it had to address in some way the local material needs of the communities it sought to represent. The difference, however, is that Pachakutik is attempting to do this in a way that breaks with old patterns of political handouts and clientelism; it is deliberately setting out to develop a new style of more participatory and transparent politics, especially at the local level. Whether and to what extent this political movement will ultimately succeed in replicating and expanding the models that have been developed in a few of its most exemplary municipalities remains to be seen.[18] In any event, the movement's concepts of participation and transparency have already seeped into Ecuador's political culture, with politicians from other parties beginning to appropriate its language. This effort to develop new political practices and new types of relationships between voters and officeholders is one of the ways Pachakutik is contributing to the deepening of democracy in Ecuador.

Leadership and Organization

The level of mobilizational capacity that the Ecuadorian indigenous movement has sustained since the first national uprising in 1990 is by all measures extraordinary and helps qualify it as the strongest indigenous movement in Latin America. The movement's strength and unity cannot be understood without examining the organizational structures that have developed over the last thirty years. Also important are the norms that guide actions and expectations within these organizations, which result from an even longer history of grassroots indigenous community experience.

Membership in CONAIE is organizational, not individual. The national organization rests atop a pyramid of organizational layers that begins at the local level and builds up to the national. At the lowest level there are individual communities, for the most part rural farming communities, which tend to make decisions collectively. Some are better organized than others, but almost all rural communities have a president who is selected by the community as a whole.[19] At the next level are the *organizaciones de segundo grado* (OSGs), or second-tier organizations, which represent a group of communities in a geographical area. These in turn belong to a provincial organization, and the provincial organization to one of three regional organizations: CONFENIAE, representing the Amazon; Ecuador Indians Unite (ECUARUNARI) in the highlands; and Coordinadora de Organizaciones Indigenas de la Costa Ecuatoriana (COINCCE) for the coast. Finally, these three regional organizations each belong to the CONAIE. Many of the OSGs in the Amazon and highlands have roots dating back to the 1960s and early 1970s, with some going as far back as the 1930s. The fact that CONAIE was constructed upon a network of preexisting organizations helps explain its relatively rapid institutional consolidation after 1986.

Membership in CONAIE and these local and regional organizations is not individual, but based on group membership in a territorially defined community. Participation is determined by delegation from below. For example, to attend a CONAIE congress an individual must be delegated from an appropriate organization at each different level: first from the local community, then the OSG, the provincial organization, and finally the regional organization. This structure creates strong incentives for leaders to maintain close relationships with and ties to their communities. While this is not a fail-safe model for preventing corruption, it does prevent the commandeering of an organization by a leader with no real grassroots base.

Norms such as alternation in leadership play an important role in facilitating unity and avoiding splits within movement organizations. It is frowned upon for one individual to stay too long in a leadership position; other people should be given the chance to lead. Another mechanism that has served to maintain unity in CONAIE between the two major regional groups—the Amazon and the highlands—has been the informal practice of striking a regional balance in the top leadership of the CONAIE.

The leadership pool of the indigenous movement has grown tremendously over the past thirty years. Increased access to education, beginning in the 1970s under Guillermo Rodríguez Lara's developmentalist military regime, was important in this regard, as was the nationwide literacy campaign initiated by the administration of Jaime Roldós (1979–81) and the bilingual education movement, which took off in the 1980s. The literacy campaign and the bilingual education movement were important training grounds for many of the current crop of movement leaders, providing them with experience as educators and administrators. The upcoming leadership is even better prepared, with more and more of them earning graduate degrees in law, education, and the social sciences. The movement, in turn, has been successful in attracting and keeping educated young people in its ranks.

In those areas where there is a sizeable indigenous population, Pachakutik is being built squarely upon this leadership and organizational foundation. In the May 2000 elections Pachakutik had its best results in provinces like Cotopaxi, Bolivar, and Imbabura, where indigenous organizations are strong. In these provinces the indigenous organizations often served as the backbone of the Pachakutik campaigns, devoting much of their personnel and organizational resources to the election effort. Not only was their people power important for campaigning, but access to indigenous communities was easier and more natural for Pachakutik than for traditional parties. In most cases, indigenous Pachakutik candidates were themselves movement leaders. With an incipient organizational structure, few economic resources, and little access to the media, it would have been difficult if not impossible for a new contender like Pachakutik to make electoral gains in the rural areas without the preexisting foundation of the indigenous organizations.

Pachakutik is developing organizational norms and structures that mirror or appropriate elements from the indigenous organizations. In most provinces Pachakutik candidates for the 2000 elections were selected in large provincial assemblies to which OSGs and other civic and community organizations sent delegates. In many cases, candidates were first nominated by their respective organizations and then voted upon by the full assembly. This is different from the practice of most traditional Ecuadorian political parties, where decisions about who is going to run on the party ticket are often made by a small group of party leaders.

In districts with active indigenous organizations several mechanisms have been developed to keep elected officials accountable to the grassroots organizations. For example, Congressman Gilberto Talahua, an indigenous legislator from Bolivar, does not unilaterally appoint his staff; the provincial indigenous organization the Federacion de Organizaciones Campesinas de Bolivar (FECAB-BRUNARI) does so.[20] The organization also has the practice of rotating the staff every six months, so that various people have the opportunity and experience of serving in the congressman's office. In an economy as poor as Ecuador's, jobs in Congress are a luxury and a privilege. By removing the appointment decisions from the individual legislator, the movement assures not only Talahua's continued accountability to the organization but also that he does not use his office and the resources that come with it to build up an individual power base apart from the organization.

Opposition versus Participation

The indigenous movement's incursion into formal electoral politics represents a new, potentially powerful tool in its efforts to improve the condition of indigenous communities and carve out a place of dignity and power for indigenous peoples within the Ecuadorian nation. However, electoral participation creates a new set of strategic dynamics within social movements. At times, electoral and protest strategies complement one another, but at other times they lead to contradictions and tensions.

Scholars studying new left parties in Latin America have observed that despite shared political and programmatic goals, it has often proved difficult if not impossible for these parties to cement permanent alliances with social movements. The way Pachakutik and the indigenous movement break down on the question of loyalty to a national programmatic agenda versus concern with obtaining particularistic resources is by focusing on local politics in small rural provinces. The movement organizations themselves must be concerned with obtaining material benefits for the grassroots. So the tension between national and local strategies can surface not only at the juncture between the political and social movements but also within the indigenous movement itself. This tension has become more pronounced as the indigenous movement has grown in stature and emerged as one of the main organizational leaders of leftist opposition to neoliberalism.

Yet another axis of tension within the indigenous movement and between it and Pachakutik is that surrounding radical versus reformist strategies. As in any movement there are different tendencies within Ecuador's indigenous movement. The radical faction asserts that real political change for indigenous people is not possible under current political conditions and that more radical change is needed. Those who hold this position tend to view electoral participation more instrumentally, if they support it at all. This tenuous commitment to the rules of the political game in Ecuador clearly can lead to tension between the social movement and its political arm.

Both these points of tension (local versus national and radical versus reformist) were evident in the moment and aftermath of the January 2000 uprising. The call that led up to the events of January 21—to dismantle all three branches of government on the grounds that they were corrupt and not serving the interests of the majority poor—was radical, even revolutionary, and responded to issues of concern to indigenous and nonindigenous alike. However, in the aftermath of January 21 the movement continued to struggle with this new national leadership role and the need to address specific sectoral interests. Together with the CMS, CONAIE announced that it would carry out a citizen's ballot initiative on a number of demands that had figured in the January 21 platform, including ending dollarization, unseating the current Congress, and removing a U.S. military base in Manta. At the same time, however, the new administration reopened talks with CONAIE. In these negotiations CONAIE brought to the table the national policy issues mentioned above as well as specific sectoral demands. The more particularistic demands included a laundry list of such things as the designation of a government printing press to publish books and other materials in native languages, a rural housing subsidy, and the establishment of a permanent "indigenous fund" to be used for development and cultural projects.[21] After several months of negotiations, the indigenous movement was set to sign an agreement that would have committed the government to making good on the various sectoral demands without addressing any of the broader national economic and political policy demands of the indigenous and social movements. In the end CONAIE did not sign the agreements, and the talks broke down, due primarily to government ineptness. However, the fact that CONAIE was ready to sign these agreements exemplifies the conflicting pressures on the indigenous leadership. They want to take advantage of their political power to make an impact on broad national policy, but they are also under intense pressure from the grassroots to deliver very concrete and visible benefits.

Negotiating these two sets of goals is also an issue in the new arena of electoral politics. In the first place, the election of indigenous leaders to public office raises grassroots expectations about their ability to deliver goods and services. This is due in large part to the nature of Ecuador's political system and political culture, in which clientelism and *caciquismo* tend to dominate and overshadow programmatic and ideological agendas. In this system, voters tend to judge elected officials more on their ability to deliver concrete goods and services than on their programmatic or ideological positions. Meeting voters' expectations then is somewhat easier for local officeholders, because their job is to build infrastructure and deliver resources. By contrast, this is not the prescribed role for national-level politicians, including members of Congress, something that is often not well understood by the grassroots voters who elected them.[22] In addition, it is difficult for Pachakutik to have an impact on national policy when their congressional delegation is so small. In coalition with other center-left and left-wing parties they have been able to achieve some of their goals, but the movement's impact on major national policy issues has been limited. Likewise, congressional politics in multiparty systems like Ecuador's by definition requires a great deal of negotiation and compromise. This presents another set of tensions and dilemmas for Pachakutik representatives, as they can either attempt to maintain an ideologically pure position, which relegates them to a marginalized position within Congress, or engage in brokering to gain some things in exchange for others, but at the risk of appearing like a traditional political party. While electoral participation can achieve some important changes by placing people in local office, the ability of Pachakutik, at least until now, to impact national policy through electoral means has been quite limited because it remains a minority party.

Pachakutik's indigenous legislators are in a difficult position, as they have few tools to retain and build grassroots support, nor are they in a position to have a major impact on national policy-making. Likewise, the indigenous movement's national-level leadership, frustrated with their inability to implement change through their national elected officials, often return to movement strategies of protest. When the level of protest reaches the point that the demands are for radical structural change, as was the case in January 2000, elected congressional representatives are put in a difficult and uncomfortable position. This difficulty was evident in the weeks before the January 21 uprising, as CONAIE insistently pressed its demand that all three branches of government be dissolved. While agreeing with CONAIE's analysis of the grave crisis facing the country, several Pachakutik representatives expressed frustration that the movement had lumped them together with other members of Congress into the category of "corrupt politicians."[23] The reluctance of all but one of the Pachakutik delegation (Congressman Talahua, from Bolivar) to participate in the marches and street protests that led up to the January 21 takeover or to officially renounce their congressional seats was viewed as opportunistic by CONAIE leadership and bases. Obviously demands for radical change will create problems for Pachakutik's elected officials because there is an inherent contradiction between demands for radical structural change through nonconstitutional means—as in the actions of January 21—and electoral participation. In the wake of the January 21 events, right-wing parties in Congress attempted to force Pachakutik legislators out of Congress for their association with the movement.

In conclusion, like other left parties in Latin America, Pachakutik has experienced the tension between delivering immediate concrete benefits to voters and negotiating national-level policy-making and politics. However, Pachakutik's relationship with indigenous and social movements is more integrated and organic than that of most other leftist parties in the region, and this makes an important difference in how these tensions are resolved. Likewise, there is an ongoing tension over strategy, with many in the movement not completely willing to jettison more radical aspirations for electoral participation. Yet the fact that Pachakutik has had some measurable success in the electoral arena and has been able to get people elected to local and national office means that there is a larger group of people who have a stake in the political process, and this has dampened the power of the more radical sectors. For democracy to deepen in Ecuador, it will be important that Pachakutik continue to be able to carve out a space for itself within the political system and that political elites not stifle or obstruct the movement's electoral efforts. Despite the difficulties, there is great potential for Pachakutik to play an important role as one facet of indigenous and social movement strategy in Ecuador. Clearly much can be achieved at the local level, and an emphasis on this in the electoral arena combined with social movement activities at the national level has the potential to serve as a constructive conduit to a division of labor between the electoral and social movements.

While more systematic work needs to be done on trends in rural voting, Pachakutik's success seems to suggest that alternative parties can make inroads among poor rural populations, thereby further eroding traditional power structures and clientelistic practices that impede democratization. However, the conditions under which Pachakutik has been able to succeed are special in many ways and therefore point to the real challenges for achieving similar outcomes in other countries where social movements are not as strong or unified.

Given the tremendous potential for transformative change at the local level, as well as the fact that revolutionary strategies are no longer viable in the post–Cold War world, it is likely that electoral participation will remain an important part of the indigenous movement's repertoire of strategies for social change. In turn, the indigenous movement's participation is vitally important for the deepening of democracy because it offers hope that new social actors can make incursions into the political arena through the formal democratic mechanisms in place. The inclusion of these new social actors is bringing into the political arena new practices that have the potential to challenge and invigorate Ecuador's political culture. What combination of strategies Ecuador's indigenous and social movements choose to employ in the future and the response from other political players and Ecuadorian society in general will have an important impact on the prospects for democracy in this small Andean nation.

3   Engendering Andean Politics

The Paradoxes of Women's Movements in
in Neoliberal Ecuador and Bolivia

⚜   In the past two decades, women from various social sectors have emerged as protagonists in social movements and electoral politics in the Andes. Women from low- and middle-income backgrounds; urban and rural women; women of indigenous, mestiza, and African origins; household workers; agricultural workers; heterosexuals and lesbians—all have played significant roles in establishing contemporary women's movements and in helping to en*gender* the broader political, cultural, and economic landscape of the Andes.[1] While women initially played roles in male-based human rights, antiauthoritarian, university, and antipoverty struggles in the late 1970s and 1980s, many women decided to create their own organizations as a way to address their specific needs and challenge sexism.[2] In the 1980s, global feminism, United Nations initiatives, and inequalities "at home" all contributed to a much-needed, increasingly vibrant, and pluralistic movement of women that has crossed all sectors of society. While in the early 1980s organized women received significant funding and ideological support from newly democratizing governments and the international development community, in the 1990s the rules of the game changed significantly. Market-based development policies in Ecuador and Bolivia, including economic liberalization, privatization, state retrenchment, and the general move toward integration into the global market economy, have contributed to a new set of relationships among civil society, the state, and the economy in each country. One result of this is that poor, urban, and rural communities have become more responsible for their own social welfare. In particular, the burden of privatization measures has been transferred "invisibly" to the realm of women's work.

Both Bolivia and Ecuador provide important examples of the successes and failures of neoliberal development. Bolivia's world-renowned neoliberal experiment, which began in the mid-1980s with the introduction of one of the harshest sets of adjustment measures ever implemented in the region, has exacted a high social cost and has affected the lives of millions of Bolivians. Until the mid-1990s, Bolivian governments succeeded in implementing World Bank and International Monetary Fund–inspired adjustment measures, often by effectively quelling opposition from social sectors. Since 1997, however, Bolivians have witnessed massive protests against neoliberal reforms and accompanying measures such as decentralization and educational reform. In Ecuador, in contrast, social opposition to neoliberal development measures has effectively blocked reforms in certain periods, particularly during the late 1990s. The coalition model of social movements and political parties, which greatly influenced the new 1998 constitution, serves as an example of how neoliberalism has catalyzed women and indigenous sectors into action. Yet despite Ecuador's widespread activism, policies such as dollarization have not been prevented.

In these national contexts, like elsewhere, international funding priorities have shifted from the earlier focus on state planning to a focus on private-sector planning and public-private partnerships (Segarra 1996). Given already existing gender biases in economic development policies, in which women's work in households and communities has been largely invisible to macroeconomic planners (Elson 1991, 1998), the neoliberal emphasis on the privatization of social welfare has helped to exacerbate the amount of work women perform in their households and communities. And whereas once women's organizations could rely upon external funding for their institutional activities and growth, leading to the establishment of hundreds of women's nongovernmental organizations (NGOs) and to what some have called the "NGOization" of women's struggles (see Alvarez 1998), in the 1990s funding priorities shifted toward market-oriented development projects such as women's microentrepreneurship and self-help community development initiatives, including food-for-work programs (Ochsendorf 1999); communal kitchens; and self-help housing-construction projects in Bolivia, Ecuador, and elsewhere throughout the Andes and Latin America (Barrig 1996). An important outcome of this has been that the poorest sectors of women have been targeted and mobilized as volunteers, rather than as paid laborers, in neoliberal-inspired social programs. While this is not a new phenomenon, the focus on self-help and volunteerism has greatly increased during the neoliberal period around the world.

In these ways, the period of neoliberal development planning over the past two decades has contributed both to women's empowerment and to their disempowerment. While some women have actually gained political visibility through their participation in the state, political parties, and/or NGOs, the majority of women have lost out economically. The historical project of women's "integration into development" (Boserup 1970) has always been "uneven and incomplete" (Vargas 1992), yet the neoliberal period has exacerbated these contradictions by creating wider inequalities among rich and poor and among women policy makers who work for the state and/or the development community and those women who are targeted as the recipients of neoliberal development policies. In addition, racial and ethnic differences among women have been overlooked, both in theory and practice (Paulson and Calla 2000). In development studies, "race" is often construed in terms of "culture," thus erasing an important form of inequality (Chua, Bhavani, and Foran 2000). Indigenous and women's movements appear separate and fragmented, both in academic research and in political action, despite the rich history of indigenous women's organizing, particularly in Bolivia, where, for example, the Federación de Mujeres Campesinas y Indígenas de Bolivia "Bartolina Sisa" has existed since the early 1980s. In Ecuador, in contrast, it has been more recently that indigenous women have created their own organizations to address their needs and to challenge both racism within women's movements and sexism within indigenous movements. The Congreso Nacional de Mujeres Indígenas y Negras (National Congress of Indigenous and Black Women), for example, was formed in the late 1990s by a group of indigenous and Afro-Ecuadorian women activists with the purpose of addressing the multiple forms of discrimination they face in Ecuadorian society.

Women activists have contributed substantially to public debates on neoliberal reform and related issues of national identity and citizenship. By "neoliberal reforms" I am referring to a set of economic and social measures designed to restructure economic and political institutions with the purported goal of improving overall economic growth and output. Most commonly, this includes economic liberalization, privatization, trade initiatives, and state retrenchment, typically in the form of structural adjustment policies (SAPs). Related measures include decentralization policies and educational and health reform, which have been implemented with an eye toward, first, radically reducing the role of the state in the economy and society; second, establishing public-private partnerships between the state and civil society; and finally, increasing the participation and responsibility of civic actors and institutions in facilitating the national development process (Albó 1996). In this sense, decentralization measures, although not necessarily "neoliberal" measures themselves, have converged well with neoliberal strategies to restructure state-civil society relations and have had a tendency to operate more from the standpoint of private capital rather than public governance. This is so despite the obvious reality that national governments, including state women's agencies, still play key roles in any national or transnational development process (Schild 2000).

In the Ecuadorian case, four strands of feminist action became visible during the political crisis of 1997.[3] These strands of feminist action serve to illustrate some of the gendered contradictions of neoliberal reform in the context of nationalist politics, contradictions that have only worsened since the financial crisis and the inception of dollarization in Ecuador in September 2001 (also see chapter 9). In the Bolivian case, women social actors have contributed to challenging the institutionalization of neoliberal state policies in Bolivia.[4] Yet while Bolivian and Ecuadorian women have challenged neoliberal development, some organized women also have nonetheless participated, however unwittingly, in the institutionalization of these very policies and, more broadly, in the formation of a new kind of "gendered neoliberal citizenship" (Schild 2000).[5] At the very least, women, like other social actors, define their political identities and negotiate with societal institutions in contradictory ways that reveal the broader contradictions of Andean cultural projects of modernity.

The Gendered Politics of Neoliberal Restructuring

Since the early 1980s, numerous sectors of women in both countries have felt specific, gendered impacts of structural adjustment policies (Moser 1989; Lilia Rodríguez 1994), including changes in household expenditures and consumption patterns; changes in family structure; continuing lack of access to basic resources such as water, electricity, and paved roads; inflationary costs of food, transportation, and education; and, generally, the increased workload of women in their homes and communities (Benería and Feldman 1992; Dwyer and Bruce 1988). As many scholars have pointed out, local women's organizations in Ecuador and Bolivia, in both rural and urban areas, have increased in size and number during the past two decades and have provided important networks for channeling resources and confronting the economic crisis on various levels (Lilia Rodríguez 1994, 1996; Lind 1992; Salinas Mulder 1994; Zabala 1995). Others have shown that these types of organizations, most of which are composed of the popular, working class, rural poor, and/or indigenous (Centro María Quilla/CEAAL 1990), have become the new recipients, or "targets," of development (Escobar 1995). Historically, such organizations have formed to respond collectively to the negative effects of economic crisis and, in some cases, to the interrelated effects of racism, sexism, and/or ethnocentrism, among others. Now that they have endured for several years or decades, often with economic aid from the state, NGOs, and/or international development organizations, they are assumed to be highly capable of distributing resources to local communities, particularly at times when the state can no longer provide this type of service delivery. In this way, their struggles for survival have become institutionalized (Lind 2003a) and, through male biases in development theory and policy design (Elson 1991), incorporated into the logic of most development policies. One result of this is that women participants have become "burnt out" (Moser 1989), underpaid, and/or poorer than they were previously, despite the development assistance.

Each country has undergone a similar set of adjustment measures since the early 1980s: while in Ecuador the restructuring process initially was less harsh, the latter period of the 1990s proved extremely difficult for the financial sector and for the majority of Ecuadorians alike. Bolivia, in contrast, began its restructuring process with a "bang" in 1985, only to experience enduring poverty throughout the late 1990s. Interestingly, during this same period Bolivia has undergone a highly innovative decentralization process as well, with local democratization as its goal. In similar although less dramatic fashion, Ecuador also has implemented decentralization measures. These two processes, neoliberal restructuring and decentralization, have both contributed to the paradoxes that women's movements face in the current period.

Since the early 1980s, Ecuadorian governments have negotiated dozens of loans and generally adhered to International Monetary Fund (IMF) and World Bank–inspired structural adjustment measures. These measures have included state downsizing; the privatization of state industries; trade liberalization; political decentralization; and, generally speaking, the move to insert Ecuador into the global economy by letting the "free market" work on its own. The government of President Sixto Durán Ballén (1992–96) accelerated the process of restructuring through its "modernization plan," which included the reduction of trade barriers, the promotion of export-led development, and the privatization of key national industries. During that period, the administration restructured and downsized social and economic ministries, laid off more than twenty thousand state employees, and implemented a World Bank/IMF–designed Emergency Social Investment Fund to address the "social costs" of structural adjustment (Segarra 1996).

When President Abdalá Bucaram (September 1996–February 1997) announced his economic policy in December 1996, Ecuador's national foreign debt reached over twelve billion dollars, and the government's budget deficit reached over one billion dollars (World Bank 1999). While President Bucaram and his brother and then–social welfare minister, Adolfo, handed out money to impoverished supporters throughout the country, Bucaram simultaneously asked citizens to accept neoliberal reforms as a "sacrifice" for the nation that was necessary to pay the twelve-billion-dollar national debt. Many viewed this as deceitful since just months earlier Bucaram had promised a lighter adjustment. His proposals during this period caused the prices of electricity, fuel, and telephone service to increase as much as 300 percent. High prices fueled protest by consumers as well as labor unions of many kinds: taxi drivers, street vendors, truck drivers, and small and large businesses, among others. While Bucaram's strategies pushed some sectors into further isolation, they catalyzed others into immediate action—a common contradictory effect of neoliberal reform (Benería 1992; Lind 1997). As a result of his policies, coupled with charges of corruption and growing mistrust of his government, Bucaram faced opposition by people of all social classes and geographic origins. Ultimately, in February 1997, Bucaram was forced to resign following an unprecedented, spontaneous mobilization of over two million Ecuadorians and a congressional vote to remove him on charges of "mental incapacity."[6]

Various sectors of women, along with indigenous activists and workers, participated actively during this period to bring political and economic stability back to the country. While organized women fought for change, the majority of women and men continued to face extreme economic hardship, which only worsened in the aftermath of the political transition. In August 1998, Jamil Mahuad (August 1998–January 2000) was sworn in as president. Like his predecessors, Mahuad sought to continue the neoliberal reforms, which led (among other things) to inflationary price rises in fuel, transportation, and other basic expenses. In addition, several major banks were forced to close their doors to their savings holders and file for bankruptcy. Met with great opposition by several political sectors, President Mahuad stepped down in January 2000. The current vice-president, Gustavo Noboa (February 2000–present), took over the presidency and, despite popular opposition to neoliberalism, proceeded to implement a broad neoliberal program that included dollarization of the economy. In the meantime, the majority of Ecuadorians have experienced significant financial setbacks from their lost savings and social security and from the transition to dollarization.

The Bolivian state, in contrast, arguably has undergone the most intense process of restructuring throughout the region. Beginning with Decree 21060, designed by neoclassical economist Jeffrey Sachs and initiated in 1985 by President Paz Estenssoro, Bolivia has undergone a series of measures including the privatization of state-owned enterprises (e.g., mining companies) and economic liberalization. These measures, now widely perceived by supporters as an example of the success of structural adjustment and by critics as an example of its failure, contributed to the layoff of over twenty-five thousand tin miners and to their (and their families') displacement to urban areas such as El Alto, Cochabamba, and Santa Cruz, as well as to the Bolivian Amazon region (McFarren 1992). In 1993, the administration of President Gonzalo Sanchez de Lozada (1993–97) initiated some additional reforms to complement the harsh structural adjustment policies. Although he continued most of Estenssoro's economic reforms, he also introduced three important social and political reforms: education, decentralization, and the laws of popular participation.

Sánchez de Lozada's decentralization measures catalyzed an intense shift from centralized state power to decentralized power in local municipalities and provinces and resulted in the establishment of over three hundred new municipalities (Albó 1996). His popular participation measures were designed to democratize political participation by (1) creating new political structures, (2) seeking a wider representation of people and interests within the new political structures, and (3) providing more democratic checks and balances among state and civil society organizations to avoid political corruption and opportunism. At the local level, new groups were formed, including *organizaciones territoriales de base* (OTBs, or territorial base organizations) and *comites de vigilancia* (oversight committees), creating a triangular structure among these new groups and the municipalities. In theory, these measures have been designed to incorporate previously marginalized voices and to strengthen democratic participation by civil society actors, beginning with local levels of participation. In practice, particularly in terms of gender, race, and class, these measures have had contradictory results, since indigenous and poor women tend to be among those who suffer the most.

Decentralization has also been an important policy strategy in Ecuador, particularly since the late 1990s. Initial studies have documented women's formal and informal participation in the newly decentralized political structures, emphasizing how women tend to become politically active initially through "informal" activities such as community organizations and networks (IULA/CELCADEL/US AID 1992, 1997; Arboleda 1994). On one hand, to the extent that women have been targeted as new participants in the local political structures, they have perhaps gained some additional political visibility and power. Yet at the same time, neoliberal policies have contributed to organized women's increased workloads and, as a result, to their economic disempowerment (Benería and Feldman 1992; Lind 1997). Thus the reforms have had contradictory effects on different sectors of women and have led to a range of political responses by women's organizations.

Women's Political Responses to Neoliberal Restructuring

Two general themes emerge in studies of Andean and Latin American women's movements in the 1990s and early 2000s. First is the "crisis of identity" that women activists and institutions are faced with as they negotiate the terms of neoliberal restructuring. Here I am referring primarily to the shifting relationships among state agencies, NGOs, and community organizations; between national and municipal or provincial governments; and among the women themselves who work in these institutions. This includes, for example, the way state women's agencies delegate responsibilities to private women's NGOs and to local municipalities, a direct result of decentralization and adjustment measures. This is also linked to the changing funding priorities for community-based women's organizations, leading to the so-called privatization of women's struggles for survival (Benería 1992; Lind 2003b). The second key theme is the shifts in power that occur within women's movements as a result of their internal restructuring, another consequence of the broader restructuring process (Schild 1998; Ríos 1998). Given these contexts, in which women activists have been faced with intensive and enduring adjustment measures, coupled with economic and financial crisis and rapid political change, how have contemporary women's movements addressed neoliberalism? How have they addressed the perceived changing role(s) of the state and the new public-private partnerships? How have they grappled with their own roles in the process and with the restructuring that has occurred within women's movements themselves?

Feminists Working within the State

Since the 1970s and 1980s, state women's agencies in both countries have played important roles in promoting gender issues from within the state—as well as in defining their primary recipients: sectors of poor women, including local women's organizations. Both the Ecuadorian state women's agency, the National Women's Council (CONAMU), and the Bolivian state women's agency, the General Office for Gender Issues (DGAG), have accomplished significant gender-based policy and legal reforms over the years. While earlier both agencies operated primarily as managers and facilitators of community-based projects, the neoliberal shift toward privatization and decentralization has meant that CONAMU and DGAG too began to delegate project management and implementation to municipalities or to civil society–based women's organizations. As a result, they are no longer necessarily directly responsible for these aspects of the process; rather, private and/or local entities are responsible. Yet despite the transfer of responsibility from the state to the local arena, a shift that is often perceived as "democratizing," they continue to define the parameters of state development policies that are implemented in and/or by local women's organizations and communities. In this sense, state women's agencies act as state interlocutors vis-à-vis their recipients, "poor women" (and sometimes "poor men"), and vis-à-vis the loosely defined women's movement, in order to complete their specific mandate to "integrate women into development." In an important sense, CONAMU and DGAG, like other state women's agencies throughout the region, continue to maintain institutional and interpretive power (Jean Franco 1989) despite their shift toward a decentralized model of state policy implementation. And as CONAMU and DGAG continue to be the primary institutions that define how women are to be "integrated into development" in each country, they maintain interpretive and institutional power in the gender and development field as well. For example, community women's organizations tend to be asked to participate in projects (with no or little pay for their labor) that are facilitated by middle-class professional women's NGOs and ultimately overseen by the state women's agency. Thus a hierarchy exists among national and local institutions, and class and educational inequalities tend to exist among the women who work in each of these institutions. An additional example concerns how poor women are brought into these projects and the consequences of their (often unpaid or underpaid) participation for their workloads. An unfortunate consequence of gender and development models has often been that poor women lose out economically, even if they gain some kind of political visibility and/or personal empowerment. Thus state women's agencies' relationships with local women's organizations—and with various sectors of women in general—are fraught with contradictions.[7]

The employees of state women's agencies, commonly feminists and/or political appointees, experience these contradictions as well. CONAMU's history, for example, is in many ways similar to that of other women's state agencies in Latin America (Placencia and Caro 1998; Alvarez 1998; Valenzuela 1998). Historically, some CONAMU directors have been self-defined feminist leaders from the NGO sector, yet most have been from traditional, non-feminist political sectors.[8] CONAMU has undergone several name changes, which reflects its growing status within the state. In late 1997, the then–National Women's Office (DINAMU) was given higher institutional status and renamed CONAMU. Its primary objective, until the present, is "to serve as the interlocutor of gender and development projects on a national level."[9] Its main focus is to design policy frameworks and to delegate project management and implementation to local women's organizations, local municipalities, and others who bid on the projects. Funding for projects is received from the Inter-American Development Bank (IDB), the United Nations International Children's Emergency Fund (UNICEF), the United Nations Development Fund for Women (UNIFEM), and other international organizations and is complemented by a minimal amount of state funding. The primary emphasis is on project design, rather than service delivery. Like other hegemonic state practices, CONAMU, as interlocutor of gender and development policy, serves to normalize a certain set of ideas about women's roles in development, while rendering others invisible or less important.[10] In particular, Western gender and development approaches have tended to view women's economic roles in isolation from their ethnic, racial, and cultural identities, thus overlooking the complexity of women's responses to societal change.

While CONAMU has power in defining who gets funding and why, it is also restricted by the conditions of development funders. It designs gender and development state policies and therefore contributes to defining the discursive and institutional boundaries within which knowledge is produced about women and development in Ecuador, yet it must frame its agenda within a context that is acceptable to international funding institutions. Educational programs on gender and development typically have been funded by foreign governments or through United Nations agencies such as UNIFEM and UNICEF. Other projects on gender and property (see Deere and León de Leal 2000) and women's participation in rural development initiatives have received funding from the IDB, the World Bank, or foreign development agencies. CONAMU and DGAG rely on this funding in order to acquire additional negotiating power with the state, since the state typically provides matching funds to the women's agency. The agenda of the funding agencies, then, largely shapes and sometimes limits the agenda of the state women's agencies. It is not surprising, then, that recently there has been an emphasis on property and women's integration into "free market" initiatives. In these ways, CONAMU itself designs its policy agenda within the complex web of state power relations (since CONAMU itself is a marginalized state agency), with the international development field, and with civic organizations and individual women in Ecuador.

As in Ecuador, the Bolivian state women's agency has played a significant role in facilitating "women's integration into development" in the context of neoliberal reform (even prior to 1985). The DGAG, part of the Vice-Ministry of Gender, Generational, and Family Affairs, located in the Ministry of Sustainable Development and Planning, has grown in institutional importance since its inception in the 1970s. During the government of President Gonzalo Sánchez de Lozada (1994–97), gender concerns were housed with indigenous and elderly concerns in the Vice-Ministry of Gender, Ethnic, and Generational Affairs, based in the Ministry of Social Welfare. When President Hugo Banzer entered office in 1997, he restructured these units: now there is a Vice-Ministry of Ethnic Affairs and a Vice-Ministry of Gender, Generational, and Family Affairs. This institutional restructuring split "target groups" according to ethnicity/race and gender (i.e., gender concerns are now housed in one institutional location, and race/ethnicity concerns are housed in another; see Paulson and Calla 2000). It also represented an ideological shift from a state focus on "gender" to one on "family." Now gender concerns are linked institutionally with (and are thus inseparable from) family concerns. As in other countries such as Chile, where there have been political battles about the usage of the term "gender" in the constitution and in the educational system (Jean Franco 1996), the Banzer administration's decision to combine gender and family concerns and to separate them from ethnic concerns reflects an ideological backlash against feminism in Bolivia.

Bolivian women's NGOs often propose agendas that the women's state agency adopts and/or rearticulates as a state policy or plan. Thus there is a fluid relationship between state feminists and activists working at NGOs or other women's organizations. Some proposals have come from NGOs such as the Center for Information and Development of Women (CIDEM), the Gregoria Apaza Center for Women's Promotion, the Women's Coordinating Committee, the San Gabriel Foundation, and the Women's Legal Office (Montaño 1996). Feminist policy analyst Sonia Montaño, a former director of the state women's agency (then called the Sub-Secretary of Gender Affairs), was also a founder of CIDEM in the early 1980s. She, in her capacity as a consultant, produced reports on gender and public policy and local governance (Montaño 1996, 1997) that the state women's agency adopted as best practice over time.

After the inception of the Banzer administration in 1997, Banzer appointed as director of the Vice-Ministry of Gender, Generational, and Family Affairs Carolina Toledo, a woman with a political-party background rather than an NGO background. Likewise, the director of DGAG, María Eugenia Díaz, is also from a political party. As leaders of the Bolivian state women's agency, their emphasis is on strengthening the state rather than strengthening a movement of women's organizations. They emphasize women's participation in state decentralization initiatives and in party reform but are not necessarily invested in strengthening the NGO-based women's movement except as a base for institutions that can carry out state plans. They therefore help to position women's NGOs as "clients" of the state in the new public-private partnership (with little recognition of the historical struggles of women's NGOs, now professionalized feminist organizations; see Barrig 1998).

Engendering Male-Based Institutions

Non-state-based women's organizations have also worked to engender and influence the agendas of male-based institutions. By making gender visible in state ministries, national and municipal development plans, policies, and political-party structures, women activists have transformed institutions and, in the process, challenged the neoliberal restructuring process. These organizations too fall within the network of women activists who have sought to work both within and against the neoliberal state. The Political Coordinator of Ecuadorian Women, for example, was established in 1996 to address state reform and the growing political crisis surrounding the Bucaram administration. The Coordinating Committee comprises feminists from the NGO sector, political parties, and the popular women's movement, most with experience in the state and/or private sector, some with previous experience in feminist organizations. A primary goal of the committee is to engender the state and political system. At the state level, this includes engendering all state ministries—in terms of personnel, policy frameworks, and project implementation. While CONAMU has worked to add a chapter on gender and development to each government's National Development Plan, the committee argues that this is not enough; rather, every section of each plan should include a gender dimension. From their perspective, CONAMU's efforts thus far have remained largely ghettoized within the larger state; the committee seeks to overcome this ghettoization by making gender an important aspect of the entire state.

To achieve this goal, the committee has set up vertical relations among expert committees and ministries with the aim of providing expertise on gender issues to policy makers within each ministry. For example, the committee on women and housing has established a relation with the Ministry of Housing, with the hope of adding a gender component to all housing policy produced in the ministry. Likewise, committees have also been set up with the Ministries of Social Welfare, Labor, Finance, and Education, as well as with other state agencies such as CONADE (Consejo Nacional del Desarollo).

To engender the political system, the committee's goal is to promote the election of feminist (and in general female) politicians and to give political-party status to the women's movement. In relation to this, the committee is pushing for an established quota system of female politicians (Vega 1998; Zabala 1999). This strategy—to engender the political and state system at large—is partly a response to some feminists' frustration with CONAMU's perceived power in and over the broader women's movement as well as with CONAMU's perceived lack of power within the broader state. This contradiction is expressed explicitly both by CONAMU employees and by CONAMU critics, including members of the committee. Indeed, it is this perceived contradiction—that CONAMU simultaneously has too much power (vis-à-vis the women's movement) and not enough power (vis-à-vis the state)—that has contributed to disagreement among feminists regarding how to proceed with feminist action within the state, alongside neoliberal state reform. Of course, this type of disagreement also stems from personal divisions and depends to some degree upon who builds alliances with whom. In this sense, political alliances are constructed, maintained, dismantled, and/or transformed over time based not solely on ideological alliances but on personal alliances as well. Just as clientelism and coalition-building were evident in the Bucaram administration at large, divergent perspectives on feminist action reflect both ideological differences and personal disagreements.

Bolivian policy makers, politicians, and NGO activists also have fought for a female quota in the political party and electoral system, with the primary goal of integrating more women into the formal political process. This move, which has followed a trend in Latin America and throughout the world to establish gender-based quotas (Jaquette 2001), was viewed optimistically by many feminists and women activists who hoped for higher female political visibility in Bolivian national politics. During this same period, Bolivia's radical decentralization policies were viewed by supporters as a related trend that could help to integrate women and other minorities (especially indigenous communities) into formal and informal politics.

Yet despite this radical movement to decentralize and establish a female quota system, preliminary studies have shown that fewer women, rather than more, are participating in the new political structures and traditional political parties.[11] Furthermore, in both countries, while the new political structures may have incorporated some women and indigenous people into their leadership, many others have actually lost power in this reshuffling. While some restructuring of power always occurs following a national policy change, clearly a decrease in women's political participation was not an intended consequence. This reveals one important paradox of women's movements in this context: should women fight to be integrated into the national political system, one that is based on an exclusionary model of citizenship (Vargas 1992; Olea 1995), or should women work outside that system in order to affect change?

The committee's strategy to engender the entire state reflects growing discontent among Latin American feminists with the effectiveness of state women's agencies in promoting gender-sensitive policies, laws, and practices. Yet at the same time, its emphasis on engendering male-based institutions during the neoliberal restructuring process raises new questions about the effectiveness of working within a seemingly culture- and gender-neutral global economic model (Jackson and Pearson 1998). The strategy to establish a female quota system is also a particularly controversial issue during the neoliberal period, when aside from the concrete economic changes women and men are experiencing in their daily lives, cultures of individualism and of the market are further promoted through the globalization process (Sassen 1998). Through this process, many women activists have questioned whether or not they would work with(in) the state, rather than in their own organizations. And even those who work in NGOs continue to be faced with issues of autonomy vis-à-vis the development field.

A New Public-Private Partnership?

Historically in Ecuador and Bolivia, fluid relationships have existed among women's NGOs and the state women's agency. In addition, a variety of relationships exist among community women's organizations and (what tend to be) middle-class NGOs and state employees. Yet during the neoliberal period these relationships have become more complicated, since the stakes for funding and support are higher and since there is no consensus over whether to work within the new public-private arrangements or outside them. Some umbrella organizations have attempted to negotiate these institutional arrangements by bringing women together from diverse political sectors. The La Paz, Bolivia–based Women's Coordinating Committee, for example, is an NGO that has focused on coalition-building among NGOs and on integrating women into national development in Bolivia since the 1980s. Most recently, the committee has focused on building a national network of local female politicians, particularly women from rural municipalities, OTBs, and oversight committees. National conferences have been held to train and build networks among elected women, with the assistance of the committee, DGAG, and several other NGOs. The committee's founder, Diana Urioste, contends that her project "helps to bring visibility to women's issues and to empower women at the local level," yet she is cautious in claiming that this is a solution in itself, given that the broader political and economic process continues to erode women's and men's livelihoods and forms of sustainability.[12] In addition to this project, the Women's Coordinating Committee represents over fifty women's NGOs and community organizations throughout the country. Urioste has participated in numerous national, regional, and international conferences over the years, and her political strategies have also changed to reflect the current political context in Bolivia.

The Quito, Ecuador–based Permanent Women's Forum serves as another example of an umbrella women's organization that has worked to negotiate and build coalitions among public and private political sectors. Established in 1994 during the regional preparatory meetings for the United Nations conference in Beijing, China (held in 1995), the forum represents organizations from a wide range of political sectors and includes women of middle-class, professional, and/or NGO sectors, among others. The forum was initiated by Guadalupe León, then director of an NGO that focused on issues of domestic violence and abuse. The forum originally relied upon institutional support from the NGO, although it was designed as an umbrella organization of women's NGOs and local organizations committed to incorporating women into community-based and other development initiatives, as well as into informal political networks. In general, the forum does not advocate women's participation in the formal political process. Rather, it operates more from within a development framework and advocates the incorporation of women into public decision-making and planning.

During the Bucaram period, the forum advocated a civil society approach to politics, in which civil society institutions, rather than the state or political parties, would be engendered. This "engendering" would occur both through women's actual participation in community-based and national initiatives and through promoting awareness of the gender dimensions of organizational structures, policies, project design and implementation, and so on, in local organizations. Interestingly enough, its original advocate, Guadalupe León, was also the labor minister during a short period of Bucaram's administration in 1996. Thus while the forum focused on strengthening civil society institutions, its leader took a place in the state.

Not only did León work within the state, but she did so during a period of heightened anger and frustration among feminists surrounding Bucaram's policies, which were laden with gendered contradictions. Perhaps the most fundamental issue for other feminist strands was that León chose to work with an unpredictable government labeled for misogynist acts, including alleged sexual harassment among high-ranking, male government officials, and for its gendered antics, including the honoring of Lorena Bobbitt as a national hero, which had already alienated several political sectors.[13] Furthermore, León's appointment further fragmented feminist politics in the state: between CONAMU, the Women's Coordinating Committee, and León's position as labor minister, feminist interests were dispersed throughout the state. However, rather than creating a stronger feminist network within the state, this led to further divisions among feminists, thus contributing to the different strands' distinct approaches to addressing change. The forum, later led by other feminists, also sent members to participate officially in the redrafting of the 1998 Ecuadorian constitution, a highly significant event for women activists. Following Ecuador's new laws requiring that social movements be "party-ized," both the women's movement and the indigenous movement were given official seats, along with the National Senate, in the constitutional redrafting meetings.[14]

Both the La Paz–based Women's Coordinating Committee and the Quito-based Permanent Women's Forum have chosen to work within the new public-private partnerships by creating their own coalitions, specifically through coalition-building and working with other political sectors to address broad national issues. Currently in Bolivia, feminist policy makers have also organized to address how they can participate in the amendment of Bolivia's constitution and, more generally, in the traditionally male-based realm of public policy.[15]

The fact that political institutions have been restructured as part of the broader process of economic restructuring has indeed contributed to schisms among the different political approaches women have taken in this context. State feminists, women working to engender male-based institutions, and women working within the new public-private partnerships may emphasize different aspects of change, but all tend to agree that they cannot avoid the restructuring process, which, most concur, is here to stay and must be addressed. Nevertheless, many women activists remain adamantly opposed to working for change at this level, preferring to work outside these institutions in opposition to neoliberalism. This has led many to observe the fragmentation of Andean women's movements, rather than their cohesion under extreme duress.

Yet despite the perceived fragmentation of the Bolivian and Ecuadorian women's movements, neoliberal policies have also catalyzed women to participate in broader unified fronts at unprecedented levels. For example, Ecuadorian women's organizations, although they constitute diverse strands of action, have all worked toward strengthening democracy and citizen practices—and reshaping biased economic policies. Bolivian women's organizations, from the Bartolina Sisas to middle-class policy organizations such as the Women's Coordinating Committee and the Cochabamba-based Women's Legal Office, address a range of issues related to the current neoliberal economic measures, the politics of decentralization, and additional issues such as the "war on drugs" and increased levels of homelessness in Bolivia's cities. Thus even as neoliberal policies have exacerbated class divisions among women and contributed to the fragmentation of the women's movement, women's organizations have created coalitions and informal networks and, often with other social groups, engaged in sustained protest against neoliberalism.

Neoliberalism, in fact, has become the political rubric under which many women's organizations have banded together to address their common concerns as women, despite longstanding historical, cultural, class, geographic, and political differences. As elsewhere in Latin America, neoliberalism has served an important political purpose for women's movements: this is so despite the multiple ways in which women and men define and understand the meaning of economic policy in their daily lives.[16] It is not a coincidence, for example, that on International Women's Day (March 8) in recent years, Andean women's organizations have organized around the theme of neoliberalism, making connections between their roles as women and neoliberal development policies, globalization, and international development.

Autonomous Feminism

The perceived fragmentation of women's movements in the neoliberal period has been best addressed by the new "autonomous feminist" movement, which challenges the foundations of "second-wave" feminism as well as issues of power, autonomy, and identity among organized women. Now a widely known regional (even global) movement, autonomous feminism has significant roots in Bolivia. Its first expression was evident in the formation in the late 1980s of Creative Women, founded by the only two out lesbians in Bolivia, both of whom are feminists with leftist backgrounds. Creative Women is arguably the most well-known feminist organization in Bolivia today because its founders, along with a handful of members, intervene in the public sphere through the use of graffiti, public performances, television interviews, and written publications and at their self-managed café, where they produce music and poetry. Their graffiti is widely known in the La Paz area, as well as in other cities and in some rural areas. Their graffiti invites people to rethink their own positions of power and complacency in Bolivian society, much as third-wave feminist graffiti and other forms of modern art did in the United States and elsewhere, by focusing on women's and men's identifications with the Bolivian state, privatization, the development field, and sexism. They question people's ways of identifying themselves through the dominant lens of society and also provide a strong critique of what they refer to as "institutionalized feminists"—NGO-based and/or professional feminists—for their perceived complacency in the "gender technocracy." Development aid has institutionalized a "gender technocracy," they argue, which has become a bureaucratized form of feminist knowledge that represents Western/northern interests more so than the interests of women in local Bolivian communities—a process they believe has been exacerbated by neoliberal reforms.

Creative Women organized the first regional conference on autonomous feminism in 1998. While its members make valid points, they often do not acknowledge their own forms of dependency upon international funding and ideologies. Considering that they too have received development funding for at least one of their written publications, and that the founders were exiled in Italy during the 1970s, they too are influenced by "northern" agendas. Yet what makes them interesting is their ability to be self-critical of feminism itself, as it has historically developed, and the ways in which they challenge constructions of identity among members of the NGO-based women's movement and women in general.

Ecuadorian feminists have also created an autonomous feminist group, Feminists for Autonomy. Frustrated with the limitations of working within the state and/or under the guidelines of international development organizations, disillusioned with party and other ideological and personal divisions among CONAMU, forum, and committee feminists, and desiring a new form of politics, a small group of feminists organized an informal group to discuss and reflect upon the political crisis stemming from the Bucaram administration. Self-defined as autonomous feminists, they maintain a strong critique of the bureaucratized structures within which they must often work if they wish to earn an income and/or receive institutional funding. Comprising feminists who have worked in NGOs or in the state and are now disillusioned with the "gender technocracy," Feminists for Autonomy is small and grassroots in nature, yet it has made its presence known through public, performative acts of protest in Quito.

One such symbolic protest that received national attention occurred on International Women's Day, 1998. The autonomous feminists dressed up as Manuela Sáenz, Simón Bolívar's liberator, and rode on horses to Independence Plaza in the central historic district of Quito. While this protest was relatively small, the symbolic move to reappropriate Sáenz's image was significant on more than one level. Known as "la libertadora del libertador" (the liberator of the liberator) for having once saved Bolívar from being captured by the Spaniards, Sáenz has recently been revived in Ecuadorian literature and popular culture as a heroine in her own right—and not just as an appendage to Bolívar. Her image has been revived in the imaginations of many Ecuadorians at a time of heightened public debate and sometimes outright conflict over national identity. By reappropriating Sáenz as a modern national hero, autonomous feminists helped to remake the nation by tapping into Ecuadorians' collective memory of resistance to Spanish conquest and rule and by engendering that collective memory.

This protest is also significant because feminists invoked a collective, historical notion of national identity yet also critiqued the boundaries within which nation-building and development have occurred within Ecuador. As they performed the nationalist image of Manuela Sáenz, they reclaimed the very project of nation building with which Sáenz is associated. In this sense, they drew from her historical representation to engender, and critique, the modern practice of nation building. They critiqued, for example, political corruption and the nation's debt burden and advocated economic redistribution and democratization of the political system. Inherent to their march was the idea that women are affected in gender-specific ways by the current economic and political reforms. Their public performance of Sáenz, an historically "invisible" heroine of the colonial independence movement, thus became a modern icon of feminists remaking the nation in the context of neoliberalism.

The Paradoxes of Women's Movements

The different strands of women's political action have simultaneously struggled for institutional spaces within the state while also questioning the premises within which the state and other male-based institutions or processes are constructed (e.g., the party system, male-based NGOs, constitutional reengineering, national development plans). One important consequence of the restructuring process is that increased class divisions have occurred among middle-class and poor and working-class women, and specifically among middle-class feminist policy makers and NGO activists and

women "targeted" by neoliberal policies. While many organized women, regardless of their class background, claim to be tired of working for little or no
pay, poor women tend to be the most "burnt out" (Moser 1989; Lind 2001).
In addition, the neoliberal development model (including gender and development policies) creates distance between "experts" and "clients," between
the professional women who design and oversee projects and the project recipients, poor women. This places organized middle-class women in the contradictory position of working for social change, often with a critical vision,
yet also finding themselves implicated in the web of power relations that the
restructuring process has helped to institutionalize. And for working-class,
poor, and/or rural women this translates into increased work in the face of diminishing resources, particularly given the state's inability to provide social
welfare. This paradox of class inequality that results from a free market model
of development is one that women activists have yet to address adequately. At
the heart of this, organized women need to rethink not only the "sites and assumptions" of their political organizing (Brodie 1994) but also how they can
more effectively challenge national and global economic models, which appear gender-neutral yet carry heavy male and Eurocentric biases (Elson 1991;
Chua, Bhavani, and Foran 2000).

It remains to be seen what will occur within the Bolivian and Ecuadorian
women's movements. In both countries, community-based women's organizations have received minimal support from state and international development aid since the initial period of structural adjustment in the early 1980s.
Initially they organized out of economic necessity; now they may be "burnt
out" and underpaid, yet they are viewed as an exemplary model of resource
distribution.[17] Decentralization and popular participation measures—which
exist to varying degrees in both countries (see Arboleda 1994)—have contributed to institutionalizing this process, by which women are incorporated
into the new political structures. While this process has had positive effects
on specific sectors of women who gain political visibility or economic independence, it nonetheless contributes to the "privatization of women's struggles" (Benería 1992). Some organizations gain while others lose; some, while
they may have economic support, are managed on the assumption that
women have endless amounts of time to participate on a volunteer basis
and/or for low wages. In addition, cuts in state spending translate into the intensification of domestic work, as women become responsible for activities
such as childcare and food distribution that were once funded externally (Benería 1992). This is one way in which the burden of privatization measures and
state budget cuts is transferred "invisibly" to the realm of women's work—in
this case, to community women's organizations. This observation resonates
with research conducted on women's organizations in Bolivia and Peru and

with other regional studies (Benería and Feldman 1992; Barrig 1996; Lind 2002).

An additional paradox concerns how women's movements position themselves within the new public-private arrangements. This paradox, faced by state women's agencies, NGOs, umbrella organizations, and community groups alike, includes, first, the concrete ways in which Ecuadorian and Bolivian women have negotiated their "place at the table" in national discussions. For example, the formation of the Congreso Nacional de Mujeres Indigenas del Ecuador (CONMIE) in Ecuador has created an entirely new political space from which black and indigenous women can create a united front and address issues of racism in relation to other issues of class and gender inequalities. As such, CONMIE is one of the first groups to address the intersection of these complex systems of oppression as they help to shape the Ecuadorian national community. Likewise, women's groups of all classes and backgrounds face the dilemma of how to develop their own strategies and not those suggested or implied by funding agencies. Once women begin to implement strategies that emerge from the neoliberal model, rather than alternatives to it, they are caught in the broader paradox of the power of development discourse in defining contemporary political and economic agendas. This is an issue that all people face, not just organized women in Ecuador and Bolivia.

Autonomous feminists have addressed this political paradox most explicitly, although arguably not most effectively. They too must work from within the institutional arrangements of neoliberalism (some out of necessity, some out of choice). They have participated in important protests, such as the Creative Women boycott of a gender and development master's program at a research institute affiliated with the public university in La Paz. They claimed that because the program received foreign funding, and given its emphasis on development studies, it was simply another part of the "gender technocracy." Many "institutionalized feminists" would not disagree. However, the divergent viewpoints lie both in their understanding of social change and in their relationship to modernity: some choose to work within it; others choose to deconstruct it and imagine a "post-development" alternative (Simmons 1997).

Clearly, all strands of women's political action have contributed in important ways to transforming national politics in neoliberal Bolivia and Ecuador. As visible actors in the anti-Bucaram protests and in drafting the new constitution, they have undoubtedly played crucial roles in transforming the political process. Although many sectors of organized women have had to deal with the consequences of dollarization and the ongoing financial crisis for their own households—including the loss of savings, being forced to give up their automobiles, having to care for needier family members, and so on—they have begun to address the complexity of this situation through their anticorruption protests. In Bolivia, women activists continue to critique President Jorge Quiroga for maintaining the neoliberal model, as well as for his government's crackdown on indigenous, labor, and coca-producer organizations. An important area of research that needs to be addressed is how women policy makers can "talk to the boys" about economic growth, structural adjustment, and the models of citizenship that underlie current decentralization measures. As elsewhere, Bolivian and Ecuadorian women have yet to bridge this gap—which indeed will not disappear without the will of male-based political sectors. Whether feminist demands will translate into policy, law, and/or cultural practice remains to be seen.

In a neoliberal context a state's plan to privatize social welfare relies (however implicitly) upon a gendered social order in which women's identities and roles are defined in terms of the market. Organized women in this context gain some but lose out on their overall project of rethinking the global economic model of neoliberalism. The difficulty ahead lies in determining how women activists can work within the institutional arrangements of neoliberal development while also addressing how neoliberal policies themselves negatively affect poor women's and men's lives in Andean cultures and societies.

II Conflict and Violence

Fernando Coronil and Julie Skurski

4   Dismembering and Remembering the Nation

The Semantics of Political Violence in Venezuela

> And the death of the people was as it has always been:
> as if no one, nothing had died,
> as if they were stones falling
> on the ground, or water on the water.

> —Pablo Neruda, *Canto General*

Violence and History

Although political violence has played a central part in the formation of nations, its historical constitution and role in national imaginaries have received scant attention.[1] All too frequently violence is not so much explained as its causes identified, its form accounted for by its function, and its function instrumentalized. Violence is thus reduced to a practical tool used by opposing social actors in pursuit of conflicting ends. Whether treated as a cause, function, or instrument, violence is generally assumed rather than examined in its concreteness. Little attention is paid to its specific manifestations, to the way its effects are inseparably related to the means through which it is exerted, and to the meanings that inform its deployment and interpretation.

Moments of political violence appear shatteringly similar in their grim outcome and in the sheer physicality of the destruction they inflict. Yet these moments, even those regarded as spontaneous outbursts, are shaped by each society's particular history and myths of collective identity and are energized by sedimented memories of threats to the collectivity. In a critique of what he called the "spasmodic view of popular history," E. P. Thompson (1971) warned against viewing popular protest as a simple reaction to increasing prices. Just as riots are not a direct response to hunger, state repression is not simply a means to control popular unrest. Seemingly spontaneous popular action develops through the enactment of shared understandings and the enunciation of novel statements in a familiar idiom, while the state's use of force as a means to control unrest draws upon a vision of the natural ordering of society that is based on quotidian relations of domination. The immediacy and apparent naturalness of moments of collective violence may conceal their intentionality and socially constructed significance.

Violence is wielded and resisted in the idiom of a society's distinctive history. When it becomes a force in contending efforts to affirm or restructure a given vision of order, it simultaneously disorders and reorders established understandings and arrangements. Aggression becomes inseparable from transgression, the rupture of conceptual and physical boundaries indivisible from the construction of new orders of significance. Violence pushes the limits of the permissible, opening up spaces where customary and unexpected meanings and practices are brought together in unprecedented ways, illuminating hidden historical landscapes in a flash, and leaving behind the opaque memory of ungraspable territories. In the crisis of meaning that violence conceives, the territoriality of nations and the corporeality of people become privileged mediums for reorganizing the body politic and forcibly controlling the movement of persons and ideas within the nation's material and cultural space.

In Venezuela, two conflicts between the state and the popular sectors in the late 1980s became landmarks in that nation's history. Both were responses to political changes and socioeconomic transformations that, since the late 1970s, have disrupted the bases of Venezuela's populist political system, based on petroleum-rent distribution, and have challenged the assumptions that long sustained it. These conflicts became nodal points in the redefinition of the discourse of democracy, as dominant and opposition forces clashed over the interpretation of events and their implications. And in the broadest context, they were conditioned at once by a colonial legacy and by a reordering of worldwide capitalist relations. As the hidden hand of finance capital and the visible hand of cultural fashion etch the indeterminate boundaries of the postmodern map of the world, the contours of this landscape reveal the hold of transformed colonial relations in the age of postcolonial empires.[2]

History and the Massacres

Toward the end of the 1988 presidential campaign, an event occurred that, although it appeared far removed from the fanfare and display of politics, was directed to a national political audience. Fourteen villagers from the border town of Amparo on the cattle plains *(llanos)* on the Arauca River, dividing southwest Venezuela from Colombia, were killed on October 29, 1988, by a government counterinsurgency brigade claiming they were guerrillas. Four months later, from February 27 to March 3, 1989, there took place a massive unplanned urban uprising involving widespread looting, against which the government used extensive force: by official count, 276 people died; a human rights organization identified 399 bodies. It was detonated by the unrealized expectations of political and economic renewal raised by the electoral campaign and anger at the abrupt adoption by President Carlos Andrés Pérez of a stringent International Monetary Fund (IMF) austerity program.

These unusual incidents of repression, protest, and revolt shook the assumptions about civilization and barbarism, leader and pueblo, and state and citizen that had ordered populist discourse.[3] To understand them, we must consider the context in which they occurred, including especially the dominant representations of the nation's history and promised future. The concept of democracy, which is the central term of Venezuela's dominant political discourse, draws on historical memories of autocratic rule and economic stagnation to validate the party-led system of capitalist promotion. This discourse holds democracy to be the nation's greatest achievement and the necessary condition for its progress. It closely links democracy to development, attributing Venezuela's rapid growth and prestige concerning political freedom and human rights to its multiparty system and construing the democratic regime as the nation's guardian, entrusted with directing the flow of oil income to benefit both pueblo and nation. This conception of democracy builds implicitly on the memory of the nation's strife-filled history of caudillo rule and military strongmen, which lasted with brief interruptions until 1958. It rests as well on the memory of armed leftist opposition to the young democracy during the early 1960s. Populist discourse has linked internal threats to democracy from right and left to the presence of foreign threats to national sovereignty. In an effort to buttress its legitimacy and strengthen its control over dissent, the democratic regime has kept alive the image of threats concealed within the polity and lurking at its borders, seeking the chance to return.[4]

In the late 1970s, the Venezuelan economy began a decline into what would become a crisis by the mid-1980s. It had experienced a short-lived euphoric oil boom, brought on by skyrocketing world oil prices, during Carlos Andrés Pérez's first term of office (1974–79). His government launched an extraordinarily ambitious program to industrialize the economy, with the stated goal of freeing the nation from its dependence on oil exports.[5] The promise of rapid development, coupled with a protected economy in which state oil-rent distribution generously supported patronage-based political parties, raised expectations and defused opposition. But the program heightened tendencies within the rent-based system: a level of consumption that far outran production, concentration of power within the state and its allied economic groups, and corruption at the highest levels of the political and economic ruling elite. Moreover, the oil boom added a factor virtually absent from the Venezuelan economy since 1930, a large foreign debt.

The unanticipated drop in world oil prices in the 1980s, the likelihood of which the country's leaders had ignored when they contracted the debt, propelled a downward economic slide.[6] In 1986, under President Jaime Lusinchi (1984–89), Venezuela signed a costly debt renegotiation agreement with the international banks. Debt repayment, rather than social and development programs, thus became the political priority. The financial sector and large economic groups with assets abroad and diversified investments at home profited; capital flight accelerated, as the wealthy deposited in foreign banks an estimated sixty billion dollars (twice the national debt), while domestic real income fell by 50 percent over this period. The debt service paid during Lusinchi's administration came to thirty billion dollars and consumed 50 percent of the nation's foreign exchange. Although these changes undermined the basis of the protectionist model and powerful business organizations made gains in their promotion of free market polices, the political elite maintained the rhetoric of populist nationalism. As the expectations this rhetoric fueled clashed with deteriorating conditions, political protest and disaffection with the nation's political leadership increased.

The rentier state's economic independence from a taxpayer base has permitted the Venezuelan political system, like those of other nations chiefly dependent on exporting oil or other primary products, to become highly state centered and unresponsive to public demands, thus discouraging the development of independent interests and organizations within civil society. Mechanisms of political reciprocity and accountability have remained restricted, elected officials obtain their position through their place in their party's hierarchy, and the expression of local demands is channeled through highly politicized structures. Presidential campaigns, then, are the occasion for the image of a dialogue between politicians and electorate momentarily to be constructed and consumed. Costly and lengthy, these campaigns orchestrate a national theater of democracy in which candidates seek to display mass support and their followers seek to position themselves favorably within the changing configuration of clientelistic ties.

The 1988 election brought two unprecedented results: for the first time in Venezuelan history a former president was reelected, and voter abstention, previously below 10 percent, now reached 20 percent. In addition, the left increased its representation in Congress, and Pérez's leading opponent made inroads in areas of Acción Demócratica (AD) allegiance. In comparison to Pérez's first victory (1973), which brought forth triumphant celebrations in the streets, this one was edged with skepticism and critique. Many wary voters had decided that Pérez might dare to bring about dramatic change, but they had weak allegiance to his party. It was widely believed that Pérez would bring an improvement in economic conditions. A leader of major initiatives during the oil boom of 1974–78, he had maintained his image as a decisive man of action who could defy domestic and international powers in defense of the nation and the pueblo. Yet unknown to the general public, Pérez was sending a quiet message to the banks at the negotiating table, where he offered to fulfill stringent conditions.

Within days of his inauguration, Pérez gravely announced the content of his inaugural promise to *sincerar* (make sincere or truthful) the economy. The free market would cleanse it of monopolies and artificial practices, allowing it to become productive. The means consisted of a strict austerity program, administered rapidly and in a large dose, like a strong medicine. He informed the public, which was largely unfamiliar with the consequences of such policies, that subsidies for basic goods would be eliminated, price controls ended, exchange rates unified and the currency allowed to fluctuate, tariffs lowered, interest rates freed, and the price of government services increased.

The Bolivarian Ideal

Venezuelan nationalist discourse conceives of history as the uncertain advance of civilization over barbarism; the nation's progress is repeatedly undermined by outside enemies and by the savagery of the land and people. This view of history as conquest of backwardness has been officialized in the epic tale of the national hero Simón Bolívar and his struggle to achieve national independence, republican rule, and social justice. The mythic account of his battle against external and internal forces and his defense of the people has been made a model for projects of national progress.

Yet nationalist discourse has suppressed from official history the elite's long resistance to the abolition of slavery and social reform during the nineteenth century, marked by caudillo revolts, rural uprisings, and its failure after the war to command broad allegiance from the population. The *llaneros,* mestizo plainsmen who had fought for Bolívar, now provided troops for the ongoing civil unrest in which rebel forces would routinely loot *(saquear)* the property of the elite. As Bolívar's ideal of republican order receded, *saqueo* was also used to describe the ruler's treatment of the state as a source of enrichment.

Only when foreign capital developed the petroleum industry in the 1920s did the economic elite offer a model of the national community that commanded broad allegiance. Popular and elite nationalism found a common ground in the project to democratize oil wealth and modernize Venezuela through state protectionism (Coronil 1997). The Bolivarian ideal of the national community was institutionalized within populist discourse and the democratic regime, offering to link the past to the hoped-for future.

The Amparo Massacre

October 29, 1988, Saturday morning: A canoe traveled up the Arauca River. Sixteen men entered a densely wooded tributary, the Caño Colorado. Peasants far from the site heard massive outbursts of gunfire, followed by shooting from military helicopters. Within hours reporters were flown to the scene by the military. General Camejo Arias, regional commander of the border counterinsurgency brigade, CEJAP, announced a successful encounter with fifty heavily armed members of Colombia's National Liberation Army (ELN), a guerrilla organization that had planned to sabotage oil pipelines and kidnap ranchers.[7] He reported sixteen guerrillas killed, although the twenty-member security brigade reported no injuries. Photos of bodies on the shore with ELN insignia lying next to guns quickly appeared in the press. President Lusinchi congratulated the general for controlling threats to Venezuela's borders and its democracy.

Two days later, the outraged townspeople of Amparo, located across the river from Colombia, spoke out, and their claims were reported in the press and taken up by various sectors. The dead men were not Colombians but Venezuelans; they were not guerrillas but unarmed fishermen and workers, family men on a fishing expedition; they were preparing not the sabotage of oil pipelines but the weekend pastime of fishing and sharing a pot of soup (*sancocho*) and rum by the banks of the river. Above all, there were not sixteen dead men but fourteen. Two had escaped by swimming through the swampy stream as helicopters searched for them overhead. With the aid of a neighboring rancher and the local police chief, they had returned home in terror the next day to tell their story. Fearing reprisal, they took refuge in the police station. The survivors were released into Congressman Walter Márquez's custody, and he began what was to become a long campaign in their defense.

Investigation of the case began on two fronts: President Lusinchi assigned it to a military court, and a multiparty congressional commission began its own investigation shortly thereafter. By placing the cause under military jurisdiction, the government shrouded it in the military's rules of secrecy and shielded it from the pressures of politicians and the press. Military judges, moreover, were likely to be personally and institutionally disposed in favor of CEJAP. In effect, Judge Ricardo Pérez Gutiérrez, a close ally of the military, obstructed the investigation and maintained a hostile stance toward the survivors. Congress named a multiparty commission on November 9, headed by a congressional ally of Carlos Andrés Pérez, to take testimony from officials and draw up an independent report.

In all likelihood, the massacre would have earned little national attention or political concern had it not occurred at the end of an electoral campaign. The president's attempt to cast the deaths in terms of the defense of democracy from external threat associated the concept of democracy with the narrow manipulation of power; appearances contrasted sharply with his campaign's effort to represent democracy in its most inclusive and popular terms. Lusinchi's stance brought to the fore the nineteenth-century image of arbitrary rule established through coercion.

Cracks immediately appeared in the official story, revealing a carelessly devised simulacrum. Government officials could not produce police records for the victims, and neither Venezuelan nor Colombian military intelligence agencies corroborated the claims of their records as subversives. Reporters and members of Congress visiting the site of the attack with the survivors filmed them reenacting their escape (they swam skillfully through the waters, disproving their accusers' contentions) and found at the scene discarded cans of acid and clothes that had been taken off the fishermen. The only shell casings they found were from M-19 rifles, the national investigative police's (DISIP's) weapon of choice (*El Diario de Caracas,* November 15, 1988, 8).

One month after the attack, the congressional commission obtained an order for the bodies to be exhumed and an autopsy performed. In the open field, with members of Congress, journalists, and family members looking on, forensic doctors found evidence that the men had been shot point-blank from behind, some tortured and mutilated, their bones crushed, their tattoos and faces burned.[8] Evidence accumulated that CEJAP's leaders had organized the ambush with the military's knowledge and were aware of the Saturday fishing outing. They had dressed several of the dead men in ELN uniforms (which lacked bullet holes) and placed a few guns next to them. This simulacrum of subversion was constructed for national, not local, consumption, for it was clear that the townspeople of Amparo would recognize the victims. The assumption was that they would be too powerless—and terrified—to counter the government's claims. Made more potent by the extremity and starkness of its elements, Amparo became a symbol of the ways power and identity were constructed within everyday life.

Once Pérez was elected president, the case appeared to reverse course. Pérez promised to change its terms, and he sought to have Amparo removed as a point of political pressure by the time of his inauguration in February. An arrest order was issued for the CEJAP members on December 30 on charges of falsifying a crime, illicit use of arms, and homicide. After President-elect Pérez assured them of safe treatment, the survivors returned to Venezuela from exile in Mexico and turned themselves in. With their assailants now detained they returned to Amparo amid celebrations, accompanied by representatives of a newly formed network of human rights activists, clergy, and political leaders. Critics noted, however, that the massacre's planners remained in power, and the pressures to obstruct the case were enormous.

During the transition period, the congressional commission forged the emerging dominant version of events. Its report to Congress of January 18, 1989, concluded that an armed confrontation had not occurred and recommended that this "different event" be investigated judicially. It questioned the contention that the victims were guerrillas and detailed the false and contradictory testimony given by the attack's planners and participants. Approved by the major parties, this report was portrayed as a validation of Venezuela's democratic processes. Acclaiming this achievement, Pérez promised to reorganize these security agencies and achieve justice for the victims.

Alternative Representations

How did the opposition depict the massacre? In this seemingly open political system, issues of presidential and military credibility are hedged by unwritten rules bound by the mandate not to question the integrity of government institutions. Only after President Pérez was in office did opposition leaders offer fuller outlines of an alternative explanation, for they felt the threat of retaliation had lessened. The opposition version of events suggested that the Amparo massacre was carried out to further the interests of a highly placed set of intelligence, military, and business figures having strong economic interests in the border region. Backed by his documentation of this and previous cases of CEJAP violence obtained through confidential contacts, Congressman Márquez argued that powerful regional interests backed the counterinsurgency brigade's ascent as a "subversive manufacturing machine." He stressed that DISIP, whose commanders controlled CEJAP, had become a politically privileged paramilitary organization involved in illicit activities in the western border area, through which it expanded its power and buttressed that of its landowner and business allies. Ideologically fueled by extreme anticommunism, the foreign-trained commandos reputedly charged ranchers for protection from subversives; at the same time, in alliance with ranchers, DISIP terrorized peasants and Indians so they would not defend their lands from encroachment by powerful landowners, many of whom were retired military men.

The Amparo attack, the opposition version claimed, had a history that included several prior DISIP and CEJAP massacres of alleged subversives. The border brigade had manufactured subversives—generally undocumented Colombian workers who were lured into ambushes and brutally killed, their bodies then displayed as those of guerrillas. These supposed subversives were used to justify continuing government and rancher support for DISIP and its autonomy in the region.[9] The previous massacres had not created a public outcry, in part because they involved Colombians or (in earlier years) Venezuelan leftists and because they did not take place during an electoral period. Each confrontation further justified DISIP's power and augmented the president's image as the defender of a threatened democracy, while spreading fear among different sectors of the population.

President Lusinchi's long-time mistress, Blanca Ibanez, had made DISIP her special province, influencing the appointment of its directors and maintaining close links to its commander of operations, López Sisco, and his ally, General Camejo Arias. Critics maintained that through a combination of patronage and surveillance she had constructed a fiefdom of power whose ties extended into the upper levels of economic and political activity, playing a role in Lusinchi's ability to silence dissent and sustain the appearance of consent to his policies.

The opposition's accusations about the Amparo massacre made unspoken reference to this reality. Their sustained criticism, seemingly focused on the abuses of an uncontrolled intelligence unit, implicated specific forms through which power was exerted during the Lusinchi administration. Within the opposition, opinions differed as to whether these forms were limited to this administration or whether power relations were at stake that outlasted any one presidency.

The Credibility of Power

Occurring at a time of political transition, the Amparo massacre jolted interpretive schemes, provoking a sense of indignation among sectors of the urban populace ordinarily uninterested in the fate of the rural people and inclined to believe accusations of their criminality. In November, student-led demonstrations against the government's cover-up occurred in Caracas and other major cities, many of which ended in property destruction and police violence. In the emerging counterinterpretation, the government was the oppressor and the pueblo the innocent victim. A crescendo of protests, in which grassroots Christian groups and activist clergy were vocal, created images of the Amparo fishermen as symbols of a martyred pueblo. They articulated a widely circulating opposition view: The Amparo victims stand for all of us. They are *desamparados*—forsaken, without legal protection, rights, or even identity. They are ordinary people, pawns in a system of inverted values. They are victims of government manipulation—deceived, used, and discarded.

The Amparo massacre resonated in the public imagination with foundational tales of civilization and barbarism on the Llanos: the Arauca River in the state of Apure, the lawless frontier ruled by force, outbursts of savagery, and the helplessness of the pueblo in the face of personalized power. Many people were quick to relate the event to the classic novel *Doña Bárbara*.[10]

Counterinterpretations of the massacre challenged not only the official version of events but the government's capacity to construct its own image. The Lusinchi administration had relied on obscuring reality to maintain its public support. While it confronted the debt crisis by denying that a crisis existed, it financed state expenditures with Venezuela's international reserves, consuming them entirely by the end of the administration. Through propaganda focused on the president's affable personality, the administration reassured the public that the state's paternalistic role would remain unaltered. But a report by Amnesty International delivered to the government in July 1988—prior to the Amparo massacre—documented the administration's escalating suppression of political protest and its constant police and military violence against the poor.[11] The state reproduced ever more overtly its official image as the protector of an anarchic pueblo, while silencing its critics as "subversives."

The Venezuelan state asserted its authority in a theatrical mode, constructing a drama whose plot reenacted the civilizing myth of the state as a scriptwriter. This simulacrum—the representation of the illusion of representing the real—rests on the controlled tension between fact and appearance, between attention to evidence and disregard for conflicting information, and thus on the willingness to allow cracks in the performance to reveal the arbitrariness of authority. Fear grows out of these cracks. As in detective stories, in which certain clues are left behind in order to induce a misreading, the visible marks of artifice in the misrepresentations of politics are not necessarily to be treated as faults, but as signs to be deciphered.

El Masacrón

With Pérez's election, many, including opposition leaders, believed he would restore the tutelary bond between leader and pueblo and halt the nation's shrinkage and backward slide. His first term of office in the 1970s saw providential wealth raise living standards and establish Venezuela as a leader of Latin American economic integration. Thus, despite Pérez's links to corruption and the debt, he represented for many the promise, which hearkens back to Simón Bolívar, that the state would battle for social justice and economic independence. The electoral campaign had raised the hope that his presidency would signal an end to regression, a reopening of the nation to progress.

On February 27, however, masses of people took over the streets of most of the nation's major cities, particularly in the capital region, protesting increasing prices and looting stores.[12] Once the government recovered from its paralyzing shock, it responded with the suspension of constitutional guarantees and a storm of bullets. Thousands were wounded and arrested, and the official death toll reached 277. At the time, unofficial estimates that circulated confidentially put the fatalities at well over 1,000.[13]

No comparable social upheaval, in terms of extent of looting or ferocity of repression, had taken place in contemporary Latin America in response to an economic austerity plan. The total reported killed in fifty different protest events occurring between 1976 and 1986 in thirteen countries was under two hundred; the most violent single incident had been the 1984 riots in the Dominican Republic, which claimed sixty lives (Walton 1989, 188). While so-called IMF riots were frequent during this span, according to John Walton they generally grew out of organized protest, such as strikes and demonstrations, and they tended to select certain targets, both political and business. The Venezuelan riots, however, did not emerge from organized efforts, although they were preceded by years of sporadic conflicts in certain cities, and the looting was aimed at a broad range of businesses, encompassing street vendors and modern supermarkets, workshops and factories.

The events that shook state authority and fragmented the social territory also disrupted established interpretive schemes, resisting the efforts of official and opposition forces to fix them with a name. Official discourse neutrally labeled the conflict "27-F" and "the events" *(los sucesos)*. The terms "the disturbances" or "the big jolt" *(el sacudón),* which suggest a passing disruption of the normal order, became widely accepted in the media. Opposition discourse introduced the terms "social explosion," "popular uprising" *(poblada),* and "the big massacre" *(el masacrón).* The stark label "the war" was common among professionals, expressing the social fracture that the middle class had experienced. It recalled as well the feared return of the civil wars that marked the nineteenth century—memories that had been kept ever-present by government leaders. This shifting vocabulary reflects the uncertain attempts to control the historical construction of events that overflowed traditional channels of contestation and categories of collective agency.

What had happened between February 2, when Pérez's spectacular inauguration took place, and February 27? On assuming the presidency, pressured by an acute shortage of funds, Pérez took up the internationalist strand of Venezuela's Bolivarian nationalist ideology in an effort to refocus the state's civilizing mission. He defined Venezuela as a leader of the debtor nations' battle against domination by international banks, a promoter of Latin America's unity against threats to its independence. This image built on the anti-colonial component of national discourse that equates national independence from foreign domination with a moral struggle. By evoking these shared assumptions, with their resonances of social justice, Pérez sought a legitimizing link with official history for the government's policies.

The crucial task in the new economic strategy, and a condition the banks made for obtaining the new loans, was to open the protective shell that had insulated the nation against international competition throughout most of the century. Ideologically constructed as a momentous historical change, this decision redefined Venezuela's place in history and the world. From this perspective, the protected and subsidized market had fostered parasitical capitalists, inefficient industries, and corrupt politicians. But lacking the oxygen of abundant petrodollars, protectionism was asphyxiating the nation. Insulation

from international competition had meant isolation from economic competence. Opening the nation to the world meant building bridges to capitalism,
allowing its rationality to flow into the nation. This policy, which meant the
decline of many small businesses, was suddenly presented as common sense. It
received the strongest endorsement from wealthy businessmen and politicians
able to retain power through the transition. This manner of pursuing modernity also made the nation vulnerable to world-market relations. The state had
created an exceptionally sheltered domestic space—a fertile ground for culti-
vating hierarchical alliances and weaving illusions of social harmony. Opening this shell also meant tearing down this web of relations and shared understandings.

With the acceptance of the curative rationality of the free market, a change
occurred in the discourse of nationalist modernization. The achievement of a
healthy economy became valorized as the nation's primary goal—above that
of forming a developed pueblo. Although these goals had coexisted in parallel
fashion in the discourse of protectionist modernization, arguments now
openly privileged the economy's demands, subordinating those of the pueblo.
The civilizing relationship that weds state and pueblo and engenders national
progress no longer appeared as a protective bond. And the dismembering of
this bond was dramatically prefigured by the Amparo massacre. The border
llaneros became the emblems of the pueblo, but they were transformed into a
subversive threat to be silenced and written upon, evoking collective memories of the conquest and rebellion.

With the ascent of a populist variant of free market discourse under Pérez,
the pueblo was presented as the undisciplined and lazy product of an unpro-
ductive economy, a symptom of the sickness caused by easy money obtained
during years of abundant oil rents. The official effort to explain the crisis
without seriously implicating the nation's ruling elite presented Venezuelans
as wanton consumers. The assumption was that if the state's protectionist
structures were dismantled, people would turn to productive work, for they
needed the discipline and instruction that the market could provide. The new
administration introduced its adjustment program using a moral language of
reform. Although it spoke of the need to reform individual behavior, it did
not address social reform, which had long been central to protectionist discourse. The latter had promised to correct social inequities by intervening in
the organization of the market. Instead, free market discourse promised to
correct economic distortions by reorienting individual behavior and perceptions.

In an oft-repeated lament, Pérez claimed that Venezuelans had been living
in a world of illusion and false expectations. They must now face reality. On
February 16 he announced "el gran viraje" (the great turn): the move from ar-

tificial to real capitalism. The government would soon cut tariffs, remove price controls and subsidies, and unify the exchange rate at market levels, thus eliminating the preferential rates that had continued to subsidize imports subsequent to official devaluations. While these measures would take time to design and implement, the expectation of their advent, together with a shortage of foreign exchange, prompted a series of escalating processes.

The reality consumers faced diverged wildly from market rationality. Confronted with the imminent dismantling of protectionism and the rising costs of imports, manufacturers cut back production and businesses hoarded products. Several weeks before Pérez's inauguration, in an effort to drive prices up, businesses withheld government-regulated food and consumer items. Angry confrontations in markets and grocery stores between sellers and consumers escalated as consumers found that basic goods were being rationed, and they accused sellers of hoarding and favoring preferred customers. These confrontations occurred above all in stores where the middle class and poor shopped, often owned by Portuguese, Chinese, and Lebanese immigrants thought by many to be avaricious and unscrupulous.

Commercial hoarding was met by consumer hoarding. Shortages and anticipated price hikes provoked consumer runs, a snowballing desire to stock up in preparation for the disruption of production or some unknown eventuality. In uncertain times, hoarding provided a vague sense of protection, but only those with means could afford to hoard to any degree. Soon, for the urban poor, their inability to purchase basic foodstuffs with their money at the store, their being told at their neighborhood grocery "no hay" (there is none), and their having to search anxiously across the city for stores rumored to have needed products fed a mounting anger. Their sense of affront at a deceptive political system reflected in the tyranny of profiteering businesses grew as supplies diminished.

In this environment, the government announced a doubling of gasoline prices to take effect on February 26 as a first step toward reaching world prices. The state oil company's income would be increased by eliminating gasoline subsidies. In this oil-exporting nation, a hike in gas prices was not a simple mercantile decision. It implicated the bond that united the national community: an imagined shared ownership of the nation's petroleum resources based on its founding legal code. The state's legitimacy was intimately tied to its ability to control the nation's formerly foreign-owned oil industry in the name of the pueblo.[14] To equate oil with other commodities on the international market, and to demand that people pay dearly for what was considered to be their national birthright, was to rupture a moral bond.

This rupture was exacerbated when the collective transportation association, arguing that fares had to reflect the increased costs of vehicles and parts, decided to raise bus and van fares by over 100 percent on February 27, in defiance of the government's 30 percent ceiling. Already resented by working-class commuters and students for poor service, the privately owned transport companies' aggressive stance now provoked outrage. Passengers had no alternative transportation to the city and were down to their last change before receiving their end-of-month paychecks. The abrupt doubling of bus fares crystallized the sense that people were being deceived and abused by both government and business, and it brought them together in the street, where both protest and the inversion of authority could occur.

Popular Expansion

Popular protest began at dawn on February 27 in the working-class town of Guarenas outside Caracas, as well as in the Caracas bus terminal, where workers and students congregated at an early hour. Protesters, some led by students chanting antigovernment slogans, initially blocked collective transport vehicles. Soon people turned against grocery stores and food markets. Leaders emerged, young men who tore locks with crowbars and smashed windows, urging people to take what was theirs. The people surging into the stores found to their outrage that subsidized staples that had disappeared from the market were stored away, waiting to be sold at marked-up prices. Some policemen, themselves poorly paid, helped looting take place in an orderly fashion or took part in it as well. A collective decision to occupy the streets and invade stores, suspending the rules regulating public movement and commerce, took shape. The street became the site for the contestation of market and political controls widely regarded as immoral and oppressive.

Diffuse and decentered, the protest multiplied in commercial areas near working-class neighborhoods, following the city's principal streets. These avenues and freeways, the channels along which news was quickly communicated to the major commercial centers by the city's numerous motorcycle messengers, were also vulnerable arteries that protesters blocked off with barriers, bringing traffic to a halt. Most public transportation ceased. Trapped delivery trucks were besieged, their goods carried off and distributed. By the end of the workday in Caracas, astonished downtown employees left their jobs to find the streets filled with people shopping for free, calmly carting off food and even large appliances.

In this *saqueo popular* (popular looting), people came down from the hills and up from the ravines, streaming toward local stores in the streets ringing the city. The term *saqueo popular* has a double meaning. The Venezuelan political and economic elite was widely accused of looting the national treasury, for it had engaged in notorious corruption and had taken twice the amount of the national debt out of the country in massive capital flight. Now it was everyone else's turn to acquire without working. Middle-class families in neighborhoods traversed by deep ravines, where looting had been initiated by slum dwellers, participated in the *saqueo*, filling their cars with goods. At this early stage, when popular action had not encountered government repression, observers related with empathy to the call for *saqueo popular.*

Looting momentarily dissolved money's ability to regulate collective life. The invasion of business establishments rendered meaningless the barriers that money normally imposes between commodities and consumers, between public and private. Amid an uncertain and dangerous situation there were overtones of a village fiesta—a sudden abundance of liquor and grilled meat shared at impromptu gatherings in the poor neighborhoods on the hills circling Caracas. Bottles of champagne and brandy made a surprise appearance at parties now enlivened by dance music broadcast throughout the hills from newly acquired audio equipment. The smoke of barbecues mixed with that of burning stores. Against the "etiquette of equality" that ruled street behavior in this self-defined egalitarian society, the poor sought to assert, even if momentarily, their image of real relations of equality.

During this initial period, when rules were transgressed and categories confused, exhilaration and fear competed for control of the situation. Exhilaration followed from the collective assertion of popular understandings over official explanation. Through countless acts of defiance, which included burning some police stations and local AD offices, people spoke about their rejection of not only their immiseration but the deceptive reasons routinely put forth to explain it and the institutions supporting it. On February 27 several hundred motorcycle delivery men, *motorizados,* surrounded the Federation of Chambers of Industry and Commerce (FEDECÁMARAS) building, the headquarters of the nation's largest business association and a symbol of the business class that had benefited from government policies. Business leaders briefly caught inside spread rumors of alarm concerning attacks on the propertied. Some took their families out of the country, and many privately called on the president to act.

"El pueblo tiene hambre" (the people are hungry), the slogan widely painted on walls, was the explanation most frequently offered by participants for the uprising. It conjured an image of shared experiences uniting strangers who were anonymously joined in the simultaneous looting briefly televised to the country and the world. Hunger was regarded as a national cause for revolt, but it was a shorthand expression referring, through the image of food, to what was regarded as unnecessary deprivation and insult in a country that had both wealth and democracy. With their revolt, people bluntly shattered the officially constructed illusion that the populace would acquiesce to economic adjustment. Reflecting with surprise on their collective action, many observed, "We are no longer a passive pueblo." They expressed a sense of moral affront at the manipulation and silencing of popular demands that was the cumulative experience of this oil- and rent-based democracy. If, as Pérez demanded, it was time to face reality, this was what it looked like from the popular perspective.

The link between hunger and revolt connected notions about political action and rights, leaders and people, that were given blurred expression during the disturbances. In a striking gesture that appropriated the most hallowed official signs of nationhood, protesters in many instances sang, as they broke open stores, the opening line of the national anthem, "Gloria al bravo pueblo que el yugo lanzó" (Glory to the angry people who threw off their yoke). They sang it both when they waved the national flag and when they faced the attack of the military in lines drawn in the streets between an unarmed people and occupying troops. This hymn to popular revolt linked anger to courage, political freedom to social justice. Invoked in official contexts, such as the state ceremonial occasion and the school salute to the flag, the hymn embalmed the *bravo pueblo* in the distant past; to sing it spontaneously in a popular assault on the street was to resuscitate it as a living critique, not a ratification of authority.

"El pueblo está bravo" (the people are angry), painted on walls and repeated by protesters, rebutted the official glorification of a silent pueblo. Popular anger was inseparable from indignation at being deceived. "Se han burlado de nosotros" (they have mocked us), and "basta del engaño" (an end to deception), declared looters and sympathetic observers (many from the middle class) at the outbreak of the disturbances. When in the polyphony of this mass upheaval, people asserted that "el pueblo habló" (the people have spoken), their actions indicated their refusal to remain passive.

A multilayered fear set in, driving people to affix blame for the worsening course of events. Two currents converged: fear of uncontrolled popular criminality and fear of official repression. Both state action and state absence were cause for terror, compounded by uncertainty as to whether the present government would be able to survive at all. In this seemingly solid democracy, no local system of political groupings was found to help reestablish order in the barrios, and no words of explanation were offered by the political leadership. Among the elite and the middle class, the fear that the disturbances were a threat to all private property and social order took hold. Some of the very wealthy left the country in their private jets. The middle class sought to band together to protect their property, often organizing armed defense groups among neighbors.

Gaps in the state's leadership and the coordination of its agencies became visible. Although the government's civilian leadership was hesitant, the military was suddenly decisive in the streets. On the morning of the second day, the military began to occupy the cities, ordering businesses to close. By the end of the day, as assaults on businesses grew bolder and extended to small factories, troops cleared the streets by opening fire on crowds of looters. People turned to the television for word from the government and found images of looting.

The president eventually spoke. He defined the disturbances as a protest of the poor that reflected longstanding social injustices (*El Nacional,* March 1, 1989). With this statement he placed responsibility on past policies and distanced himself from those (like some members of Pérez's cabinet) who blamed the upheaval on subversives, criminals, or illegal immigrants. With grim business leaders at his side, he declared a general wage raise and a four-month freeze on firings—both measures that business had until then opposed. However, Pérez offered no purpose around which to unite as a nation, no promise for the future; rather, he underlined, as on many occasions, the exceptional ties he had built in the international arena. The audience to which he was primarily speaking, in effect well outside the borders of the country, sat in the government and bank offices of Venezuela's creditors; he sought to communicate that Venezuela required concessions on its debt in order to avoid future upheavals but that he was well in control of the present situation.[15] To his domestic audience he issued a demand for acquiescence. Pérez tersely announced that constitutional guarantees, including freedom of the press, were suspended and that a curfew would be in effect from 6 P.M. until 6 A.M. until further notice. His role as an international leader remained, but now he was a leader without a pueblo.

The suspension of guarantees led to a sharp escalation of state violence against the poor. When Minister of the Interior Alejandro Izaguirre, a seasoned AD leader, appeared on television on March 1 to announce government measures, he was rendered speechless on camera, unable to use the traditional language of populism in this conjuncture. Disney cartoons replaced him without explanation. The eruption of the pueblo into public view deeply troubled the Venezuelan political leadership. On March 1, at the height of government violence, AD's president and founder, Gonzalo Barrios, lamented that the international media had televised abroad "the horror, the primitiveness, the uncontrollability, from a civilized point of view, of the looting that took place in Caracas" (Tarre Murzi 1989, 143). He regretted that the events had shown "the entire world the other face of Venezuela, the face of the slums, of the hungry masses, of marginal people" (*El Nacional,* March 4, 1989). This was the face that the government violently sought to conceal.

State Repression

The state's actions slowly took form, as it attempted to control, define, and conceal the events under way. Ten thousand troops were airlifted into Caracas, which, because of its valley location, had been cut off by road from the rest of the country, interrupting its food supply. With a naturalness that stunned the barrio population, the military and police forces undertook to drive people out of the streets and mark territorial boundaries that the poor must not cross. Scenes of soldiers and police firing on looters in barrios were not televised nationally but were broadcast on U.S. and European news, bringing an unwelcome shock of recognition to Venezuelans with satellite dishes, who discovered a disturbing new image of the nation through the eyes of the international media.

The militarization of the conflict under the suspension of most constitutional guarantees meant that "order" was reestablished in the barrios by means of massive violence, both indiscriminate and directed, even though, as critics later argued, the constitutional guarantee of the right to life had not been suspended. The military displayed its presence, stationing tanks to protect government and corporate offices, major shopping centers, and the borders of wealthy neighborhoods. But outside of a few shopping centers, these had not been targets of the looters. Rather, these outposts signaled the boundaries to be defended against the "marginals" (barrio residents).

Government repression brought to an end the disturbances' expansive phase, marked by popular occupation of the street. Pockets of gunfire directed at government forces by "antisocials" in certain barrios and housing projects became the focus of government attention. They were presented as revealing the true face of the disturbances: the anarchic and criminal effort to subvert democracy through violence. In the context of deep collective fear, the idea hardened that despite broad social participation in the looting, the disturbances emanated from the feared *cerros* (hillside barrios) ringing Caracas.

According to dominant notions, the very poor and the criminal, living in subhuman conditions in the shanties and housing projects, lead a basically lawless existence. The *cerros* are regarded as the haven for various categories of *antisociales: malandros* (thugs), drug dealers, dark-skinned foreigners, and urban guerrillas. The disturbances were soon constructed as the unleashing of this marginal, primitive mass upon the city center. At this moment of crisis, otherness was projected onto the city's barrios, as if the residents of these socially diverse areas in their entirety constituted a threat to the civilized order. As General Camejo Arias had said of the border region where the Amparo massacre had occurred, "everyone there is a criminal."

Collective fears fragmented the urban population along the lines they traced. Many barrio residents feared that marauding savagery might emerge within their midst. Neighboring barrios, often situated higher up the hill and populated by recent immigrants, might attack their homes and property. The army and police, attempting to divide the poor through the spread of panic, planted rumors that mobs of impoverished foreigners and criminals were leading night assaults on houses.[16] Although the rumored assaults never materialized, barrio residents stood guard on their rooftops and in the streets, drawing gunfire from the troops. Although people in the barrios sought to defend themselves from their neighbors, people in wealthy districts armed themselves against the barrios. Residents of luxury apartments bordering the barrios formed armed brigades with police approval, and Rambo-style groups of wealthy youths brandished sophisticated automatic weapons that the upper middle class had been bringing into the country for some time.

The government's armed agencies deployed violence in multiple forms, communicating in practice to the poor the distinct forms of otherness by which they could be encompassed. The military faced the barrio population as a military enemy, the police confronted it as a criminal gang, and the intelligence police treated it as a subversive agent. Their cross-cutting attacks created confusion and panic, fragmenting the poor yet more. After the initial exhilaration of defiance, most of the population hoped for the reestablishment of order and an end to uncertainty and destruction; they often welcomed the young soldiers of rural origin who were posted in their neighborhoods. But military officers responded to subversion by defining the barrios as its source. Their population became the enemy to be controlled, driven back, broken. The death of an army officer leading a search for snipers was made the symbol of democracy under siege, one that political and entertainment figures elaborated upon in televised statements and during the broadcast of his military funeral.

Police and security forces used the period of suspended legality to round up criminals, settle personal accounts, raid houses, and terrorize certain barrios. Policemen who knew the criminals and illegal aliens in a neighborhood sought them out in their houses and the streets, in some cases shooting them down or taking them away to unknown sites. For these operations some agents did not use their official weapon but an unregistered personal gun called a *cochina* (dirty one; literally, female pig).[17]

Security forces also used a tactic developed in demonstrations and on the university campus to provoke incidents and turn public opinion: masked gunmen known as *encapuchados* (hooded ones) in civilian clothes shot at people, often from motorcycles, creating panic. It was impossible to determine whether they were police, criminals, or subversives. Terror became faceless.

The morgue was the site for the encounter between the poor and their own invisibility, as people sought in vain to recover the bodies of relatives and friends. Some knew that a person's body had been sent there after witnessing their death. Others arrived after fruitless quests at overflowing jails and hospitals. Unclaimed decomposing bodies were stacked in morgue hallways where, defying rules and the stench, relatives searched. The city ran out of coffins. Eventually indifferent morgue workers told family members to end their vigil. Loads of cadavers, they said, had been taken en masse to an unmarked mass grave in the Caracas public cemetery—in garbage bags.

Images of bodies tossed into trucks, dumped in garbage bags, and buried in unknown sites by tractors took hold in the collective imagination. Repeated and magnified in the barrios, they objectified for the poor their own erasure, the futility of attempting to establish their individual claims. Just as bodies were erased, so were the casualty figures. After initial estimates of several hundred dead in Caracas, the media quickly stopped giving numbers. The government, denying unofficial estimates of over 1,000 dead and hundreds wounded and maimed, maintained the 276 figure.[18] Because conditions were chaotic and people alarmed, the tendency was to hold exaggerated notions of the deaths involved, which rumors placed in the thousands. However, the government never released the names of the dead and resisted legal efforts by newly formed groups of victims' families, such as the Committee against Forgetting and the Committee of Relatives of the Innocent Victims of February–March (COFAVIC), to exhume bodies from the mass graves. Soon after the massacre, COFAVIC fully identified 396 bodies. The government, however, refused to acknowledge this information and did not alter the official figure even after COFAVIC later identified three of the 68 bodies exhumed from La Nueva Peste, expanding its own list to 399.

The Nation's Primitivity

The startling suddenness of the popular protest brought candid commentary, yet its complexity and newness defied description. Uncertain on a changing ground, commentators sought the stable footing of established foundations. One such premise, concealed in normal times, concerned the country's intrinsic backwardness. It was as if by overflowing the riverbed, the masses had uncovered the hidden but familiar bedrock of a primitive national identity. Evaluating the nature, source, and significance of this backwardness became the obscure object of literary and political attention, distinguishing oligarchic and populist views of the nation. For the elite, the upheaval brought repressed understandings of this troublesome issue to the surface. At the height of the crisis, when people gained control of the streets, submerged populist assumptions converged with the oligarchic conception of the pueblo as a backward mass. Although under ordinary conditions populist rhetoric depicts the pueblo in positive terms as virtuous, albeit ignorant and in need of guidance, during this crisis the element of ignorance was brought to the fore in order to present the pueblo as savage: prone to lose control if not adequately harnessed and ready to plunge the nation into chaos if not swiftly repressed. It is not surprising, therefore, that journalists could employ the image of the pueblo as an uncontrolled river without qualms.

Ambivalence toward the pueblo did not disappear but was displaced. According to journalist Alfredo Peña, popular protest had been justified. The problem arose because the masses, without adequate political or trade union organizations, had no adequate means of expressing themselves. Although Venezuela's economic crisis was less serious than Argentina's or Uruguay's, the masses in those countries remained controlled because they had representative parties and trade unions: "Without leadership they [the masses] become anarchic or overcome their leadership, overflow the riverbed—and the unruly come to lead the movement" (*El Nacional,* March 4, 1989). The masses were right in being upset, Peña reasoned, but wrong in their form of protest.

In the congressional debate of March 6, the leader of the moderate left party Movement toward Socialism (MAS), Teodoro Petkoff, suggested that the protesters were not organized workers but people pushed to the edges of society—to prostitution, drugs, and alcoholism. Petkoff argued that the Venezuela that had "erupted like a volcano" on February 27 was not "the Venezuela of workers organized in trade unions or associations. No, it was another Venezuela, it was the unorganized Venezuela, the Venezuela that has been piling up in a huge bag of wretched poverty." According to him, the Venezuela that "came down from the hills or up from the ravines" was "a Venezuela of hungry people, of people who are not part of the conventional organization of society." This Venezuela had produced "the roar of a wounded animal." He blamed the politicians of the ruling parties for having created this other Venezuela, labeling them Doctor Frankensteins: "They created a monster, and this monster came out to complain, came out to demand its share of the immense petroleum booty of all these years."

As hidden assumptions surfaced during the riots, they took on novel meanings and were recast by changing conditions. The opposition between civilization and barbarism now equated rationality with the free market, the domain of the modernizing elite, and backwardness with state protection, the province of the needy masses, corrupt politicians, and inefficient businessmen. This division was concretized in the layout of the cities, as borders between rich and poor neighborhoods became military and moral battlegrounds, frontiers separating different kinds of people. In ever more binding ways, the ruling elite established its fraternity across international lines, for its overriding concern was with international financial flows rather than with the organization of the domestic market. It interpreted popular protest as a reaction against capitalist rationality, denying the multilayered critique of injustice it contained—a protest at once against new free market measures and against a politically constructed economy characterized by corruption, inflation, scarcity, and the hoarding of basic goods.

Bodily Inscriptions and the Body Politic

Having represented the pueblo as a barbarous mass blind to the force of reason, the governing elite found justification for using blinding force against it. The ferocious deployment of state power at the center stage of national politics blocked from view the significance of popular protest as a critique of the social order. Through the display of force, the government represented the protesting pueblo as a hydra-headed threat that included subversives, foreigners, drug dealers, Cuban agents, guerrillas, and common criminals—all dangerously invisible.[19] Mass killings were thus a way of constructing the pueblo as irrational and the government as the sole defender of reason. Through the massacre the logic of the Spanish Conquest was reinscribed on new bodies. The nation was split in two.

The elite confronted the fractured body politic by enunciating its own contradictory relationship to the pueblo, deepening national divisions while calling for unity. The defense minister directed the removal of alien elements at the same time that politicians called for renewed communication with the pueblo. Employing the paternalistic terms of elite discourse, ex-president Rafael Caldera reprimanded the national political leadership for having distanced itself "from the pueblo who feel, who live, who sometimes express themselves in an improper fashion, and sometimes look for forms of expression that border on barbarism, but that must be understood. We have to reestablish communication with them" (Tarre Murzi 1989, 138).

As violence provoked a crescendo of fear, Minister of Defense Italo Alliegro became the public hero in the reestablishment of order. By the time troops had been withdrawn and the media had redefined the riots as vandalism and resistance as subversion, Alliegro's smiling face had appeared on magazine covers and his name was topping popularity polls. At the moment officially construed as a historical crossroads in the nation's ascent toward modernity, the death of the pueblo was made to appear inconsequential, inscribed in the collective imagination through images of the poor as an anonymous mass of savages, as refuse to be discarded in garbage bags, as if the poor, in death as in life, were one mass.

The Barbarism of Civilization

Corporeality has served as a privileged medium for the political imagina-tion in Latin America, as states that have but partial control over their popula-tions and territories have inscribed on their subjects' bodies assertions of power directed to collective audiences. These inscriptions encode not only the reasons of state but the unquestioned foundations of these reasons, the bedrock of common sense that renders natural the social landscape. Physical violence, like printing, is a vehicle for making and encoding a history whose specific form and significance cannot be understood outside that history. Crises reveal that these assumptions are not reproduced unchanged but reinterpreted and transformed through the present. In making history, people remake their his-tory, recasting the past through a contemporary optic. The waking terrors of the living are the nightmare through which the past is imagined.

A colonial history that engraved upon bodies the denunciation of the vic-tim's crimes informed the Amparo massacre. Similarly, a tradition of conquest weighed upon the state's treatment of the *masacrón* victims as an anonymous mass. But both instances reconfigured the present in the past's terms *and vice versa,* making salient suppressed conceptions of the poor as disposable savages. In accord with shifts in domestic and international conditions, the terms of nationalist discourse acquired new accents: "I would have killed all those sav-ages, as I am sure they would have killed us if they had a chance. They hate us." So said Sofia, a wealthy lawyer and Harvard-trained businesswoman, as she shaped her arm into a machine gun and pointed her finger toward the slums that surround her office in a skyscraper overlooking the hills from which looters had descended.

For the last half-century, state affluence held social conflict in check. But as the ascent of free market ideology displaced the moral economy of protection-ism with the morality of capital, a rupture of customary bonds uniting leaders and masses, state and people, pushed the poor to the border of the body politic. In this new configuration, boundaries have become frontiers separat-ing the civilized from the barbarous. Without state protection, people are free to choose progress. Hand in hand, the logics of conquest and the free market converge to impress upon people the changing meaning of their social anonymity.

The characteristic exercise of state power in Venezuela proceeds dramatur-gically, by means of performances designed to establish an account of reality through the persuasiveness of power; they intend less to convince than to pro-duce acquiescence (Coronil 1997). When the reproduction of state authority is so deeply intertwined with the construction of its representation, politics centers on the artifice of its making. The makeshift or contrived character of certain political representations, visible in the theatrical display of state violence during both massacres, may actually express a form of constructing power rather than a deficiency in its organization.[20]

In each massacre the state attempted not simply to represent reality but to show that it had the power to write the plot, to decide who belongs at center stage, who is at the margins, who is in the audience, and who is shut out. When people dared to act, the state countered by turning them into actors in different dramas. By transforming peasants into guerrillas and protesters into savages, the state sought simultaneously to control their actions and to redefine the pueblo as the chorus in the wings of the theater of populism. At the margins of this official drama, however, people spoke lines of their own making, challenging the plot of a modernizing project dependent upon their silence. Less than four weeks after Pérez's second inauguration, in response to the state's attempt to make commodities reflect the unmediated rationality of the free market, people responded with fury by "spontaneously" freeing commodities from the market. This spontaneity at once revealed the hidden activity of sedimented memories and experiences and made explicit a popular critique of relations or rule embedded in quotidian life. Through their actions, people pried open a space through which to glimpse a different social imaginary by ignoring the state's drama (which they called the "farce") and attacking for a moment the theater itself.

It will be as difficult to remember as it is hard to forget just how order was reimposed. While people inscribed with their bodies their presence upon the state, the state inscribed its power upon their bodies. To achieve the reestablishment of stability, the state can no longer assume that there are compliant actors or a passive audience; it must modulate its actions in accord with its memory and its altered perception of what the pueblo might do. As the state presents the drama of modernization on stage, people murmur in the aisles, walk out, and talk outside. We may be able to hear these voices questioning the assumption that the death of the pueblo may take place "as if no one, nothing had died, as if they were stones falling on the ground, or water on the water."[21]

Violence and Modernity

Are these, then, just further exotic tales about the violent character of distant others, a confirmation of the premodern character of contemporary Latin America? A myth central to modernity, whose course passes from Kant to Hegel and Foucault (1979), contends that as heirs to the Enlightenment, modern states establish their authority by embodying not divine will or force but reason. The modern state, Foucault asserts, having domesticated the bloody theater of violence of the ancien régime, replaces publicly inflicted physical punishment with a myriad of disciplinary procedures that permeate the body politic and engender the modern soul. From this perspective, violence as a reason of state marks the premodern domain, in which the state writes its texts on the bodies of its citizens, presumably because premodern souls grasp its reasons concretely.

These events demand the reconsideration of a viewpoint that divides history into ascending stages and is blind to the violence through which modern states secure their hegemony. The forms of state violence may indeed vary in different societies, in part reflecting how their mechanisms of social control—what Gramsci called their "trench systems"—protect states from political and economic threats. State violence is thus inseparable from other forms of social violence, the exceptional deployment of state force from the quotidian practice of social domination. But whenever states violently reproduce the conditions of their existence by imposing the standards of their rule through force, we may glimpse how myths of authority are grounded on the terrain of history and how, as Benjamin suggests, documents of civilization are at the same time documents of barbarism (1969, 256).

Political violence thus can be understood as an opaque historical artifact, a set of practices and cultural forms whose meanings can only be deciphered by understanding the historical memory and social relations of the society within which it arises, takes form, and achieves effects. As violence becomes embodied in practices and objectified in institutions, technologies, and icons, it becomes modular; commoditized and taught in multiple forms, it circulates in markets that cross boundaries.[22]

Listening to violence entails exploring a terrain in which the construction of meaning is contested through the deployment of competing modes of meaning-making. If, with de Certeau, we view society as constituted by "heterogeneous places" in which a "forest of narrativities" engenders multiple conceptions of reality (1984, 183, 201), we may hear a multitude of submerged voices speaking through a variety of semantic fields. Narrativities of violence form a dense forest with deceptively homogenous contours. While Foucault posits the existence of a clear correlation between types of society and forms of state violence, our analysis suggests that these typological correspondences may be partial and shifting, for the surface similarity of the elements composing the forest of violence obscures how the power of these forms derives from their complex coarticulation with each other on heterogeneous social terrains.

In the Amparo and February massacres state violence took place at once as a spectacular theatrical performance and as a hidden technical operation. Postcolonial societies, by making particularly visible the ongoing imbrication of heterogeneous historical forms of subjection, illuminate the emerging imperial landscape of the contemporary world. At a moment in history when the globalization of space is being achieved through simultaneous integration and fracture, inclusion and exclusion, transmuted colonial relations remain dynamic forces within processes of global change. The events analyzed here are moments in this worldwide reordering of body politics. Through them we may glimpse the movement from a world organized by what Tom Nairn calls the uniformed imperialism of direct political control and territorially fixed markets (1977, 356) to one shaped by what may be called the multiform imperial controls of fluid finance capital, a world of increasingly deterritorialized markets and shifting political, economic, and cultural boundaries. The Venezuelan riots and massacres, as people who lived through them know, are inseparable from the hidden violence of postmodern empires.

5   State, Esprit Mafioso,
   and Armed Conflict in Colombia

Mafias, Politics, and the Esprit Mafioso

〜 M. A. Matard-Bonucci offers a conceptualization of mafia useful for an analysis of Colombian politics: the mafia is not a formal organization, but a form of behavior and a mode of power.[1] There are four key historical conditions that help explain the growth and consolidation of models of mafia power and behaviors. First is a situation in which the nation-state has not established a firm presence in certain regions and local forces contest an exclusionary central power. The classic example of this dynamic is Sicily, with insularity appearing to be an important sociocultural element explaining the emergence of the mafia. Insularity should not be understood as isolation, but as a relationship with a centralized political power that helps to define social and political identities. Clientelism is a critical aspect of this relationship, with the "clientele" as an early form of mafia. Groups of "clients" have a "protector" in the region, defend his person and patrimony, are the docile instruments of his caprices and ambitions, and at the same time carry out crimes in his name, almost certainly enjoying the immunity that comes with his protection.[2]

A second factor is the existence of a personalized mediation with centralized political powers, which provide mafias with a "social function." In the case of southern Italy, the exclusion of a poverty-ridden region led to the creation of a relation with the center that was controlled by a local elite, which assumed representation of the region and used private violence to maintain its predominance. A third factor is that dependency is mediated through the use of economic resources and political power. Mafias represent both new and old forms of relationships, that is, precapitalist and feudal relations in a modern context.[3] Mafias are thus the result of modernization processes within precarious situations of modernity.

Finally, private violence is used as a mechanism of social control and the exercise of power. In the case of Sicily, social power emerged from sources beyond those found within the formal legal system. Real power in the social and political life of Sicily was found in the use of force and violence to control economic resources and remained apart from institutional schemes.[4] A long history, during which power and material force were the exclusive preserve of local barons and violence was exercised on their behalf, contributed to the development of "mafia sentiments," which, more than an organization, were an ample and common part of the social psychology of Sicily during centuries.[5]

The "esprit mafioso" emerged out of the ancient customs of powerful noblemen, the aristocrats who dominated the island of Sicily during centuries and were accustomed to using power and violence to protect their own self-interest. This constituted, not only in Sicily, a privileged position of immunity before the laws of the country that, until the eighteenth century, included trials before their own tribunals, distinct from those of lower social classes. The mafia is a medieval sentiment that arises from a belief that an individual can be assured the protection and integrity of their person and property through their own worth and influence, independent of the actions of the authorities or the law.[6] The esprit mafioso took root in Sicily, and despite social progress and political democracy, it has been difficult to eliminate among the majority of the population. It suggests that to achieve success in life, one must have the valor to oppose authority and if necessary the law, or at least support those who can do so and not suffer formal legal consequences.

An additional factor that historically helped legitimate the esprit mafioso in Sicily was a revolutionary peasant movement, long excluded from the social and political life of the nation. In the wake of the political struggles of the mid–nineteenth century, "peasants did not cease in thinking of how to arm themselves or preserve their arms in the hopes of the 'great day,' while the bourgeoisie only thought of defending itself with private and public guardians."[7] The esprit mafioso was not mechanically derived from models of organization and rebellion among Sicily's popular masses. Rather, its development was the result of the circumstances of their exclusion and the ways by which this exclusion was transferred from the level of general social and political struggles to the individual and group. The essence of that transference was the sense that one must oppose the violence and injustices that are encountered in daily life, even if that means recurring to violence and force to preserve personal prestige.

Finally it is important to note the relationship between the mafia and the economy of those areas where such relations developed. In southern Italy, the citrus boom played an important role in the diffusion of the mafia in the countryside. The introduction of the *gabela,* a form of extortion imposed on the citrus industry, contributed enormously to the strengthening of the mafia. The blurring of legal and illegal capital in the economy is a constant in the social and economic history of the mafia and one of its greatest triumphs.[8]

Unlike the Italian case, mafia power in Colombia expanded as a result of the illegal drug economy in a regional environment without the need of a center. That is to say, it did not require a mediating role with the state; on the contrary, it strengthened its territorial control based on an illegal and global-ized market. That is why drug trafficking has deepened the fragmentation of centralized power in Colombia, combining forms of "para-institutionality" in the exercise of both force and justice while intervening in the electoral arena. In the context of the internal conflict, it is also creating a new strategic situa-tion for itself in the name of defeating the guerrillas. In this way, drug traf-ficking is situating itself so as to capitalize on an eventual reordering of power by the state. At the same time, traffickers continue to seek to legitimize their social power, just as they do with the capital obtained from trafficking, which is usually laundered through legitimate businesses in the rural sector. Private power is thus being used to create a new public order.

Two Scenarios of Esprit Mafioso, Armed Conflict, and Social Control

The premodern structure of Colombia's state is found in its weak capacity to control territory and exercise a monopoly of force in both the city and the countryside. During much of the nineteenth and twentieth centuries, Colom-bia's regions developed politically and economically with little national inte-gration. First, geography conspired to inhibit integration by making trans-portation between regions—particularly between the capital, located on the isolated high plateau of the central cordillera, and other departments—ex-tremely difficult. Each region developed its own economic base and trading links with the external world. Second, continual civil wars among civilian elites mobilized local private armies. Although many of the wars, such as the War of One Thousand Days (1899–1903), involved struggles among national elites, they also provided opportunities for local conflicts to manifest them-selves. In this context, national institutions such as the military and the judi-cial system failed to develop a strong local presence and were more often than not swept up into these conflicts.

The current conflict needs to be understood in this historic context. As the insurgency involving the Revolutionary Armed Forces of Colombia (FARC) and the National Liberation Army (ELN) developed from the 1960s onward, local dynamics came to the fore. Each guerrilla force filled vacuums in parts of the country where state institutions were weakest and developed ties to both the local society and the economy. Local landowners and party bosses either made deals with these forces or organized the fight against them. The relative isolation of the insurgents allowed the state and national elites to downplay their importance. Only in the 1980s, with the growth of new social move-ments, the growing economic power of drug trafficking, and a growing guer-

rilla presence in the cities (particularly in the now-defunct April 19 Movement, or M-19), did the state appear increasingly under siege. After a failed
hard-line response during the administration of President Julio César Turbay
Ayala (1978–82), President Belisario Betancur (1982–86) initiated a peace
process and political reforms aimed at opening up the democratic system.
While leading to a new constitution in 1991 and the incorporation of various
guerrilla groups into the political system, most notably the M-19, these efforts were quickly overwhelmed by the local dynamics influencing the guerrillas, the intensification of the drug wars, and the growing organization and
national coordination of paramilitary forces under the umbrella of the paramilitary United Self-Defense Forces of Colombia (AUC), led by Carlos Castaño. Despite renewed efforts to revive the peace process during the Pastrana
administration (1998–2002), the entrenched interests and local dynamics
that had developed by the late 1990s made it very difficult for all armed actors to agree on a path to peace.

A weak state has been a key factor in explaining the two types of colonization of the countryside that have predominated historically. The first pattern
of colonization is based on the large ranches and *latifundio* (large feudal-like
landholdings) that are sustained by patrimonial social relations. This phenomenon has been developing more recently into enclave economies that depend on commercial agriculture, similar to the situation that existed in areas
dependent on banana exports at the start of the twentieth century. Politically,
in these zones domination is based on clientelistic relations that functionally
mirror the relations found on *latifundio*. Regional political control in these areas revolves around families whose origins can be historically traced to contraband and illegal economic activities in the seventeenth century that allowed
them to create a monopoly of political control. Colombia's Atlantic coastal region provides an example of this historic dynamic. A second pattern of colonization emerged out of the large population that was displaced due to the
political violence or economic expropriations carried out in the mid–twentieth century. This population occupied areas with low agricultural productivity. By the late 1970s, they had increasingly found in the coca economy a
source of income that allowed them to accumulate capital and migrate to
other, more productive zones.

In the diversity of these regional scenarios there emerged distinct forms of
articulation with narco-trafficking. In areas based on the first pattern, a
process of symbiosis developed between export capital derived from drug trafficking and money laundering carried out through the purchase of agricultural lands. This process not only led to a further concentration of land ownership but also created political consequences, including an increase in armed
conflicts. It is especially in these areas that there is the strongest development

of private armed groups that act parallel to those of the state and have become key actors in Colombia's violence. These private armies first emerged to defend private property from common delinquents and threats from the guerrillas and over time developed into organizations with a separate and semiautonomous identity. In areas following the second pattern, relations developed between peasants and the early phases of the drug trade, that is, the growing and processing of coca. In this context, the growing political and military power of insurgents introduces a new dynamic, with the latter increasingly taking on an intermediary role with drug trafficking. These regional dynamics, and their economic, social, and political consequences, can best be observed by examining two of Colombia's regions: the departments of Magdalena and Putumayo.

Magdalena

The department of Magdalena, on Colombia's Atlantic coast, has three important geographical features that are linked to different economic activities: the Sierra Nevada of Santa Marta, a marijuana-producing zone since the 1970s; the Magdalena River valley, historically a center of cattle ranching, with small towns that depend on this activity; and the central plains along the Ariguani River, a largely agrarian area dedicated to such products as rice and bananas. These physical zones create diverse ecosystems and an ecological equilibrium in the water, plant, and animal resources of the area. The Magdalena River delta includes, for example, streams, canals, swamps, and flooded plains, all fed by the Magdalena River, all contributing to a rich ecosystem. Needless to say, these resources have been transformed due to the patterns of colonization and the economic and social relations that have resulted from them.[9]

The Magdalena River has historically been an important transport system, linking the interior with the Atlantic. The extensive delta system at the mouth of the river has been ideal as an entrance point for contraband and illegal arms since the colonial period. The abandonment of this zone by the state, the exclusionary nature of large landholding patterns in the region, the development of a subculture that privatizes the use of public resources, and the lack of consciousness regarding exploitation of economic resources in an ecologically fragile region have all contributed to a dynamic of conflict and methods of social control peculiar to this region. Around the delta itself, there can be found large cattle ranches and *latifundio* that commercialize bananas, rice, and African palm. For the most part, these land-tenure patterns create labor practices based on premodern forms of social control, including personal dependence on the part of workers and small landholders on large landholding patrons. The use of force and political manipulation extends even to electoral processes, which are used to legitimate the power of local elites. The result has been a true "geography of power," in which the interrelation of territory, resources, and social control becomes the basis of political power.[10]

Historically, low population densities, the weak state presence, rebellious indigenous populations, and the isolation of towns in the area have, since colonial times, made the area vulnerable to external attack. These same factors have been important in fomenting illegal activities in the region, which had become a major source of income by the end of the colonial period.[11] Between 1850 and 1950, the economy of the Caribbean coast developed according to global trade economic cycles. At the same time, the geographic and demographic factors mentioned earlier undermined the possibilities of economic development and social cohesion.

In the nineteenth century, much of Magdalena developed as a frontier region, with most towns emerging along the trade routes of the Magdalena River, which remained the primary mode of transportation and communication in the region. Cattle ranching developed largely as a result of the lack of a significant labor force and a social structure still based on patrimonial domination. Only after 1905, with the dramatic increase in banana exports, did Magdalena witness an increase in commerce. Nonetheless, the enclave nature of the banana industry did not result in an equal development of the area. Only in those areas where banana plantations were formed—Ciénaga, Fundación, and Aracataca—did significant export-oriented commerce develop. By the middle of the twentieth century, the port of Santa Marta had still not been fully integrated into the national economy, largely due to a lack of effective transportation. Because of the lack of a railroad connection (controlled by the United Fruit Company), and the growth of the rival ports of Cartagena and Barranquilla, Santa Marta remained largely an export enclave for bananas.[12]

Today, the Caribbean coast has the highest rates of poverty in Colombia, and its per capita gross national product (GNP) is below the national average. In 1996, half the population lived in poverty.[13] Socioeconomic statistics demonstrate the extreme underdevelopment of the region. While the illiteracy rate in Colombia is 11.2 percent, in the Caribbean states it reaches a dramatic 21.4 percent, with several states, including Magdalena, having illiteracy rates of over 48 percent. Moreover, only 19 percent of the population in this region has access to health care.[14] Poverty is clearly linked to land-tenancy patterns. Over 78 percent of the land is owned by large landowners, who represent only 26 percent of all landholders in Magdalena.[15] Although most of the land of the northern coast is arable and capable of producing a wide range of agricultural products, it has largely been dedicated to cattle ranching, an activity that is not highly productive, uses little labor, and thus has a limited impact on economic development in the region. Moreover, overgrazing, deforestation, and a growing population have contributed to soil erosion and threatened the ecological balance of the region. Faced with this environmental threat, the Colombian state has failed to offer solutions, preferring to rely on private actors and voluntary agreements.

Drug Trafficking

By the end of the 1960s the Sierra Nevada of Santa Marta had become the epicenter of a marijuana boom. The isolation and poverty of the rural economy were important elements in the development of this boom, as were the weakness of the state and a complex geography favoring contraband. The expansion of this boom brought with it a new wave of migrants from other departments, particularly Santander and Tolima. The rapid changes brought about by this economy, including access to new wealth, created new conflicts that led to violence. The lack of legitimate institutions to resolve conflicts and the fact that many of those involved in the drug trade came from lower-class sectors previously denied access to the region's sources of wealth led to an unprecedented wave of violence. In addition, the participation of the region's prominent families in the marijuana trade opened the way for this illicit economy to have a growing influence in the political arena. The buying of votes, made possible by the large sums of money controlled by drug traffickers, allowed those involved in the marijuana trade to acquire political power, including election to local councils or Congress.[16] Inevitably, security forces, including the police, were corrupted by this trade. As the power of marijuana traffickers expanded, their private power, based on mafia codes of conduct, was used to dominate the public sphere.

A typical example of this dynamic involves the drug trafficker José Cuesta, who came from the coffee-growing area of Caldas and was very influential among migrants from the departments of Santander and Tolima.[17] Cuesta made a name for himself as someone willing to resolve disputes, filling the void left by an absent state. He managed to survive the violence in the zone and by the 1980s had gained control of the coca trade in the Sierra Nevada area. Faced with the growing presence of guerrillas (ELN and FARC) in these areas, he emerged as a sponsor of paramilitary self-defense forces (*autodefensas*), gaining legitimacy as someone able and willing to control insurgent threats. Using his economic power to control votes, he developed close relationships with political elites, including a senator, and expanded his activities into legal economic enterprises, by the late 1990s effectively gaining control over much of the private transport industry in the region, developing an "ecotourism" business, and managing much of the infrastructure in the Santa Marta area.[18] Finally, he was designated a "justice of the peace," increasing his respectability as an upright citizen of the area. In many ways, the history of José Cuesta evokes the corrupt practices of the ruling elite of the province of Santa Marta in the colonial era, when those involved in contraband were admitted as respectable members of local society. Now as then, the isolation of the area, poverty and inequality, and a lack of resources conspire to blur the line between what is legal and respectable, and what is illicit and forbidden.

The private power of drug traffickers is also inserted into the public sphere through the purchase of lands and the provision of security. This process is best seen in the southern part of Magdalena, an area dominated by extensive cattle ranches. The area is today controlled by paramilitary forces, and in particular by Antonio Corrales, who made his reputation engaging in "social cleansing" *(limpieza social),* that is, physically eliminating common delinquents, cattle rustlers, and other social undesirables. His organization gradually "evolved" into a self-defense force, finally associating itself with the paramilitary forces of the AUC. In the area of Santa Marta, paramilitary forces are commanded by Pepe Torres, who has had difficult relations with José Cuestas. Finally, in the western part of Magdalena, near the town of Remolino, paramilitary forces are controlled by the drug trafficker "El Ciempiés," whose influence in drug trafficking and recruitment extends into the marginal neighborhoods of Barranquilla. This complex panorama suggests the confluence of persons involved in drug-trafficking activities, the paramilitary forces of Carlos Castaño, and cattle ranchers.[19] In economically depressed towns and rural areas, the AUC has found fertile ground to recruit members, extending its private and mafioso model of social control.

As illicit activities have increased in the region, ranchers from traditional oligarchic families, such as Juancho Noguera from Aracataca, have been assassinated, even though many of them initially sponsored the self-defense forces in the region. The arbitrary and criminal activities of these groups have included the violent displacement of traditional families, as drug-trafficking groups look to take over their lands. While these actions have created uncertainty, they appear to follow a logic that, within the context of regional violence, is rational and that aims to create a new security situation.

Insurgency

Insurgents maintain an important presence in areas around the Sierra Nevada de Santa Marta, which is the only mountainous zone of the area and thus provides a higher level of protection for guerrillas. The Nineteenth Front (Frente José Prudencio Padilla) of the FARC and the Frente Francisco Javier Castaño of the ELN operate in the region, with the latter acting mostly in the southern area of Santa Marta. After 1997, the ELN increased its presence in the lake regions of the area. The apparent objective of the ELN was to insert

TABLE 5.1 Violence against the Civilian Population in the Cienaga Grande of Santa Marta Area, 2000

Date	Site	Events
January	Lower Magdalena river towns of Santa Rita, Tenerife, Remolino, El Banco, Guachada	Selective assassinations that provoke the displacement of 500 people
February 7	Remolino	Assassination of 3 people and destruction of houses
February 13	Buena Vista, Nueva Venecia, Remolino	Death threats and displacement of 1,100 peasants. Disappearance of 20 peasants in Remolino and the displacement of 3,000 peasants
Late February	Trojas de Cataca	Massacre of 7 persons
November 22	Nueva Venecia, Pueblo Viejo	Thirty-six people identified as assassinated, with up to 80 people unidentified

SOURCE: Report of the Comisión de Organismos de Derecho Humanos sobre las Masacres en la Ciénaga Grande de Santa Marta (January 19, 2001), Bogotá.

itself into an area that has high indices of poverty and unresolved conflict over the management of fishing resources; that is an important corridor between the Caribbean and other areas under the ELN's control; and finally that has a difficult geography that makes it ideal as a refuge as well as a place to hold hostages kidnapped from nearby cities. The arrival of the ELN was made palpable with an ultimatum to fishermen of the region who engaged in the *boliche* method, that is, large-scale and indiscriminate fishing of waters that dramatically reduces fish populations and thus negatively effects small fishing communities. The ELN's warning of reprisals against those who engaged in this method not only announced their presence but also highlighted the inability of state institutions to resolve a conflict that had long been a sore point among the population.[20] The incapacity of local institutions to manage the lake environment was most notable in 1995, when, during the construction of the road between Ciénaga and Barranquilla, salt and fresh water were mixed, causing a drastic fall in the fish population.

The lack of legitimate institutions clearly helps the guerrillas establish a relative level of acceptance based on norms and rules enforced through the use of military power. The entrance of the guerrillas in the zone has led to a series of massacres and confrontations involving the paramilitary (see table 5.1).

It is clear that both the guerrillas and the paramilitary forces respond to a specific regional dynamic. As table 5.2 notes, guerrilla and paramilitary actions focused on three conflicts that were sharpest in the Ciénaga. As armed

TABLE 5.2 Conflicts and Violent Actions in the Delta Area of Magdalena

Conflict	Guerrilla Actions	Paramilitary Actions
Water resource usage by large landholders and contamination near the Sierra Nevada (Aracataca and Fundación)	Attacks in Trojas and Aracataca	Massacres and displacements
Use of *boliche* fishing	Threats issued against *boliche* fishermen	Massacre of Nueva Venecia
Conflict over the management of canals	Interventions in the control of canals	Selective assassinations and displacements in Santa Rita

SOURCE: Field interviews.

groups attempted to consolidate their power, they manipulated and endangered the lives of civilians to assure their control over the population.

The strategic advance of paramilitary forces in the region responds to two specific goals: consolidating themselves in an area where they exercise important political influence; and creating a strong position from which they can advance a military solution to local conflicts, a strategy that has significant support from important sectors of local society and the state. The military offensive launched by the AUC at the end of 2000 against ELN positions near the Sierra Nevada of Santa Marta was an attempt to dislodge the guerrillas from their positions and achieve a total victory. The offensive was accompanied by the massacre of El Morro and attacks along the ELN's corridor linking the Sierra with other regions, resulting in the displacement of some seven hundred families.

By 2001, the paramilitaries had made important political and military advances in Magdalena. Politically, the AUC had learned to use its force to condition the electoral process, forcing candidates out of races to create a single option in elections for mayor, town council, and other positions, as well as pressuring voters on election day to vote for candidates approved by the paramilitaries. As a result of this strategy, the AUC effectively controls a third of the municipalities in the department. Simultaneously, as it gains economic control over the district of Santa Marta, a new strategy of social control is being implemented.

The paramilitary is not merely a reaction to the presence of guerrillas; it represents an independent political and military project of social control that extends the economic structures linked to cattle ranching *latifundio* and an agroindustrial sector that receives capital directly from drug trafficking. Although the relation between these agricultural sectors and drug trafficking has often been noted, the case of Magdalena suggests some interesting peculiarities. First, important sectors of the traditional political class are directly involved in the management of drug-trafficking activities, a situation reminiscent of the colonial era. Second, the move on the part of the paramilitary forces in the region toward acquiring political power through electoral pressures involves them directly in the management of a series of local and regional resources. Third, this unprecedented circumstance allows the AUC to use the cover of legitimate institutions to strengthen its private control of all aspects of citizens' lives, including the use of public spaces to protect, manage, and strengthen the private interests of drug traffickers. Fourth, these circumstances deepen the trend toward the privatization of dispute resolution, impeding the possibility that community demands can be publicly aired, debated, and resolved in public institutions. In effect, this deepens the traditional exclusion of the poor from the political arena and makes it even more improbable that public policies can be adopted to improve the social and economic conditions of the poor in the region. Finally, all of the above trends create a situation in Colombia controlled by actors whose strategic goal is an authoritarian transformation of the Colombian state, a situation that favors drug-trafficking interests searching to legitimate their activities through their leadership of a private strategy of counterinsurgency.

Putumayo

Putumayo is an Amazonian department near the Colombian border with Ecuador.[21] The central and lower regions of the department are marked by a dynamic of colonization resulting from violence in other parts of the country, a crisis in the agrarian sector of the economy, and a flight of peasants from regions that have undergone aerial fumigations of poppy (the key ingredient for the production of heroin) and coca crops. As a result of this accelerated process of colonization, the area has seen a rapid and indiscriminate destruction of its dense tropical forests. Between 1983 and 1996, Putumayo lost 355,832 hectares of forest, or 17.07 percent of its forest area. Among the areas worst affected are the lower Putumayo, including the Valle del Guamuez, which in this period lost 70 percent of its forest, and San Miguel, which lost 44 percent of its forest area.

The lower Putumayo has seen the most dramatic levels of conflict, which revolve around two dynamics. First, the fumigation of illicit crops has dramatically accelerated. Between December 22, 2000, and the first week of February 2001, 29,000 hectares in Putumayo were fumigated, an equivalent of 67 percent of all lands fumigated in 1999. Second, there has been an intensification of the fighting between paramilitary forces and guerrillas disputing control of the region. The AUC entered Puerto Asis at the end of 1997, motivated in part by the peasant marches carried out during 1996, which it perceived as an indicator of social support for the guerrillas. During the initial stage of the paramilitaries' presence, there was a wave of selective assassinations of community leaders, church activists, and in general anyone thought to have links with the guerrillas. At the same time, the paramilitaries attempted to systematically displace the guerrillas' control of the commerce in coca paste and threatened shop owners in urban areas who refused to pay for the "protection" offered by the paramilitary forces. Peasant leaders who had led the 1996 marches were also threatened, and many were forced to leave the region.

By the end of 1998, the AUC entered the area of La Hormiga, Valle de Guamuez. Apparently, paramilitary forces had carried out intelligence operations prior to their entrance to the zone in order to detect possible supporters of the guerrillas and evaluate the terrain. The attempt to dislodge guerrillas from the area began with an effort to remove municipal authorities in a bid at gaining control of coca-paste commerce and developing links between local commercial activities and the economic interests of the paramilitary groups. To this end, these forces engaged in a high level of violence in an attempt to signal a change in the control of the region. The massacres thus have a symbolic function, announcing the power and presence of the paramilitaries. Simultaneously, the guerrillas of the FARC reacted with selective assassinations and massacres of their own in an attempt to neutralize the entrance of the AUC or regain control of areas lost.

The process of reverting guerrilla control in the lower Putumayo began with intelligence operations that focused on identifying the urban militia structure of the FARC, supporters of the guerrillas, and the places that were important in the commercialization of coca paste. At the same time, the AUC was interested in identifying the taxes and fees that the service and commercial sector paid, with the purpose of gaining control of these structures of payments, in the best tradition of the classic *gabela*. Once this information had been ascertained, those involved in the local economy were notified of the change in the structure of power in the region and their new obligations. In the process of controlling the coca-paste economy, guerrillas had opted to eliminate the intermediaries in its commercialization. Behind the elimination of these intermediaries was an attempt to gain control of their profits, although the public argument of the guerrillas was their lack of confidence in this sector and its possible links with paramilitary groups.

The structure of "services" provided by the urban militias of the guerrillas has been a focal point of counterinsurgency strategy. Some estimates put the number of militia members at four to five times the number of combatants. As one union leader noted, "What are the militias of the FARC and ELN? They are instruments that allow them to place bombs, kidnap, and assault in the cities."[22] Generally the militias are directed by former guerrilla combatants who have developed physical problems as a result of combat with the armed forces. These militias are considered the principal obstacles in developing counterinsurgent actions, making it difficult for the armed forces to disarticulate the activities of guerrillas. In this sense, paramilitary actions have a specific logic within the context of the war: to undermine the militia structure of guerrillas and thus weaken their capacity to wage war.

An additional function of the militias is to exercise social control over the population. Gathering information and watching the movement of people within the town are some of their key occupations. In some areas, the militias facilitate the commercialization of coca paste by peasants. As the militias have been drawn into this activity, developing economic interests of their own, they have increasingly helped delegitimize the guerrillas, as arbitrary and despotic behavior undermines the ideals of guerrilla struggles. As middlemen in the commercialization of coca paste, the militias of some zones have become key actors linking insurgent groups with the drug economy, taking the place of a multiplicity of intermediaries that channeled part of the capital derived from the local commercialization process into such diverse economic activities as bars, prostitution, and arms trafficking. Traditional intermediaries (*chichipatos*) are usually the first to suffer economically when groups linked to the insurgents decide to enter the trade themselves. These intermediaries in turn become available as a social base to paramilitary groups, who usually allow them to continue in their role as long as they pay a tax to the local AUC. The relation between the intermediaries and paramilitary groups is clearly one that emerges only as a result of guerrilla actions.[23]

The illegal economy and the war also intersect in the area of prices. Normally, guerrilla intermediaries offer lower purchase prices for coca paste in order to increase their own profit margins. Many producers risk their lives, given that guerrillas impose a "death penalty," by selling their coca to non-guerrilla intermediaries who promise market value for their product. Here again, the expansion of paramilitary forces in the Amazonian region is linked to the illegal economy. While guerrillas manipulate market prices to their own advantage, the AUC is much more flexible, allowing demand and supply to fix the price of coca paste without intervention, as long as intermediaries are willing to pay their tribute.

Another problem that peasants face comes from the fact that guerrilla intermediaries often do not pay promptly for their products, undermining the legitimacy of the guerrillas and reminding many peasants of state agencies that did not pay for legal crops, a situation that initially led many peasants into the coca economy. In many cases guerrillas will pay peasants in "certificates" that can be used in small stores to buy necessities. Merchants are then forced to wait for payment from the guerrillas for the certificates, usually having to accept less than face value. A difference thus emerges between the role that guerrillas used to play as defenders of peasant interests and providers of security for recent colonizers of the zone, and their more recent role as armed middlemen in the drug trade, who underpay for products, are late with payments, and use strong-arm tactics to quiet complaints.

Although the entrance of the guerrillas into drug activities was a pragmatic reaction to the coca economy, it opened the way to an increasing delegitimization of insurgent groups and new opportunities for the entry of paramilitary groups into the area. The guerrillas have reacted to these challenges by imposing new rules of behavior backed by armed threats and attempting to demonstrate their continued military and political power, as with the "armed strike" that was declared by the FARC in Putumayo from late September to November 28, 2000. The strike was a political disaster for the FARC for a number of reasons. First, there were no clear objectives offered to the population, beyond a rejection of the paramilitary presence. Second, despite an attempt to send a message regarding the implementation of Plan Colombia, the strike proved exhausting for both the FARC and the population. By weakening both groups, the strike lessened the possibility of effective resistance to antidrug efforts. This created ideal conditions for the government's plan to initiate an aerial fumigation program, which effectively started in the area in December 2000. Third, the strike resulted in the destruction of property such as cars and an oil pipeline (causing serious environmental damage) and a prohibition on transportation that created food shortages, hitting poor peasants hardest. The result thus appeared self-defeating for the population of Putumayo. Finally, the strike was lifted unilaterally by the FARC without having gained any significant benefit for the people of the region but having generated serious resentment due to the high costs suffered by the population. The strike demonstrated the profound political crisis of a guerrilla group that substitutes unclear demonstrations of force for specific political objectives. Moreover, the absence of a political project and concrete proposals for regional development has led to a growing preference for the use of force and an authoritarian and arrogant approach toward the civilian population.

Comparing the Two Scenarios of Conflict

Both Magdalena and Putumayo evidence a strong absence of a legitimate state presence. However, the ways in which this absence is manifested are distinct in the two regions. In the Atlantic coast region, the exercise of power is based on premodern relations articulated with state actors through the clientelism of the two traditional parties. This pattern traditionally allowed the state a minimal level of institutional control. With the growth of drug trafficking, illegal private actors have increasingly displaced the state in the area of social control. The exercise of power by these new actors has been carried out through the use of violence, the creation of personal ties of loyalty, and the payment of various forms of *gabela,* in a pattern that cuts across the entire region. The internal war affecting Colombia has, moreover, dramatically reduced the institutional capacity of the state to carry out even its minimal functions, while at the same time the premodern and privatized social relations that characterize illegal actors involved in the violence have become their strongest weapon.

Colombia's armed conflict is not one involving a struggle between a modern state attempting to impose its legitimacy through the use of force and an insurgent group. The support, both implicit and explicit, by sectors of the state for private groups engaged in violence and atrocities evidences a pattern of social control reminiscent of the premodern era. At the same time, this relationship crystallizes the prevalence of an esprit mafioso in a context of modernization without modernity. By substituting for the legitimate exercise of state power the atrocities and cruelties carried out by private actors, a subculture is emerging that is based on values of order enforced through premodern private powers. This subculture, with deep roots in drug trafficking, is increasingly demanding its acceptance in society as legitimate. Its primary function is to castigate and warn its enemies or their potential friends. In this sense, it embodies practices characteristic of medieval warriors, with vengeance as a necessary value in the code of honor. This code, typifying what Lawrence Stone has termed the medieval "society of *hacendados,*" has an increasingly high level of acceptance among the diverse sectors of political and economic power in Colombia.[24]

"Security for investment" is one of the pragmatic slogans formulated by these sectors. Rather than a formula for the development of a modern state, it posits an authoritarian model of development using premodern methods to guarantee security. As their legal counterparts do, these illegal investors aspire to insert themselves into the global marketplace and attract foreign investors. In the areas of both security and investment, they obtain the support of a variety of organizations that see in their private mechanisms a better likelihood of security being provided than the state can offer. This situation leads to an important question: what is the state in Colombia at the start of the twenty-first century if not the very predominance of these private interests, which have proved incapable of creating symbols of a unifying national identity and culture and which are now affected by these same mechanisms of private power that they tolerated for so long? The Colombian conflict is nothing more than the result of a long history during which multiple forms of private power were created and armed.[25] In this context, the esprit mafioso has become a symbiosis between the historic legacy of drug trafficking's attempt to legalize and legitimize itself through land ownership and the implementation of a successful counterinsurgency strategy based on the privatization of power. For significant sectors of the country's political elite, the esprit mafioso is becoming the primary ethic in the exercise of public power. It is worth remembering that in the Sicilian context the mafia, with its use of violence as a mechanism of economic control and strength, permitted the creation of an order whose rules, though unstable, helped define a structure of power.

What might be the final result of this dynamic in Colombia? The growing fragmentation of national political power and the self-sufficiency of regional power groups that challenge the national state are a key part of this situation. Behind this self-sufficiency lies the power and resources provided by drug trafficking, which accommodates itself to this fragmentation and, as we have seen, gains strength in diverse regions. An increased level of centralization would thus appear to be, at least in the long term, a possible response on the part of all armed groups as well as the state to the ungovernability that fragmented power presents. While the guerrillas are supposedly fighting to capture centralized state power, the response of the paramilitary forces is more complicated. These forces developed with the direct and indirect support of state power and thus have up to now not attempted to attack the central state. Moreover, it is clear that a significant sector of the state still is convinced of the military usefulness of paramilitary forces in diminishing the insurgent challenge, believing in their instrumentality. Nonetheless, this new actor has begun to acquire a level of power that has led to a growing demand for political recognition. How the central state will respond to this challenge remains to be seen, although an accommodation that requires an authoritarian recomposition of the state is a possibility. It is quite likely that paramilitary forces will attempt to occupy any new political spaces created by a centralized redefinition of state power.

The esprit mafioso in Colombia is also to be found among the country's guerrillas. Insurgents have increasingly become less interested in convoking diverse sectors of society and articulating a common vision based on participation and autonomy. Instead, guerrillas have focused on using social groups in an instrumental way, to merely advance their own particular interests. Moreover, there is an increasing use of violence to advance the nonpolitical interests of insurgents. These include resolving personal disputes or obtaining special benefits from individuals, taking over the role of intermediary in the commercialization of coca paste, promoting marches and mobilizations advanced by the guerrillas, and finally ensuring that the sale of coca paste occurs in only those places authorized by the guerrillas.

The growing personalization of military power ascribed to guerrilla commanders throughout the country has also contributed to an esprit mafioso, in-sofar as this personalization has been accompanied by the predominance of clientelistic relationships with the local population and a tendency to resort to force when problems or resistance emerge. Although these characteristics bring the guerrillas closer to mafia models of violent behavior, it should also be remembered that they still maintain political and military practices and a public discourse that emphasizes their role as an insurgent force attempting to combat the formal structures of the state.

Violence and Social Control

The esprit mafioso is growing and is permeating Colombian society as a whole. Values such as vengeance and the violent settling of scores are an increasing part of everyday life. These values often produce schizophrenic results: most Colombians condemn drug trafficking; however, when a trafficker attempts to "legalize" his situation by buying land and acquire legitimacy by supporting those who promote "order" in the community, he is accepted or at least not openly questioned. The large profits generated by the global trade in drugs have clearly contributed to a new regional economic dynamic, creating employment and income without the need for government-directed development. This new source of income has also modified expectations in these regions, which traditionally focused on demands for state support of infrastructure or assistance in creating sustainable development. The drug economy created huge profits for individuals, but with a loss of social order and personal risk. In the past, community organization was by necessity a vehicle of survival for those settling areas of colonization, helping colonizers confront a range of difficulties. Today, the drug trade has created perceptions of immediate profits in the present, undermining the idea of an uncertain future that requires organization, social protests, and pressures on the state to provide economic and social benefits.

Economic globalization and the discourse of free trade have helped demonstrate to many the goods available from a highly profitable activity, creating new consumer expectations among a population that could previously not imagine such bounty. Local economies that were economically backward and isolated, never imagining direct market access to consumer goods without the intermediation of state agents, have now been dollarized and inserted into consumer markets. These changes did not come without a significant cost. The absent state cannot provide security or collect taxes. Its premodern condition does not allow it to construct affirmative cultural referents, which in turn makes the use of force the primary mechanism to resolve conflicts and regulate behavior. Even with its use of force, the state does not act to realize and consolidate a strategic monopoly. Rather, it acquiesces in and tolerates private violence to resolve conflicts, which may be effective in the short term but over time tends to contribute to the state's delegitimization. As a result, state policies have weakened the ethical mechanisms and symbols that could strengthen its actions against those that violate the law or corrupt public policies, with Colombian society paying a high cost.

Amid the violence, drug trafficking is perceived in two ways: either as a mechanism of support for the guerrillas, which thus requires a strong response (the position of those who support Plan Colombia), or as a source of financing for the creation of a new structure of power, based on the intermediation of capital from drug trafficking. Colombia's war is thus not just one involving economic and military disputes. The demands of war are forcing the different armed actors involved to construct their own structures of security and control in local environments, in most cases sacrificing the interests of local communities. Armed conflict is thus becoming an end in itself, substituting trust in military leaders who are intolerant of civil society and merely interested in gaining control over noncombatants for the possibility of constructing democratic spaces and participation.

The Changing Map of Colombia's War

The map of war in Colombia is rapidly changing. The south is undergoing strategic changes, with the insurgency gaining influence over an ample area of the Amazonian region and attempting to gain control over the frontiers that border Venezuela, Brazil, Ecuador, and Peru. The strategy increases the guerrillas' mobility and helps defend their financial base. While Plan Colombia envisions government forces gaining control of a territory the size of Putumayo (24,885 kilometers) over a two-year period, the insurgency has expanded its "theater of operations" to include over 400,000 kilometers in the Amazonian region. A third of the nation's territory is thus experiencing a structure of power based on a war economy and authoritarian methods of control, with draconian regulations governing all aspects of daily life.

A variety of factors has seriously weakened the peace process, including the consolidation of paramilitary forces, which enjoy ample support from important sectors and which successive governments have been unable to confront in an effective manner; the perception that the United States prefers policies that emphasize military solutions to Colombia's problems—a perception that only deepened in the aftermath of the September 11 attacks in the United States and its subsequent emphasis on antiterrorism as an integral part of national security; and finally a hardening of positions in both the state and society, as confidence in peace talks was shaken by an increase in kidnappings, extortion, and attacks against civilian targets. As confidence in the peace process waned during 2001, important sectors of Colombian society pressured President Andrés Pastrana to take a harder line with the guerrillas. Increasing attacks on the population and a general acceleration of violence significantly raised the costs of negotiating in the midst of the conflict, ultimately leading to a breakdown of negotiations in early 2002. Moreover, pressure from Washington to intensify the military aspects of Plan Colombia and combat international terrorism created a dynamic that made the peace process increasingly unsustainable. This dynamic also led insurgents to question the usefulness of the peace process as a mechanism to end the conflict, based on the belief that the Colombian government is not representative of society and lacks the ability to move the process forward.

Insurgents, in the meantime, attempted to increase their area of operations, their financial strength, and their military readiness in order to improve their bargaining position. Authoritarian methods of social control, attacks against civilian targets, and the lack of serious proposals concerning the country's problems created a legitimacy problem for the guerrillas and also came at a high political cost, as in Putumayo. On the other hand, the unfolding of the war, with its strong paramilitary component, reduced the government's negotiating leverage and had a negative impact on the peace process, reducing confidence among all actors. The growing U.S. intervention in the name of fighting drug trafficking, the economic crisis that took hold in the 1990s, and the weakness of the traditional parties have all contributed to a regime crisis that insurgents have learned to use to their own advantage. At the same time, civil society remains weak, unable to coordinate a response to violence, and lacking conditions for fuller development.

The situation in Colombia has begun to approach that of the worst period of the "Violencia" (1948–55), when the polarization of the countryside was such that civilian populations were ascribed to one side or the other and thus considered legitimate targets. With the state absent from this growing polarization, it has become just another armed faction in the war, losing its role as mediator and organizer of public over private interests. The peace process effectively obscured the complexity of the drug economy, treating it as a largely marginal issue, even as its role in the dynamic of war has been increasing. While drug trafficking is an extremely difficult problem to address, given its international dimension, external pressure from the United States has focused attention on coca eradication, which as a policy has failed, only contributing to an intensification of conflict. With hard-line policies being adopted by President Alvaro Uribe Vélez, elected in 2002, it is worth remembering that a purely military approach that does not recognize the complex intersection of interests and local conditions behind armed conflict, evident in places such as Magdalena an Putumayo, is unlikely to succeed.

6   Collateral Damage

The U.S. "War on Drugs" and Its Impact on
Democracy in the Andes

෨ The dramatic increase in drug trafficking poses real dangers to countries throughout the Western Hemisphere. Drug trafficking in the Andes breeds criminality, exacerbates political violence, and hence greatly increases problems of citizen security. It has corrupted and further weakened local governments, judiciaries, and police forces and rends the social fabric, particularly in poor urban areas where both drug abuse and drug-related violence are rampant. Illicit drug abuse—a minor problem in Latin America a decade ago—has reached epidemic proportions in cities such as Caracas, Medellín, and Lima. The physical and moral damage to individuals, communities, and societies of the illicit drug trade is creating new challenges for Andean societies, already struggling to overcome endemic poverty and injustice.

As the world's largest consumer of illicit drugs, the United States also confronts a myriad of problems stemming from illicit drug abuse and drug-related violence. The policy response developed in Washington, however, is largely driven by domestic political considerations and a desire to be "tough" in combating the illegal drug trade—hence, the drug war rhetoric that prevails today. Through its diplomatic and economic leverage, the United States has to a large extent dictated the policies adopted by the Andean governments, often over the objections of both local governments and important segments of civil society, at times draining scarce resources from other national priorities. Apart from breeding resentment and tensions in bilateral relations, the U.S. approach to international drug control has also left a path of "collateral damage" in its wake.

This chapter explores such collateral damage in three Andean countries—Peru, Bolivia, and Colombia—and in two principal areas: first, the influence and role of security forces and their relationship to civilian-elected governments in the postauthoritarian regime period; second, the way in which the drug war exacerbates existing problems of political violence and fosters human rights violations. The U.S. government's war on drugs clearly hinders efforts to put civilian-military relations on a new footing and as such constitutes an obstacle to the strengthening and deepening of democratic governance in the Andes. U.S. drug policy is detrimental to efforts to reduce military roles and missions, to eliminate the military's role in maintaining internal public order, to enhance civilian control over military forces, and to increase both the transparency and the accountability of military forces. Moreover, the counternarcotics mission provides the military with a task that is likely to lead to human rights abuses, and the "confidential" nature of counterdrug programs further exacerbates patterns of impunity.

With the transition to civilian-elected governments in South America have come widespread efforts to reduce the power of local security forces, limiting their authority to the control of national borders, and to enhance the control of civilian-elected governments over local militaries and intelligence services. Washington, its claims to the contrary notwithstanding, erodes these efforts by relying on the Latin American military and police forces to play the lead role in combating the illicit drug trade, providing the resources, training, and doctrinal justification for militaries to play a significant role in domestic counternarcotics operations, a law-enforcement function reserved in most democracies for civilian police. The dominant role assigned to local security forces in the drug war is detrimental to the region's fragile transition toward more democratic societies following decades of often brutal military rule. In following this policy, the U.S. government legitimates Latin American security forces in a fundamental internal security role, now directed at "new enemies," and confirms them as actors in domestic politics. More often than not, U.S. support is provided prior to any meaningful institutional reforms that would ensure greater civilian control or respect for human rights.

U.S. officials often justify the embrace of local militaries as necessary to confront the firepower of drug traffickers and the rampant corruption among police forces. Yet the long-term consequences of this approach may be even more detrimental than drug trafficking itself to prospects for democratic consolidation and regional stability. Nor is it clear that bringing in the military will allow local governments to circumvent the very real problem of corruption. As former Bolivian president Gonzalo Sánchez de Lozado once said: "When you have a corrupt chief of police, you fire him. When you have a corrupt chief of the army, he fires you."[1] The lack of accountability and transparency of the region's armed forces makes rooting out the inevitable corruption that accompanies antidrug efforts even more difficult and controlling potential human rights abuses next to impossible.

Through its drug policy, the United States has forged unholy alliances with militaries that have deplorable human rights records. In Bolivia, U.S. drug policy pits coca farmers against the Bolivian police and army, generating conflict, violence, and human rights abuses. In Peru, the U.S. government provided counterdrug aid to the Peruvian National Intelligence Service (SIN), responsible for death-squad activity and significant setbacks to democracy in that country between the April 1992 *autogolpe,* or presidential self-coup, and Fujimori's dramatic fall from power nine years later. Perhaps most disturbingly, in the name of fighting drugs, the U.S. government has become directly involved in Colombia's brutal counterinsurgency campaign and is providing millions of dollars in economic assistance and training to Colombian military forces, some of whom are allied with the right-wing paramilitary groups responsible for the majority of human rights abuses being committed in that country today. Washington has slid down the slippery slope of increasing involvement in yet another counterinsurgency quagmire in Latin America.

The Illicit Drug Trade

The Andean region is the source of the bulk of illicit drugs that ultimately wind up on U.S. city streets. Cocaine, derived from the leaf of the coca plant, is produced primarily in the Andean countries of Colombia, Bolivia, and Peru. The coca leaves are mixed with easily obtainable chemicals and other products to make coca paste, which is then transported to laboratories and processed into powdered cocaine. Colombia has also become the principal supplier of heroin to the eastern United States. A broad network of dealers and transportation routes is in place to export these illicit drugs to the United States and other areas of the world.

The areas under coca cultivation, drug-trafficking cartels, and trafficking routes have proliferated since the drug war was launched. Coca production can be compared to a balloon: squeezing it in one area merely causes it to pop up somewhere else. In Peru, for example, coca production used to be confined to the Upper Huallaga Valley. Coca-eradication efforts and the mysterious spread of a fungus in coca-growing regions led to new production areas in the lower and middle Huallaga, the Apurimac river valley, and elsewhere. Just as the Peruvian Air Force and the U.S. Southern Command (SouthCom) began intercepting airplanes flying with coca paste from Peru to Colombia for refinement into cocaine, coca production in Colombia exploded.

A similar trend has occurred with cocaine production and trafficking. Following the crackdown on Colombia's Medellín cartel, the Cali cartel quickly replaced it. Once most of the Cali cartel leadership was behind bars, a "democratization" of the drug trade in Colombia took place, as smaller, regionally oriented networks of drug traffickers—much more difficult to infiltrate and dismantle—took root around the country. Drug mafias have since proliferated in Mexico, Bolivia, Peru, Venezuela, and Brazil. Traffickers have adapted quickly to drug control strategies, developing new methods and routes to circumvent detection.

Fortune magazine once described the cocaine trade as "probably the fastest growing and unquestionably the most profitable" industry in the world.[2] In fact, the illicit drug trade has become an escape valve for Andean economies, which have fared poorly over the last two decades. Particularly in the boom years of the mid- to late 1980s, when the cocaine trade took off, coca and cocaine dollars helped alleviate Peru's and Bolivia's severe balance-of-payments problems and at least partially compensated for the lack of new loans and investments. In recent years, as coca-eradication efforts have succeeded in reducing overall coca cultivation in Bolivia, the local economy in the Cochabamba area has bottomed out and malnutrition and related diseases have skyrocketed in the Chapare coca-growing region—clear indicators of the dependence on the revenues derived from the coca trade. Even in Colombia, with the largest economy of the three, the drug trade has helped lubricate the economy and provides substantial, though risky, employment opportunities.

As the gap between the rich and poor has widened following a decade of free market reforms, for many of the region's poor coca production has become a means of survival. In Bolivia, following neoliberal reforms that devastated the tin industry and led to widespread factory shutdowns, people flocked to the Chapare region. In Colombia, peasants forced off their land as a result of political violence and poor urban dwellers with no prospect of legal employment make their way to the southern coca-growing regions, either to plant coca or work as *raspachines,* or harvesters of coca leaves. There are simply too many poor people, and too much land suitable for coca production, to put a lid on illicit coca production. Likewise, rampant unemployment and underemployment in urban areas ensure a steady supply of recruits for other stages of the drug industry, from those who transport coca paste to others higher up in the drug-trafficking ranks.

U.S. International Drug Control Policy

As a result of these conditions, the Andean region is the frontline in the U.S. war on drugs. Successive U.S. presidents have sought to target the "source" of production: the coca leaf, a traditional crop among Andean peasant communities. While the roots of the drug war go back to the Nixon administration, the launching of the "Andean Initiative" by President George H. W. Bush in 1989 focused attention on source-country efforts. The stated objectives of the five-year strategy were to strengthen the political will and institutional capabilities of the Andean governments to combat drugs, increase the effectiveness of local law enforcement and military antidrug activities, and work with these countries to disrupt and dismantle drug-trafficking organizations. The thrust of the source-country approach is to make the illicit drug trade more dangerous and costly, thereby driving down production and availability, driving up prices, and ultimately discouraging U.S. citizens from buying and using illicit drugs.

A final objective of the Andean strategy was to strengthen and diversify the legitimate economies of the Andean countries so that they could overcome the destabilizing effect of eliminating coca and cocaine as a major source of income. However, economic assistance was originally to be provided only after success was obtained in significantly disrupting the coca and cocaine trades. Security assistance, on the other hand, was front-loaded in the five-year plan. The Andean Initiative was centered on a dramatic escalation of support for military and police forces in the region, promotion of a direct hands-on role for both local and U.S. military forces in combating drug trafficking and production, and an enhanced role for some local intelligence services in domestic intelligence-gathering operations.

At the outset of his administration, President Bill Clinton promised a different approach to the drug war by proposing treatment on demand for drug users and education at home. Administration officials largely dropped the use of war metaphors and paid greater lip service to promoting democratic institutions and economic development in drug-producing countries. But the administration soon reversed course, following the path laid out by Bush's Andean Initiative. Approximately 65 percent of the federal drug control budget continued to be allocated annually for supply-side efforts at home and abroad, and the Andes remained the centerpiece of U.S. international drug control policy.

By the mid-1990s, the Clinton administration—backed by the Republican-controlled Congress—had dramatically increased funding for international counternarcotics assistance. As the 2000 presidential and congressional elections approached, Congress approved another major infusion of aid for international drug control efforts. In addition to nearly $300 million approved through the normal appropriations procedure, an emergency supplemental aid package for "Plan Colombia" was legislated, amounting to $1.3 billion over a two-year period, making Colombia the third-largest recipient of U.S. military assistance in the world. Nearly $1 billion was allocated for the Colombian armed forces—almost $2 million a day. (A small portion of that package was provided for counternarcotics efforts in Bolivia and Peru and for "forward operating locations," or FOLs, military bases used to refuel sophisticated U.S. aircraft involved in aerial surveillance of the Andean region to gather counternarcotics intelligence.)

With the advent of the George W. Bush administration, U.S. drug policy has come full circle. In the spring of 2001, the new administration presented its "Andean Regional Initiative," another nearly $1 billion aid package for fiscal year (FY) 2002 that is remarkably similar to the former President Bush's

"Andean Initiative."[3] While still targeting Colombia, the latest program is designed to address the spillover effects of the U.S. drug war in Colombia by providing increased assistance to its neighbors, including Peru, Bolivia, Ecuador, Brazil, Venezuela, and Panama. The U.S. Congress approved $625 million for the Andean Regional Initiative for FY2002 and shortly thereafter began considering a request for FY2003 of over $600 million.

In short, several billion dollars have been allocated to Andean counterdrug efforts in recent years. Yet there is hardly a dent in overall coca production, and cocaine and heroin are just as cheap and readily available on U.S. city streets as they were when the Andean Initiative was first launched. Washington is losing its self-proclaimed war on drugs in the Andean region. Yet with no "enemy" to declare formal victory, the war continues unabated at a high cost to U.S. taxpayers and, most significantly, to the people of the Andean region.

The Pentagon's Role

Security assistance—aid to local military and police forces—is one of the principal tools for U.S. agencies waging the drug war abroad. While the Drug Enforcement Administration (DEA) is the primary agency engaged in on-the-ground antinarcotics activities overseas, in 1989 the U.S. Congress designated the Department of Defense (DOD) as the "single lead agency" for the detection and monitoring of illicit drug shipments into the United States and expanded its funding for training and equipping local security forces. In addition to the provision of military hardware, the U.S. military runs an array of counternarcotics-related training programs. U.S. training programs take on many different forms, and training teams can be as small as a single officer or as large as an entire platoon. In FY1998, for example, SouthCom carried out at least 2,265 "Deployments for Training" in Latin America and the Caribbean involving over forty-eight thousand U.S. personnel (Isacson and Olson 1999). In addition, U.S. Special Forces also carry out their own training deployments, often numbering in the hundreds per year. In-country training is supplemented by instruction at U.S. military facilities. Among the U.S.-based facilities used for counternarcotics instruction is the former School of the Americas at Fort Benning, Georgia.[4] It offers officers an eleven-week course that provides instruction in planning, leading, and executing drug-interdiction operations, including infiltration and surveillance techniques, patrolling, and demolition and close-quarters combat (Zirnite 1997). In 1999, the last year for which figures are available, the United States trained a total of about thirteen thousand Latin American military and police, either in the region or on U.S. bases.[5]

A vital part of their instruction, U.S. officials stress, is human rights training. However, training is provided regardless of the human rights record and political will for human rights–related reforms exhibited by recipient forces. Human rights groups point to other inherent problems with U.S. military counternarcotics training programs. The jungle warfare–type training that DOD provides to Latin American security forces is not well suited for drug control efforts, which should be oriented toward sound investigations and criminal prosecutions. Inadequate or illegally obtained evidence continues to be a major obstacle to successful prosecutions, while the killings that occur during violent drug raids often provoke controversy when potentially innocent individuals are involved, such as in the shooting of a civilian aircraft in Peru in April 2001 in which a U.S. Baptist missionary and her infant daughter were killed.

Despite the wide array of DOD counternarcotics programs in place today, the U.S. military's role in counternarcotics efforts was met with some resistance in the Pentagon. Many DOD officials were concerned about becoming involved in a mission that was seen as deviating from the U.S. military's traditional role and that could potentially be detrimental to military readiness in other areas of the world. U.S. military officials were, in short, reluctant recruits to the war on drugs.

However, SouthCom embraced the drug mission enthusiastically. In the wake of the Cold War, the drug war provided the rationale for maintaining SouthCom's budget and troop levels as other areas of the world rose in importance on the Pentagon's agenda. SouthCom officials also viewed the drug war as converging with its previous roles and mission; the low-intensity conflict strategies honed during the years of conflict in Central America were quickly adapted to carry out the new mandate. Perhaps most importantly, the drug war provided SouthCom with a means of not only maintaining but expanding military-to-military relations throughout the hemisphere.

Expanding Military Missions

Counternarcotics training, whether conducted in-country or at U.S. facilities, is viewed by many Pentagon officials as an important opportunity to foster closer ties with South America's armed forces, one of the key goals of DOD's post–Cold War strategy for the hemisphere. In a series of interviews conducted by the Washington Office on Latin America (WOLA) in 1990 and 1991, U.S. military officials with responsibility for U.S. security policy toward Latin America underscored the need to not only maintain but expand relations with militaries across the hemisphere—a strategy they have pursued ever since. They also stressed the need to enhance military capabilities, even as civilian-elected governments took hold: "Currently, in SouthCom's view, the U.S. military's part in promoting democracy . . . is neither to work for a reduction in Latin American military forces nor to attempt to delimit the role of armed forces in Latin American societies. Rather, the U.S. military role is to continue to strengthen military capabilities on the assumption that democratic values will be transmitted. Enhancing host nation capabilities appears repeatedly throughout SouthCom documents as a goal for counterinsurgency, anti-narcotics, and nation-building activities" (Call 1991, 41). In following this policy, the Pentagon is seeking to strengthen the very forces that many local governments are trying to keep back in the barracks after decades of military rule and that remain one of the principal obstacles to establishing effective civilian rule in the Andean region.

Some local analysts point out that by circumventing civilian institutions, the U.S. government may be undermining people's faith in those institutions at a time when democratic developments remain delicate and when curbing military autonomy remains critical to future democratization. In some Andean countries, the civilian government's control of military forces is tenuous at best, and local militaries are increasingly flexing their muscle. For example, in Colombia—which does not have a history of military rule—the military's powers have steadily expanded as insurgency movements have grown. In August 2001, for example, a law was passed and signed by President Andrés Pastrana that, according to one journalist, "allows the military to supercede civilian rule in areas declared by the president to be 'theaters of operation' and reduces the chance that army troops could be subjected to thorough human rights investigations by civilian government agencies."[6]

Since the Andean Initiative was first launched, military power and influence have grown in different ways throughout the Andean region. In Ecuador, a popular uprising and military coup in January 2000 led to the ouster of the sitting president. In Bolivia and Venezuela, military officials have entered power through elections. When former dictator General Hugo Banzer was elected president, he announced his intention to elevate the Bolivian military's role in the country, paving the way for greater military involvement in counternarcotics operations. Hugo Chávez, one-time coup plotter and now president of Venezuela, has "militarized society to a level not seen since democracy was restored in 1958," according to one international observer.[7] A faction of the military allied with disgruntled civilian sectors nearly ousted Chávez in a failed coup attempt in April 2002. All of these examples provide a potent reminder of the extent to which military forces across the Andean region continue to see themselves as the arbiters of political power.

In Peru, President Alberto Fujimori relied on the active support of the Peruvian armed forces and the SIN to consolidate his authoritarian rule. The power and political influence of the Peruvian military expanded significantly following the 1992 *autogolpe,* as was evident in its increasing role in the judicial realm, the impunity with which it operated, and its role in helping President Fujimori secure reelection in 1995 and again, via widespread fraud, in 2000. Until it was dismantled in 2001, the SIN functioned as the regime's political police. It was responsible for the systematic harassment, intimidation, and blackmail of its perceived political opponents; carried out widespread illegal wiretapping and other surveillance; and was the principal agency involved in manipulating the courts, Congress, and the electoral apparatus to favor executive-branch policies (Youngers 2000). Yet both the Peruvian military and the SIN were courted by U.S. officials as important allies in the drug war and received significant U.S. economic support toward that end.

In short, the allies chosen by Washington as it wages its drug war in the Andes represent some of the most dangerous elements of their societies. In this context, the drug war's collateral damage is quite clear: an enhanced role for local military and intelligence forces in domestic operations that lack sufficient mechanisms for civilian control and accountability. These forces are beefed up at the expense of civilian institutions upon which the future of democracy in these countries depends.

Overcoming Local Opposition

The Andean Initiative's potential dangers to the consolidation of civilian rule initially generated opposition among many Latin American governments. However, the U.S. Congress put its full weight behind ensuring the use of U.S. diplomatic and economic leverage to coerce cooperation from reluctant drug war partners. In 1986 it enacted a "certification" requirement for drug-producing and -transport countries. By March 1 of each year, the administration must "certify" to the U.S. Congress that those deemed to be drug-producing or -transport countries are cooperating with U.S. efforts to control drug production, trafficking, and use. Countries that are not certified face a full range of sanctions, including the suspension of all U.S. foreign assistance not directly related to antidrug programs, U.S. opposition to loans by multilateral development banks, and possible trade sanctions. While numerous countries have been granted a "national security waiver," only Colombia has faced the full weight of U.S. sanctions as a result of "decertification."

Andean countries initially balked at Washington's demand that local militaries play a prominent role in counternarcotics operations and at U.S. insistence that the war on drugs be made a top priority, even in the face of the severe economic crisis that engulfed the Andean region at the time. Andean leaders not only had scarce resources but also feared that some of the political and economic challenges they faced could be deepened by a large-scale crackdown on the coca and cocaine trade.[8]

Even some local militaries objected to this new role. Both Peruvian and

Colombian military officials, for example, repeatedly claimed that counterinsurgency objectives took precedence over counternarcotics objectives and saw the two as conflicting, rather than complementary. In the Peruvian Huallaga, the military had adopted a strategy of trying to win "the hearts and minds" of the local population in order to erode any support the Shining Path had among the local population. Eliminating their economic livelihood only risked pushing them into the hands of the guerillas. As one former Peruvian military commander said, "There are 150,000 peasants growing coca in the zone. Each of them is a potential subversive. Eradicate his field and the next day he will become one."[9]

Despite local resistance, the U.S. government used the threat of decertification and the significant disruptions in both aid and trade with the United States that such an action would cause to bring local governments on board. The Andean militaries in Colombia, Bolivia, and Peru were eventually enticed with the economic and political backing offered by Washington and, like SouthCom, found in the drug war a convenient raison d'être for maintaining troop levels, budgets, and political influence. For the Colombian military, the benefits of adapting to the drug war rhetoric are more than obvious from the U.S. aid now flowing into their coffers. More than ten years after the Andean Initiative was first launched, all of the Andean militaries are now actively engaged in the U.S. war on drugs.

Human Rights and the "Narco-Guerrilla" Theory

Among those militaries are those responsible for some of the worst human rights violations in the hemisphere today. As a result, another unintended consequence of the U.S. war on drugs is that Washington is at least indirectly fueling human rights violations and, in Colombia, contributing to the region's most brutal counterinsurgency campaign. U.S. support for abusive forces is taking place even as overall levels of human rights violations have declined markedly across the region and most countries have significantly improved human rights records.

International antinarcotics accords include provisions relating to the protection of human rights. The 1990 Declaration of Cartegena, for example, requires that "the parties act within the framework for human rights" and states that "nothing would do more to undermine the war on drugs than disregard for human rights." Bilateral agreements between the U.S. and Latin American governments often include clauses on human rights, and administration documents, such as the annual International Narcotics Control Strategy Report, stress the compatibility between antinarcotics programs and respect for human rights. Nonetheless, both the Bush and Clinton administrations have, at different points in time, downplayed the gravity of the human rights situation in countries such as Peru and Colombia in order to obtain congressional support for counternarcotics assistance.

The "narco-guerrilla" theory, which first gained prominence in the early 1980s, has allowed the counternarcotics and counterinsurgency missions to blur, creating greater risks that local forces that receive U.S. counterdrug assistance become involved in human rights abuses. At a 1984 Senate hearing, federal officials warned that international terrorists were turning to drug trafficking to finance their operations.[10] The alleged link between drug traffickers and insurgents became an implicit component of the first Andean Initiative, as administration officials depicted drug traffickers as irrevocably tied to leftist subversives. By the mid-1990s, U.S. officials pointed to Colombia as the center of narco-guerrilla activity. In an April 2, 1998, statement, Representative Benjamin Gilman boldly exclaimed, "The frightening possibilities of a 'narco-state' just three hours by plane from Miami can no longer be dismissed." In the wake of the September 11, 2001, attacks, the term now used most frequently is "narco-terrorist."

While links between drug traffickers and guerrillas clearly exist, the reality on the ground is more complex. No one disputes that the Revolutionary Armed Forces of Colombia (FARC) gains significant resources from the illicit drug trade. It has virtual territorial control of vast areas where coca plantations thrive, providing it with a very important and steady source of income that allows it to advance militarily and maintain a steady flow of recruits. However, the guerrillas are one of many actors—including elements of the armed forces and right-wing paramilitary groups—involved in the lucrative drug trade. In fact, drug mafias are most closely associated with right-wing paramilitary groups, with whom they have historic ties. These in turn often have close ties to members of the Colombian security forces. The implications for U.S. policy are formidable.

Supporting Peru's Intelligence Service

Abusive army units are not the only ones who have benefited from U.S. largesse; local intelligence services have also. During the years that military dictatorships prevailed across the Latin American region, intelligence services were often the source of the worst manifestations of state terror, and since the return to civilian rule those agencies have largely evaded reform by civilian-elected governments. The character of intelligence and the uses to which it is put depend on whether those in command answer to democratic civilian authority. Yet Andean intelligence services continue to operate with significant autonomy, are not accountable to the public, and often operate with a Cold War mentality that fails to distinguish legal political activity from insurgent or criminal activity.

Perhaps the most blatant case is that of Peru, where the U.S. government provided political and economic support to Peru's intelligence service, the SIN, despite its involvement in death-squad activity and the antidemocratic activities previously described. U.S. officials claimed throughout the course of the 1990s that the SIN played an important coordinating role in counternarcotics efforts, leaving Washington with little choice but to support it. U.S. officials even claimed that the SIN was effective in its efforts, meeting publicly with SIN officials, praising their work in the press (and lending political support even as the SIN's involvement in sinister activities was growing), and providing economic support via the State Department and the Central Intelligence Agency (CIA). The de facto head of the SIN and President Fujimori's top security adviser, Vladimiro Montesinos, was long rumored to be on the CIA payroll.

This relationship appears to go back to the 1970s, when Montesinos was thrown out of the Peruvian army and spent one year in jail after an unauthorized visit to Washington, where he was suspected of selling information to U.S. agents. He then launched a lucrative law practice defending accused drug traffickers. In 1978, he defended Colombian drug kingpin Evaristo Porras Ardila, a former member of the Medellín cartel. The following year he defended Jaime Tamayo, another Colombian trafficker. During the trial it was revealed that Montesinos had served as guarantor for rental contracts on two houses utilized by Tamayo as cocaine laboratories. Later, Montesinos defended one of Peru's most notorious drug traffickers, Reynaldo Rodríguez López, known as El Padrino.[11]

In 1990, Montesinos was introduced to Fujimori by his campaign chief, Francisco Loayza. After helping Fujimori avoid a judicial trial for tax evasion, Montesinos quickly became his top security advisor.[12] Within a short period of time he had taken over control of the SIN and was being portrayed as the architect of the Peruvian government's war against terrorism and drug trafficking. Although he held no formal title within the government, by the mid-1990s U.S. officials would refer to Montesinos as Peru's "drug czar." Although in other countries Washington was quick to dictate who should control narcotics policies, in the case of Peru, U.S. officials publicly lamented that they had no choice but to work with Montesinos. Privately, they pointed out that he indeed got things done—he was viewed as "Mr. Fixit."[13]

Throughout this period, credible allegations repeatedly surfaced linking Montesinos to unconstitutional acts, human rights violations, and drug trafficking–related corruption. Montesinos is considered to be the mastermind behind the April 1992 *autogolpe,* when Fujimori shut down the Peruvian Congress and judiciary, suspended the country's constitution, and subsequently adopted draconian antiterrorist legislation. He is also considered to be the key

organizer of a death squad (known as Grupo Colina) responsible for some of
the worst human rights atrocities that took place during the Fujimori government. In addition, numerous individuals claimed under oath that Montesinos
demanded bribes in order for drug-trafficking operations to go forward unim-
peded by authorities.

Periodically reports surfaced regarding the wealth that Montesinos has accumulated. For example, in December 1999, local journalists discovered that
Montesinos's bank account in Lima contained 275 times the annual income of
a high-level government adviser. Yet every time these allegations arose, U.S.
officials publicly stated their confidence in the integrity of Peruvian government officials and refused to back calls for investigations. The unwillingness
of U.S. officials to support investigations into allegations of wrongdoing by
Montesinos provided him with crucial political support when he was most
vulnerable to criticism.

Shortly after Montesinos emerged as Fujimori's right-hand man, Peruvian
journalist Gustavo Gorriti reported that the CIA was providing counternarcotics aid to an SIN antinarcotics unit involved in death-squad activity. In-
quiries by members of the U.S. Congress revealed that the U.S. State Department had provided small but steady amounts of assistance to the antidrug
unit of the SIN until the late 1990s. The CIA was also believed to have channeled aid to the SIN, although it refuses to deny or confirm such reports.
Most disturbingly, credible reports say that the CIA paid Montesinos at least
one million dollars a year in cash for a ten-year period, allegedly for counternarcotics programs—and that such money flowed right up until September 2000, when Fujimori was forced to announce new elections in which he
would not run, along with the dismantling of the SIN.[14] According to the
U.S. ambassador to Peru, John Hamilton, it was not until Fujimori's surprise
announcement that all communication with Montesinos allegedly ceased and
the SIN was informed that all programs with the United States would be dis-
continued. He also acknowledged that the CIA had an "official liaison relationship" with Montesinos.[15]

In short, Washington maintained ties to Montesinos and to the SIN long
after serious and credible allegations of his link to the drug trade and to human rights violations had been put forward and months after his role in steal-
ing the 2000 presidential elections had become evident. With the fall of the
Fujimori government, the prosecution of dozens of officials implicated in corruption and other scandals, and the subsequent capture of Vladimiro Montesinos, more and more information is being revealed as to the corrupt practices of the Peruvian "drug czar," who amassed a known fortune of nearly
three million dollars.

Over the course of the Fujimori administration, U.S. officials consistently spoke out in defense of human rights and democracy; yet it is now clear that through the drug war, the United States was supporting the very forces that were undermining democratic institutions. U.S. drug policy exacerbated trends toward increased concentration of power in the hands of the president; suppression of legal political dissent and independent reporting; and the steady elimination of mechanisms of transparency and accountability within government, which allowed for massive official corruption to go on for years unnoticed. In short, as a result of drug war politics, the U.S. government became an accomplice, albeit indirectly, of authoritarian rule.

Fueling Violence in Bolivia

Perhaps nowhere is the direct collateral damage of the U.S. war on drugs more evident than in Bolivia. With no guerrilla groups operating in the country, no murky line between counterinsurgency and counternarcotics efforts blurs the picture as in Colombia. In other words, human rights violations that result from antinarcotics operations are just that. While current abuses pale in comparison to the killings and disappearances that occurred under some of Bolivia's military dictators, a disturbing pattern of detentions, mistreatment, and abuse of the local population prevails in Bolivia's primary coca-growing region, the Chapare. Moreover, the primary victims are not drug traffickers but poor farmers who eke out a subsistence-level income through coca production. The antinarcotics efforts that have led to such abuses are rooted in Law 1008, adopted by the Bolivian Congress on July 19, 1989. Passed under U.S. pressure, Law 1008 gives the government sweeping powers to control coca production and drug trafficking. Social unrest, conflict, and violence in the Chapare have clearly increased as a result of U.S. pressure on the Bolivian government to comply with Law 1008 and to meet annual coca-eradication targets.

The Bolivian antinarcotics police, the Mobile Rural Patrol Units (UMOPAR), are trained and funded by the U.S. government, which provides everything from uniforms to the cost of feeding UMOPAR detainees in some police prisons. The UMOPAR commit a litany of abuses: arbitrary searches and arrests, theft, and mistreatment of detainees during interrogations. A study conducted by the Andean Information Network (AIN), a nongovernmental organization based in Cochabamba, Bolivia, revealed startling statistics: 60 percent of those detained stated that they had been threatened by the police during their arrest, and 44 percent affirmed that they had been tortured and/or beaten.[16] Bolivian officials implicated in abuses are rarely, if ever, sanctioned.

Massive sweeps, where hundreds may be detained at one time, often lead to arbitrary detentions. Detainees are typically held for several days and then released without being charged or presented before judicial authorities. Often, they are not allowed to notify family members of their detention. Other detentions are not indiscriminate but target those actively opposing coca-eradication activities. Following two investigative missions to Bolivia, Human Rights Watch concluded that antinarcotics police carry out arrests "intended to suppress peaceful and lawful protest activity" and detain coca-grower federation leaders in order "to secure advantage in negotiations with them over government policy."[17] In late 2001 and early 2002, the Bolivian government detained almost all of the coca growers federation's top leadership, charging them with crimes that would have kept them behind bars for life. In the face of escalating violence and decreasing public support, the government finally released them.

In 1998, then-president Hugo Banzer launched a plan to eliminate all illicit coca within his five-year term in office and brought the army into on-the-ground operations to carry out his mandate alongside local police forces. The "zero coca" policy served to intensify the cyclical patterns of violence that plague the Chapare. In May 1998, Banzer announced the transfer of the Armed Forces High Command to Cochabamba, the city closest to the Chapare. Approximately five thousand army troops moved into the area, mostly young conscripts who had no experience in diffusing face-to-face conflicts or social protests and who were unprepared for the severe living conditions of the tropics. The soldiers' presence led to greatly increased tension and a sharp increase in violent confrontations. With U.S. financial support, the Bolivian military is reinforcing its existing infrastructure in the Chapare region to house and train its troops, ensuring military control of the region for the foreseeable future.

As the Bolivian government pursued its "zero coca" policy, the situation in the Chapare continued to deteriorate, culminating in a massive protest in September and October of 2000. Coca growers blocked the main roads in and out of the region for nearly one month. Food supplies rotted on trucks, and all other commerce ceased. The military responded with its strongest use of force yet, firing indiscriminately into the crowds of protesters. Two civilians were killed, seventy-eight wounded, forty-eight illegally detained, and sixteen tortured. Five members of the security forces and one soldier's wife were also found dead in the rain forest. No serious official investigations of abuses by state forces have gone forward, though coca farmers are on trial for the other killings.[18]

The cycle continued the following year, with steadily escalating protests and violent repression beginning in September 2001 and continuing through February 2002. Over that period, ten coca growers were killed as a result of excessive use of force by security forces. Four members of those forces were killed, apparently by angry coca growers. Over 350 protesters were injured or detained.[19]

Although the Bolivian government has declared victory in its "zero coca" strategy, forced eradication efforts continue. To avoid eradication, in recent years coca growers have planted more coca in with other plants and under trees, where it cannot be detected via aerial surveillance. While accurate statistics are not available on coca production in the Chapare, it is clear that coca is being replanted at a rapid rate. The lack of effective alternative development efforts and pervasive poverty not just in the Chapare but throughout the country ensure that coca will continue to be grown despite the military presence.

Although Bolivia has witnessed 182 coups since it gained independence in 1825, the U.S. government has expressed no reservations about bringing the military into domestic operations that previously pertained to the police. The most significant collateral damage of the drug war in Bolivia, however, is violent social conflict and a range of human rights abuses. Despite millions of dollars and years of coca-eradication programs, the drug trade continues to flourish and coca production continues, while drug war–related abuses abound. The cyclical patterns of violence that have developed in the Chapare as a result of the U.S. war on drugs will no doubt continue well into the future.

U.S. Involvement in Colombia

Although the Bolivian government in recent years has consistently met U.S. coca-eradication targets and other counternarcotics objectives, it has faced cuts in U.S. assistance as funds are diverted to Colombia. In Colombia, the U.S. drug war is inextricably intertwined with the military's counterinsurgency campaign. The number of victims of political violence killed on any given day in Colombia has almost doubled in recent years, to twenty per day.[20] Over 70 percent of these killings are attributed to right-wing paramilitary groups, often allied with the country's security forces; the rest are attributed directly to the Colombian security forces and to the insurgents. The tactics of the FARC in particular have become increasingly brutal, and this organization is responsible for widespread killings and kidnappings. In addition, political violence has forced more than one million Colombians from their homes—over three hundred thousand in 2000—mostly fleeing paramilitary rampages.[21] Paramilitary groups are responsible for hundreds of massacres of civilians a year.

The ties between paramilitary and state security forces are well documented. Human Rights Watch reports "compelling evidence that certain Colombian army brigades and police detachments continue to promote, work with, support, profit from, and tolerate paramilitary groups, treating them as a force allied to and compatible with their own."[22] Despite periodic pledges on the part of the Colombian government to combat paramilitary activity, the Colombian armed forces have failed to take adequate steps toward reining in the paramilitaries. Apart from a handful of high-profile cases where significant international pressure was brought to bear, the Colombian military has failed to prosecute and punish members of its ranks implicated in paramilitary activity and other human rights atrocities. Moreover, the military high command has punished those who have spoken out against collaboration with paramilitary groups and has promoted those who have fostered paramilitary activity.

U.S. policy toward Colombia underwent important changes beginning in mid-1997. The Clinton administration began to move beyond a narrow focus on drug trafficking in Colombia to take into greater account the devastating impact of political violence. Growing U.S. recognition of the insurgent threat turned Colombia into a top national security priority, and, over the course of 1998 and 1999, political support among U.S. policy makers for a more direct U.S. role in the Colombian counterinsurgency effort grew considerably.

The U.S. military steadily increased its support to its Colombian counterparts, carrying out a range of training and assistance programs that appear to go well beyond counternarcotics support, including training, manning radar sites, and intelligence gathering. According to a 1998 *New York Times* investigation: "The separation Washington has tried to make between those two campaigns—one against drug trafficking, the other against the guerrillas—is breaking down. Officials say more United States training and equipment are going to shore up basic deficiencies in the tactics, mobility and firepower of the Colombian military, rather than for operations directed at the drug trade."[23]

In late 1998, U.S. Secretary of Defense William Cohen and Colombian Minister of Defense Rodrigo Lloreda announced stepped-up military collaboration and the formation of a bilateral working group, intended to facilitate increased U.S. training, sharing of aerial and satellite intelligence date, and U.S. support for the restructuring and modernization of the Colombian armed forces. According to press reports at the time, then–SouthCom commander General Charles Wilhelm stated that the agreement highlights the close relations between the two militaries, that U.S. assistance is not restricted in any way, and that it could be used to combat both drug trafficking and guerrillas.[24] General Wilhelm himself claimed that he had become a "crucial adviser" to the Colombian high command and was assisting with an ambitious reorganization of the Colombian armed forces.[25]

In mid-2000, the U.S. Congress approved the $1.3 billion emergency aid package for Plan Colombia described previously, the bulk of which was geared toward shoring up the Colombian armed forces in their war against the FARC in the southern coca-growing region of the country. It included equipping and training three army counternarcotics battalions and the provision of sixty sophisticated helicopters to allow ground support for aerial herbicide campaigns.

The emergency aid package, however, coincided with a serious effort on the part of the Colombian government to restart peace talks with insurgent groups. Washington adopted a two-pronged strategy, publicly expressing support for the Pastrana government's efforts, while privately urging for more military action. Few in Washington believe that the war can be won militarily. Many argue, however, that an El Salvador–type strategy must be pursued, whereby the U.S. military provides the assistance, training, and intelligence necessary for Colombian troops to bolster significantly their ability to confront the guerrillas. That, in turn, is intended to change the correlation of forces, increasing the political clout of the military and eventually forcing the guerrillas to negotiate from a position of weakness.

The September 11, 2001, attacks, followed by the collapse of the faltering peace process in February 2002, bolstered the position of those arguing for a military approach and a direct U.S. counterinsurgency role in Colombia. The FY2003 aid package announced by the administration includes nearly one hundred million dollars to equip additional army battalions to protect oil pipelines in the northeastern part of the country. The administration has also requested congressional approval for eliminating restrictions on providing U.S. assistance and intelligence for counterinsurgency purposes, erasing the previously murky line between U.S. counternarcotics and counterinsurgency support.

Some of Colombia's neighbors have become alarmed at the escalating U.S. involvement in Colombia and the potential "spillover effects" of U.S. military aid. Ecuador in particular has raised two issues: the potential environmental impact of dumping large quantities of herbicides into the fragile Amazonian ecosystem and the potential flood of refugees fleeing political violence and human rights violations as the conflict intensifies.[26] The aerial eradication program funded by the U.S. government has also generated significant controversy within Colombia because of the potentially devastating health and environmental consequences of spraying toxic herbicides on a massive scale and because of the government's failure to provide adequate economic alternatives for those growing coca. The governors in the areas most affected by the aerial spraying have actively campaigned—in Colombia and Washington—against the program.

The eradication program tends to target small coca farmers, while *ras-*

pachines, or coca-leaf harvesters, are some of the primary victims of drug sweeps on the ground. Coca-growing regions have become a melting pot of people from all over Colombia: those fleeing right-wing paramilitary or leftist guerrilla violence, peasants forced off their land, and young men with no prospects for employment in urban shantytowns. With no other economic alternative, they are willing to face the jungle region's harsh living conditions in order to eke out a subsistence-level wage through the region's main economic activity: coca. Coca, in other words, is an economic necessity for many. As bluntly stated by one local bishop, Belarmino Corea, "The people fear that if they stop growing coca, they will die of hunger."[27]

When their coca crops are eradicated, as in the case of the small farmers, or they are forced off coca fields, as in the case of the *raspachines,* there are three options: go deeper into the jungle to grow more coca, become farmhands of drug traffickers who manage large coca plantations in more remote areas, or join the ranks of the FARC. In short, U.S. coca-eradication efforts in Colombia are counterproductive. Colombia is the only country in the Andean region that has accepted the use of chemical herbicides to eradicate coca; yet since the program got underway in 1995, coca production in Colombia has increased by more than 150 percent.[28]

In contrast to the other Andean countries, the collateral damage of U.S. policy in Colombia stems from a very real war with high costs for the civilian population. U.S. officials claim that the situation would likely be even worse without U.S. assistance. Yet each day that the war is prolonged, another twenty people lose their lives—more than seven thousand people a year. Another several hundred thousand are forced to flee their homes. The main contact that many Colombians have with the state in the worst areas of violence is with the forces of repression that have refused to sever their ties to brutal paramilitary groups. U.S. support provided to the Colombian military comes at the expense of aid to civilian institutions and development programs, which remain woefully underfunded but which ultimately are the only viable means of creating a truly democratic, and peaceful, country.

In the post–September 11, 2001, foreign policy–making environment, the U.S. war on drugs is increasingly being folded into the broader war against terrorism. Casting it as a war against "narco-terrorism," however, exacerbates the worst elements of the U.S. war on drugs and hence poses even greater risks to democratic consolidation in the Andean region.

In making local military forces strategic partners in the so-called war on drugs, Washington is expanding their role and mission precisely when it should be seeking to reduce their power and influence, particularly in maintaining internal public order, a task that should correspond to the police. Through the provision of training, intelligence-gathering capabilities, and military hardware, the U.S. government emboldens local militaries and some-times reduces the ability of civilian governments to exert control and effective oversight over those forces. Assigning them a task that is inherently "confi-dential" in nature also hinders civilian oversight, transparency, and accounta-bility. The Colombian military provides a case in point. Since it began receiv-ing significant U.S. assistance, its powers have expanded and the ability of civilian courts to oversee its conduct has declined markedly.

In Colombia, billions of dollars in U.S. counterdrug assistance are fueling the region's only significant counterinsurgency war, hence exacerbating the most serious human rights crisis in the hemisphere. In Bolivia, the human rights crisis in the Chapare coca-growing region is a direct result of U.S. drug policy. And in Peru, through its counternarcotics program, Washington sup-ported the most sinister element of the authoritarian Fujimori regime: the SIN, or the national intelligence service. The "collateral damage" of the U.S. war on drugs is not evident on U.S. city streets—where illicit drugs remain as cheap and readily available as ever—but is far too evident to the people of Colombia, Bolivia, and Peru.

7 State, Elites, and the Response to Insurgency

Some Preliminary Comparisons between Colombia and Peru

At first glance a comparison of insurgent violence in Colombia and Peru would appear to yield few elements for a useful comparison. Despite the fact that both countries are in the Andean region, there are significant differences in the historical sources and trajectory of violence in both cases. Insurgency in Colombia has a much longer history than in Peru; the ideology, tactics, and strategy of the groups involved are different, as is the political, economic, and social context of conflict. However, on one of the key variables involved in understanding political violence, namely state power and capacities, there is a significant point of comparison that can provide important insights into the choices and strategies of political actors. In a largely historical-structural analysis, I focus here on the different responses of one key actor, namely socioeconomic elites, to a similar problem, expanding insurgencies in the context of weak states, and suggest that a complete understanding of how states respond to violence requires a fuller appreciation of the structure of elites and their relation to the state.

State Power

Beginning in the late 1970s, political analysts refocused attention on the state as both a political actor and an arena of political conflict.[1] Much of the literature that has emerged since this period focuses on two questions: what criteria can we use to measure the strength of the state, and what is the relation between the state as a political actor and economic elites? Although this is not the place to review this extensive literature, it is important to note that by the late 1990s there were primarily three schools of thought on this issue: those emphasizing the state as a cultural construct (Geertz), as structure (Skocpol 1979), and as a rational actor (Bates). If any consensus has been reached it is that an understanding of the state and state power must be multidimensional, encompassing the varied arenas and ways in which state power is expressed.[2] While there needs to be a recognition of the dimensions of state power, clearly which approach is favored should also depend on the questions asked. In examining state power in the context of political violence, key elements to consider are the resources and capacities of state institutions. In this regard, the structural framework adopted by Theda Skocpol's analysis of states and social revolutions may be most useful. Skocpol's framework suggests three policy arenas that are especially useful in considering state power in the context of internal conflict.

The first arena to consider might be termed the organizational-bureaucratic arena. How efficiently does the state plan and implement its public policies? Are state institutions organized according to professional criteria? Does the state bureaucracy have an effective presence throughout the national territory? A second arena involves state-society relations. To what extent is state authority viewed as legitimate, resulting in voluntary adherence to state laws and regulations? Do state institutions penetrate society? That is, are policy goals realized on the terrain of society? Do social actors participate and assist in the realization of these goals, or is societal resistance and/or co-optation of state policies the norm? A final arena to consider concerns international relations, insofar as states interact with other states and the results of those interactions affect their resources and capacities. Does the state's position in the international political economy put it at a disadvantage in trade patterns and/or make it vulnerable to financial shocks that in turn weaken the resource-extractive capacity of the state? Is the state subject to hegemonic domination due to its political, economic, or military position? Are there historic conflicts with neighboring states that have led to wars? Have patterns of alliances improved or worsened the state's international position?

While each of these arenas involves a different set of issues, it is also clear that they overlap, insofar as weakness/strength in one arena is likely to have a spillover effect in other arenas. It should also be clear that state power is not fixed but relative and ever changing depending on the different mix and conjunction of factors at any given moment. The framework of state power outlined above requires a detailed historical-structural analysis across time to evaluate qualitatively the strength or weakness of the state. What follows is a very summary and preliminary evaluation of state power in Peru and Colombia during insurgency. In the case of Peru, the emphasis is on 1980–93, that is, the period during which the Shining Path (SL) and the Tupac Amaru Revolutionary Movement (MRTA) were active. For Colombia, the period considered is 1990–2000, when there were two large insurgencies, the Army of National Liberation (ELN) and the Revolutionary Armed Forces of Colombia (FARC), with the latter rapidly expanding its actions across the country. In both cases, I suggest that the state ranks low on the criteria of state power outlined above.

The Organizational-Bureaucratic Arena

The history of state development in Colombia and Peru has not favored strong organizational-bureaucratic capacities. In both cases, centralized state systems relied on local brokers to implement state power. Power in the Peruvian highlands revolved around *gamonales,* mestizos or whites who dominated the indigenous population usually in concert with local military caudillos.[3] The state had a low extractive capacity, with private firms collecting taxes until the mid-1960s. An enclave mining economy in the highlands and a plantation system on the coast, both dominated by foreign capital, produced limited revenue for the state (Dobyns and Doughty 1975, 219). The coup led by General Juan Velasco Alvarado in 1968, which inaugurated the Revolutionary Government of the Armed Forces, signaled an important change. The military instituted sweeping changes, including nationalizations in the mining sector and the most radical agrarian reform in the hemisphere after Cuba. The reforms reshaped the organizational-bureaucratic arena of the Peruvian state by simultaneously expanding the public sector and, through the agrarian reform, eliminating the system of local power brokers. Nonetheless, the reforms fell far short of creating a modern state structure.[4] While eliminating the power of traditional landowning oligarchs and foreign mining companies, the military was not successful in creating new mechanisms of political intermediation between state and society. The result was a political vacuum that was quickly filled by extremist groups, particularly SL. Similarly, a large public sector became a source of state weakness rather than a sign of state strength as inefficiency, corruption, cronyism, and a growing public debt in the 1980s contributed to a deepening economic crisis that ended in the worst recession since the 1930s. Under these circumstances, the ability of the state to plan and implement public policies was limited.

The size of the state sector is clearly not an indicator of state strength. Although the policies of the military increased the size of the state, it did not put into place policies that increased state capacities. The state was larger by the time of the García administration (1985–90) than it had been in the past, but its vulnerabilities had reached a critical stage, as hospitals lacked medicines, teachers went unpaid, and military equipment was unusable due to a lack of spare parts. Along with economic vulnerabilities, the actions of insurgencies in this period also had a nefarious effect on the organizational capacities of the state.[5] Attacks against infrastructure, private companies, mayors, and government officials throughout the country made the implementation of development programs virtually impossible.

Colombia also began from a point of strong local power brokers, although its pattern is quite different from Peru's. The historic dominance of the country's two traditional political parties, Liberals and Conservatives, was based on a network of clientelist relations that provided privileges and services in return for loyalty. Under this arrangement, the state became superfluous.[6] Even the provision of security, as we shall see, was partisan, something that limited the intrusion of the armed forces into the political life of the country, while other Latin American nations underwent cycles of military intervention. The pattern of economic development by the end of the nineteenth century did not favor a strong state either. The coffee economy developed around small and medium-sized peasant landholders and commercial entrepreneurs who had little use for the state and saw in the central government a potential threat rather than a partner in development.[7]

Like Peru, Colombia did not experience the "national-populist" phase that most of the region underwent in the 1930–60 period, and that was critical in the rise of the developmentalist state. In Peru, oligarchic forces with the backing of the military prevented the American Popular Revolutionary Alliance (APRA) from coming to power. In Colombia, the assassination of Jorge Eliécer Gaitán and the persecution of leftist-populist groups effectively blocked the possibility of a national-popular project. While in Peru a sector of the military intervened to impose a developmentalist state, with only limited success, Colombia's political and economic elite used the accords of the National Front to maintain a monopoly on political power, thus limiting state development. Although the 1970s witnessed a gradual expansion of the public sector in Colombia, the country largely avoided the "developmentalist" phase of state formation, with its *dirigiste* assumption of state-directed development and redistribution.[8] As a result, Colombia maintained macroeconomic stability at the cost of both the state development and the national integration that populism achieved elsewhere.

The State-Society Arena

Both Colombia and Peru have a complex and diverse geography with sharp regional and ethnic divisions that have made the formation of a common national identity difficult. A long history of regionally based rebellions and movements and a "complex web of social relations" are also characteristics of these societies, although the latter should not be confused with strong civil societies, which both nations have traditionally lacked.[9] Together these factors have hindered the ability of the state to establish legitimacy, penetrate society, and ensure voluntary adherence to laws and regulations. During much of Colombia's history, the state was viewed in instrumental terms by the two dominant parties in a zero-sum game that usually ended in civil war. Through the National Front these societal organizations agreed to mutually co-opt the state, sharing resources and dividing spoils between them. The ex-

clusionary nature of this societal co-optation of the state left a number of social groups out of the scheme, from leftist parties and supporters of the former
dictator General Gustavo Rojas Pinilla to peasants and labor organizations.[10]
The success of the *paros cívicos,* or civic strikes, and the rapid rise of the M-19
at the end of the 1970s and in the early 1980s were obvious symptoms of this
dynamic. The end of the National Front and the constitution of 1991 were
clear attempts to rebuild state legitimacy, although the persistence of clientelism, corruption, and dominance of the two parties continued to hamper
this effort.[11]

The capacity of the Colombian state to penetrate society and ensure adherence to state laws and policies has been limited by illegal groups that command significant resources and, through both social support and violent intimidation, violate and impede the implementation of such laws and policies.
A long history of organized crime and mafia groups exists in Colombia, and
since the 1970s, largely due to the growth in narco-trafficking, these groups
have grown dramatically, gaining control of territory, wielding political influence, and commanding significant economic resources (see chapter 5). This
was coupled with the rapid expansion of insurgents in this same period, who
by 2000 were estimated to control up to 40 percent of the nation's territory.
The ability of these groups to corrupt state officials and challenge the state's
monopoly on violence has not only effectively restricted the reach of state
power in Colombian society but in many ways co-opted the state itself. Either
through support, bribery, or intimidation, violent groups have gained influence over mayors, judges, bureaucrats, and other state officials, thus reducing
and restricting the policy autonomy of state institutions.[12]

In the Peruvian case, traditional landowning elites had long used the state
apparatus to protect and advance their interests until the military intervened
in 1968 to carry out its radical project of reform. Since the colonial era, the
criollo elites of the coast had had little interest in penetrating the Andean
sierra with its large indigenous majority, preferring to rely on hacendados
and, when necessary, local military caudillos to maintain control. The state in
early Republican Peru was in many ways a Lima state. In the wake of the War
of the Pacific (1870) and the Chilean invasion, the power of local elites and
military caudillos increased, a situation that the central state did not attempt
to reverse until the 1920s. Moreover, for much of Peru's history, the state had
little need to intervene in economic affairs, given the open-market nature of
the economy.[13]

Part of the Velasco-era reforms was an ambitious effort to refound state-
society relations, establishing new corporatist structures and relationships.
The effort foundered as social organizations that had emerged among popular
sectors, with the approval of the military, co-opted the corporatist scheme. By

the mid-1970s the labor, peasant, student, and neighborhood organizations created by the state had been co-opted, largely by leftist parties and organizations.[14] The legacy of this social co-optation was a powerful popular movement during the 1980s that through strikes, protests, and elections exercised unprecedented influence over state policy-making. Out of this same tumult emerged a small Maoist party in the poorest department of Peru, Ayacucho, that throughout the decade carried out its war "from the countryside to the cities." SL's strategy was aimed at generating power vacuums (vacíos del poder) across the national territory by directly attacking the state's presence. At the end of the decade, most analysts were increasingly concluding that SL had achieved its objective, as vast swaths of the national territory lacked representatives of the state, from mayors and policemen to development planners (see chapter 12).

The International Arena

Colombia and Peru are developing nations in the sphere of influence of the world's only remaining superpower. This situation puts both states in a vulnerable position in the international arena, although they have managed this situation in very different ways. Since independence, Colombia has never had a significant war with a neighbor or been invaded, even though it did lose part of its territory (Panama). War and conflict can be a double-edged sword when it comes to state power. In the European experience, war was an important element in the formation of nation-states, strengthening national identity and tying nation to state through the creation of symbols, heroes, and common experience. External wars also force the marshalling and centralization of resources, leaving behind an important legacy for state power.[15] On the other hand, a loss in war, especially if accompanied by a loss of territory, can weaken the authority and legitimacy of the state and might even result in the disappearance of the state. Colombia's lack of a significant war experience has meant that it has not received the benefits of war for state formation, but neither has it suffered the consequences of a military defeat. Peru, on the other hand, has experienced both defeat and conquest (the War of the Pacific [1870]) and victory (the War with Ecuador [1942] and subsequent border conflicts). While Peru's defeat had a significant impact in the late nineteenth century on state formation, both wars produced a pantheon of military heroes and symbols that have been important in strengthening national identity. Above all, war and the tensions with neighbors that were the legacies of those wars elevated the position of the armed forces in national life by reaffirming the military's self-identity as a "tutelary institution."

Both Colombia and Peru have been vulnerable to pressures from the United States, which has significantly curtailed the policy autonomy of these states. The most obvious policy area where this has occurred involves drug trafficking. The imposition of a supply-side antidrug policy, beginning in the 1980s, was carried out through the process of certification and conditionality that the United States imposed on both countries. U.S. policy favored a military approach to the problem; along with a new role for its own military, funds, training, and other programs were directed to the militaries of both Colombia and Peru. The introduction of Plan Colombia, later expanded to Plan Andino, was another indication of this approach.[16] The hegemonic dominance of the United States in the hemisphere and the high level of importance attached to the drug issue not only made it impossible for either state to consider alternative policies but made it extremely difficult for either state to avoid cooperating in the programs designed by Washington.

It is in the economic area where both states have suffered their greatest vulnerabilities. Trade patterns, the role of foreign investors, and external debt have often been sources of weakness in the international arena of state power for developing states. For much of their history, Colombia and Peru have had relatively open markets based on primary-product exports, an economic model that accentuates their vulnerability to trade patterns, including the price of and demand for their exports.[17] Moreover, open-market development increased the domestic influence of a powerful external actor, multinational corporations (MNCs), in the internal dynamic of both Peru and Colombia. In Peru, the mining sector has historically been the area with the greatest foreign presence, in Colombia the petroleum and banana sectors. The influence of MNCs on their "home governments" and their control of important sectors of their "host" countries' economies can give them significant leverage over states.

Since the 1970s, international financial institutions have increasingly come to exercise extraordinary influence over the domestic policy-making process of developing countries. This influence emerged as a result of the financial crises that had affected much of the Third World by the end of the 1970s. The oil-price shocks of 1973 and 1979, the exhaustion of import-substitution industrialization, and an oversized and inefficient public sector were among the factors that brought on this crisis in Latin America. Peru was one of the first countries to experience this financial crisis in Latin America. In 1977, a serious balance of payments deficit and an inability to meet debt payments led to the arrival of an International Monetary Fund (IMF) "team" in Lima, which designed one of the regions first austerity packages, including a series of monetary and fiscal goals to be overseen by the IMF. Through the early 1980s, Peru's debt payments reached 70 percent of its export income as a neoliberal program was instituted during the administration of Fernando

Belaúnde (1980–85). With the election of Alan García in 1985, Peru's position toward international financial organizations shifted. Unilaterally limiting debt payments to only 10 percent of export income, the García administration soon found itself cut off from new credits, a situation worsened by a dramatic decline in foreign private investment and capital flight. The García administration's effort to defy international financial institutions proved disastrous for the state, as revenue declined and the worst economic crisis since the 1930s took hold.

Until recently, Colombia had generally managed to avoid the financial vulnerabilities that have afflicted other states in the region. While most of Latin America underwent a debt crisis, Colombia combined macroeconomic stability with steady growth and low debt. A traditionally conservative fiscal and monetary policy, policy continuity, and a gradual diversification of exports helped Colombia avoid the dramatic swings in economic performance of Peru and other Latin American countries. Nonetheless, by the 1990s Colombia had begun to experience some of the same vulnerabilities as other states in the region. The accelerated opening of the Colombian economy during the Barco administration (1986–90), and continuing through the 1990s, broke with the traditional gradualism of Colombian economic policy. The impact has been dramatic. Privatizations, declines in the prices of key exports, especially coffee, growing external competition, and the deteriorating security situation created a crisis in both the agricultural and manufacturing sectors. By 1999, Colombia suffered the highest unemployment rate in Latin America, a negative growth rate of 5 percent, and sharp cutbacks in public spending. That same year, Colombia signed its first accord with the IMF, which set specific macroeconomic targets and reorganized the country's growing debt.[18] Colombia's state thus began to experience the weakness that comes with declining economic resources and capacities, as well as the loss of policy autonomy to external actors.

State Weakness and the Response to Insurgency

As Joel Migdal has noted, to a large extent state weakness is merely a manifestation of underdevelopment; it therefore should not be surprising that, although their specific historical trajectories are different, both Peru and Colombia as underdeveloped countries share this common characteristic. For a comparativist, the most interesting and useful comparisons do not simply involve contrasting similarities or differences but noting how similarities and differences interact. Of special usefulness are contrasts between policy choices where structural or institutional conditions are similar. A comparison of Peru and Colombia's counterinsurgency policies thus offers a rich opportunity for developing a number of useful comparisons. While both situations involve "weak" states facing insurgent challenges, the policies adopted to deal with this challenge were ultimately quite different.

In both Colombia and Peru, the armed forces faced significant limitations that not only impeded a military victory over the guerrillas but led to the rapid growth of insurgency, in terms of both number of combatants and territorial presence. Peru confronted a very structured, ideological Maoist insurgency with strong millenarian characteristics. Within a few years of initiating its armed struggle in 1980, SL quickly expanded beyond its initial area of operations in Ayacucho. By 1988, it had developed armed "columns" in every department of the country, including urban cells in the shantytowns of Lima. The number of actions, primarily assassinations, destruction of infrastructure (electric towers, bridges, etc.), and bombings, rose over tenfold in this period.[19] Colombia's guerrillas, tracing their roots to the 1950s "La Violencia" period, have been largely peasant based and have traditionally controlled large swaths of rural and sparsely populated zones in the southern and western parts of the country. The growth of insurgency here was even more dramatic than in Peru, expanding significantly beyond traditional areas of operation. By 2000, the government estimated that the FARC had over sixteen thousand combatants, double the number of fighters estimated in the mid-1990s; the ELN was estimated to have forty-five hundred combatants, slightly over one thousand fighters more than in the mid-1990s.[20] Guerrilla actions, ranging from kidnappings and destruction of infrastructure to assassinations and assaults on police and military barracks, also dramatically increased. While the growth of insurgency in both Peru and Colombia resulted from a variety of factors, in both instances the armed forces were incapable of detaining its rapid expansion. Lack of equipment, particularly helicopters and light weapons; inadequate counterinsurgency training; unclear goals; contradictory interpretations of the nature of insurgency; a largely defensive military strategy; and tense and often conflictive relations with local populations, including human rights abuses, were among the problems both militaries faced in confronting insurgent challenges. Nonetheless, the states' responses to this challenge varied considerably.

The Societal-Centered Approach

The state response to insurgent violence in Colombia can best be characterized as "abdication and privatization," a process in which state actors provide the legal framework, legitimacy, logistical support, and on occasion armaments to private societal actors in order to combat insurgents. Beginning in the 1960s, pressures from regional elites confronted by guerrilla attacks led the state to adopt the first in a long series of laws and regulations permitting and encouraging the formation of self-defense organizations. Colombia has a long history of armed civilian groups, and clearly the prior normative framework is important in understanding the ease with which the state ceded security authority to private actors. While the precise relation between state security forces and paramilitary organizations varies across time and regions, for the most part the relation is decentralized and involves mostly midranking officers.[21] One of the first laws authorizing the formation of self-defense groups was expedited in 1968 (Law 48), calling for their organization and supervision under the armed forces.[22] By the late 1970s, self-defense groups expanded rapidly and took on a more offensive and "preventive" approach to insurgency that included assassination of leftist political activists, union and peasant leaders, and journalists. The more aggressive strategy coincided with the implementation of the National Security Statute (Decreto 1723) by the Turbay Ayala administration (1978–82), which inaugurated the most repressive period in recent Colombian history. Forced disappearances, torture, and massacres occurred throughout the country, carried out by both regular military forces and self-defense groups. The Magdalena Medio became a special target of the new paramilitary offensive. A traditional stronghold of the Communist Party, with a significant FARC presence, the Puerto Boyacá area in particular witnessed a long and vicious war that resulted in the expulsion of all leftist presence in the region.[23]

The emergence of drug trafficking in the 1980s had a dramatic impact on the development of paramilitary forces. The formation of the Muerte a Secuestradores (MAS) in 1981 by members of the Medellín cartel to protect the narco-elite and their growing landholdings from both peasant resistance and guerrilla attacks changed the nature of the paramilitary phenomenon in Colombia. Along with the new resources these actors injected into paramilitary groups, they also helped create new regional alliances, linking sectors of the security forces, traditional party cadres, drug traffickers, and local elites behind private violence. This growing connection with drug traffickers, as well as the audacity and cruelty of paramilitary massacres, such as the war of extermination waged against the Unión Patriotica and a series of massacres in Urabá and Córdoba in the late 1980s, created the first attempts to begin to delegitimize paramilitary forces. President Virgilio Barco publicly called such groups "criminal bands," and the Supreme Court later overturned the 1968 law and other regulations that authorized paramilitary groups.[24]

Despite these efforts, paramilitary organizations continued to occupy a central role in the state's response to violence. In the early 1990s the organization Perseguidos por Pablo Escobar (PEPEs) emerged, with the specific purpose of tracking down Escobar and his associates, just at the moment when the Colombian state had declared them a major threat to national security.

Carlos Castaño, who would later become leader of the paramilitary forces, was a key figure in this group. Rumors have long linked the PEPEs with both Colombian security forces and the U.S. Special Forces and intelligence agencies attempting to capture Escobar.[25] Throughout the 1990s paramilitary groups grew dramatically, and the Colombian state, including the armed forces, demonstrated at best ambivalence toward these groups. The Gaviria administration in 1993–94 authorized (Law 62, Decree 356) the creation of security cooperatives known as "Convivir," which once again legitimized the privatization of security. Although the administration argued it was merely responding to the security needs of citizens and not endorsing paramilitary organizations, it was clear that within the context of Colombia's recent history of violence, the state was openly abdicating its claim on a monopoly of legitimate force. The 1990s witnessed the most rapid growth in paramilitary groups yet, with a tenfold increase registered by the end of the decade.[26] Moreover, the creation of United Self-Defense Forces of Colombia (AUC) in 1997, under the leadership of Carlos Castaño, has allowed them to develop a national discourse and present what appears to be not only a military strategy but also political, economic, and even social strategies. As the FARC in particular made significant military advances in the 1990s and the armed forces appeared unable to defeat the insurgency, the AUC entered the battlefield and made significant inroads. However, the primary strategy of paramilitary forces, both in the late 1990s and in earlier periods, was to attack the civilian population that they believed either were or could potentially become supporters of the guerrillas. Not surprisingly, paramilitary forces had become the major violators of human rights in Colombia by 2000.

The State-Centered Approach

The "abdication and privatization" model of counterinsurgency adopted in Colombia contrasts sharply with the approach followed in Peru. Faced with the rapid growth of insurgency and an ineffective military response, Peru moved in the opposite direction of Colombia. Rather than cede and abdicate state authority, the Fujimori administration (1990–2000) attempted to reconstruct state power through a process of "authoritarian reengineering," providing state institutions with the capacities and resources sufficient to implement a highly repressive counterinsurgency strategy directed by the state. The strategy was predicated on the support of key national and international elites, the civilian government, and the armed forces, as well as a military that had long intervened in the political arena, creating a civil-military alliance that sustained the regime for a decade. There were three elements to this strategy: new institutional powers and resources for the security apparatus of the state that effectively increased its presence in civil society; explicit and implicit restrictions on democratic institutions and norms; and finally a series of economic and social policies that attempted to increase the state's penetration of civil society.

The budgets of state security agencies dramatically increased in the 1990s: the budget of the National Intelligence Service (SIN) was reportedly fifty times greater in 2000 than it was in 1990, and the total budget of the armed forces by 2000 represented 32 percent of all state spending (contrasted with only 13 percent spent on education).[27] Along with increased budgets came new powers and missions. The SIN expanded its "psycho-social" campaigns through the media, increased wiretapping and surveillance of opposition figures, and created a special paramilitary group (Grupo Colina) charged with eliminating suspected Shining Path sympathizers. Death-squad activities in Peru were carried out directly by active-duty members of the SIN or the military who responded to orders received directly from the chain of command, including the de facto head of the SIN and presidential advisor Vladimiro Montesinos.[28] In the armed forces, the structure of promotions and budgets was centralized in the hands of the presidency. In addition, a series of "special powers" was provided to the military, the most notable of which was the expansion of the jurisdiction of military tribunals to try civilians accused of terrorism. The armed forces were also granted power to "intervene" on university campuses (violating their autonomy); to set up *zonas de rastreo,* areas in which the military would carry out house-to-house searches while blocking off an area; and finally to assist *rondas campesinas,* peasant patrols of localities, in coordination with the military, in detecting guerrilla activities.[29] Admittedly, the widespread rejection of Shining Path's ideology and methods among the vast majority of Peruvians created an acceptance of the state's approach within civil society. Moreover, many nonrepressive elements, including amnesty programs for surrendering fighters and improved police tactics, also contributed to the state's effective response.[30] The result of this strategy was not only a security apparatus with more power but also a large and extensive presence in civil society.

In order to carry out its strategy, the Fujimori regime early on had identified democratic norms and institutions as impediments to its plans. The 1992 self-coup *(autogolpe),* or the suspension of the constitution and the closing of Congress by the president, was in part an attempt to undermine what was perceived as an obstacle to the effective implementation of counterinsurgency plans. A series of democratic rights, including habeas corpus, was restricted or eliminated by regime decree. The 1993 constitution also weakened institutional checks on executive power, reducing the oversight capacity of Congress, restricting judicial autonomy, and ending the process of decentralization begun in the 1980s. Moreover, the press was either co-opted through bribes and extortion or repressed. Journalists, human rights workers, and opposition figures were the target of threats, illegal detentions, and occasionally physical violence.[31] The absolute personalization of power within the regime and repression of the opposition thus ensured limited criticism and the unobstructed implementation of counterinsurgency measures.

A final element in the Fujimori strategy was the implementation of a series of social and economic policies meant to increase the state's penetration of civil society and also reduce the possibility of autonomous societal organizations. These measures were aimed at ensuring an increased state presence on the terrain of society, demobilizing possible challenges to state authority, and increasing the policy-implementation capacity of the state. In addition to the policies noted earlier, the regime set up an elaborate clientelist system to provide social services that was directly linked to the Ministry of the Presidency. Preexisting social programs, which had long been controlled by parties of the left, were co-opted by the ministry, reducing autonomous political spaces. Neoliberal economic restructuring, which included extensive privatization and a reduction in both state subsidies and the public sector, played an important role not only in demobilizing civil society but in increasing the efficiency of the state as well as the economy. A "small and strong state" was the slogan of neoliberal reformers, who argued that a large and "bloated" state would necessarily be a weak state, thus linking economic reforms with the security situation.

Elite-State Configurations

How can we explain the different counterinsurgency models adopted in Peru and Colombia, particularly given that in both cases the state has traditionally had limited capacities and resources? The hypothesis I suggest here is that the crucial variable in explaining this difference is the nature of the elites in the two countries, particularly their relations with both the state and the political regime. The society-centered "privatization" model of counterinsurgency long favored in Colombia reflects the fragmentation of the elite and its weak links with the state in general and the armed forces in particular. By contrast, the state-centered "authoritarian" model adopted in Peru in the 1990s was the result of a civil-military alliance forged by elites and the security apparatus; it indicates how Peruvian elites have traditionally viewed the state as the focal point of power politics in the country. Clearly, many factors contribute to the structure of socioeconomic elites and their relation to the state, and only a brief synopsis of the two cases can be offered here. Geography, resource endowments, and ethnic/racial cleavages, to cite just three factors, have played important roles in both cases. The structure of elites is also likely to be notable in political society, insofar as party systems reflect social structures and cleavages. Finally, both the membership and, more broadly, the structure of elites are likely to change over time as changes in the economy and society take hold.

There are four key elements to the structure of elites in Colombia that have favored a society-centered approach to counterinsurgency. First, Colombia's elite has traditionally had a heterogeneous economic base, a reflection of the economic diversification the country experienced in the twentieth century. Coffee, industry, mining, cattle ranching, and petroleum are among the dominant economic activities in Colombia (one can clearly include the "narco-elite" here as well), and while there are important connections among the elites involved in these activities, each sector has its own elite structure and *gremio* (sectoral organization).[32] While conflicts among *gremios* have existed, they have generally not been open. Second, elites in Colombia have a deeply regional character and identity, linked to the specific economic activity of each zone, for example, cattle ranching in the coastal departments. The social structure and particular vision of socioeconomic elites, in terms of their perception of society, politics, and economics, thus vary considerably depending on local or regional conditions.

The heterogeneous economic base and regional diversity of the Colombian elite have historically made it difficult for them to forge a common political project and impeded the development of a hegemonic class with a vision of national identity and a program of state modernization.[33] Intraelite conflicts with a strong regional, economic, and ideological content plagued Colombian politics throughout the nineteenth century. Both these conflicts and the political pacts that often put an end to them, especially in the twentieth century, were carried out on the terrain of society, involving private partisan armies and gentlemen's agreements to divide power, with little interest in using the state for anything beyond sectoral or private goals. The state was largely a source of funding for private initiatives or for clientelist/patronage politics and, as mentioned earlier, not the source of the significant "developmentalist" economic or social policies found elsewhere in Latin America. Moreover, there appears to be at least some evidence that elites were aware of the dangers of the state as an instrument of political power or social change. The swiftness with which General Rojas Pinillas was removed as he began to develop and use the state to build a political project suggests the wariness with which traditional elites viewed this possibility. With the end of the National Front in 1974, partisan conflict not only failed to reemerge as in the past, but the two traditional parties continued the policy consensus of the National Front. The growing unity and consensus among the national political elite had an important impact in a variety of policy areas, most notably making it possible to launch a peace process in the early 1980s. Nonetheless, the consensus among the national political elite (see chapter 11) has also been accompanied by a fragmentation of the party structures themselves, as local party bosses have gained growing power, and a distancing between national political elites and traditional socioeconomic elites.

Finally, an important link in understanding the elite preference for the "privatization" model lies in their historically strong antimilitary sentiments. From the independence period onward, Colombian elites have had a profound distrust of the armed forces. The two-party system and the lack of military regimes clearly contributed to this attitude, as Francisco Leal Buitrago notes.[34] The social distance between elites and the military further deepened this distrust. A military career was never seen as a mark of social distinction by elites, and conscription was generally restricted to the lower and middle classes. The Colombian armed forces, absent from direct participation in politics for most of the nineteenth and twentieth centuries, never developed an institutional identity revolving around nation building, limiting the possibility of developing an autonomous political project. The professionalization process came relatively late to the Colombian military (1907), in part because of the long history of the elites' reliance on private partisan armies and their disinterest in, and distrust of, a strong military establishment.[35] Although since the end of National Front the military has increasingly developed autonomy in a number of areas, this has resulted in challenges to presidential policies and not elite interests.[36]

While Colombian elites, faced with a weak state and insurgent challenges, opted for a society-centered counterinsurgency strategy, in Peru elites facing these same circumstances opted for a state-centered counterinsurgency program. A number of factors tended to favor this development. First, the state in Peru has been at the center of vigorous contestation among different sectors of society with alternative political projects. A significant populist challenge after 1930 from the APRA party, and from the 1960s through the 1980s a powerful leftist political option, threatened to use the state apparatus to implement decidedly anti-elite programs. During the Velasco military regime, the state not only acted as an agent of change but also undermined the political and economic power of Peru's economic elite, sweeping away the agrarian oligarchy, carrying out nationalizations, and heavily regulating economic activities. As a result, the state has been the primary arena of political conflict in the twentieth century as different political projects (populist, socialist, neoliberal, radical military) competed to capture state power to implement their programs. The weakness in this approach to politics has been that with rare exceptions, societal organization has been neglected, resulting in the collapse of these projects once state power is achieved, due to the lack of sustainable social support.

Second, Peru's socioeconomic elite is largely a Lima elite. In part this is a legacy of the colonial period, when Lima was a viceroyal capital concentrating not only administrative power but also ecclesiastical, economic, and social power. The Spanish and later their *criollo* descendants preferred to settle on the coast rather than in the largely indigenous and mestizo highlands, and they remain there today. The socioeconomic and demographic shifts of the twentieth century have only accentuated this concentration. Most of the country's industrial and financial activity takes place in Lima, which also concentrates close to a third of the national population. With the socioeconomic elite established in Lima, the stage was also set for a highly mercantilist relation to develop, one in which elites used their influence and contacts in the traditionally centralized state structure to extract privileges, grants, and monopolies from governing officials. The result has been a dynamic, prevalent during and since the colonial era, in which the administrative structure of the state is an important arena in which the elite can establish and maintain contacts and relationships, lest they lose their privileges to competing individuals or groups.

Finally, with the exception of the Velasco period, the armed forces in Peru have a long and close relationship with the country's elites, having blunted populist and socialist challenges to the socioeconomic and political order of the country since the early twentieth century. Moreover, the armed forces have played a crucial role, as noted earlier, in the construction of national identity and have defined for themselves the role of "tutelary institutions," that is, institutions that represent the historical continuity of the nation and are above the "politics" of civilian groups or parties. The longest period of uninterrupted democratic civilian rule in twentieth-century Peru was twelve years (1980–92). This long history of military interventions and regimes in Peru has led to the vision, shared by both members of the armed forces and civilian sectors, of the military not only "embodying" the nation but also acting as the ultimate arbiter of political disputes.

These factors are crucial to understanding the preference for the "authoritarian reengineering" approach adopted in the 1990s. Elites played a crucial role in fostering the Fujimori regime's authoritarian project, backing the regime's effort to impose "order" through authoritarian state policies. The financial sector and civilian technocrats helped the regime establish contacts with international financial organizations that provided needed credits and investment and assisted in the planning and implementation required to restructure the state along neoliberal lines. Each of the ministers of the economy during the Fujimori period came from the business sector, and each played a crucial role in reforming the state structure. The reforms introduced in the labor sector, reducing the power of unions, and in the agrarian sector, essentially fostering a reconcentration of land ownership, were viewed as necessary not only to attract needed investment but also to weaken areas where the left was traditionally strong. The business sector fully supported the 1992 *autogolpe,* and the main *gremios* remained fervent supporters of the regime throughout the Fujimori decade, contributing heavily to the Fujimori reelection efforts in 1995 and 2000.

In a comparative analysis of counterinsurgency approaches, it is important to look beyond merely the strength or weakness of state structures. Both Colombia and Peru confronted growing insurgencies under conditions of state weakness, a situation common to underdevelopment. Nonetheless, each developed a very different way of combating insurgency. The key explanatory variable behind their divergence is the configuration of the elite structure, including its relation with the state and political regime and its ability to forge and carry out a common political (or hegemonic) project. In essence, the historical experiences of these two different elites shaped their relations with the state and other political actors, which in turn created and/or limited their ability to construct the alliances and adopt the visions needed to deal with insurgent challenges.

An important lesson to bear in mind when comparing these two models is that although in one country (Peru) a model contributed to the defeat of insurgency, in both cases the methods employed signified horrendous costs for the civilian population and democratic institutions. The human rights situations in Colombia and Peru were the worst in the Western Hemisphere during the periods considered here. Massacres, torture, arbitrary detentions, and forced disappearances were part of the daily reality that citizens in both countries faced. In Peru, abuses were carried out largely by the armed forces and, by the 1990s, the intelligence services as well. In Colombia, the situation is more mixed, with the armed forces and paramilitary forces implicated and, by the mid-1990s, the latter group actually responsible for the largest share of abuses. Clearly neither model of counterinsurgency provides a guarantee for respecting human rights, and both weaken democratic norms and procedures. In Peru, democratic institutions were directly undermined by the self-coup carried out in 1992, and the regime's later development accelerated the trend toward authoritarianism, creating one of the most corrupt regimes in recent Latin American history. Although Colombia managed to preserve its democratic institutions more successfully than Peru, the inability of those institutions to extend meaningful guarantees of security to their participants had the effect of restricting their relevance to an increasingly reduced number of citizens.

In a similar vein, it is also important to underline the fact that both approaches responded to the historical conditions of individual countries, that is, the particular relation between states and elites, as well as the nature of insurgency; it would thus be erroneous to conclude that one response to insurgency could emerge or be applied in another case with a similar outcome. This is especially relevant for the lessons drawn out of the Peruvian experience. The relative "success" of Peru's response might seem to offer a model of effective counterinsurgency. However, in addition to this approach's very high cost, it would be difficult to apply in a situation with a different historical configuration, such as in Colombia. Peru's success required state capacities, and state-elite and state-society relations, that are not found in Colombia. The broader lesson here is that effective responses to insurgency, in addition to respecting democratic norms, must take into account the specific conditions and causes that lie behind each internal war.

In considering the impact of counterinsurgency on democratic procedures and norms, much of the traditional focus, particularly by the human rights community, has been on the role of the state and its security forces. While this has a long-standing basis in international law and the policies of both international governmental and nongovernmental organizations, one of the implications of the argument presented here is that analysts need to look beyond state actors in assessing responsibility for human rights violations. If we consider states as autonomous institutions operating in political vacuums, then an exclusive focus on security forces might be analytically justifiable. However, states are in fact structures embedded in their societies, the result of social configurations involving societal relations across time and space. Clearly, degrees of responsibility vary. From a policy perspective, a focus on the matrix of resources and logistics that allows human rights violations to continue, whether the military-paramilitary connection or the operations of the military itself, is likely to lead to the points most vulnerable to change in the short term in response to political pressures at the national or international level. However, those political and social actors that actively support and encourage policies, institutions, and practices that violate internationally accepted democratic norms also bear some responsibility. Dealing with this dimension of democratic accountability is far more difficult, given that social actors and structures are removed from daily and routine violations of human rights. Nonetheless, there needs to be greater accountability. How that might be accomplished remains an ongoing challenge for the international community.

Mark Ungar

8   Human Rights in the Andes
The Defensoría del Pueblo

Keeping track of human rights in the Andes means keeping track of the state and society. While the region's states are being weakened by increasing economic and political pressures, their societies are becoming more aware of constitutional rights and the growing threats to them. Throughout the Andes, mediating between the state and society on human rights is the Defensoría del Pueblo, an independent national ombudsman mandated to investigate rights abuses, receive complaints from citizens, initiate legal recourses, and formulate policy. Although one of the region's newest institutions, the *defensoría* has been thrust to the forefront of human rights as the principal gauge of state abuses and citizen demands.[1]

The *defensoría* is a clear breakthrough for human rights because it will help make state agencies more efficient, accountable, and responsive to both specific cases and general popular concerns. The region's governments may be gambling that the agency will relieve political pressure and improve state functioning without threatening real interests. But the momentum behind *defensorías* may become more powerful than expected as they grow adept at using power, publicizing issues, and developing societal alliances. The *defensoría* already enjoys high levels of public popularity and credibility as a new and politically untainted institution, and its ability to link once-separate issues has put it in a highly visible and vocal advocacy position.

Despite such hopeful assessments, however, the *defensoría* may founder on political interests and popular expectations. First of all, the practices and powers of state institutions and officials readily sabotage the *defensoría*. Even many hard-won successes in resolving cases and enacting laws are more than countered by government decrees and ongoing state practices. In particular, the abusiveness of security forces and the inefficiency of the judicial system negate such efforts. Second, as the *defensoría* becomes a voice for society it may be silenced by the same deeply rooted structural problems that muzzle society in the first place. In advancing the rights of women, pensioners, and indigenous people, for example, the *defensoría* will ultimately have to address why such groups face persistent, systemic discrimination—a task well beyond its political and institutional means.

The first years of the Andes' five *defensorías* have brought out both their power and their pitfalls. When the agency focuses on specific cases or uncontroversial issues, such as public education programs in Bolivia and consumer rights in Ecuador, it easily meets its goals. But when taking on a politically charged issue, it often falters. Peru's former *defensor* Jorge Santistevan de Noriega was thus attacked when he waded into electoral politics, as was Colombia's when he became too involved in the civil war. But while taking on bigger issues is riskier in the short term, it may actually strengthen the *defensoría* in the long term by enabling it to stake out real authority with a wide reach. Those agencies that limit themselves to safer issues may ultimately be condemning themselves to being just another reform serving more to validate than to challenge the system. As the "the magistrate of persuasion," the *defensoría* has to harness its main power—as the arbiter between state and society on human rights—into concrete change. No other approach is likely to succeed in democracies far better at adopting human rights laws and institutions than making the changes in practice that matter. So while the *defensorías* in Peru and Colombia have taken more risks, they will probably end up stronger than those of Ecuador, Bolivia, and Venezuela.

Increasingly, studies of democratization and human rights in Latin America are turning their attention to the issues addressed by institutions like the *defensoría*. Some analyses focus on the continuing impact of authoritarianism (Loveman 1998), while others point out the state's inefficient, limited, or biased functioning (Przeworski 1991; Stotzky 1993; O'Donnell 1993; Migdal, Kohli, and Shue 1994). Addressing the complaint that "justice, law, and citizenship in the real lives of citizens" (Holston and Caldeira 1998) are being ignored, though, others have begun to connect state institutions with the ever-changing daily dynamics of democratic societies. As political and societal conditions become even more unpredictable, in particular, change itself needs to be more central in assessing human rights conditions. The agencies, laws, and organizations formed to protect rights must constantly adapt; even the most carefully written provision has little effect if it loses applicability to state practices and societal needs. At the nexus between the state and society, the *defensoría* captures this sense of change and so deepens understanding of the politics and pressures of human rights in contemporary Latin America. This is particularly true in the Andes, afflicted by more societal divisions, inequality, economic frailty, and political instability than most of the region.

Formation of the *Defensoría*

An independent office often with constitutional ranking, the *defensoría* has a defined set of official powers but a wide range of informal ones. It is not a judge or a prosecutor and cannot detain individuals, pass rulings, or impose punishments. But it can formulate legislative bills and administrative reforms, develop strategies for rights protection, mediate conflicts, and promote adhesion to international rights law. Either on its own accord or on behalf of an aggrieved party, the *defensoría* also investigates abuses by the police, in the prisons, and throughout the judiciary. When denouncing specific violations and pushing the government to prosecute violators, it has at its disposal a range of legal mechanisms: *amparo,* which is the general legal complaint against a state action; habeas corpus, which is a petition against illegal detention; and, in some circumstances, challenges to laws' constitutionality or enforcement procedures.

With these powers, the *defensoría* is in a strategic position within both the state and society. In the state, it is authorized to expose and promote resolutions to problems in the public administration and with public services such as water, electricity, and transportation. All state agencies are obligated to cooperate with the *defensoría* and implement agreed-upon changes. If the responsible officials do not cooperate—or do not implement the changes in good faith—the *defensoría* usually has the authority to go to the head of the agency or to Congress, request the dismissal of the obstructionists, and sometimes emit public censure. Most of these offenses find their way into newspaper articles, special studies, and the *defensoría*'s annual and very detailed reports to Congress. In some cases, the agency will muster up affected sectors of society to put pressure on the state. Within society, the *defensoría* also monitors social, political, economic, and institutional conditions that may be generating systematic violations. To resolve them, the agency may act as a mediator or conciliator between groups or between the state and the complainant. In mediation procedures, it controls the process without applying pressure or making recommendations, while in conciliation it does formulate recommended solutions.

In each Andean country, the *defensoría* grew out of a combination of international pressures, the state's limitations, and broad popular movements to strengthen human rights. The idea was not to replace but to support other state agencies, increasing access to them while taking on issues they could not absorb. Most specifically, the *defensoría* is intended to relieve the tension arising from the contradictory obligations of the Ministerio Público (MP; attorney general), which is in charge of both prosecuting crimes and protecting detainee rights. An autonomous agency, it has authority to impede arbitrary detentions; recommend whether a case proceeds to trial; and investigate the rights obligations of the judiciary, the police, and the public administration. But despite different reforms intended to improve and streamline its functioning, the MP remained internally incongruous because of its simultaneous responsibility of prosecuting defendants and protecting their due process rights.

In December 1992, Colombia became the first country in the region to formally establish a *defensoría,* following its introduction in the 1991 constitution. Peru adopted a *defensoría* in its 1993 constitution, building on the prototype *defensoría* created within the Ministerio Público in 1979, which was turned in 1989 into the more official Fiscalía Especial (special prosecutor) for human rights. It did not pass the necessary establishing (organic) law until 1995, however, and did not appoint its first *defensor* until the following year. Similarly, Bolivia created a *defensoría* in its 1994 reform of the constitution but created an organic law in 1997 and appointed its first *defensor* in 1998. Ecuador originally placed *defensoría* functions within the Constitutional Court but then established a *defensoría* in its 1996 constitutional reforms, enacting an organic law and appointing a *defensor* in 1997. The agency was part of a larger rights framework that included the 1999 National Plan for Human Rights, which strengthened protections for minorities and tightened restrictions on the police, and the 1998 constitution (adopted in August 1999), which contains new human rights provisions such as a prohibition of amnesty for those guilty of egregious abuses.

TABLE 8.1 Defensorías del Pueblo in the Andes Region

Country	Year Legislated	Year Installed
Bolivia	1994	1997
Colombia	1991	1992
Ecuador	1996	1997
Peru	1993	1996
Venezuela	1999	1999

TABLE 8.2 Role of Defensorías del Pueblo

Authorities	Obstacles
Investigate abuses in the judiciary, police, public administration, prisons, public and private services	Civil strife
Collect information, issue reports	Police and extrajudicial violence
Formulate policy and legislation	Societal divisions and expectations Popular legal norms
Initiate legal recourses: *amparo,* habeas corpus, unconstitutionality	Political uncertainty
Speak for citizens, work with nongovernmental organizations (NGOs), mediate, arbitrate conflicts	Executive manipulation Bureaucracy, lack of cooperation Judicial inefficiency

In Venezuela, finally, a *defensoría* was first proposed in 1991 by the constitutional reform commission headed by former president and sitting senator Rafael Caldera. Part of the bill, significantly, would have allowed states to establish their own *defensorías,* while parallel proposals would have created the position of *defensor vecinal* at the municipal level. Political turmoil and resistance held back these efforts until 1999, when a *defensoría* was included as part of the new "citizen" branch of government created in a constitution engineered by newly elected president Hugo Chávez. Restructuring the state and adding new rights guarantees—such as the exclusion of rights cases from the military court system—the constitution was in part a response to previous

Structure of the *Defensoría*

Since the *defensoría* must be independent, the appointment of its head, the *defensor,* is critical. In most countries, that appointment is made by Congress, usually with a two-thirds vote. Most serve a period of five years, with the possibility of a single additional term, and may be involuntarily removed only for "serious" infractions, also through a two-thirds vote. Otherwise, the *defensor* is accountable to officials only on designated matters.

To maximize impact and minimize bureaucracy, most *defensorías* gear their structure toward deconcentration, coordination, and specialization. Based in the central office with the *defensor* and usually a *primer defensor adjunto* (first adjunct defender) is a set of specialized committees responsible for functions like public education and complaint processing—often prioritizing cases through the use of parallel "urgent" and "ordinary" procedures. *Defensoría* branches around the country usually replicate this structure, with some deploying mobile units to more isolated areas. But while decentralization brings services to as much of a country as possible, it also risks getting the *defensoría* caught up in local politics. So regional offices must follow central-office directives, staying centered on uniform standards.

Also located at both the central and regional offices are adjunct *defensores* specializing in particular populations, such as children and the elderly, or particular issues, such as health. Adjunct *defensores* on women are the most common, with the same authorities and limitations as the agency at large. Even when their intervention is limited to assistance and advice, for example, these *defensores* have expanded their work to range from common societal abuses, such as sexual assault, to "abuses of omission," such as faulty implementation of protective laws.

Political Interests and State Power

While the *defensorías* were created as part of democratic reform, their actual functioning has been shaped more by the politics of specific governments and the use of state power. Like candidates outside traditional parties, much of the *defensoría*'s popularity rests on its lack of affiliations. But this also means that it is less skilled at the politics needed to get things done, with dependence on state funds, overlaps with other agencies, and lack of patronage networks forcing the *defensoría* to navigate among officials operating on their own turf. In some cases, such as Bolivia and Colombia, governments eager for a fresh approach to chronic problems have given the *defensoría* some leeway. But when the agency then takes those same governments to task, the usual response is negligence, stalling, or attack.

Political pressure is the most transparent method of such responses. When weak parties, legislatures, and other democratic institutions are changing or confronting a strong executive dominating the political agenda, the resulting imbalance can severely weaken the *defensoría*'s functioning. Under Peru's Alberto Fujimori administration (1990–2000), for example, the *defensor* was sharply rebuked by the supreme military council when he asserted in December 1996 that the arrest of General Rodolfo Robles, charged after criticizing the government's human rights record, was illegal. Fujimori did concede that the arrest may have been "an error," but he nevertheless took no action to stop Robles's trial.

The less obvious but more pernicious threats to a *defensoría*'s work are the entrenched powers and practices of state agencies. Governments are now elected, but many powerful state agencies, like the police and the courts, still evade accountability or exact a price for it. Democracies' internal security forces can be just as violent as ruling militaries, particularly when dealing with problems like drug trafficking. Latin America's authoritarian regimes were more repressive, but blame was more easily affixed on its leaders; under many current democracies, the laws are better, but responsibility and redress are more diffuse and state agencies are more skillful at eluding oversight. Even the newly overhauled state of Hugo Chávez's Venezuela continues to run on patronage and intimidation.

Together, politics and state power may constrain the *defensoría* to a role of public advocacy and information collection that only marginally affects institutions and practices. Such a prognosis seems to be confirmed by the fact that, so far, *defensorías* do far better when dealing with specific matters and other independent agencies. Only a few cases of torture plucked out of larger patterns of police violence tend to be resolved, for example, while deferring to congressional committees or concentrating on nonthreatening forms of popular education have had more resonance than criticisms against powerful ministries.

Pressures and Obstacles from Governments

While governments may see the *defensoría* as a boost for their government's popularity, they are more likely to see it as a threat or a convenient object of blame. Such reactions could be foreseen in executive resistance to such agencies' very formation. Ecuador's president first rejected the *defensoría* and other reforms for not being in accordance with "the purpose of the Executive Function."[2] In Peru, the agency was first introduced in 1994 and approved by Congress in May 1995, soon after Fujimori had been reelected to a second term. The government's support of the bill was due in part to its election-year efforts to counteract criticism of its liquidation of democracy in its April 1992 "self-coup." Soon after the bill's approval, in fact, it was retracted. During the ensuing debate, the agency was castigated as a "superpower" and a "grand inquisitor" that would make Peru ungovernable by spawning an enormous bureaucracy that would overpower all state agencies through its power to monitor them and oblige their cooperation.[3] A revised bill that reduced the *defensoría* was then passed in August. Subsequently, the agency was subject to constant attack, reaching its heights with the *defensor's* involvement in the highly controversial 2000 election. When he called for an inquiry into the president's registration drive after receiving hundreds of complaints of false voter signatures, for example, the president's congressional allies retorted that the *defensor* himself should be investigated for partisanship and accused his office of being a center of radicalism.

A less brazen form of government pressure is exercised through funding. Because of this, many countries specifically give control of the *defensoría's* budget to Congress or the courts—often with explicit rules that the *defensoría* should not make decisions based on financial reasons. But such regulations have not always worked as intended. Soon after appointing the country's first *defensor,* the Ecuadorian government instigated his resignation by denying him an adequate budget and reducing his term in office.[4] Such manipulation also occurs with special programs. When Peru's *defensoría* began a campaign to promote the rights of the handicapped in early 1999, it did not get any funds from the Ministry of Finance and Economy.

Learning from these experiences, as well as those of other agencies, the *defensoría* rarely relies completely on formal procedures. The *defensoría* writes annual reports to Congress, for example, but, as many Ministerio Públicos have discovered, such reports do not necessarily generate change. Since some members of Congress see themselves as the overseers of the MP—Bolivia's general prosecutor complains that "the constitution is misinterpreted to make Congress appear to be the head of the MP"—they often balk at implementing directives on rights concerns.[5] One way to get around such blocks is to appeal to domestic and international opinion. Citing cases before the Inter-American Human Rights Commission and a U.S. congressional report on the lack of judicial independence in Peru, for example, the country's *defensor* pushed for action on these issues in order to avoid further reprobation.

Institutional Practices and Repression

Far bigger obstacles than political interests are the practices of state institutions. Because its own powers are limited, a *defensoría* depends on its ability to cajole the machinery that administers justice. Since no *defensoría* can monitor all daily activities in the street, prisons, police stations, and courts, it needs the cooperation of those who do. But throughout the region, a range of responsible officials carries out or allows systematic abuse of all basic rights. The courts are slow and inefficient; public defenders are overwhelmed and ineffective; the police are repressive and powerful; and prisons are mired in inhumanity and violence.

The most unwieldy block of these institutions are those comprising the criminal justice system, which picks up where the *defensoría* leaves off. The majority of complaints to the *defensoría* regard the judicial process, in fact, which a *defensoría* can and does use to publicly pressure judicial officials. But it still steers the vast majority of its cases, either directly or through the MP, into the appropriate legal channels. It then has to rely on these channels to protect the rights, make the rulings, and impose the remedies needed for a satisfactory resolution. As in all of Latin America, however, the judiciaries of the Andean countries are slow, corrupt, discriminatory, and insufficiently independent (see Méndez, O'Donnell, and Pinheiro 1999). Untrained personnel do much of the judges' work; files and information are haphazardly collected; and trials, not surprisingly, take years to begin and complete. Such chaos has pushed emergency recourses such as *amparo* into regular use. In Venezuela, where the average criminal trial lasts over four years, the provision that judges must decide *amparo* petitions within forty-eight hours has caused an "amparicitis" by lawyers eager to avoid the usual delays. This has overloaded the courts and spurred the outright dismissal of nearly 90 percent of *amparos,* sometimes years after the filing. In Ecuador, the *defensoría* has warned about severe bottlenecks of unresolved *amparos* in areas such as the city of Guayaquil but has been able to do little more than urge area judges to quickly resolve them.[6]

Courts also have to contend with threats, bribery, political attacks, and dissolution of independent support agencies such as the judicial council. This council (the Consejo de la Judicatura or Magistratura) was created to shake up the judicial process through its authority to select, monitor, and discipline judges, as well as to formulate budgets. While only a few countries had councils at the beginning of the 1980s, twelve had them at the end of the 1990s, including all of the Andean countries. But even with their wide-ranging powers, like the *defensoría* they have been forced to withstand executive attacks, judicial ineffectiveness, institutional rivalries, and counteraccusations from officials being investigated. In Bolivia, Congress severely curtailed the council when it became too inquisitive of corruption in the courts. In Venezuela, the constituent assembly that wrote the 1999 constitution dismissed over 120 judges, overhauled the Supreme Court, and eliminated the judicial council. In a bad omen for Venezuelan democracy, the two latter measures were taken *after* the popular referendum endorsing the constitution. In Peru, the entire judicial council resigned in 1998 in protest of a law restricting its authority to investigate judges and dismiss those found guilty, which came on the heels of previous restrictions like a March 1998 law that dissolved its power to appoint prosecutors.

The experience of the Ministerio Público, the overworked prosecutor that the *defensoría* was created to support, also provides a preview of how a legal body can get tangled up in political and state practices. Despite its powers, most MPs have been hindered by a shortage of funds, poor cooperation, and the historical manipulation of past presidents. Constantly juggling their many tasks, in many countries the MP has abandoned some of them, such as criminal investigation, to the police. Weak MPs then allow rights abuses to multiply. In Venezuela, one MP official said that although *fiscales* (public prosecutors, who make up the MP) must be present at each detainee's statement to the police, they are in one part of the police station while confessions are being extracted under torture in secret basements.[7] The Venezuelan MP's power to open a *nudo hecho*, the pretrial investigatory process against a state official accused of a crime, has also been sidelined. Though designed to be completed in under a month, the procedure is conducted in secret and is often delayed for up to six years "by uncooperative police [or] indifferent or recalcitrant judges, . . . and neither the [MP] nor the victim has the legal means" to move it forward.[8] Such delays often result in acquittals of guilty officials, since it is highly difficult to produce witnesses and evidence for trial after such a long period of time, or in their permanent immunity when the statute of limitations runs out before the *nudo hecho* ends. Venezuela's MP tried different ways to speed the procedure, but his efforts were blocked—often by the same officials who steadfastly dismissed the idea of a *defensoría* as just "more bureaucracy."[9]

Such practices exist throughout the region, generating systematic abuse of due process rights. Most vulnerable are criminal defendants, of course, the vast majority of whom rely on public defenders. With the sole exception of Costa Rica, no Latin American country has an adequate number of public defenders. In Venezuela, each one had an average of under sixty-nine cases in 1979; by 1995, that average had shot up to well over three hundred.[10] Despite legal requirements of scheduled visits, two-thirds of those awaiting trial report never even having met with their defenders.[11] The first meeting between them is often at the detainee's investigative declaration, at which point options such as challenging the detention order are no longer available. But reforms intended to ameliorate this situation have had limited impact.

Such patterns are common throughout the region, and in no country do the numerous government and private legal-aid centers begin to make up for them. In Peru, defendants' rights were severely eroded by antiterrorism laws, which dominated the first years of a *defensoría* concerned about the thousands of unfounded arrests and unfair trials under such laws. Soon after presenting Fujimori with a list of those convicted of terrorism or treason without sufficient proof in March 1999, the *defensor,* Jorge Santistevan, was named to a special presidential commission that reviewed hundreds of cases of those presumed innocent of these charges and later sponsored legislative bills to allow those who repent terrorism to appeal to the judiciary to lift mandates of detention and interrogation. Combined with international pressure, this work led to the release of about five hundred prisoners. Conscious of provoking a counterattack, though, Santistevan was careful not to overplay his hand. To avoid cornering the military into admitting error, for example, he did not directly challenge the arrangement by which those deemed innocent would be exonerated rather than pardoned. Peru's experience with terrorism and antiterrorism laws galvanized these efforts. But in countries struggling with the more pervasive problem of common crime, progress is slower. Although most countries are beginning to hire more public defenders, improve their working conditions, and restructure their operations, they still fall short of demand.

Moreover, sharp increases in arrests for common crime, coupled with the slowness of the judicial process, have made the region's prisons among the most crowded and violent in Latin America. Despite penal-code reforms and new rights guarantees, penitentiary rights abuse remains endemic. In Peru, where over 70 percent of inmates at any given time have not been tried, overcrowding and rioting have become the norm. Colombia's 168 prisons pack over forty-three thousand inmates—nearly half of whom have not been sentenced—into spaces allotted for fewer than thirty thousand.[12] In Venezuela, among a population of about twenty-five thousand housed in facilities designed for just over fifteen thousand, the annual number of killings nearly doubled in the 1990s. In every country, the *defensoría* has been at the forefront of pressing for action.

An increase in riots and escapes, along with mounting international criticism, finally pushed governments to take more than ad hoc measures. A 1997 law passed by Colombia's legislature required freeing inmates who had served 60 percent of their prison terms unless they were charged with serious crimes such as terrorism or drug trafficking. Ecuador adopted a similar plan, allowing the freeing of 40 percent of inmates charged with use or possession of small amounts of drugs. A provision in the country's new constitution also allows judges to order the immediate release of unconvicted prisoners who have been in jail for more than a year. By the end of 1999, this law had led to the release of about six hundred of the twenty-one hundred entitled inmates. In Bolivia, a former justice minister introduced new bail laws, hired more public defenders, and released thousands of debtors from prison. While such changes were positive, the ability of a minister to bring them about only underscored the *defensoría*'s limitations. That minister is gone, but the *defensoría* is responsible for seeing those changes through.

In comparison, though, the region's courts and prisons are far more amenable to reform than are its police forces, whose persistent violations of constitutional guarantees have made them a central concern of each Andean *defensoría*. While more studies expose law-enforcement abuses (Chevigny 1995; Pinheiro 1996), they are outpaced by the changing patterns and causes of abuses. During both authoritarian and democratic eras, first of all, the number of police forces in each country—judicial, intelligence, military, specialized, provincial, and municipal—has grown rapidly. Aided by the availability of authoritarian-era laws, governments continue to step up police power to control crime, armed insurgencies, and volatile societies. Even when such threats diminish, police continue to expand their official and unofficial powers and use them in ways that often neutralize constitutional guarantees.

In Bolivia, the police were reorganized into more clearly defined limits after the 1982 transition to democracy. But the reemergence of their historical role in suppressing demonstrations and strikes, as seen in recent protests over government policies, has stretched those limits. The huge antinarcotics operations of the 1980s also rekindled the police's military training and militarized approach to internal order. The *defensoría* has not shied away from these practices, even implicating Policia Técnica Judicial (PTJ) officials in the beatings and torture of detainees. But, as with nongovernmental rights organizations, such action has fueled its public image as less a check on police power than a "protector" of criminals at the cost of public safety. Recalling her trip to an otherwise routine neighborhood meeting, the country's *defensora,* Ana María Romero de Campero, remembered being surrounded by a crowd who raucously chanted "Defensoría of Delinquents!"[13]

The National Police of Colombia (PN), involved in serious rights abuses such as organizing paramilitary groups and killing suspected guerrilla sympathizers, also has a history of repression. Repeatedly militarized since its founding in the 1890s, the PN has been notorious for its weak coordination and accountability. During the 1948–53 civil war, for example, it deteriorated into small units controlled by local powers—a practice reemerging as violence and corruption again fragments the country. Impunity is also the norm, as seen in the 1994 military court acquittal of Naval Intelligence Network officials charged with dozens of extrajudicial killings, despite strong evidence against them. Sometimes security and police forces have even refused to carry out arrest warrants, such as when the attorney general had to use its own Technical Investigation Unit to capture a major ally of the powerful paramilitary United Self-Defense Forces of Colombia (AUC).

After Venezuela's transition to democracy in 1958, a government besieged by both conservative opposition and a left-wing rebellion put pressure on judges to jail guerrilla suspects, repeatedly suspended constitutional rights, and strengthened the police through decrees and laws. In particular, the powerful PTJ was granted extensive investigatory powers and placed in the executive branch's Justice Ministry—an affiliation unusual among democracies, which usually put judicial police in nonexecutive agencies with investigative authority, such as the MP. Even after the guerrillas were defeated, police agencies continued to emphasize preventative detention and forced confession. Their rights abuses continued to rise, particularly during the six suspensions of basic constitutional rights—including the right of assembly and the right to the inviolability of the home—during the 1990s.

In Ecuador, most complaints to the *defensoría* have been against the police and armed forces, charging them with torture, beatings, arbitrary detention, and disrespect of constitutional tribunal rulings.[14] Despite government admission of responsibility in several detainee deaths, reports continue of torture, mistreatment, and disappearances, particularly by the National Police. Of the nine hundred complaints received between October 1998 and March 1999, over 50 percent were regarded as illegal preventative and arbitrary detentions.[15] Also continuing to rise are the death tolls from the police's questionable firearm use and the extrajudicial killings of crime suspects.

The police violate constitutional rights in the judiciary as well as on the street. Officially subordinate to judges, judicial police oversee most criminal investigations and carry out routine procedures like inspecting crime scenes, retaining evidence, and questioning witnesses. But they often ignore the rule that they can take only an "informative statement" from a detainee and admit that many cases hinge on little more than confessions—many of which are coerced. Many officers destroy evidence, defy court orders, protect indicted colleagues, harass political activists, accuse public defenders of advising their clients to withhold incriminating information, "use false witnesses, invent facts . . . bring false charges against innocent persons," and shake down sus-

pects "to not bring charges."[16] In Venezuela, officials concede that "in the pretrial activities of the police, there are no judicial controls except for the presence of the prosecutor in the declarations to the police"—a requirement rarely
met.[17] With inadequate resources and overloaded dockets, judges themselves
"tend to base [their] decisions on police actions without an investigation of
them and without a deep conviction regarding the veracity or falsehood of the
facts," while police officials often ignore rulings against them.[18]

Rising levels of crime aggravate such practices. In the early 1990s, Latin
America's homicide rate was 22.9 for every one hundred thousand inhabitants, while after 1995 the regional rate jumped to nearly 29.[19] But the reaction from Latin America's anxious leaders has largely been a combination of
ad hoc policies and new public-order laws that do not generally address
crime's socioeconomic causes. Downplaying abusive policing and the criminal
system's chaos as unavoidable by-products of the crime surge—rather than as
parts of the larger problem—Andean governments first turn to harsh measures and "extraordinary" police operations such as mass detentions.

In Ecuador, "states of emergency" are the favored crime-fighting response.
During the one extended over Guayas province for most of 1999, the police
detained hundreds of people and held many for over two days without charge.
In Venezuela, massive police sweeps of poor urban barrios began in the 1970s,
increasing in the 1990s as the national homicide rate rose by 73 percent
(nearly fivefold in Caracas).[20] In Peru, increases in urban gang violence, organized crime, and attacks in wealthy areas have also prompted tough anticrime
measures. Equating national security with crime prevention, in 1998 the government adopted ten decrees, many based on antiguerrilla measures linked to
rights abuses. But while crime rose from 155,000 reported crimes in 1990 to
a height of 289,000 in 1994, it declined to 192,000 reports by 1998—suggesting that politics and police power motivated the anticrime laws as much
as crime itself.[21] These laws weakened basic rights and accountability by
transferring many enforcement powers from civilian to military courts and
the notoriously abusive National Intelligence Service (SIN), forming a new
SIN body to coordinate police intelligence, and prohibiting courts from sub-
poenaing interrogating police officers in many cases. These decrees also increased arbitrary and biased prosecutions, as Decree 895 did by creating the
crime of "aggravated terrorism" and giving the police power to detain suspects for up to fifteen days and allowing military tribunals to try accused
civilians. Decree 900, which transfers competence to hear habeas corpus petitions in many cases from the dozens of Lima-area criminal judges to one specialized judge, stifles use of this recourse.

Seeing the popularity of these policies, governments tend to ignore the resulting increases in extrajudicial killings; torture; raids; illegal curfews;

threats; extortion by both individual officers and "mafias"; and extensive networks in the trafficking, distribution, and sale of arms and narcotics. Anemic internal police discipline, broad legal impunity, and the concentration of such abuses in poor urban areas only fuel them further. And with judiciaries, legislatures, and other institutions unable or unwilling to check such problems, the *defensoría* finds itself limited. Even as Peru turned its attention toward regular street crime at the same time the *defensoría* began functioning, for example, police tactics consistently outmaneuvered the agency. According to national law, police officers may only arrest people with a judge's order or in the case of a crime being committed en flagrante delicto. Yet they regularly conduct massive sweeps, such as one in a poor neighborhood in June 2001 that netted three hundred people in a search for a single suspect. With the legal maximum of twenty-four hours that a suspect can be held before being put at the disposition of a judge, such large numbers of arrests invariably cause the police to violate this rule as well. Supported by political and public opinion, though, they argue that it is more effective to detain and then investigate, rather than the other way around. To avoid judicial approbation, they describe such action not as "detention" but as "intervention." Enjoying both political and legal cover, asserts *defensor adjunto* Samuel Abad Yupanqui, these practices become an "engrained part . . . and accepted notion of policing."[22]

The adoption of progressive new penal process codes throughout the Andes underscores the need to stem such practices. While penal codes specify crimes, penal process codes lay out the procedures under which they are investigated and prosecuted. Given the police's power and the judiciary's disarray, such codes are an essential part of civil rights protection. Bolivia's and Venezuela's new codes have important changes, such as emphasizing the presumption of innocence, changing trials from bureaucratic written procedures to open oral ones, strengthening the MP and judges, clarifying the police's role in criminal investigation, having verdicts made not just by judges but by panels of judges and citizens, and providing language assistance.[23] Peru added prohibitions of disappearance and torture to its penal code, and Colombia's code was supplemented with proscriptions of disappearance and massacre. In Venezuela, the benefits of the new code are seen in the dramatic drop of nearly 40 percent in the prison population. While able to help promote those codes' positive provisions, however, the *defensoría* is unlikely to have much impact on their negative ones. Bolivia's *defensora* has criticized the allowance of clandestine agents (*agentes encubiertos*) in the new code, for example, stating that their use in drug operations and phone tapping violates basic rights such as equality before the law and the right to be tried by a competent authority. Even more damaging are political attacks on the codes for "coddling" criminals, which have led to a sometimes violent popular backlash in countries such as Venezuela.

New process codes are sapped not just by state practices but by other laws. Drug laws have proved particularly immune to legal checks and institutional oversight. Venezuela's 1984 Organic Law of Substances, Narcotics, and Psychotropic Drugs widened police discretion in conducting searches and generated an increase in raids of private homes without court orders.[24] Police agencies derived judicial powers from the law's vague definition of investigatory authorities and the courts' failure to clarify them. Bail laws often exclude drug defendants, while bureaucratic incompetence often keeps many detainees incarcerated beyond their sentence time. Bolivia's 1988 anti-trafficking law, Law 1008, for example, violates due process by prohibiting pretrial release and has fostered discrimination against indigenous people and male campesinos.[25] In countering these trends, the *defensoría* has to carefully balance peasant communities and law-enforcement agencies, both of which are suspicious of it. *Defensoría* officials in Bolivia's coca-producing region of Chapare, for instance, faced retaliation after accusing police of illegal shooting, beatings, and collusion with traffickers.

Drug laws and other special public-order measures further threaten human rights when the military is involved. In Bolivia, the armed forces control many coca-producing zones and have been accused of beatings, illegal confiscation, and violent raids. In Peruvian areas under emergency law, the rights of personal liberty, inviolability of the home, and freedom of movement are restricted. The government resisted international and national pressure to ameliorate the 1995 amnesty designed to deflect prosecution of military and police officials accused of rights violations.[26] As in other countries, impunity and acquittals characterize many of the cases against officials that have been brought to trial. As with some other issues, though, the *defensorías* have successfully challenged military abuses by taking on specific problems and individual cases. Estimating that 80 percent of recruits were forcibly conscripted, Peru's *defensor* worked with the human rights groups Legal Defense Institute (IDL) and Asociación Pro–Derechos Humanos (APRODEH) to help eliminate compulsory military service.

The *Defensoría* as Societal Voice

With such inefficiency and abuse causing widespread disillusion and distrust in state institutions, the *defensoría* has been given the role of citizen voice as well as that of institutional watchdog. No matter how alienated they become from the state, citizens still need it to protect their constitutional rights. The *defensoría* expresses those needs by speaking to and for marginalized groups, resolving specific cases, gathering information, gauging public opinion, mediating conflicts, and expanding into new issue areas. Applying these authorities to the range of human rights, it can also make politically potent links between problems that officials prefer to approach separately, such as when the *defensorías* of Colombia and Peru blame political conflict for the economic suffering of women and indigenous people. In the process, a skillful *defensoría* acquires legitimacy, influence, and trust. In Bolivia and Peru, polls consistently give the agency, along with the church and the press, the highest levels of public confidence. Over five hundred people lined up outside the central office of the *defensoría* in Peru on its first day of operation, with similar responses greeting each regional office opening. In its first year, Colombia's *defensoría* received 10,000 complaints; in its second year it got 16,417, and in its third 25,409.[27]

The *defensoría* builds such trust by becoming a voice for marginalized populations. Special seminars on the elderly and youth have helped these populations organize and express their concerns, such as through the consumer defense organizations that Ecuador's *defensoría* helped form in twenty provinces. Responding to pleas from an indigenous community, Peru's *defensoría* pushed the Agriculture Ministry to fulfill its obligations, even accusing the National Agrarian Office of violating the Law of Communities. Colombia's *defensoría* has brought attention to the overlooked problem of child abuse. Estimating that nearly eight million children suffer from some form of abuse—with sexual exploitation alone rising 600 percent between 1996 and 1998—a 1999 *defensoría* report singled out a lack of state funds and increases in poverty for blame. A 1999 agreement between the *defensores* of Bolivia and Argentina even focused attention on the nearly absent rights protections of Bolivian immigrants in Argentina.

In particular, the special offices and adjunct *defensores* on women's rights have highlighted social and economic abuses against women. Publicizing the high rates of violence and poverty that women suffer, Colombia's *defensoría* has urged the president to empower the Women' Equality Office to develop and implement policy. The women's *defensor* has also pushed the government to give priority in housing to female-headed households and carried out studies on the safety and health of women in prison.[28] Supported by several nongovernmental organizations (NGOs), Peru's *defensoría* worked against a government sterilization program targeting poor women, during which medical officials reported that they were given bonuses for sterilization quotas. Its efforts led to enforcement of a seventy-two-hour waiting period for sterilization operations and a dramatic drop in their number.[29] The *defensoría* has also been at the forefront of antirape campaigns, estimating over six thousand cases of rape annually in Lima alone (although some rights groups assert this to be the monthly figure). Linking women's rights and police abuse, the *defensoría* has also acted on the hundreds of complaints it receives by women charging police agencies with illegal and inadequate responses to domestic violence, such as dismissing accusations because of a lack of visible wounds.[30] These and other effective, well-targeted efforts stem from *defensores'* meticulous information gathering, careful confidence building within the social group, and knowledge of how policy decisions are made.

In addition to group advocacy, *defensoría* officials have found success in broadening their mandate into less traditional rights issues, such as the environment. Backed by the *defensoría,* for example, a major Bolivian environmental rights group based in Cochabamba denounced the local government's development projects as a violation of the national Environment Law by citing their adverse impacts. In an era of decentralization and privatization, the functioning of public utilities is another nontraditional but particularly rewarding rights issue for *defensorías.* With nearly three-quarters of all complaints to Bolivia's *defensoría* about the public administration, in fact, the agency has made state services a principal focus. Often prompted by individual complaints, Peru's *defensoría* has documented and charged public utilities and energy companies with price-fixing, overcharging, and violating certain laws. Colombia's *defensor* also has charged utilities with violations, such as illegally altering the terms of payments of users. On these and other issues, new concerns and still-unformed laws allow the *defensoría* to not only gain public support but seize new authorities within the state.

With both traditional and nontraditional rights issues, information and education are particularly important to the *defensorías* because they allow the comparison of conditions in different areas. Among the Bolivian *defensoría's* biggest contributions are its popular Educación Radiofónica de Bolivia radio programs; its information gathering through its six regional offices; and special provincial seminars that expose discrimination, judicial inefficiency, and problems in schools and public services—all critical for a poor, geographically dispersed, and linguistically fragmented population. Such efforts provide a basis for effective policy by revealing imbalances that ultimately direct resources to needier regions. With their limited budgets to carry out all this work, every Andean *defensoría* depends on the growing numbers of NGOs in the region—which also helps forge their alliances with society. Many of the cases brought by the *defensorías* throughout the region, in fact, have relied on NGO material. With evidence gathered by the Comisión por la Vida y por la Paz Social, for instance, Ecuador's *defensoría* complained to the Defense Ministry about military operations in certain regions, linked to abuses such as the 1998 murder of a union activist.

Despite such progress, however, this public advocacy role can turn the *defensoría* into a victim of its own success. As with any official, of course, personal biases and views can cloud the agency's work—which is particularly problematic for an agency based on neutrality. Bolivia's *defensora,* for example,

highlights her commitment and work on behalf of the Church, while catego-
rizing as "aggressive" the rights efforts of groups such as homosexuals.[31]
While such favoritism may be politically astute, taken too far it will undermine the agency. Beyond individual beliefs, though, the *defensoría's* public
role is harmed by problems out of its control. In particular, progress on questions of inequality and discrimination is stymied by their structural causes.
Some types of rights protection illicit hostility from the public; some indigenous and community legal practices encouraged by *defensorías* are at odds with
national laws they are supposed to uphold; and societal problems themselves
may simply overwhelm the agency.

Most seriously, the *defensoría* is easily pulled into structural problems whose
solutions are neither easy nor necessarily popular. This has been clearest
around the public panic over crime, which turned many sectors of society—
such as shantytown dwellers, the unemployed, immigrants, and youth—into
automatic suspects. Rising up to "control" these groups, a job that the state is
seen as forfeiting, is vigilante justice meted out by gangs or spontaneous gatherings, usually in poor neighborhoods and sometimes led by off-duty police
officers. Most victims are individuals accused of specific crimes, ranging from
robbery to murder, but in some areas self-appointed death squads target entire
groups. In 1996, the regional *defensor* in Colombia's Caldas department publicly called on the police to investigate up to eighty deaths in a spasm of such
"social cleansing." But while it is a serious threat to human rights and thus a
legitimate concern for *defensorías,* vigilantism is also something that grows out
of popular frustrations and attraction to draconian law-and-order measures.
The *defensoría,* therefore, risks being cast on the wrong side of an issue that
even governments will exploit for their own political ends.

Another outgrowth of the crime rates, and of low confidence in state agencies, is an astronomical increase in private security forces, which probably
outnumber government police in many cities. Their poorly trained and paid
employees, many with shady pasts, frequently commit abuses. And the increasing tendency for municipal forces in cities like Lima to employ these
agencies on contract further complicates the situation. After it hired a security firm that was implicated in massacres and other abuses, for example, the
Colombian government responded by prohibiting these businesses from having powers such as collecting evidence and receiving military weaponry. But
with army officers still continuing to support these organizations, such a
strategy only drives illegal action underground—making it more difficult for
the *defensoría* to counter it.

Freedom of expression, another of the region's beleaguered human rights,
can also pull a *defensoría* in over its head. Throughout the Andes, the media
has been under attack by laws, threats, and other intimidation and censorship

efforts. During the Fujimori period in Peru, journalists who exposed rights violations or were critical of the government received death threats and faced legal reprisals, including arrest on trumped-up charges of contempt and obstruction of justice. The Peruvian *defensoría* worked with reporters in rural areas arrested for "apology" for terrorism and pushed a reluctant Fujimori to meet with the Inter-American Press Society. Reflecting the effectiveness of promoting individual cases, Colombia's *defensoría* took up the case of a journalist beaten by the police in February 1999 while attempting to report on the eviction of street vendors.

Because of their human rights mandate, *defensorías'* uneven protection of human rights activists displays their limits most prominently. Members of Bolivia's Permanent Assembly of Human Rights (APDH) have been threatened, arrested, and tortured by police officials; associates of Peruvian organizations like the Lima Bar Association and the National Coordinating Committee of Human Rights have been regularly harassed; and Venezuela's president has attacked rights groups ever since one of them documented abuses by the military in its December 1998 flood-recovery efforts. In most of these cases, the *defensoría* is unable to attain enough information or cooperation to even initiate legal action. Colombia's *defensor,* for example, has assiduously investigated dozens of assassinations of rights activists, political figures, and government investigators. Blame is usually placed on the military or paramilitary groups, but the military often shrugs it off by blaming rights organizations themselves. After the May 1998 killing of a top state official, military officials gave false information to the attorney general implicating the Justice and Peace rights group, subsequently raiding its office and threatening its employees. The government responded with measures like installing bulletproof glass and security cameras in some rights organizations' offices but has only slowly carried out its promise to cleanse government files of false accusations against those same groups.

As with crime, indigenous rights is another issue that presents *defensorías* with a conflict between legal standards and political demands. During the 1990s, Bolivia, Colombia, Ecuador, and Peru enacted constitutional provisions recognizing indigenous legal practices. Allowing those communities to administer justice in their regions has brought benefits like adoption of harmonious rather than adversarial proceedings. But indigenous law frequently clashes with national law, such as when it lacks predetermined punishments for specific crimes, allows trials for witchcraft, and passes down sentences of forced labor or collective punishment.[32] Such conflict puts rights agencies in political as well as legal binds. In Ecuador, internationally supported indigenous communities scored big victories against oil companies operating in the Amazonian region. But when the leader of the Confederation of Indigenous

Nations of Ecuador (CONAIE), instrumental in this work, joined in the un-constitutional January 2000 revolt against the government, a warrant went out for his arrest. The MP and other agencies would not carry out the arrest, however, knowing that it could trigger potentially violent acts such as high-way blockades. Again, legal standards and the public will may squeeze a *defensoría* trying to balance them.

A *defensoría*, finally, may simply be overwhelmed by any one of these prob-lems—particularly when taking it on in a highly public and political manner. Reporting that about 1.2 million people have been displaced from their land by the country's internal violence, Colombia's *defensoría* condemned the gov-ernment for having "no policy to put a stop to this atrocity" and bluntly as-serted that the very "recuperation of the State's credibility" rides on its ability to come up with a working solution.[33] But the state's response has largely been one of poor coordination, low funding, and even harmful actions such as compelling displaced persons to return home without providing for their safety.

Such tactics, of course, are especially risky when *defensorías* cannot make up for the state's inadequacy. This has happened on a number of issues, such as when Colombia's agency took on the task of providing public defense and when Peru's decided it would document and register criminal and terrorist detainees. Sometimes a *defensoría* can ease out of such responsibilities, but do-ing so on issues that have become integral to the agency may smack of failure. In Colombia, above all, the *defensoría*'s public advocacy has been consumed by the civil war. Provincial *defensores* document killings and kidnappings, help stem violence through actions such as convincing soldiers to leave particular towns, relay communities' fears of attacks to the Defense Ministry, and when possible warn of imminent violence. Drawing up "maps of risk," the Colom-bian *defensoría* reported 194 massacres in 1998 alone—47 percent by paramil-itary groups and 21 percent by leftist guerrillas—and also uncovered "diffuse massacres," in which individuals were killed at separate times in a municipal-ity to avoid the attacks being reported as a massacre. *Defensoría* officials have met with both left-wing and right-wing armed groups, documented mas-sacres by the military, and accused the government of refusing to publicize *de-fensoría* warnings of imminent paramilitary attacks. But with little physical security beyond their own persuasive abilities, *defensoría* officers in the field face constant threats and obstacles and usually end up quitting or being pro-moted to safer areas.

Political uncertainty, state practices, societal demands, legal conflicts, and institutional pressures all make the Andes' Defensorías del Pueblo walk a thin line between success and failure. Without the rest of the state to implement the reforms and resolve the cases a *defensoría* brings to it, human rights protection is unlikely to improve. And when a *defensoría* does make progress, as with new rights issues, it risks triggering backlashes from both state and society. Through controlling budgets, browbeating the media, and manipulating policy, governments are not hesitant to attack *defensorías* in the name of public order, national policy, or even democracy.

As with progress on human rights in the past, the *defensorías* will therefore have to depend on their skill in collecting information, shaping public opinion, utilizing legal procedures, and taking advantage of political openings. Despite new constitutions, laws, and governments, that is, the Andes' *defensorías* demonstrate that human rights work must be in sync with a changing state and society. Above all, they must be willing to challenge power, which might make the *defensorías* of Peru and Colombia stronger in the long run than those in Bolivia, Ecuador, and Venezuela. Written rights guarantees are not a goal but a tool for bringing about political oversight, alterations in state practices, functioning citizen channels, and consistent protections for society's most vulnerable groups. The transition out of military rule was a change that allowed the creation of rules and institutions to promote human rights, but engagement with the state and society is now needed to make those rules and institutions work.

III Political Change and Democracy

Liisa L. North

9 State Building, State Dismantling, and Financial Crises in Ecuador

History repeats itself.
Another July Revolution:
the military tired of so much corruption.

—Colonel Fausto Corbo, January 21, 2000

Colonel Fausto Corbo, one of the four hundred or so army officers ranging from lieutenants to colonels who supported the indigenous uprising that led to the deposition of President Jamil Mahuad on January 21, 2000, was referring to the parallels between that event and the young officers' revolt of July 1925—the Revolución Juliana or July Revolution. Both political cataclysms were preceded by acute economic crisis and the crash of the country's banking system, which, in 2000 as in 1925, were blamed on corrupt politicians in the pockets of equally corrupt bankers. Moreover, young officers preoccupied with the integrity of the nation-state were protagonists on both occasions. The officers' political allies, the outcomes of their actions, and the international context of the two rebellions were, however, very different.

Certain enduring features of Ecuador's postindependence political-economic evolution have made state building and the pursuit of incorporative reforms particularly problematic. These features relate to its regional divisions, the composition of its dominant classes, and patterns of social-political organization among its subordinate classes.

The Andean highlands were the seat of the country's postindependence traditional landlord class, which reigned over an indigenous population locked into servile labor relations (Guerrero 1993). As late as 1956, it was possible to find press advertisements for highland estate sales "with horses, sowed land, and *huasipungueros,*" that is, indigenous peasants who, for their labor on the estates, received small plots of land for subsistence cultivation in lieu of wages (Saad Herrería 2000, 64). Ecuador's "modern" financial-commercial-landlord elite, on the other hand, emerged on the coast in the course of two agricultural export cycles that were associated with the halting expansion of capitalist social relations in the countryside. These were the cacao cycle, which lasted roughly from 1860 to 1920, and the banana cycle of 1948 to 1972. The elites' principal institutions—their chambers of agriculture, industry, and commerce, as well as their banks—were clustered in the cities of Quito and Guayaquil, the highland capital and the major coastal port, respectively. Leading members of these institutions, in turn, have enjoyed privileged direct access to public policy-making up to the present day.[1]

Middle-class political and other organizations have also been historically fragmented along regional lines while the rural and urban popular masses have been divided along both regional and ethnic lines. Indeed, scholars of Ecuador's politics have typically referred to their forms of political participation as atomized, diffuse, heterogeneous, dispersed, segmented, and the like. Despite the foundation of both socialist (1926) and communist (1931) parties and their notable organizational efforts, subordinate classes remained deeply divided and, for the most part, mobilized into elite-dominated coalitions through populist leaders such as José María Velasco Ibarra from the early 1930s to the early 1970s (Maigushca and North 1991) and Abdalá Bucaram in the1990s. In turn, the middle classes were for the most part "encapsulated within elite-dominated parties" (Conaghan 1988, 99). Moreover, given the different characteristics and policy needs of highland and coastal societies (e.g., between cheap imports for coastal consumers dependent on the health of, first, the cacao and, then, the banana export economy and tariff protection for highland textile industries), the country's regionally based elites have displayed a remarkable capacity to mobilize subordinate classes to political action in defense of their own private economic interests by appealing to regional concerns and sentiments (Quintero and Silva 1991).

The July Revolution represented the first serious and relatively broadly supported challenge to the dominance of the coastal "plutocracy" whose members, during the 1980s and 1990s, became key players in the pursuit of neoliberal reforms in general and the financial crisis of Mahuad's presidency in particular. The outwardly oriented coastal export elites, on the basis of their control of cacao export production and marketing, had achieved political dominance vis-à-vis their then more inwardly oriented conservative highland counterparts through the Liberal Revolution of 1895. Twentieth-century political regimes—whatever their specific forms—have been structured to a significant degree around competition between these two regionally based dominant classes. They nevertheless have repeatedly manifested the capacity to mount a unified front when challenged by popular mobilization or redistributive policies—land reform most importantly—that could have permitted the sustainable development of domestic markets, thereby reducing Ecuador's catastrophic dependence on exports.

State Building and State Dismantling

In July 1925, the young officers' actions were supported not only by Ecuador's incipient urban working and middle classes but also by highland elites and even a few notable members of the coastal elite. Indeed, the "ideologue" of the revolution was Napoleón Dillon, the president of the Quito Chamber of Commerce and the founder of the country's first modern textile factory (Drake 1989, 135–39; Rebecca Almeida 1994, 34), although specific demands and the coup itself originated from the Liga Militar, which had been formed in October 1924. The *liga*'s program was focused on strengthening the power and authority of the central state and resolving an acute fiscal crisis that was blamed on the coastal banking and import-export "plutocracy." Indeed, the specific target of generalized opprobrium was the Guayaquil-based Banco Comercial y Agrícola. It was the bank of the great cacao interests, and as the most important of the private banks licensed to emit Ecuador's currency (the *sucre*) at the time, it had become the principal lender to the chronically deficit-ridden governments of the day.

Despite strong opposition from the coastal plutocracy, the July events eventually led to the foundation of a set of financial and other state institutions, a Central Bank among them (in 1927), under the tutelage of a mission headed by U.S. economist Edwin Kemmerer. Moreover, the constitution of 1928, which emerged from the revolution, for the first time in the country's history included principles for social legislation: the twelve-point program of the officers referred, among other things, to the promotion of the interests of both the working classes and the indigenous population, progressive tax reform in favor of "the proletariat," and the taxation of "flight capital" (Paz y Miño Cepeda 2000, 25–26). Little of that program was translated into effective policy.

The "social question" at the time pertained to the wretched state of working-class living conditions in general and to the misery of coastal workers in particular: they were bearing the brunt of the cacao crisis of the early 1920s, and hundreds of strikers and protesters had been killed by the army in Guayaquil in November 1922. That "question" also referred to the servility and racial oppression of and denial of citizenship rights to the then majority indigenous population that labored on the highland estates: localized highland indigenous peasant rebellions had taken place in 1921 and 1923.[2] However, neither the coastal nor the highland rural laboring masses, who formed the majority of the population at the time, were organized, nor were they participants in the July Revolution.

Nevertheless, a socially diverse alliance of highland elite groups, along with urban-based popular and middle-class sectors from both the highlands and the coast, supported the July 1925 revolt. In stark contrast, in January 2000, young officers lent their support to a predominately indigenous uprising led by the mainly rural highland- and Amazonian region–based Confederation of Indigenous Nations of Ecuador (CONAIE), which had been formed in 1986. Some prominent individuals, including liberation-theology-inspired members of the Catholic Church, also adhered to the rebellion. CONAIE, however, had neglected the construction of broadly based political alliances, counting only on the Social Movement Coordinator (CMS), which incorporated the workers of publicly owned petroleum and electrical-sector enterprises in addition to "certain groups from the south of Quito," one of the poorest areas of the capital city (Ortiz Crespo 2000c, 30). The absence of organized support in the coastal region was particularly glaring; the middle classes, rather than joining the rebellion, chose to watch it on TV screens in the safety of their homes. Even the Ecuadorian Federation of Evangelical Indians (FEINE), which claimed the allegiance of a significant proportion of the indigenous population, failed to support the rebellion. Yet ambivalent sympathy for the Indian cause was widespread. In a survey taken as the events were unfolding, "71 percent of those polled said they were in favor of the indigenous movement and 64 percent approved the takeover" of the congressional buildings by the CONAIE at the same time that, contradictorily, 79 percent favored "maintaining the constitutional order" (Collins 2000b, 46).

CONAIE's program demanded the dissolution of all three branches of government—the executive, the legislative, and the judiciary—and their replacement by a National People's Parliament backed by provincial and district parliaments; a "total change" in economic policy from the neoliberal model to a "fair, responsible, environmentally sustainable economy that recognizes plurinationality and cultural diversity [and is] productive and democratic [and] directed toward human development; and democracy . . . under the principles of AMA KILLA, AMA LLULLA, AMA SHUA" (Declaration 2000, emphasis in the original).[3] These were revolutionary demands indeed. In comparison, the declarations of Colonel Lucío Gutiérrez, the military head of the January 21, 2000, movement, were considerably more vague. He referred to a "tenacious and implacable Pacific Junta against a new form of slavery to break the chains that bind us to the most appalling corruption. We are here to overthrow that disgraceful model in order to change the structures of the state and strengthen democratic institutions. We are acting peacefully in order to recover the self-esteem, pride, and honesty of the Ecuadorian people, to check the corruption and impunity sponsored by the government." Colonel Gutiérrez also appealed to "the Church, the communications media, businessmen and bankers, and other opinion leaders, workers, women and men" who love Ecuador, to unite behind the coup and provide "ideas to change the country" (*El Comercio,* January 22, 2000).

Lacking any elite allies or organized social support beyond the CONAIE and the CMS, the junta of the Government of National Salvation (Gobierno de Salvación Nacional) lasted an ephemeral twenty-four hours on January 21–22 before the military high command took charge. To the relief of the bankers and businessmen to whom Colonel Gutierrez had appealed, it arranged the constitutional succession of Vice-President Gustavo Noboa to the presidency. Thus the attempt to place the "social question" on the policy agenda again and reverse the neoliberal-inspired dismantling of central state institutions that had begun to be established in the wake of the 1925 July Revolution failed. The U.S. government, the Organization of American States (OAS), and the international financial institutions (IFIs) made it clear to the generals (who in fact had earlier also demanded Mahuad's resignation) that they would not tolerate a military government and that the constitution had to be respected. Otherwise, the country would be boycotted and could expect no economic assistance or cooperation in dealing with its worst economic crisis of the twentieth century, including a gargantuan foreign debt—which, at $15.2 billion, exceeded the gross domestic product (GDP) and soaked up about 45–50 percent of the public budget before Ecuador defaulted in September 1999.

Washington had also denied recognition to the governments of the July Revolution, but its leverage at the time was limited: the bulk of Ecuador's public debt was internal, most of it owed to the Banco Comercial y Agrícola, and no powerful international or hemispheric organizations existed to deliver credible threats. Moreover, the international climate of the 1920s favored state building—or at least the creation of central banking and related institutions—as a consequence of the financial chaos that followed World War I (Rebecca Almeida 1994, 23–24). Thus, coastal bankers and import-export interests were placed on the defensive by the July Revolution. By contrast, in 2000, bickering coastal and highland elites, shaken by the events of "black Friday" (January 21), united to defend the constitutional order and deepen the neoliberal reforms that were initiated in the mid-1980s under the presidency of León Febres Cordero, the right-wing leader of the essentially coast-based and misnamed Social Christian Party (Partido Social Cristiano).

Most remarkably, the new government agreed to pursue the official dollarization of the financial system that had been announced by President Mahuad on January 9. With that decision, the role of the Central Bank—perhaps the crowning achievement of the July Revolution—was gutted. It would no longer be able to regulate exchange rates or control the money supply, which would become entirely dependent on the country's export earnings (see, e.g., Acosta and Juncosa 2000; de la Paz Vela 2000).

With the decisions to deepen neoliberal reforms and adopt the U.S. dollar as the official currency for all transactions, Ecuador in the year 2000, mutatis mutandis, was reverting to the basic doctrines of the Liberal Revolution of 1895—that is, to the doctrines that the July Revolution of 1925 had attempted to reverse by assigning, as argued by Juan J. Paz y Miño Cepeda, an interventionist and at least mildly developmental and reformist role to the state as the representative of common interests (Paz y Miño Cepeda 2000, 73–74). During the following decades, conflicts regarding the utilization of the state to serve broad public rather than narrow private interests were resolved, for the most part, in favor of the powerful regionally based private economic groups that have continued to dominate state policy up to the present date. Symbolic of the outward-oriented coastal elite's remarkably rapid recovery of initiative was the elimination of the working-class representative in the Central Bank's directorate. Within three years of the bank's foundation, he was replaced by a representative of coastal agricultural interests (Rebecca Almeida 1994, 103).

Key Moments in State Building, 1925–79

With the possible exception of the elected civilian government headed by Galo Plaza Lasso (1948–52), the most coherent efforts to strengthen state institutions and address the "social question" after the July Revolution were undertaken by military dictatorships. These were the regimes headed by General Alberto Enríquez Gallo (October 1937–August 1938), a four-man junta (July 1963–March 1966), and General Guillermo Rodríguez Lara (February 1972–January 1976). The last of these regimes was replaced by a military "Triumvirate" (1976–79), which, under the tutelage of the country's remarkably shortsighted economic power groups, turned policy sharply toward the right. At the same time, the Triumvirate established the conditions for the transition to the electoral democracy that has manifested increasing signs of fragility since, at least, the conflict-ridden and corrupt presidency of Abdalá Bucaram (August 1996–February 1997). Popularly known as "El Loco," he was driven out of office by the combined opposition of the country's social movements and elites.

To review the erratic history of state building and socioeconomic reform in Ecuador, General Enríquez's brief interlude in power took place in the midst of the acute social and political conflicts that saw fifteen heads of state rotate through the presidential office in the course of the 1930s depression. The participation of members of Ecuador's Socialist Party was "decisive" in his government (Moreano 1991, 194), which expedited the country's first labor code, limited the privileges of foreign corporations (e.g., by eliminating tax exemptions), attempted to strengthen the Central Bank, and maintained political liberties that allowed the left to organize not only among the urban but also among the rural working classes and the coastal and highland peasantries (see, e.g., Cueva 1990, 103). Moreover, indigenous communities were recognized through the Law of Communes (Ley de Comunas), which opened the door to indigenous political organization at the local level. In contrast to the mildly reformist, nationalist, and inclusionary policies of the military dictatorship, the civilian elites who managed to divide the armed forces and arrange the deposition of Enríquez in mid-1938 spearheaded "a purge of the democratic wing of the army" and turned to widespread repression (Cueva 1990, 104).

Following the recovery of the export economy during World War II, the government of Plaza Lasso, supported by U.S. advisors, began to construct the modern "developmentalist state." Active government intervention—to construct the road and port infrastructure and extend the agricultural frontier—created the conditions for the "banana boom" (1948–65). Neither the highly unequal distribution of land nor the prevalence of precapitalist social relations in agriculture was addressed by the government, but both land and credit policies in the newly opened-up agricultural areas favored small and medium-scale banana producers. The province of El Oro, where such policies set the general tone of social and economic transformation, ranked fourth in 1974 among Ecuador's (then) twenty provinces on most social and economic indicators as well as on per capita productivity.[4] By 1999, the country was divided into twenty-two provinces and 214 cantons. Clearly, the country's military influenced the manner in which the agricultural frontier was settled in El Oro, a strategic border province that had been occupied by Peruvian forces during the 1941 war between the two countries.

It remained for the simultaneously reformist and repressively anticommunist military government of the mid-1960s, tutored by U.S. advisors inspired by the Alliance for Progress and pressured by social agitation in the countryside, to address the "social question" in the agrarian sector. Not only was land ownership highly concentrated, but precapitalist social relations, in the form of *huasipungeros,* still prevailed in the indigenous zones of the highlands. However, by the 1960s, some *huasipungueros* had been organized into the Ecuadorian Federation of Indians (FEI), established in 1947 under the aegis of the Communist Party. In December 1961, between ten and fifteen thousand FEI-affiliated highland Indians took over the streets of Quito in a peaceful but "threatening" demonstration for agrarian reform (Guerrero 1993, 91–92). Meanwhile, agrarian organization and conflict had also erupted in the coastal areas: John Forrest Uggen (1975) documented eighteen strikes and land invasions during 1960–63 in the province of Guayas alone, that is, in the rural seat par excellence of the country's Guayaquil-based elites.

The agrarian reform law decreed by the military government in July 1964 was designed to defuse such conflicts by abolishing precapitalist social relations and promoting the creation of a rural middle class, through some land redistribution but principally by extending the agricultural frontier through colonization. That law also created the Institute of Agrarian Reform and Colonization (Instituto de Reforma Agraria y Colonización [IERAC]), which functioned, at times for the better and at times for the worse, until 1994, when it was abolished by a neoliberal-inspired agrarian development law. As mild as the 1964 reform law may have been, it was resisted by the most traditional sectors of the highland landlord class, and both coastal and highland landlords joined forces to ensure that neither agricultural workers nor peasants were represented in IERAC's executive council (North 1985, 434–38). Meanwhile the junta's efforts to promote industrialization, reform customs administration in the port of Guayaquil, and raise import taxes earned it the enmity of the coastal elites. Once the danger of social revolution was apparently dampened by some reform or at least the promise of reform—combined with the repression of left and popular groups that, if left free to organize, might have built up the capacity for ensuring the implementation of the new agrarian law—highland and coastal elites joined forces once again and "resorted to economic sabotage" to oust the military junta (Isaacs 1993, 3). They engineered a transition to a civilian government that they could more easily control (Cueva 1991, 156, 160; Moreano 1991, 190). Nevertheless, conflict in the rice-production zones of the coast reached such alarming proportions that, in 1970, the elected government of Velasco Ibarra issued Decree 1001, which abolished *precarismo* (precapitalist tenancy relations) and led to some land redistribution in those areas.

With the petroleum export boom on the horizon, in 1972 reformist and nationalist sectors of the army again led a coup, this time to ensure that the foreign exchange earned from oil would be spent on national social and economic development rather than falling into the hands of foreign corporations and their local allies among Ecuador's dominant classes. The coup makers ambitiously promised that the new government would not only "'carry out a real and effective agrarian reform,' distributing land to those 'who genuinely and directly work it,' but that 'it would undertake all the necessary steps to eliminate the economic, political, social, cultural, military, and ideological aspects of the country's dependency'" (quoted in Cueva 1991, 167).

The military's agrarian reform law (1973) fell far short of the promises made, since coastal and highland landlords, with the support of all other elite sectors, succeeded in watering down the draft proposals presented by the military government (North 1985, 439–41). Indeed, one prominent scholar of Ecuadorian agrarian policies has argued that all the reform laws since 1964 were fundamentally oriented to facilitate the growth of "modern [large-scale] business farming" (Redclift 1978, 24). The Rodríguez Lara government, however, did renegotiate contracts with the foreign petroleum companies, thereby ensuring for Ecuador the resources that allowed the regime to undertake infrastructure construction programs, expand public education and health services, and provide generous subsidies for import-substitution industrialization (ISI) as well as agricultural modernization. These policies favored the expansion of urban middle classes, which prospered with economic diversification and the rapid expansion of public employment. At the same time, the dominant classes "conserved the bases of their power intact" (Cueva 1991, 169).

In fact, both coastal and highland elites benefited immensely from the subsidies provided to the private sector for modernizing their old enterprises and establishing new ones. Nonetheless, they perceived the Rodríguez Lara government as dangerously statist and menacingly reformist and united yet again to force the resignations of progressive ministers and ultimately of Rodríguez Lara himself. He was replaced in 1976 by a Triumvirate composed of the heads of the three branches of the armed forces. The Triumvirate, in turn, issued a new law of agrarian colonization (1977) for the Amazonian region, but it did not cut back on investment in education, public health, rural electrification, and the like or on subsidies to the private sector. The availability of foreign exchange from the export boom facilitated particularly capital-intensive forms of ISI and agricultural modernization (Larrea Maldonado and North 1997, 920–21), and when petroleum income began to decline, not only the state but also the private sector turned to aggressive borrowing abroad: Ecuador's total foreign debt grew from $1,263.7 million in 1977 to $3,544 million in 1979 (Ortiz Crespo 2000b, 54). This set the stage for the ongoing fiscal crisis of the state and for the private sector's repeated demands for state assistance under the civilian governments of the 1980s and 1990s.

Despite the very high growth rates of the petroleum boom years, between 1974 and 1982, the percentage of wage workers in the economically active population (EAP) actually fell in both rural and urban areas; approximately one hundred thousand jobs were lost in the countryside, and 62 percent of the remaining agricultural labor force was underemployed around 1980 (PNUD 1999, 39). Thus, while genuine agrarian reform was blocked, wage employment in agriculture was reduced, and few jobs were created in new industrial activities. Nevertheless, as long as overall growth rates remained high, truncated agrarian reform was compensated to some degree by public and private construction booms. They provided employment for unskilled workers in the rural areas and urban centers to which both indigenous and mestizo peasants migrated in increasing numbers, either periodically or permanently. This was the case because the amount of good-quality agricultural land that was redistributed under the terms of the 1973 agrarian reform law remained paltry while the support programs necessary for making land-reform beneficiaries' enterprises viable—extension services, reasonably priced credit, favorable or at least predictable access to markets, and so on—were not forthcoming. Indeed, the modern agricultural sector or business farmers received almost eight times more support than the traditional sector, which was composed largely of indigenous highland peasants (Larrea Maldonado 1992, 157).

The fundamental weakness of all the military-led efforts to strengthen public institutions, undertake redistributive reforms, and sponsor a socially more benign pattern of development (through progressive-tax, industrial-promotion, agrarian, and other policies) resided in their lack of organized social and political support that might have countered the power of the country's dominant classes. Nevertheless, since these dictatorships did not engage in repressive excesses equivalent to those of the southern-cone military regimes of the 1970s and 1980s, the majority of Ecuadorians remember the last military government quite nostalgically as a *dictablanda* rather than a *dictadura,* that is, as a soft rather than a harsh dictatorship (Isaacs 1993, 4–6). Indeed, the democratically elected civilian governments of the 1980s and 1990s—and the country's economic elites—have tended to be viewed as both more corrupt and incapable of ensuring basic living standards.

With regard to the capacity of the dominant classes to block the military's reformist initiatives, several scholars have analyzed their evolution into monopolistic and/or oligopolistic regionally based networks that set the limits to, if not the agenda of, public policy. The banana boom allowed coastal elites to recover from the crisis of the cacao cycle and the depression, and that sector's profits were increasingly concentrated in the hands of a small number of export enterprises based in Guayaquil. David P. Hanson (1971) found that by the late 1960s, ten coastal "business empires," integrated through family ties and/or interlocking directorates, had consolidated to incorporate the region's largest commercial (especially import-export), financial, agricultural, industrial, and media interests. Industrial establishments at the time were recent "additions to established 'family empires'" (Hanson 1971, 85) that engaged in portfolio diversification to minimize risks (Conaghan 1988, 41). Guillermo J. Navarro's study of the concentration of capital in the mid-1970s found two "economic super groups" of national dimensions based in Guayaquil (1976, 80–97), while Catherine M. Conaghan provides evidence concerning the ways in which the largest business groups of both the coastal and highland regions associated themselves with multinational capital during that decade (1988, 57). Her survey of seventy industrialists also found that the great majority of them emerged from the traditional dominant classes and perceived redistributive policies as threatening since the elites and the urban middle classes constituted their domestic market (Conaghan 1988, 46, 68–70).

The transition from military to "democratic" civilian rule in Ecuador thus took place within a society in which "rent-seeking commercial-financial-industrial groups that emerged out of, or were linked to, the traditional landlord classes penetrated directly into the state apparatus" (Larrea Maldonado and North 1987, 924) and were accustomed to equating their private interests with national interests. This was an elite that saw the state's role as "simply that of maintaining 'order and vigilance.'. . . While highly dependent on the state for subsidized development, industrialists espouse[d] laissez-faire principles. Confronted with popular demands for political participation and economic equality, capitalists call[ed] for more production and exclusion of the people from its benefits. As they demand[ed] preferential access to and security from the state, they den[ied] the legitimacy of similar claims by other social actors" (Conaghan 1988, 70). The transition evolved in the midst of deepening economic and social crises; a weakly developed, regionally divided, clientelistic, and personalistic party system without citizen involvement or loyalty; the steady weakening of labor organizations as full-time employment became an increasingly scarce commodity; deepening social inequalities; and the gestation of highland- and Amazonian region–based indigenous movements that achieved notable organizational coherence by 1990, when the first of the indigenous rebellions that punctuated that decade's history took place (see, e.g., Zamosc 1993).

The "Washington Consensus" and the Dismantling of the State

The first post-transition civilian government (1979–84), headed by Osvaldo Hurtado following the death of president Jaime Roldós in a plane accident, pursued a standard set of stabilization policies. It resisted the full-scale application of the neoliberal structural adjustment policies (SAPs) embodied in the "Washington Consensus" and favored by the elites who had perceived the Rodríguez Lara regime as statist and menacingly reformist. The country's dominant classes also viewed Hurtado, a reformist Christian democrat, as a dangerous "socialist"—even as a "communist"—and fended off just about all government efforts to respect the campaign proposals on which the Roldós-Hurtado team had been elected to power, including tax, administrative, agrarian, educational, and political reforms (Mills 1991).

In his efforts to obtain private-sector cooperation in the midst of the debt crisis that erupted in 1982, Hurtado was persuaded to take measures that may be considered a prelude to the bank salvage operations pursued later by

President Mahuad in the late 1990s. Specifically, in 1983, Hurtado agreed to prevent the collapse of the "modern" private sector by converting its $1.6 billion debt into *sucres*. To place into perspective the extent to which the private sector had engaged in borrowing abroad, its foreign debt in that year doubled all the assets of Ecuador's private banks (Canessa Oneto 1999, 28).

It was Hurtado's successor to the presidency, coastal business leader and Social Christian Party head León Febres Cordero (1994–98), who began to implement the neoliberal agenda in a forceful fashion. His policies made him the darling of the IFIs and the U.S. government, which invited him to Washington in 1986 to congratulate Ecuador as a model of good economic management. To be sure, Febres Cordero turned to deficit financing and "populist" measures as petroleum prices plummeted later that same year and a major earthquake destroyed the pipeline that carried petroleum from the Amazonian production fields to the coastal port, cutting off all oil exports for six months (Estupiñan de Burbano 1991, 342). However, it is not in the "populist excesses" of his last two years in power but in his policies toward the private sector, public institutions, and state security that Febres Cordero's enduring legacy lies.

Hurtado's "sucretization" of the private-sector debt was criticized by various progressive commentators. However, it was Febres Cordero's decision to delink the "sucretized" debts from exchange-rate variations and extend their repayment period from three to seven years that became the "gift of the century"—adding up to more than $1.3 billion—to the benefit of a small number of enterprises that included foreign banks (Acosta 1994, 234–35). That favor to his business allies also seriously weakened the position of the Central Bank, which had to assume the dollar payments while the *sucre* was devalued (Jácome 1994, 24–25, 16n). But the Central Bank was only one of several key public institutions that suffered damage during the Febres Cordero presidency; others included the national social security system (IESS), the state petroleum corporation (CEPE), the public electricity company (INICEL), and agencies that had provided subsidies for basic consumption (Roldós Aguilera 1991, 343–45). It would appear that the government deliberately weakened those (far from perfect) institutions in order to buttress later arguments in favor of privatization.

At the same time that the viability of the social and economic institutions of the state was being undermined, a minor guerrilla insurgency provided the Febres Cordero government with an excuse for engaging in egregious human rights abuses and setting up new police institutions that were not dismantled during succeeding administrations. According to a highly respected human rights leader, "torture became routine," Febres Cordero's "most fatal legacy" being "the establishment of a carefully structured repressive apparatus" that

included four new police units, one of which operated in a "clandestine criminal fashion" directly under the control of the Ministry of the Interior. Furthermore, members of these units worked as private guards, while retired police and military officers were often contracted by the private security firms
that began to proliferate in Ecuador in the mid-1980s. Thus public security
institutions became informally linked to private security enterprises, some of
which, in turn, began to provide legal cover for the operation of various
"armed groups" of the extreme right.[5]

While the Hurtado and Febres Cordero administrations' private-sector
bailouts set part of the stage for the financial debacle of the Mahuad presidency, its proximate causes lay in the 1994 General Law of Financial Institutions. This law was passed during the tenure of another president of the political right, Sixto Durán Ballén (1992–96), as part of a program to modernize
and liberalize financial markets. By eliminating the possibility of intervention by the Superintendency of Banks and leaving supervision of the numerous new banks that were created under the auspices of the new legislation at
"minimal levels," the law "was an invitation to disaster: a series of unscrupulous bankers concentrated credit in their own real or fictitious enterprises,
channeling the savings of their clients toward their own personal enrichment"
(Ortiz Crespo 2000b, 51).

As the country's banks were left to largely regulate themselves, Durán
Ballen's government also pushed through new agrarian legislation, sponsored
by the US-AID–supported think tank of the landlord class, to guarantee
property rights and liberalize land markets. Effectively, the redistributive
clauses of all earlier legislation were eliminated by the 1994 Law of Agrarian
Development, and IERAC was abolished, to be replaced by a new National
Institute of Agrarian Development (INDA). Nevertheless, in response to a
second highland- and Amazonian-wide indigenous *levantamiento*, or uprising,
directed specifically against the proposed law, communal property was left
with some protection, and Article 36 recognized the right of indigenous and
Afro-Ecuadorian peoples to the possession of their "ancestral lands." That
concession had the greatest potential impact in the Amazonian region, where
for decades various indigenous peoples had been protesting the expansion of
the petroleum industry, and in the northwestern province of Esmeraldas,
largely populated by people of African descent (Navarro, Vallejo, and Villaverde 1996, 32–39).

In brief, as post-transition civilian governments pursued the SAPs favored
by the IFIs and major donor nations by slimming down the state, they also
grappled with the foreign debt (which, as noted, reached $17.4 billion and ab-
sorbed 45–50 percent of the public budget by 1999); unstable export markets; chronic budget deficits (generated not only by subsidies but also by the

incapacity or unwillingness of successive governments to raise taxes); and natural disasters (el Niño in 1982–83 and again in 1997–98, the earthquake of 1986, and economically damaging volcanic activity in 2000). Public expenditure as a proportion of GDP fell from 20.5 percent in 1982 to 11.0 percent in 1992, and social services deteriorated with dramatic cutbacks in education and health budgets. During the same time, the informal sector burgeoned as formal employment opportunities in both public and private institutions dried up: wage employment as a proportion of total employment declined from 65.7 to 55.7 percent in the urban sector, and from 38.5 to 33.7 percent in the countryside (Larrea Maldonado 1998, 188–89), undermining the bases for union organization. Not surprisingly, income distribution also worsened in a country historically characterized by profound social inequalities: from 1988 to November 1993, "the income of the top decile rose from twenty-four times that of the bottom decile to thirty times" (Larrea Maldonado 1998, 194).

The mostly rural indigenous peoples (perhaps 20–25 percent of the total population) were particularly affected by these policies and trends: in 1995, 73.2 percent subsisted below the poverty line and 36.7 percent in conditions of indigence, in contrast to 54.9 and 19.0 percent of the nonindigenous, respectively (PNUD 1999, 44). Indigenous grievances found expression in the *levantamientos,* or uprisings, organized by CONAIE. The confederation initially focused its agenda on ethnic cultural claims and obtained a commitment to state support for bilingual education from the Democratic Left Party government of Rodrigo Borja (1988–92), which tried to resist at least some aspects of the neoliberal agenda into which it was locked by both domestic elite and international pressures. However, constituency pressure forced CONAIE to take on the agrarian agenda, and during the June 1990 *levantamiento,* it demanded, among other things, the resolution of seventy-two land conflicts between peasants and estate owners (Zamosc 1993, 289). The Borja administration subsequently responded positively to some indigenous territorial claims in the Amazonian region and agreed to a mostly highland-focused debt-for-land swap program administered by the Ecuadoran Populorum Progressio Fund (FEPP), a church-linked NGO that sponsors rural development programs (Navarro, Vallejo, and Villaverde 1996). These initiatives, nonetheless, did little to arrest the declining living standards and discontent of an indigenous population that had benefited, over the previous decades, from the expansion of public education and the decline of direct landlord control at the local level and that, for the first time in the country's history, was nationally organized.

All these trends—from the dismantling of state institutions and increasing control of the policy agenda by the country's rentier elites to further declines in living standards and the consolidation of indigenous organizations—came to a head during the presidency of Jamil Mahuad. In order to win the second round of the presidential elections of 1998, he established a working relationship, so to speak, with the coastal plutocracy. Shortly before his deposition, it was revealed that Mahuad's campaign had been largely financed by Guayaquil-based bankers who, in light of subsequent events, were clearly aware of the infirm state of the financial institutions they owned: in October 1999, a few months after his arrest on corruption charges, Fernando Aspiazú, the principal owner of the Banco del Progreso, admitted that he had contributed three million dollars to Mahuad's campaign chest (Saad Herrería 2000, 134).

The Culmination of the Crisis of the State and Society

As noted earlier, the 1994 financial-sector modernization law opened the floodgates to risky and corrupt practices, which included loans to "ghost" or fictional enterprises owned by the principal shareholders of the banks. Those practices ultimately undermined just about the entire private banking system. As Mahuad was inaugurated in August 1998, the devastating effects of the 1997–98 El Niño—combined with declining revenue from traditional (banana and petroleum) and new (flower and shrimp) exports—were taking their toll on the economy. In this context, when one bank (Banco de Préstamos) had already been forced to close on August 28, and the collapse of Ecuador's largest bank (Filanbanco) was imminent, the national congress passed a law (in November) that established the Agency for the Guarantee of Deposits (AGD). It provided 100 percent public protection for all deposits—large and small—in the financial system, but without empowering the AGD to touch the bankers' other assets (de la Paz Vela 2000, 16). Subsequently, the government pulled together a rescue package for Filanbanco, whose principal owner, Roberto Isaís, like Aspiazú, was a prominent member of the Guayaquil-based coastal elite: the package added up to about seven hundred million dollars, an amount equivalent to the entire public education budget for the year. Isaís then proceeded to sell a bank he owned in Miami and establish Ecuador's largest brewery.

On November 26, Congress also passed a law eliminating income taxes, replacing them with a 1 percent tax on financial transactions. As the tax began to be applied in January 1999, it provoked a 30 percent drop in dollar deposits and a 17 percent drop in *sucre* deposits in the national banking system, further weakening it as a whole (Hurtado 1999, 24). In March, in an attempt to save the system from collapse, the president first of all decreed "the most radical measure of the century" (Ortiz Crespo 2000b, 52). He froze half of all deposits in savings and checking accounts and all moneys in long-term deposits, taking two-thirds of the money supply out of circulation and effectively confiscating the personal savings of several million Ecuadorians to shore up the financial institutions owned by a few dozen families. Second, in order to raise government revenue to deal with the fiscal crisis of the state, he proposed to reduce government subsidies, on which the country's increasingly impoverished popular sectors had come to rely.

Mahuad did not succeed in either endeavor: another very large bank, Aspiazú's Banco del Progreso, was forced to close its doors while massive protests —spearheaded by CONAIE and taxi, lorry, and bus drivers' federations in March and then again in July—forced the president to revoke his proposals to reduce gasoline, gas, and electricity subsidies. In response to the March protests, Congress passed new tax laws that included the reintroduction of modest income taxes, and the government took various steps to open access to frozen bank accounts for certain groups of depositors and some institutions (including cooperatives). Meanwhile, an international team of experts was contracted to conduct an audit of the banks (May–June).

Without delving in greater detail into the health of individual banks or the breadth of strikes and protests—which included doctors, teachers, and others in addition to the indigenous organizations and the *choferes* (bus and taxi drivers)—suffice it to note that by the end of 1999, twelve financial institutions had passed into the hands of the AGD. The state thus became the proprietor of "70 percent of the net worth and 60 percent of the assets" of the country's banks (Ortiz Crespo 2000b, 52). However, before the AGD interventions were executed, Ecuador's private bankers, according to the estimates of a prominent local economist, Alberto Acosta, had received more than $2.2 billion dollars from the Central Bank, a sum equivalent to 15 percent of the country's gross domestic product (Saad Herrería 2000, 32). Thus Ecuador's "crony capitalism" reached extreme proportions under Mahuad, but the debacle of his presidency was made possible by the neoliberal adjustment policies pursued by previous administrations under the guidance of international banks and major donor governments, with the United States in the lead among them.

As the financial and economic crises worsened during Mahuad's brief but destructive passage through the presidency, and as the natural disasters to which the government was incapable of responding took their toll, living standards plummeted. Poverty and indigence rates, as noted earlier, had increased in the course of the 1980s and 1990s, and by 1998, when Mahuad won the presidential elections, 62.6 percent of the population lived below the poverty line (82.0 percent in the rural areas and 48.6 percent in the urban centers) (INEC 1998). By the end of 1999, according to the preliminary estimates of the Sistema Integrado de Indicadores Sociales del Ecuador, poverty affected 68 percent of the population (91 percent in the rural areas and 53 percent in the urban) as the vegetative economic growth of the decade (0.7 percent per year between 1990 and 1998) turned negative: −8.8 percent during 1998–99 (PNUD 1999, 17). Although many Ecuadorians responded to their deteriorating living standards (and also increased levels of criminal violence in both urban and rural areas) through strikes and protests, many others simply left the country. According to the Ministry of Foreign Affairs, in early 2000, there were approximately one million Ecuadorians registered in the country's consular offices abroad, and up to two million others may have left through illegal channels. If that was in fact the case, then almost 25 percent of the total population of about 12.4 million may have emigrated over the past two decades, with the numbers rising steadily during the 1990s (Barragan and Velasquez 2000, A3). According to other estimates, 10 percent of the country's economically active population had emigrated by the beginning of the twenty-first century (Acosta 2002). Even if these numbers are overestimates, an increasingly large proportion of Ecuadorians lived off the remittances of relatives who had left to seek work in Spain, the United States, Italy, and even Australia.[6] In 2000, remittances became the second most important source of foreign exchange after oil, reaching US$ 1.3 billion and 10 percent of GDP (Economist Intelligence Unit 2001, 8).

To return to the evolution of the financial crisis and popular protest, since the Central Bank printed more and more money in an effort to save the banks, inflation rates began to soar despite the very depressed state of the economy. Thus the *sucre* was once more placed under severe pressure. This, in the context of the generalized economic crisis, led President Mahuad to announce the adoption of the U.S. dollar as the country's official currency on January 9. He did so after having decreed a state of "national emergency" three days earlier, when CONAIE was already organizing meetings across the highlands in preparation for another national *levantamiento* (the fifth since the first in 1990). The events linked to that uprising and their outcome have already been discussed. What remains to be stated is that the coastal elites—to an important degree—succeeded in deflecting attention away from their own corrupt practices by claiming that the collapse of Guayaquil-based banks was essentially caused by central-government mismanagement and favoritism toward highland-based financial institutions. These accusations were then used to mobilize support among all classes of coastal society for decentralization proposals that would further weaken central state institutions.

Regional, social, and ethnic cleavages were dramatically reflected in the results of the municipal and provincial elections of May 2000. Social Christians and Roldosistas (Bucaram's right-wing populist vehicle) swept almost all positions on the coast. In the highland and Amazonian regions, the indigenous people's Pachakutic party won provincial *prefecturas* (governorships) for the first time in its history—five in total—and the Democratic Left (ID) registered important gains (Ortiz Crespo 2000a, 32–33). Significantly, the two retired generals who resigned their congressional seats to support the January 21 uprising won their campaigns: Paco Moncayo was elected mayor of Quito, with strong support from the capital's poorest districts, and René Yandun became the prefect of the highland province of Carchi, both running on the ID ticket. The popular opposition victories persuaded President Noboa to back off from the most severe aspects of proposed austerity measures, but the fundamental neoliberal direction of his administration, including dollarization, was not altered.

Ecuador's twentieth-century history and recent developments in the country contradict both liberal theories concerning the relationship between market freedoms and political democratization and Marxist expectations with regard to sociopolitical evolution. First of all, since the July Revolution of 1925, military dictatorships rather than elected civilian governments have most consistently pursued inclusionary policies that could have led to domestic market development and social progress. In fact, the country's dominant political-economic elites repeatedly blocked the military's efforts to, for better or worse, engage in nation building. When in power, those elites often proved themselves more repressive than the military—as in the case of the Febres Cordero administration—and almost always more rapacious, corrupt, and shortsighted, as in the case of the Mahuad presidency. In this regard, the support lent by young officers to the indigenous uprising of January 2000 was consistent with the military's past history and ideological propensities (see Fitch 1998, 61–105; Paz y Miño Cepeda 1993).

Second, the capacity of Ecuador's rentier elites to pursue their private short-term interests, rather than broader national interests, was facilitated by the market liberalization policies embodied in the SAPs of the "Washington Consensus." Imposed on a country where the state had never achieved a significant degree of autonomy vis-à-vis the dominant classes, deregulation, trade liberalization, and privatization policies led to public and political deinstitutionalization that increased elite capacity to extract resources from the state, withdraw capital from the country for saving and investment in safer havens abroad, and eventually provoke a financial meltdown. The dismantling of public institutions has been discussed earlier. With regard to political deinstitutionalization, as all political parties were constrained by external forces to follow the same policies, the incipient party system of the early 1980s was discredited and destabilized. Too incoherent or too penetrated by the elites, opposition parties could not develop the capacity to hold governments accountable to the broader public. Neither did the expected improvements in economic performance—competitiveness, enterprise modernization, and growth—materialize as public controls were eliminated. The culmination of these trends was expressed in the adoption of the U.S. dollar as the country's currency, a very questionable decision from the vantage point of economic development, social welfare, and political stability (see, e.g., Luque 2000; Sachs and Larraín 2000).

Third, rather than the urban working class, indigenous peasants eventually established the most coherent and powerful mass organization in the country, overshadowing the urban workers' and employees' union organizations, the student movement, and the left parties that had led popular protest in the past. The agrarian question thus remained on the policy agenda, and not only with respect to indigenous land claims. Although 61 percent of Ecuador's 12.4 million people were considered urban in 1999 (PNUD 1999, 17–18), that figure is misleading since it includes the residents of a large number of small cities and towns whose economic and social health depends on the surrounding countryside; in 1990, they made up more than 12 percent of the 55.4 percent of the population then classified as urban (PNUD 1999, 178). Moreover, not only the residents of small urban centers but even many medium- and some large-city marginal sector dwellers depend partly on agricultural production for their subsistence since they work as agricultural laborers at least part of the time and/or own or have relatives who own small plots in the rural areas. Consequently, rural conflict is likely to become more acute, especially in light of the fact that Ecuador's elites, over the last decade or so, have come to depend increasingly on old and new agricultural exports (from bananas to flowers) as industrial activity and revenue from petroleum exports have declined. In this respect, there is a policy lesson to be derived from the fact that the highest rural living standards in the country were registered in the province of El Oro, where small and medium-scale banana producers had obtained access to land and support programs in the past (Larrea Maldonado and North 1987).

Finally, the proposition that Ecuador's economic woes derive from the incoherent and incomplete implementation of SAPs—which was essentially the belief of the Noboa administration, the IFIs, and the U.S. government—has to be at least briefly addressed. Although there is no doubt about policy incoherence during the 1980s and 1990s, the historical record, as presented here, suggests that the sources of the country's instability and acute socioeconomic problems derive from the inequitable distribution of political, social, and economic resources and, indeed, from the weaknesses of the central state. To the extent that SAPs continue to reinforce the power of the country's myopic business elites and deepen dependence on volatile export markets, they are likely to worsen rather than relieve distributional inequities and conflicts.

In this context, the decision to dollarize was particularly worrisome since it made the country's money supply entirely dependent on historically fickle export markets. Moreover, given the strength of the U.S. dollar and currency devaluation among Ecuador's neighbors, already by mid-2001 cheap imports from neighboring countries were beginning to displace local production. At the same time, exports such as flowers and bananas were becoming noncompetitive in international markets served by cheaper nondollarized producer countries (see, e.g., Economist Intelligence Unit 2001, 7–8). Thus yet other socioeconomic crises loomed on the horizon as Ecuador entered the twenty-first century.

Margarita López Maya and Luis E. Lander

10 The Struggle for Hegemony in Venezuela

Poverty, Popular Protest, and the Future of Democracy

Prior to the 1990s, Venezuela was considered to be one of the few politically stable democracies in Latin America. The defeat of the dictatorship of General Marcos Pérez Jiménez in 1958 marked the beginning of the construction of a democratic political system through a series of pacts and implicit agreements among different social groups. Violent groups of the left and the right were subdued in the 1960s, and by the 1970s, two parties—Democratic Action (AD) and the Social Christian COPEI—had become the predominant political actors. AD and COPEI alternated in power and steadily penetrated other social organizations to the point, critics charged, of asphyxiating them. The system degenerated into what some have called a "partyocracy"—a dictatorship of two parties—and in the 1980s, under charges of massive corruption, both parties lost much of their credibility. Meanwhile, emerging social groups began to question the excessive rigidity of the system and argued for deepening political democracy. This weakening of the political system converged with the severe economic decay that became evident after the debt crisis that hit the region in 1983. Today, the strong two-party system that distinguished Venezuela from the rest of Latin America has disappeared. In its wake, old and new emerging actors seek to lead the rebuilding of a new hegemony and to establish a new political system with the necessary legitimacy to reconstruct and stabilize the country's principal institutions.

The recomposition of hegemony in Venezuela is occurring in a context in which the social structure and sociopolitical relations in the country have been radically transformed. Two decades of devastating socioeconomic crisis in the 1980s and 1990s have radically altered Venezuelan society. In the 1960s and 1970s, democratic institutions acquired consensus and, with the aid of industrial-led development funded by petrol revenues, established solid roots. Since the late 1980s, however, the social forces and actors that helped to construct or later became advocates of that system have lost legitimacy in the eyes of an increasingly impoverished population, who saw their aspirations for social mobility and well-being dashed by an entrenched economic crisis. As the central role these actors once played in Venezuelan political life has faded, new groups and actors have emerged and sought to construct an alternative project based on a different model of economic growth and the consolidation of a new political order. This has been a highly conflictual process, affecting ordinary citizens' daily lives through increased crime rates and political violence.

This chapter analyzes key social and economic indicators over the past twenty years in order to illustrate the context in which different groups in Venezuelan society have sought to redefine power relations and the dominant sociopolitical model. The successive failures of the hegemonic actors of the old political system to overcome the prolonged process of social and economic deterioration created the conditions that led, first, to the collapse of the political system and, second, to the emergence of a charismatic leader (former lieutenant colonel and now president Hugo Chávez) who has sought, via elections, to construct a new hegemonic project.

The Impoverishment of the Venezuelan People

The collapse of the Venezuelan political system is rooted in the socioeconomic crisis of the last twenty years. Since the late 1970s, the model of development based on import-substitution industrialization (ISI) and sustained by rents derived from the petrol industry experienced a process of slow decline. It has not been replaced, however, by an alternative model that promotes economic growth and improves the declining living standards of the bulk of the population. Three attempts have been made to halt this decline, each based on austerity and structural adjustment programs devised by advocates of the neoliberal model. This model is premised on the notion that the role assigned the state under ISI—a key regulator of diverse aspects of social life, especially economic activity—should be eliminated in favor of the free market. Neoliberal policies include the liberalization of national economies to the international market, the privatization of public enterprises, the deregulation and "flexibilization" of the labor force, and the elimination of universal social policies in favor of targeted social programs. As we shall see, each of these efforts lasted only a very short time, and each failed to stop the recession. Independent of the question of whether the failure of structural adjustment programs in Venezuela is due to political factors or to flaws intrinsic to the neoliberal model itself, the fact is that the majority of the Venezuelan population have seen continuous declines in their standard of living over the past twenty years, which they attribute to the collapse of the petrol rent-based model and the implementation of neoliberal policies. This perception has had irrefutable implications for the delegitimization of the old political system and its principal actors.

TABLE 10.1 Macroeconomic Indicators, 1979–99

Year	GDP (in millions of bs.,1984)	Growth (as variation of GDP)	Inflation (as variation of CPI)[a]	Exchange Rate (bs./$)	International Reserves (in US$ millions)[b]
1979	494,942	1.50	20.40	4.30	8,819
1980	474,205	–4.19	19.70	4.30	8,885
1981	467,395	–1.44	10.40	4.30	11,409
1982	451,781	–3.34	7.80	4.30	11,624
1983	420,099	–7.01	7.00	9.90	12,181
1984	410,067	–2.39	15.70	12.65	13,723
1985	415,349	1.29	9.10	14.40	12,341
1986	431,594	3.91	12.70	22.70	11,685
1987	459,613	6.49	40.30	30.55	9,402
1988	477,564	3.91	35.50	39.30	6,555
1989	460,813	–3.51	81.00	43.05	7,411
1990	492,170	6.80	36.50	50.58	11,759
1991	532,605	8.22	31.00	61.65	14,105
1992	556,669	4.52	31.90	79.55	13,001
1993	558,202	0.28	45.90	106.00	12,656
1994	545,087	–2.35	70.80	170.00	11,507
1995	566,627	3.95	56.60	290.00	9,723
1996	565,506	–0.20	103.20	476.50	15,229
1997	601,534	6.40	37.60	504.25	17,818
1998	602,558	0.20	29.90	564.50	14,849
1999	565,888	–6.10	20.00	648.25	15,379
2000	584,195	3.20	13.40	699.75	20,471
2001	599,968	2.70	12.30	763.00	18,516

SOURCE: Baptista 1997; IESA 2000; BCV 2002; and the authors' own calculations in growth for some years. Bold type indicates years in which adjustment programs were applied.
  NOTES: a. Variation in December to December consumer price index (CPI), metropolitan area of Caracas.
  b. Exchange rates and international reserves are as of last day of December of each year.

Table 10.1 illustrates the general macroeconomic trends in Venezuela since 1979, which marks the beginning of the downward turn in the economy. Data is available up to 2001, which includes the first three years of the Chávez government (1999–). It is worth noting that in 1999, Chávez's first year in office, the agreement signed by the previous government of Rafael Caldera (1994–99) with the International Monetary Fund (IMF) expired, and no new agreements have been signed since. The years in which adjustment programs were applied appear in bold.

The second and third columns of table 10.1 indicate gross domestic product (GDP) and its annual variation. These indicators clearly reveal the erratic nature of the Venezuelan economy since 1979, with growth and recession alternating year by year, resulting in a virtual stand-off between the two. The extreme dependency of Venezuela's economy on the export of petrol and its derivatives explains this economic trend to some degree. However, while most of the years with a growth rate of 5 percent and higher correspond to periods of significant growth in petrol-related economic activities, years with more modest growth rates are not related to this variable (as in the case of 1992). By the same token, a decrease in petrol activities does not necessarily correspond with a drop in GDP. At the same time, in 1984, 1989, and 1996—representing the first years of the three macroeconomic adjustment programs applied in Venezuela—there is either a drop in GDP (1984 and 1989) or stagnation (1996); in the subsequent three years, there is economic growth in two cases (only slight growth in 1986–87 and modest growth in 1990–2001), while in the third, 1997–98, there is an economic downturn. For the Venezuelan case, then, it cannot be argued that there is a direct relationship between adjustment measures and GDP performance. What is clear from table 10.1 is that in the first year of the adjustment there is a significant increase in inflation rates followed by a reduction in these rates, but since 1984 inflation has not gone below the double-digit mark. The consumer price index for this twenty-three-year period demonstrates that a product that in 1979 cost 100 *bolívares* in 2001 cost 39,380 *bolívares*! Another factor in the inflation rate is the continued devaluation of the *bolívar.* In 1979, one dollar equaled 4.3 *bolívares;* in 2001 one dollar was worth 763 *bolívares,* a devaluation rate of 17,744 percent. The social impact of these macroeconomic indicators is reflected in the employment trends data.

Table 10.2, which contains a breakdown of employment statistics from 1983 to 2001, indicates a clear downward trend in formal public employment. People displaced from public jobs are not finding work in the private sector; indeed, informal employment has increased much more rapidly than formal employment in the private sector. During the initial period of this series, the informal sector comprised approximately 40 percent of the economy, and after 1994 it increased substantially to around 48 percent and higher in subsequent years. The high percentage of informal-sector employment, which shows a general upward trend, stands in contrast to the employment trends between 1969 and 1979, prior to the collapse of the rentier model of development, when the average annual rate of increase of informal employment was just 0.1 percent (Valecillos 1992, 124).[1] In addition, unemployment rates increased by over 2 percent at the beginning of each adjustment program. In subsequent years, however, the unemployment rate varied considerably in each case.

The situation of economic decay, an expanding informal sector, and rising unemployment is reflected in the shifts in income and the distribution of wealth. In 1979, the average annual income was the equivalent of $5,345 in

TABLE 10.2 Employment Sector Trends, 1979–98

Year	Economically Active Population (EAP)	Unemployed as a Percentage of EAP	Formal Sector		Informal Sector % employed
			Public (% employed)	Private (% employed)	
1983	5,407,292	10.30	22.67	36.03	41.30
1984	5,716,207	13.40	21.78	36.42	41.80
1985	5,915,573	12.10	20.18	39.52	40.30
1986	6,107,115	10.30	19.38	39.12	41.50
1987	6,321,344	8.50	18.86	42.44	38.70
1988	6,572,049	6.90	18.71	43.19	38.10
1989	6,900,588	9.60	19.68	40.62	39.70
1990	7,154,622	9.90	19.85	38.65	41.50
1991	7,417,929	8.70	19.07	40.43	40.50
1992	7,537,817	7.10	18.05	42.35	39.60
1993	7,546,241	6.30	16.80	42.60	40.60
1994	8,025,928	8.46	16.40	34.29	49.31
1995	8,608,653	10.22	17.57	33.99	48.44
1996	9,024,627	12.43	17.13	34.24	48.63
1997	9,507,125	10.65	16.96	35.57	47.47
1998	9,699,330	11.28	16.33	35.47	48.20
1999	10,259,161	14.50			
2000	10,416,528	13.20			
2001	11,088,892	13.50	15.03	33.37	51.60

SOURCE: IESA 2000; OCEI 2002; and the authors' own calculations for some percentages. Bold type indicates years in which adjustment programs were applied.

1997; after twenty years of sustained economic deterioration, average annual income dropped to $3,049.[2] Income inequality also increased in this period. In 1979, the income of the richest 5 percent was 41.58 times higher than that of the poorest 5 percent; in 1997, it was 53.11 percent (Baptista 1997).

Another indicator of the situation of economic decay is poverty levels (see table 10.3). While there are different methodologies to measure poverty, each leading to different statistics, each reveals a general trend of increasing poverty over the past twenty years. For the data in table 10.3, households in poverty are defined as those whose per capita household income is below the cost of two family baskets; households in extreme poverty are defined as those whose per capital household income is below the cost of one family basket. The data reveal a steady increase in both poverty and extreme poverty. More specifically, in the first year of the three adjustment programs, poverty and extreme poverty increased dramatically in relation to the previous year. In addition, the percentage of households living in extreme poverty toward the end of the period under examination is higher than the percentage living in poverty during the 1980s. By the end of 1997, both percentages were nearly

TABLE 10.3 Households in Situations of Poverty and Extreme
Poverty, 1980–97

Year	Number of Households	Households in Poverty (%)	Households in Extreme Poverty (%)
1980	2,806,679	17.65	9.06
1981	2,880,084	22.82	10.71
1982	3,019,932	25.65	12.14
1983	3,130,682	32.65	14.95
1984	**3,183,339**	**37.58**	**18.90**
1985	3,211,477	34.77	16.60
1986	3,412,139	38.88	17.67
1987	3,541,504	38.84	16.61
1988	3,659,369	39.96	16.77
1989	**3,821,954**	**44.44**	**20.07**
1990	3,859,923	41.48	18.62
1991	3,914,165	35.37	16.01
1992	4,032,402	37.75	15.52
1993	4,190,519	41.37	16.81
1994	4,396,784	53.65	27.52
1995	4,396,354	48.20	22.95
1996	4,549,363	61.37	35.39
1997	4,468,445	48.33	27.66

SOURCE: IESA 2000. Bold type indicates years in which adjustment programs were applied.

triple what they were at the beginning of the series; that is to say, today nearly 50 percent of all families are poor, and more than one-quarter live in extreme poverty. Recent statistics from the Economic Commission on Latin America (CEPAL) confirm the downward trend of the impoverishment of Venezuelan society, though the absolute and relative numbers are different due to the distinct methodology employed in comparison to that used in table 10.3. According to CEPAL, the percentages of households living in conditions of poverty are 34.2 for 1990, 42.1 for 1994, 42.3 for 1997, and 44.0 for 1999. For the same four years, the percentages of those living in extreme poverty are 11.8, 15.1, 17.1, and 19.4. Both indicators are higher than the average levels in Latin America (CEPAL 2002).

This brutal and ongoing process of pauperization of Venezuelan society has been the driving force behind the diverse expressions of violence the country has witnessed over the past decade. As pauperization has advanced—and with it the concomitant delegitimization of the political process and its principal actors—there has been a dramatic increase in social mobilization, popular protest, and a struggle for the construction of a new hegemony.

Violence in the Social and Political Spheres

By the late 1980s, in the context of this growing socioeconomic crisis, the rate of violence rose significantly. Once a country with a very low level of violence in Latin America, Venezuela today has a relatively high level of violence, with homicide rates similar to those of Mexico and Brazil (Briceño León et. al. 1997). At the same time, popular street protest, which began to increase by the mid-1980s, became increasingly confrontational and violent, and illegal forms of protest became increasingly common (López Maya 1999a). Particularly after the Caracazo, a new phase in social behavior is evident, marked by greater violence in daily life as well as in the political realm. However, in contrast to other countries in the region, violence in Venezuela is primarily unorganized and unstructured, diffuse and limited primarily to the sphere of quotidian life (España 1994). In the political arena, growing violence and contentiousness have not yet led to situations in which social or political actors seek to employ violence in a systematic way in pursuit of their objectives. With the exception of the two failed coups d'état in 1992, in which violence was utilized as a political instrument, violence has not been employed as a political strategy by political and social actors. However, in the three years the Chávez government has been in power, political confrontation has become increasingly aggressive, though as of this writing the situation has not evolved into systematic expressions of violence. Nevertheless, there have been isolated violent incidents, such as the assassination of two peasant leaders, whose authorship remains unclear. It should also be noted that this new reality of greater day-to-day and political violence generates feelings of generalized fear and anxiety in the urban population, which in turn nurtures attitudes and behaviors favoring measures that propose to deal with these problems based on violence (Briceño León et. al. 1997).

Diffuse Violence

Homicide and violent crime statistics indicate the dramatic shifts in the daily lives of Venezuelans since the Caracazo. Since the late 1960s, when the democratic system was consolidated and armed insurgent groups eliminated, to the 1989 riots, Venezuela registered low levels of criminal and political violence. While violent activities began to increase in the 1980s, it was the implementation of a macroeconomic adjustment program, the popular uprising that followed, and the bloody repression exercised by the state to subdue it that led to an abrupt rupture of the basic understandings of Venezuelan society, in terms of both the country's democracy and how common people go about their daily lives. The new neoliberal discourse of the government of Carlos Andrés Pérez, coupled with the government's violent repression of the

Caracazo, signified a break with the hegemonic discourse of union and harmony that helped legitimize Venezuelan democracy in the past (see chapter 4). This rupture seems to have directly contributed to the dramatic expansion of daily violence registered by numerous indicators (Ugalde et al. 1994; Sanjuán 1997; Briceño León et. al. 1997). Field research also suggests that the Caracazo led ordinary Venezuelans to perceive violence as a permanent situation (Scotto and Castillo 1994).

Table 10.4 illustrates a dramatic rise in the homicide rate per one hundred thousand inhabitants and the variation in percentage terms in Caracas and in Venezuela nationwide. While some years show a decline relative to previous years, homicide rates have never returned to the pre-1989 level. Other indicators of the increasing violence in daily life are assaults and property crimes (Sanjuán 1997). These indicators have also increased, although not as dramatically or in as sustained a manner as is the case with homicide rates. At the same time, the statistics for these types of crime are usually less reliable than homicide statistics, since in societies in which the criminal justice system is mistrusted, many victims do not report the crimes committed against them, and they remain undocumented.

Another indicator of the increase in daily violence is the number of homicides perpetrated with the use of firearms. While in 1988 72.2 percent of

TABLE 10.4 Homicide Rates in Venezuela and Caracas, 1986–2001

	Venezuela		Caracas	
Year	Rate x 100,000 Inhabitants	Rate Increase (%)	Rate x 100,000 Inhabitants	Rate Increase (%)
1986	8		13	
1987	8	0.0	14	7.7
1988	9	12.5	19	35.7
1989	13	44.4	45	136.8
1990	13	0.0	44	−2.2
1991	13	0.0	46	4.5
1992	16	23.1	68	47.8
1993	21	31.3	91	33.8
1994	22	4.8	96	5.5
1995	21	−4.5	88	−8.3
1996	22	4.8	83	−5.7
1997	19	−13.6	64	−22.9
1998	20	5.3	63	−1.6
1999	25	25.0	81	28.6
2000	33	32.0	101	24.7
2001	32	−3.0		

SOURCE: Centro de Estudios Para La Paz 2002. Rate increases based on authors' own calculations.

TABLE 10.5   Car Thefts, 1990–96

Year	Rate of Car Thefts without Violence X 100,000 Inhabitants	Rate of Violent Car Thefts X 100,000 Inhabitants	Total Rate of Car Thefts X 100,000 Inhabitants
1990	151	34	185
1991	149	41	190
1992	149	47	196
1993	172	70	242
1994	157	82	239
1995	123	85	208

SOURCE: Sanjuán 1997, 225, 228.

homicides were committed with firearms, in 1989 this number increased to 85.6 percent, and to 89.3 and 91.6 percent in 1996 and 1997 respectively (Jiménez and Maestre 1998). The increase in violence is also reflected in the data referring to car theft. Table 10.5 illustrates that while there was a declining trend in car theft without violence after 1993, the cases of car theft in which violence was exercised against car owners have increased. More recent statistics indicate that violent crime in general has increased dramatically. In 1990, violent crimes represented 16.0 percent of total crimes committed, jumping to 36.0, 33.8, and 21.1 percent in 1999, 2000, and 2001 respectively (Centro de Estudios Para La Paz 2002).

Violent crime impacts not only the immediate victim but also victims' families, eyewitnesses, and the population in general through media coverage of such events. In one study, 17 percent of those surveyed in Caracas reported being victims of robbery at gunpoint in 1995, 3 percent had been physically assaulted, 11 percent had witnessed the physical assault of another individual, and 10 percent said a close relative had been a victim of homicide (Briceño León 1999). This abrupt increase of violence in daily life, coupled with the sensationalistic media coverage of such events, has created a profound sense of insecurity in the residents of Caracas. Thirty-three percent of Caracas residents report feeling insecure in their own community or neighborhood; 66 percent say they feel very insecure in other parts of the city; and 61 percent say they feel insecure when riding public transportation (Briceño León 1999).

Popular Protest and Weak Institutions

In addition to the increase in daily violence in the years after the Caracazo, Venezuelan society has experienced years of sociopolitical turbulence. In the context of neoliberal adjustment, the erosion of democratic institutions, and the shattering of the hegemonic order in place since 1958, there has been a dramatic rise in the number of violent or confrontational street protests.[3] It is not an easy task to quantify and classify the magnitude of popular protest. In order to do so, we draw upon the information contained in the database *La base de datos el bravo pueblo,* which reviews and classifies the news that appears in the Caracas daily *El Nacional.* The information contained in this database reflects a bias one would expect from a print-media publication, which often provides greater coverage of "newsworthy" protests—that is, those that are highly original, violent, or otherwise deemed of "public interest" by the media. The print media is also biased in that it tends to report on protests that occur in the capital city and not those that occur in rural areas. These limitations aside, this database is the most reliable source available for an analysis of popular protests in Venezuela over the past decade. It also offers a window into the way intellectuals and the middle and upper classes of Venezuela view what is occurring in terms of politics on the street.

The figures in table 10.6 reveal that for the years prior to 1989, with the sole exception of 1987, the reports of violent protests were less than 15 percent of the total for each year. The atypical showing of 1987 is due to one specific event that took place in the city of Mérida, where government repression, which led to the killing of one student, unleashed a wave of riots and violent protest there and in other cities throughout the country (López Maya 1996b). By 1989, the year of the Caracazo and the first adjustment program implemented by the Pérez government, the number of violent protests had increased to 25 percent of the total; it continued to represent about 30 percent

TABLE 10.6 **The Nature of Popular Protest, 1985–99**

Year	Conventional	Confrontational	Violent	Total
1985	206	41	15	262
1986	51	16	3	70
1987	36	15	32	83
1988	70	17	16	103
1989	75	85	53	213
1990	39	54	30	123
1991	8	36	31	75
1992	13	56	64	133
1993	52	64	58	174
1994	49	65	73	187
1995	64	62	63	189
1996	53	122	98	273
1997	81	44	50	175
1998	77	67	22	166
1999	43	239	72	354

SOURCE: *Base de datos el bravo pueblo,* 2000.
  NOTE: Based on news reports from *El Nacional.*

TABLE 10.7 Distinct Forms of Protest in Venezuela, 1985–99

Year	Protests	Highway Blockades	Land Takeovers and Occupations	Riots	Fires	Lootings
1985	12	1	16	6	3	0
1986	10	2	8	4	1	0
1987	21	3	2	7	16	6
1988	13	5	6	16	4	3
1989	24	13	18	39	11	26
1990	22	4	4	29	7	7
1991	11	3	3	29	16	4
1992	10	12	10	44	18	10
1993	21	13	10	50	26	16
1994	25	30	21	61	29	13
1995	27	15	14	42	18	9
1996	28	29	17	69	25	16
1997	21	18	7	21	12	1
1998	23	20	1	18	0	0
1999	38	56	26	49	8	5
TOTAL	305	224	163	504	194	116

SOURCE: *Base de datos el bravo pueblo*, 2000.
NOTE: Based on news reports from *El Nacional*.

of the total in subsequent years until 1992. In that year, when two failed coups d'état took place, the number of violent protests reached 48 percent of total protests. In 1994, the first year of the second Caldera government, this percentage dipped slightly to 39 percent and then fell to 36 percent in 1996, the year in which the adjustment program known as "La Agenda Venezuela" was launched. In 1997, 1998, and 1999, violent protest declined overall, though with some variation, to 28.4, 13.3, and 20.3 percent of the total, respectively. According to a recent report by the human rights group the Venezuelan Program for Human Rights Education and Action (PROVEA), 2000 and 2001 registered the fewest number of peaceful protests repressed by police forces since 1989 (PROVEA 2001). While the number of street mobilizations and popular protests has increased during the Chávez government, the decrease in the use of repression against them has contributed to reduce the use of violence on the part of the protesters themselves.

Table 10.7 highlights some of the types of protests employed by the population between 1985 and 1999. The data reveal the prevalence of riots over the more conventional, peaceful forms of protest employed frequently in the history of Venezuelan democracy. Also worth noting is the high number of reports referring to nonviolent protests that utilize illegal methods, such as shutting down public highways and land invasions and occupations, which give these protests a confrontational content. The height of such illegal protest activity coincides with the same years as the peak of confrontational and violent protest activity shown in table 10.6. Also notable is the high number of riots reported in 1993, when President Pérez was forced to resign from office. The combination of the statistics in tables 10.6 and 10.7 clearly demonstrates the atmosphere of social upheaval experienced in urban Venezuela since 1989.

Since the end of the 1980s there has been a rupture of what some have called the democratic consensus reached in 1958 and consolidated by the late 1960s (Luengo 1994). In this context, diverse and contradictory alternative proposals made by different political actors and social forces of different natures have begun acquiring greater legitimacy. A hegemonic struggle is taking place in which these different actors are seeking to establish a leadership role in society in order to assert their political and economic proposals. In the context of this struggle, those social groups that possess directly or have access to economic and political resources deploy those resources in the multiple outlets at their disposal. It is illustrative to note in this regard the way in which the print and the broadcast communications media have been utilized to portray favorably certain projects and the actors who support them. In the context of the vacuum left by the disintegration of the traditional political parties, associations representing the middle and upper classes, which self-identify as "civil society," have developed their own strategies to ensure that their demands and aspirations are heard. Their access to resources, thanks to their educational status and their family and social networks, facilitates their participation in this process.

In contrast, the participation of the vast majority of the population, which is increasingly poor and marginalized, remains restricted to the use of their only resources: their ballots and their disruptive power in the streets (Piven and Cloward 1977). This has led in the last several years to the surprising electoral victories of candidates who manage to represent politically the interests and aspirations of the marginalized sectors of society. The election of Aristóbulo Istúriz as mayor of Caracas in 1992, the ascent of the Causa R in the 1993 elections, and the electoral victory of Hugo Chávez Frías in 1998 are eloquent examples of this (López Maya 1997; López Maya and Lander 1999). At the same time, it is through the politics of the street, which disrupts the daily routines of millions of people and which further contributes to the erosion of already delegitimized institutions, that these sectors manage to introduce their demands and aspirations into the public debate. The principal demands of popular protests over the past decade have given rise to what we refer to as the "agenda of the poor," which may be grouped in three different categories: demands that refer to the lack or deterioration of public services; those that are related to the deterioration of income and wages; and those that seek to expand the spaces for the exercise of democracy and respect for human rights.

Three Years into the Chávez Administration

With the presidential victory of Hugo Chávez in November 1998, Venezuela entered a new phase in its process of transition. Chávez's victory—and the results of the five subsequent electoral processes that have taken place in the first three years of his administration—confirm that the traditional political elite of the past forty years has been displaced from its hegemonic role in the Venezuelan political system. This fact alone is surprising, because despite the weakness and decomposition of that elite in recent years, there was little evidence that new actors or social groups existed that could displace them so definitively in such a short period of time. The two pillars of Venezuela's bipartisan system, AD and COPEI, have been reduced to empty shells that lack new leaders and social support, with the exception of some regional or local backing that may allow them to maintain some presence in the political system. In the local elections of July 2000, an important number of mayors were elected on the AD ticket, and twenty-four governors from AD and one from COPEI were elected.

Since its beginnings, the political project led by President Chávez included a plan to convoke a Constituent Assembly as a means of "refounding" the Republic. This proposal was the procedural means by which Chávez and the new social groups supporting him would establish the institutional bases of a new hegemony. On the day he was inaugurated as president, Chávez decreed the date of the first referendum in April 1999, asking Venezuelans to approve the creation of a Constituent Assembly, which would write a new constitution. In July, the Constituent Assembly members were elected, and within a period of about three months, they presented their new proposed constitution to the public; it was approved via referendum in December of that year. An analysis of the new constitution will identify the strengths and weaknesses of the principal contours of the new political and economic order that has emerged. In addition, a brief evaluation of the economic and social performance of the Chávez government during his first three years in office will offer clues about the model of development that his government is seeking to implement in Venezuela.

Venezuela's New Bolivarian Constitution

The possibility of designing a new constitution that enjoyed a high degree of legitimacy was undermined as the new government sought to get it approved as quickly as possible in order to assure a favorable outcome. This generated tension and conflict, as well as dissatisfaction with some aspects of the constitution itself. The deficiencies of the new text will become clearer with time, but it is possible to engage in an initial evaluation of its strengths and weaknesses. It is worth noting, however, that in spite of the criticisms, in the two years since the approval of the constitution, it has gained acceptance and legitimacy.

One of the strengths of the constitution of 1999 is Title III, which refers to duties, human rights, and guarantees. Compared with the constitution of 1961, this title expands and updates the concept of human rights and gives international treaties constitutional status (Article 19). For the first time, the rights of indigenous peoples and environmental protection are recognized and incorporated into the constitution. The changes introduced in the judicial branch are also positive and have elicited broad consensus. Article 254, for example, guarantees the financial autonomy of the judiciary by establishing that its budget cannot be less than 2 percent of the total national budget. The constitution also establishes mechanisms for citizen participation in the designation and promotion of judges, free access to the administration of justice; and the restriction of the jurisdiction of military courts to military crimes, excluding cases of human rights violations from being heard in these courts. A new institution, Citizenship Power, was created that, along with the office of the comptroller and the attorney general, comprises the new Human Rights Ombudsman. The role of this latter institution is to promote, defend, and uphold the rights and guarantees established in the constitution and in international human rights treaties and conventions, as well as the "legitimate, collective and diffuse interests of the citizenry" (see chapter 8).

Several articles in the new constitution introduce new democratic and participatory practices in Venezuelan politics. Participatory mechanisms of direct democracy have been introduced, including different types of referenda that permit consultations with the population on key issues of public concern, the revocation of elected officials, and the approval or derogation of some laws. The constitution also establishes the right to vote for active-duty members of the military. The creation of the post of vice-president, a close advisor to the president and coordinator of public administration, allows for smoother functioning of the executive branch.

While the new constitution establishes the right of each individual to freely pursue economic activities, and property rights are guaranteed, it also recognizes the right of workers and communities to create associations of a social and participatory nature dedicated to any type of economic activity designed to improve popular economies, which are to be promoted and protected by the state. The constitution likewise recognizes the collective property rights of indigenous communities, as well as their right to participate in traditional economic practices based on reciprocity, solidarity, and exchange. In other words, the constitution of 1999 recognizes and grants legal protection to economic activities that are distinct to classic economic activity as conceived in capitalist systems. The breadth and strength of these types of activities will depend largely on the will of the government to promote such alternative economic practices. In this regard, with the approval of an enabling law in 2001, a new law of cooperatives and another for small and medium-sized industries were passed. New financial institutions to support the economic activities of the popular sectors have also been created, such as the Peoples' Bank and the Women's Bank.

One of the most alarming aspects of the new constitution is the change in the relationship between the armed forces and the civilian government, which weakens the principle of subordination of the military to civilians. In fact, in the new constitution the military is subordinate only to the president, who maintains the title of commander in chief of the armed forces. Military promotions are the exclusive purview of the armed forces, in consultation with the president only in the case of ranks higher than colonel or navy captain. The greater concentration of power in the hands of the president, along with an expansion of existing executive-branch powers, has also been criticized. For example, the president now has the power to legislate on any issue by obtaining approval from the National Assembly for an enabling law. Previously, the president could only legislate on economic and financial issues in times of emergency when authorized by Congress through special legislation. The enabling law of 2001 is one example of how this power is being used; once it was passed, President Chávez promulgated forty-nine laws, many of which were extremely polemical, particularly those such as the Land Law, the Liquid Hydrocarbons Law, and the Fishing Law, which affected the interests of powerful sectors of Venezuelan society. Those groups began to orchestrate a systematic campaign to challenge not just the laws but the very legitimacy of the government itself, which culminated in the aborted effort to topple the Chávez government via a coup d'état in April 2002.

The new constitution also prohibits the public financing of political parties, a popular measure given that this practice became associated with vast networks of clientelism and political favoritism controlled by AD and COPEI. It is possible, however, that the medicine will turn out to be worse than the illness itself. Two dangers exist if political parties are forced to rely exclusively on the finances that they are able to raise on their own. First, the restriction of the state's regulatory role in this regard undermines equal opportunity in terms of political competition. Second, the cutoff of public funds could inadvertently lead parties to adopt illegal means of financing. Parties that have members in public office might be tempted—more so under these new conditions than before—to siphon state resources to finance their activities. The private financing of campaigns and other political activities, made more necessary by these new measures, may give wealthy private individuals or corporations greater leverage to impose conditions on the political groups they support financially. Another problematic measure is the expansion of the presidential term from five to six years and the possibility of immediate reelection for a second term, which undermines the notion of democratic alternation in power and strengthens the likelihood of personalistic and authoritarian leadership.

The new constitution has been the object of other criticisms as well.[4] Some experts suggest that the excessive detail of some of its titles and chapters make it too rigid an instrument. Minimal attention to the issue of decentralization of public administration and the establishment of a unicameral Congress have also been criticized. For entrepreneurs and advocates of neoliberalism, the intervention of the state in the economy permitted in the new constitution is excessive. Some economists and Central Bank officials complain that the new constitution has restricted the autonomy necessary to maintain a stable currency. The new name given to the country—the Bolivarian Republic of Venezuela—was also the object of significant debate and dissatisfaction, even within the Constituent Assembly itself, which finally approved the name under strong pressure from the president.

Economic Management in Chávez's First Three Years

Despite the lack of clarity in the new government's economic model, its oil policy has demonstrated high levels of coherence. From its early days in office the new government carried out changes in oil policy that contributed to a significant rise in petrol prices on the international market. These changes have also helped improve the overall performance of the economy since 1999. Aside from oil policy, however, the new government has adopted economic policies that are not that distinct from those of its predecessor. Maritza Izaguirre, who led the Ministry of the Treasury during the final years of the Caldera administration, remained in her post during the first few months of the Chávez government—an indication that in the economic field, few changes were forthcoming. Yet the government continues to advocate resistance to neoliberal policies and has continued to search for alternative economic policies. The laws approved within the context of the enabling law are an example of this.

Since his presidential campaign, Chávez has received the support of individuals and organizations who opposed the "oil-liberalization" policies of the past decade, several of whom were recruited to work in the Ministry of En-

ergy and Mines (Lander 1998).[5] The Chávez government has also implemented important changes in the board of directors of Petróleos de Venezuela
(PDVSA), the state-run oil company. A clear shift from the oil-liberalization
policy came in March 1999, when the government agreed to fully implement
the production cuts agreed to by the Organization of Petroleum Exporting
Countries (OPEC) and other independent oil-producing countries. These
cuts, coupled with the initial recovery of the Asian economies by mid-1999,
led to an increase in international oil prices: in February 1999, Venezuelan oil
cost on average $8.43 per barrel; nearly a year later, in January 2000, it cost
$23.34 per barrel, and the average price by midyear was more than $25 per
barrel.[6] Despite the decrease in oil prices after the September 11 terrorist attacks on the United States, the average annual price of Venezuelan oil in 2001
was slightly higher than the estimate for that year's budget, at $20 per bar-
rel.[7] Throughout 2000 and 2001 the oil-liberalization policy was being overturned, and the government adopted programs to significantly reduce production costs and revise the policy of internationalizing the oil sector.[8]

The new legal framework for the oil industry will clearly have a long-term
effect. Under the rubric of the first enabling law, passed in September 1999,
the executive passed the Organic Law of Gaseous Hydrocarbons, followed by
the Organic Law of Liquid Hydrocarbons, enacted under a second enabling
law passed in December 2001. These two new laws annul all previous legislation on these matters. This legislation pursues two principal objectives. First,
by establishing a new fiscal regime for the industry, it seeks to revert the declining share of oil revenue that goes to the state's coffers. (In the early 1980s,
70 percent of government revenue came from oil exports; in 2000 only 40
percent did.) Second, it seeks to reestablish a leading role for the Ministry of
Energy and Mines in the design and implementation of public policies in the
oil sector. During the 1990s, with oil liberalization, this role had been
usurped by the top leadership of PDVSA (Lander 2001).

The new oil policy, while representing a clear effort to defend Venezuela's
national interests, and which could therefore be characterized as nationalistic,
is not sufficient to sustain a development model oriented toward improving
the living standards of the popular sectors. This would require other ingredi-
ents in the government's economic and social policies to ameliorate practices
that exacerbate poverty and maintain the marginalization of millions of citizens. In this regard, the Chávez government has been less successful.

Nevertheless, in the first three years of President Chávez's administration,
there has been a minor improvement in basic economic and social indicators.
Based on an analysis of macroeconomic trends, the Venezuelan Central Bank
(BCV) notes that 2000 marks a reversion of the negative trends noted in pre-

vious years. There was moderate growth in 2000 and 2001, though growth was slower in the latter year (with the growth rates at 3.2 percent and 2.7 percent respectively) (see table 10.1) (BCV 2000, 2001). In 2000, inflation decreased to 14.2 percent, and to 12.3 percent in 2001—the lowest inflation rates on record in the past fifteen years. The current account shows a surplus, and international reserves are at a satisfactory level. The fiscal deficit decreased from 2.6 percent of GDP in 1999 to 1.8 percent in 2000, but it increased to 4.0 percent in 2001.

In social terms, the situation is similar. In its October 2001 annual report, the human rights group PROVEA (2001) notes that during the first three years of the Chávez administration, health and public education improved, as did indicators of the population's nutritional and caloric intake. Access to free medical care has improved, and matriculation levels in all spheres of public education are up. Several problems persist, however. In the area of public health, there was a resurgence of dengue in 2001. Unemployment continues to be very high, at 13.1 percent, and the informal sector employs 48.1 percent of the economically active population.[9] These numbers are nearly identical to 1999, when Chávez won the presidential election.

The possibility of continuing these general trends toward social and economic improvement in 2002 is threatened by the international fallout of the events of September 11. The impact of the terrorist attacks on oil prices was almost immediate. The year 2001 closed with a drop in oil prices, despite the efforts of the OPEC nations to stabilize them. Given Venezuela's high dependence on oil revenues, this will have negative repercussions on the country's economic, social, and political prospects.

While conditions seem propitious for the consolidation of a new hegemony, the social and political groups that support the construction of a new national project and the alliances they have sought to build suffer from internal contradictions and tensions. The first of these alliances, the Patriotic Pole, was created in November 1998 in the context of regional elections. Initially, it comprised the Fifth Republic Movement (MVR), Homeland for All (PPT), Movement toward Socialism (MAS), and a handful of small leftist groups. Conflict among these groups was evident in the context of debates over the design of a common programmatic platform and in the infighting over political differences and bureaucratic posts. There were also conflicts within some of the groups that composed the Patriotic Pole, which added another dimension of tension to the situation. The MVR, the largest party in the alliance, has faced several internal challenges both because its membership included individuals from civilian and military sectors and because of its rapid growth as a party organization. As a relatively new organization created primarily for electoral purposes, it also faces the difficulty of consolidating its party structures. Indicative of these tensions was the split in the MVR in early 2000, in which one important faction, formed mainly of military officers and others who supported Chávez in the failed 1992 coup attempt, split from the MVR and supported the presidential candidacy of Francisco Arias Cárdenas—one of Chávez's coconspirators in the failed 1992 coup attempt. This group has now become one of the leading opposition groups to the Chávez government.

MAS has also suffered internal crises. Several of its most notable historic leaders split from the group when the party decided to support the presidential candidacy of Chávez in 1998. Another split occurred during the first year of Chávez's government due to disagreements with the Chávez administration. A third split occurred in the context of internal elections to choose new leadership in late 2001. After each split, the dissenting factions have joined the opposition to the Chávez government. The PPT, once considered a "strategic" ally by Chávez, has been a key source of leadership for the current government; several ministers and other important government officials were drawn from its ranks. But there have been moments of serious disagreement between the PPT and President Chávez. Some PPT leaders, including the party's former general secretary Pablo Medina, have left the party and joined the opposition.

In addition to these political parties and the solid electoral constituency coming from the popular sectors, the new hegemony is also supported by the military. The presence of active-duty and retired military officials in government posts at diverse levels is greater today than at any other period since the establishment of democratic rule in Venezuela in 1958. This presence has been an important source of stability and support for the transition process, but it has also been the source of unresolved tensions between the civilian supporters of the Patriotic Pole and the military sector. It is important to note that at the moments of greatest tension, the personal, direct intervention of President Chávez was required to calm the waters. For example, after the devastating floods that rocked parts of Venezuela in December 1999, confrontations between the governor of the state of Vargas and the military forces deployed to the area were aired publicly in the press, and it was only after Chávez stepped in to mediate in favor of the governor that the situation was resolved. In this instance, the authority of the civilian sector was reinforced. However, new tensions became evident in early 2002 when some high-ranking military officials publicly demanded President Chávez's resignation. The definitive solution to these tensions will not be found until the role of the military sector in the new political order has been institutionally defined. This is clearly one of the Gordian knots facing the new regime, and it will substantially influence the democratic character of the new hegemonic project.

While in each of the electoral processes carried out in Venezuela since

1998—six in total—Chávez and the forces that support him have demonstrated that they have strong popular support, by late 2001 the political polarization evident since this process began had become more extreme. In the final months of 2001, the opposition became increasingly belligerent, organizing numerous street protests, using extremely harsh language, and demanding nothing less than the immediate resignation of President Chávez. This exacerbation of the conflict started with the approval of the package of forty-nine laws under the rubric of an enabling law. Because the government failed to submit these laws to a broad public debate, powerful sectors of society rejected them all. On December 10, 2001, the opposition organized a successful nationwide civic strike. Convoked by the Federation of Chambers of Industry and Commerce (FEDECÁMARAS), the opposition demanded a review of all forty-nine laws, arguing that the rights to consultation and participation guaranteed in the constitution had not been respected. A more transparent process of public consultation and a clearer exposition of these laws' content might have avoided such a confrontation, but Chávez demonstrated little willingness to negotiate or compromise. On January 23, 2002, at the commemoration of the forty-fourth anniversary of the defeat of the Pérez Jiménez dictatorship, there were massive street protests both in favor of and against the Chávez government. Celebrating the date that democratic government had been installed in Venezuela, the opposition protesters warned about the authoritarian tendencies of the government. Ten days later, on February 4— the date of the failed coup of 1992, which had been declared a national holiday by the president—Chávez supporters organized a huge protest in downtown Caracas. Opposition forces dressed in mourning, carrying black flags and banging on pots. Press coverage of these events by both the national and international press was clearly unbalanced; opposition protests were presented as massive and popular, while the February 4 protests were practically ignored. This biased coverage has contributed to fomenting a distorted version of reality in which, presumably, the Chávez government lacks popular support and Chávez's removal from government is imminent. This was evident after the failed coup attempt in April 2002, in which Chávez was removed from office only to resume the presidency two days later.

The trends suggested by this analysis seem to suggest that Venezuelan society will face greater polarization and confrontation in the near future. In the context of possible economic difficulties, an unfavorable international situation, and a political scenario marked by weak institutions and intolerance on the part of different actors, the ability of the new hegemonic project to consolidate itself seems increasingly unlikely. With its weaknesses and defects, the emerging hegemonic project represents an effort to include and expand citizenship rights to those sectors of Venezuelan society that have found themselves on the margins of the processes of globalization and neoliberalism. The failure of this political project could mean the long-term postponement of the satisfaction of the needs and desires of the popular sectors that have been at the center of the official discourse and the object of some of its key policies.

Francisco Gutiérrez Sanin and Luisa Ramírez Rueda

11 The Tense Relationship between Democracy and Violence in Colombia, 1974–2001

~~ Among the many possible definitions of democracy, one of the best and most parsimonious is "protected consultation" (McAdam, Tarrow, and Tilly 2000). In this perspective, democratic governments ask the population to express its preferences, while being prevented from castigating undesirable opinions by a system of strong individual and social protections. Colombia has one of the world's oldest consultative traditions, which includes an early institutionalization of mass politics, regular elections, and strong parties that have created practices and perceptions shared by significant sectors of the population. Along with these elements, an equally notable and indeed eminent characteristic of the system has been a tradition of insecurity and lack of protections: civil wars, exclusionary institutions and/or informal political relationships, and in the last two decades a humanitarian tragedy of incredible proportions. There are a variety of ways to understand the tension that exists in Colombia between the two poles of democracy as outlined by Doug McAdam, Charles Tilly, and Sidney Tarrow. The political imagination of party elites is limited to the horizon of electoral practices, but elections unleash waves of violence and massacres with lugubrious regularity. There are real institutional guarantees for all political forces, but at the same time the specter of an alternation in power has been enormously traumatic. No one can impede a person from expressing an opinion (there is no *ex ante* control), but manifesting an opinion that challenges a powerful individual or group can lead to one's assassination (savage *ex post* control). There is freedom of association, but being a member of a labor union has become a high-risk endeavor.

This contrast is so abrupt and shocking that there always exists the temptation to reduce the situation to a simple reality: democracy is merely a façade, behind which exists a brutal and well-organized repression and "system of war" (to use the phrase of Richani 1997). On the other hand, others recur to the image of Colombia's democracy as a city under siege from violent elements, who are carrying out a voluntaristic war "against society." By contrast, we believe that a useful characterization of the Colombian political regime requires that one grasp the coexistence of consultation and lack of protections as representing two levels of social and institutional configurations that are each mutually irreducible. At times they are contradictory tendencies, at other times they develop along parallel lines, and yet at other moments they are mutually reinforcing. The ways in which they interact are not easily predictable, as in the case where consultations and protection always develop mutually.

In the period under consideration in this chapter, the dynamic tension between these two poles deepened dramatically. The political system simultaneously opened and closed. On the one hand, consultations expanded, incorporating new sectors of the population and creating new local and regional governments (departments and municipalities) closer to the needs of the population; as a result of successive political reforms, the influence of long-standing clientelist practices was reduced. The 1991 constitution, a genuine and important effort to modernize and democratize the country, attempted to capture this reformist initiative and provide the legal mechanisms and channels to make these changes irreversible. At the same time, the new constitution increased the checks and balances among governmental powers, making it more difficult for presidents to abuse their power.

By contrast, the system of protections, already significantly precarious by the late 1970s, rapidly deteriorated. In the 1980s and 1990s, the armed forces increased their autonomy from civilians in all areas linked to security (Dávila 1998; Leal Buitrago 2002). These decades witnessed two political genocides, the first at the national and the second at the regional level: the systematic assassination of over one thousand members of the Patriotic Union (UP) by drug traffickers, paramilitaries, and forces linked to the state; and the assassination of close to five hundred members of Hope, Peace, and Liberty (EPL), largely at the hands of Colombia's largest guerrilla movement, the Revolutionary Armed Forces of Colombia (FARC). Certainly, the traditional parties were not spared from such bloodletting. Added to this was a spiraling number of massacres against the rural population; selective assassinations of social movement and union leaders; and growing restrictions on basic liberties, including freedom of expression and protest. We believe that the tension between consultation and protection has been converted into a benchmark of political life in a number of countries in the semiperiphery, as electoral practices are expanded through democratic transitions or impositions from abroad. The Colombian case, however, has a number of peculiarities, beginning with the fact that Colombia is an example of a "first-wave" democracy (Mainwaring 1999; Huntington 1991) in the Third World.

This chapter attempts to explore the results of this tension, keeping in mind the context of institutional transformations as well as the dramatic social, economic, and cultural changes that have occurred over the last two

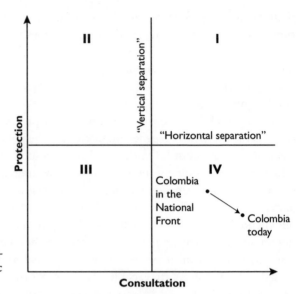

Figure 11.1. The place and evolution of Colombia in the democratic space.

decades. The analysis revolves specifically around two key questions. The first is taxonomical and related to the type of political regime that exists. Is Colombia a democracy? The answer is clearly not easy, as figure 11.1 suggests.

Figure 11.1 represents a two-dimensional space divided according to levels of consultation and protection. It should be obvious that those systems in quadrant I are democratic and that those in quadrants II and III are not. Existing criteria, both procedural and substantive, offer a comfortable "vertical division" between Type I regimes, that is, those of advanced industrial capitalism, and those of Type II and III. In the first category are those with consultation, and in the second are those with no consultation. Repression may be highly arbitrary, with widespread fear, as during the Argentine dictatorship of the 1970s, or there may be a relative degree of tranquility, with little open repression, at least for those who do not directly challenge the regime (e.g., the late Franco period in Spain or the last half of the 1980s in Poland). What these regime types nonetheless have in common is a lack of free and fair elections.

On the other hand it is much more difficult to establish a reasonable "horizontal division" between regimes. Colombia is located in the unclassifiable quadrant IV. Over the past several decades its place within this quadrant has shifted, as consultation (as in the constitutional reform of 1991) and the lack of protections have increased simultaneously. The spatial anomaly of quadrant IV has a clear theoretical corollary: there are no good explanations or adequate categories for a long-term coexistence of violence and genuine elections. We must therefore be content with noting this anomaly and focusing our attentions on a second question, which is more dynamic and related to the political system.

The second question is process-oriented. Can we speak of "democratization" in the Colombian context during the last twenty years? Has there been an "opening" of the political system? Clearly, there is the problem of operationalizing the term "opening" (Gutiérrez 2001b). The nature of the governing coalitions should be spelled out, including institutional frameworks, informal restrictions, and the general insertion of the "act of governing" in social dynamics. Though this litany may sound forbidding, it boils down to several simple questions. Has the coalition in power broadened or narrowed? Do opponents have more or fewer rights (protection)? Does the system allow alternation in some reasonable sense (consultation)?

Unfortunately, in the Colombian case such questions are rather ambiguous. In 1974, the starting point of the period under consideration, the basic political cleavage seemed to be between the defenders and the adversaries of the Liberal-Conservative alliance in power (the National Front). Other important cleavages—class and modernity-tradition, among others—basically overlapped with this one. Overwhelmingly, Colombian social science literature identified the "opening" of the system with the presence of new, "nontraditional" political forces (this, by the way, was an important motivating force behind the 1991 constitution). However, as we will see, the complex political processes that developed during this period operated over the political space in such a way that they separated cleavages that previously overlapped. As a consequence, "opening" the political system in Colombia can mean two things that today are different (but that were more or less identical at the beginning of the period): first, the evolution of power constellations around consultation and protection; second, the evolution of the participation of new political forces. It might appear logical to simply evaluate the first aspect as a function of the second, by studying the level of democracy through the lenses of political outcomes. This is not possible, though, because the political and the "substantive" cleavages no longer overlap. They are intermingled, but distinct. Actually, the possibility of considering them separately allows us to study the dynamic relation between the consultation-protection cluster and the political outcomes, and to observe the changing mutual impacts between sets of restrictions and incorporations, on the one hand, and sets of performance of political challengers in different arenas, on the other.

The National Front

Colombia has a long history of consociational pacts. The last one, known as the National Front, lasted from 1958 to 1974 and emerged as a solution to a civil war between the two traditional parties, the Liberals and the Conservatives, that resulted in two hundred thousand civilian deaths. The National Front had three key characteristics worth noting here. First, this pact developed a system of institutional exclusions, which included a provision that only members of the traditional parties could be elected to governmental positions.[1] Although both the Liberal and Conservative Parties maintained their majorities throughout the National Front period, the severe restrictions on political competition were continuously expanded. Moreover, when the bipartisan system was at the point of losing a presidential election in 1970 to the populist Alianza Nacional Popular (ANAPO) party of former military dictator Gustavo Rojas Pinilla, it responded to this challenge by fraudulently manipulating the results. Second, the two political parties that crafted the National Front had always been multiclass in character and at least since the start of the twentieth century had functioned as a mechanism of social mobility. At the same time, they were pyramidlike organizations, reflecting in some way the socioeconomic and regional structure of the country. Although many different political forces and social sectors could express and transmit their demands through the traditional parties, especially the Liberal Party, outcomes tended to have a high probability of favoring socioeconomic elites and local/regional notables. As a result, the institutional closure represented by the National Front signified a high level of social exclusion and blockage of channels of social mobility.

Even so, it is important not to overemphasize this dynamic. During the National Front, aggregate inequality declined, and as a result of reforms carried out in 1968, the beginnings of a tenuous welfare-state system were initiated. A sporadic and uneven development of social movements also occurred, focused on demanding basic structural changes. The rise of the National Peasant Association (ANUC) in this period is a good example of this dynamic (Zamosc 1986). Unfortunately, these efforts did not result in significant changes in the socioeconomic structure of the country. In contrast with other Andean countries, a real agrarian reform did not take place, despite the reformist drive of some forces within the political system that could not, however, muster the clout to realize the reforms. Frequently, social protests, strikes, and demonstrations were repressed—not with the brutality of recent times but nonetheless using laws and regulations designed to combat insurgency. To the extent that political elites believed the National Front to be indispensable, there emerged a growing equivalency in the mindset of elites between opposition to the Front and opposition to democracy. The Front agreement and the practices surrounding it simply did not provide elites with the necessary understanding and mechanisms to distinguish between antide-

TABLE 11.1 Abstention Rates in Senate and Presidential Elections, 1974–94

PRESIDENCY

Year	Election	Total Eligible Voters	Total Votes	Abstention Rate (%)
1974	Presidency	8,964,472	5,212,133	42.00
1978	Presidency	12,580,851	5,075,719	59.66
1982	Presidency	13,734,093	684,392	50.19
1986	Presidency	15,611,274	7,229,937	54.00
1990	Presidency	13,903,324	6,048,076	57.00
1994	Presidency	17,146,597	5,821,331	66.01
1994	Presidency (second round)	17,146,597	7,427,742	56.68

SENATE

Year	Election	Total Eligible Voters	Total Votes	Abstention Rate (%)
1970	Senate	7,666,716	3,967,006	48.26
1974	Senate	8,925,330	5,106,775	42.78
1978	Senate	12,519,719	4,169,834	67.00
1982	Senate	13,721,607	5,579,357	59.00
1986	Senate	15,839,754	6,869,435	57.00
1990	Senate	13,779,188	7,654,150	44.46
1991	Senate	15,037,526	5,512,703	63.35
1994	Senate	17,028,961	5,566,407	67.32

mocratic challenges and protests against institutional restrictions and/or simple social demands.[2]

A third characteristic worth noting is that the National Front introduced a series of distortions into Colombia's political life, which was already affected by high levels of personalism and factionalism. As a result of the explicit intent of the Front to impede a confrontation between the parties over access to governmental posts and budgets, the solution settled upon was an equal division of administrative posts, along with electoral positions, between the traditional parties. In effect, the level of interparty competition and belligerency was reduced, but at the cost of stimulating intraparty competition and factionalism, as well as administrative rigidities and a growing loss of ties between the population and the party organizations and their symbols. Thus, clientelistic practices were developed in which the main protagonist and referent was no longer the national party, but regional or local factions, generating a high level of particularistic demands. At the end of the Front period, electoral abstention reached 70 percent, an alarming indicator for any electoral system. (Abstention rates remain high. See table 11.1.)

When President Alberti Lleras Camargo was forced to offer members of Congress a supplementary and individualized budgetary allocation that they could dedicate to their pet projects (the so-called *auxilios parlamentarios,* or parliamentary assistance), in exchange for the approval of his reform package in 1968, a circle had closed. In exchange for a relaxation of the hierarchical and pyramidal structuring of the political system, a slow but methodical disorganization of the parties would take place, largely at the hands of regional and local political forces (again, this is especially true in the Liberal Party). Political incentives for party members were increasingly concentrated in obtaining immediate material benefits, something that both voters and candidates increasingly came to accept and expect. The political learning behind this process developed quickly, and as a result it has been difficult to end, particularly since the system worked well and those individuals who learned how to use the rules of the game tended to triumph.

The accumulation of these processes gave rise to two factors important to consider in the context of the questions raised earlier. First, the political stability achieved and the rapid decline of violence, two very tangible results of the National Front period, were obtained at the cost of a trivialization of political competition. At the end of the pact, there was a clear perception among large sectors of society that Liberals and Conservatives were largely the same and that the only true opposition was one that rejected the bipartisan system. However, it was precisely this form of opposition that was excluded from the political system. In terms of the conceptual framework outlined earlier, there emerged improved levels of security and protection, at the cost of consultation. It is almost as if in Colombia there were informal limits, the effect of which is that the sum of the "quanta" of protection and consultation is constant. If one progresses on one dimension, the other quickly deteriorates.

Another important result is that instead of producing reforms that addressed large-scale issues, integrating the national economy via public policy, the reforms that were most often adopted addressed particularistic demands, often with an illegal component to them. These policies resulted in territorial vacuums and "gray" areas in the institutional life of the country. This tendency favored the installation of political intermediaries who were very efficient but disloyal—or at least agnostic—regarding the formal rules of the game, generating in turn a growing vulnerability of the system to penetration by organized crime. As the demands of socioeconomic elites for a more active and confrontational counterinsurgency strategy increased, due in part to the growth of guerrilla movements and their activities in this period, there was a tendency to either ignore or even actively protect illegal practices directed by state agents against opponents of the political system. During the second post-Front presidency, namely that of Julio César Turbay Ayala (1978–82), the political regime became the latch linking formal and informal democracy, that is, increasing the compatibility between democratic institutions and the ambiguous and/or openly illegal behaviors that emerged from the government's counterinsurgency program. The immediate and direct costs of these policies were an abrupt criminalization of political life, a deteriorating level of individual and social protections, and a growing chorus of protests against these processes.

Democratic Formality and Informality

As Colombia's political system was undergoing these changes, important socioeconomic changes were occurring.[3] The country's economy was shifting from a reliance on coffee to mining; a dramatic growth in the importance of the illegal economy took place; access to education expanded while urbanization accelerated; the middle class grew and was strengthened; and finally, the role of the media expanded, contributing to the development of an active and independent public opinion. It was clear to most analysts that these changes could not be adequately incorporated into the system through the National Front. Thus, in addition to the endogenous changes in the political system taking place, these exogenous factors created pressures for further change.

During the government of President Turbay Ayala various events would have a profound effect on political development over the next two decades. The drug-trafficking business underwent a redefinition as a result of the move away from marijuana and toward a preponderant reliance on coca. This change brought with it significant organizational shifts in the structure of drug trafficking, including an extension of its reach throughout Colombian society and its ability to penetrate state institutions by becoming directly involved in counterinsurgency efforts. Those in favor of a hard-line military strategy against insurgency found among drug traffickers a willing ally with ample resources. While social and state actors sought out these organized crime syndicates as a mechanism to take actions against the guerrillas outside the legal system, drug traffickers attempted to combat those groups with which they had economic or military conflicts, or that obstructed their exploitation of peasant labor and takeover of peasant lands.

In many ways, the Turbay government marked several profound shifts in the basic institutional design of the political system. The political system between the end of the National Front and the 1991 constitution transformed the mechanisms of articulation between what was within and what was outside the law. Colombian *democracy* thus functioned not only within the system but also outside it through the inclusion of extrasystemic actors (not only guerrillas but also drug traffickers and paramilitaries); the explicit or implicit creation of "antisubversive pacts"; and the "incorporation of new territories," particularly those areas where the state was traditionally weak, into national accords. As a result, during the 1980s the Colombian state lost the monopoly of force, not only through its usurpation by armed groups but also through its delegation by state actors, creating the conditions for the formation of a new consociationalism. This new consociational system, with a strong regional base that does not easily relate to the national-formal political level, includes traditional elites, state agents, and organized crime syndicates. At the same time, the FARC, with its long tradition of "combining all forms of struggle," became increasingly involved in drug-trafficking networks (see chapter 5). Regional political pacts were also developed among political elites during this period, resulting in an overrepresentation of underpopulated rural areas in the political system (Gutiérrez 1996) and a strengthening of political intermediaries precisely in those zones where the line between legal and illegal activities was most diffuse and fluid.

By the end of the 1980s, the fall of the Berlin Wall and the growing demands from international actors for an economic restructuring of the economy made democratic informality costly. Nonetheless, at least three idiosyncrasies of the Colombian system gave the demands for neoliberal modernization a more complex and less obvious result than elsewhere in Latin America: an extraordinarily stable consultative tradition; a growing insurgent challenge; and finally an organized, powerful, and politically connected criminal syndicate that emerged just as the National Front was coming to an end. Colombia's elites opted for a gradual opening of the economy, and until the mid-1990s the economy did not suffer the extraordinary adjustment crises felt elsewhere in the region.

An additional transformation, related to the above, is the incredible capacity of accommodation by institutional structures to changing realities. The ability of institutions to adopt incremental adjustments in their policy-making processes and behaviors quickly became a way to govern amid growing instability. Both the ongoing internal war and the growth of illegal activities forced institutions to adjust to these new realities through a process of adaptive learning and the development of new rules of the game that were far from conforming to the basic behaviors of protected consultation. As a result, the line between illegal and legal behaviors and rules became increasingly blurred. Along with the "informal" rules that had long been a part of Colombia's reality, two new elements began to define the political system: the gray area of "there are no rules," which opens the way to improvisation, corruption, and abuse of power; and the chronic instability that has affected state and social institutions since the early 1980s.

A final shift that occurred in this period was a significant increase in political competition. This phenomenon is difficult to quantify, in large part be-

TABLE 11.2 Number of Lists Registered and Seats Disputed in the 1991, 1994, and 1998 Elections

	1991	1994	1998	Seats Disputed
Senate	143	254	314	102
House of Representatives	487	674	692	163
TOTAL	630	928	1006	265

SOURCE: R. Juan Carlos Rodríguez 1998.

cause much of this new competition has taken place within the traditional parties, which have witnessed an explosion of long-standing factionalism. If the number of lists of congressional candidates presented by both parties is a reasonable indicator, the results speak for themselves.

The new competition was in part the result of an expansion of education that took place in the early 1980s and that created political activism among a whole new generation of persons with new ideas, programs, and worldviews. Without question, both the expansion of drug trafficking and the internal war were also factors, insofar as they created new interests and polarized society.

With most of this new competition emerging within the bipartisan system, there has been no clear change in the expression of political preferences. What has changed significantly is the emergence of "new faces," both social and regional, within state and societal institutions. Although there is still a significant overrepresentation of landowners and cattle ranchers in Congress, there is much more diversity than in the past. It is likely that a similar process has been occurring at the local and regional levels as well. Most importantly, factions within traditional parties have gained increased autonomy in relation to the national leadership of the parties, as they have fostered and developed their own network of intellectuals, lawyers, and leaders; their own source of financing; and in some cases their own security forces. While before the 1980s factions were considered mere "dissidents" within the party, still dependent upon the party and confronting a well-oiled party machinery, this relation has been altered. By the 1990s, party factions had become small local groups, with a very diffuse identity (which is not the same as not having any identity), sense of independence, and access to resources independent of the center of the party, all of which distances them from the traditional world of party dissidents (Gutiérrez and Dávila 2000).

The changes in the political system since the Turbay presidency described here resulted in a growing gap between political elites on the one hand and socioeconomic elites and the middle class on the other, both of whom increasingly lost confidence in the political system throughout the 1990s. While economic elites still had "their" politicians, the loss of confidence in the traditional party structure was apparent at many levels. The problem that emerged was a "deterioration in collective relations," not a "burning of bridges." In the local elections of 1994, the upper-class sectors of Bogotá voted overwhelmingly for independent third parties, in an electoral switch that was much more rapid and complete than that of any other social sector (Gutiérrez 1995). The very negative pronouncements by the Business Council (Consejo Gremial) against the administration of Ernesto Samper (1994–98) suggested the degree to which relations between socioeconomic elites and the traditional parties had deteriorated. The Samper presidency represented an important turning point, not merely an aberration. The events surrounding accusations of links between Samper and drug traffickers during the 1994 electoral campaign, and the unprecedented tensions generated with the United States as a result, created a high level of dissatisfaction with the party system and, along with the factors mentioned earlier, contributed to the growing distancing of the upper class from the traditional parties. Tensions thus reached a high point, and insofar as actors had neither absolute power nor an ability to control events, it was difficult to reestablish traditional relationships.

These tensions are also notable in the various attempts to change the rules of the game in Colombian politics. A common element in all of the various political reforms introduced since 1970 is the conscious effort to limit traditional political practices. Aside from several specific reforms, such as the popular election of mayors, there were two important accomplishments. First was the dismantling of the National Front, which required a large number of adjustments in the political system, the last of which occurred in 1986. The end of the consociational system, which explicitly excluded third parties from attaining political power, formally ended, although a degree of consociational inertia might have continued to permeate the system for some time. Second, the 1991 constitution attempted to institutionalize an anticlientelist ethos in the political system. A series of rules that explicitly attempted to impede clientelistic practices was adopted. In short, if there has been a predominant tendency in the *formal* political system since the early 1980s, it has been to restrict, limit, and reduce the power of the traditional party system, although it is also clear that some events have helped the traditional system survive. Significant social sectors, and in particular socioeconomic elites, have attempted to "retire" the traditional party system, along with the politicians associated with that system. Have they been successful?

New Political Forces and Their Impact on Colombian Politics

Have independent third parties grown?[4] To what extent is "traditional politics" still dominant? What is the role of these new parties in the political system? Do these parties have a chance for significant victories within the Colombian political system? Will this system enter a period of political disorder with the entrance of these new political actors? And, more fundamentally for our concerns here, is the success of new forces linked to the democratization and opening of the system? The answers to these questions depend on the specific electoral arena examined. The trajectories experienced in the electoral and legislative arenas go in opposite directions. For the executive branch, elections have come to have a growing importance. The popular election of mayors since 1988 has become an important part of the legitimacy of the political system. Since 1992 there have been popularly elected governors, although with reduced powers. Even so, governors have on occasion managed to mobilize their populations behind specific issues, such as regional peace initiatives. The level of popularity and general acceptance of local and regional authorities have been high throughout the 1990s, even though a number of these authorities have been the target of corruption investigations. This tendency contrasts sharply with the skepticism that exists in most opinion polls toward basic governmental institutions such as the parties and Congress. Mayoral and gubernatorial elections have become an ideal electoral niche for independent third parties to develop their skills (Miguel García 2000), becoming the primary arena where nontraditional parties have achieved their victories.

The national executive has largely not shared in these positive tendencies, with the exception of an increased level of electoral participation. While presidents usually start their terms of office with considerable political capital, they quickly lose this advantage. At the end of their mandates, the tendency has been for presidents to leave office with low popularity ratings and to leave the office of the presidency with low levels of confidence. Since 1970, when an independent third party almost captured the presidency (Gustavo Rojas Pinilla of ANAPO), independents have not been able to break the hold of traditional parties on the presidency. Even dissident factions within the two traditional parties have not had luck advancing their candidates. Luis Carlos Galán in the 1980s and Noemi Sanín in the 1990s, the former in the Liberal Party and the latter in the Conservative Party, saw their efforts stymied by the traditional leaderships of their parties.[5]

In the legislative branch, the tendencies are more complicated, although there are also fewer analyses of this electoral arena. Local legislatures are increasingly being questioned. Department assemblies, which had become important centers for debate, decision-making, and corruption, have increasingly become known just for this latter characteristic. Municipal councils, while not suffering the same declines in confidence, are increasingly seen as impediments to the realization of goals and programs developed by mayors, and efforts have been made to reduce their powers. What appeared to have

TABLE 11.3 Evolution of the Vote: Presidency, Lower House,
and Upper House

Year	Presidency	House of Representatives	Senate
1974	5,212,133	5,100,099	5,106,775
1978	5,075,719	4,180,121	4,169,834
1982	684,392	5,584,037	5,579,357
1986	7,229,937	6,909,840	6,869,435
1990	6,048,076	7,617,758	7,654,150
1994	5,821,331	5,486,394	5,512,703
1994 *(second round)*	7,427,742	5,576,174	5,566,407

emerged by the late 1990s was a "local authoritarianism" based on a confrontational dichotomy between "efficient" mayors and "corrupt" councils. At
the national level, electoral participation in congressional elections has increased since the 1980s, although there has been some falling off in comparison with presidential elections (see table 11.3). In general, Congress has become increasingly vulnerable to attack. The 1991 constitution revoked the
existing congressional mandate, and the 1990s witnessed a series of scandals
that have gradually reduced legislative legitimacy. Connections between
members of Congress and organized crime syndicates, erratic legislative
records, the enrichment of members of Congress through a variety of legal
changes and rule-fixing, and vote buying by the executive in exchange for
funding of pet projects in congressional districts—these have all affected congressional legitimacy and made Congress one of the least respected institutions in the country. This situation has led to numerous efforts, mostly semi-
or even antidemocratic in character, to reform Congress, including a proposal
by President Andrés Pastrana in 2000 to call for a referendum to revoke Congress's mandate.

While the general impression may be that some of the reforms introduced
by the 1991 constitution, along with an inclusive electoral system, have created a high level of disorder in the legislative branch and increased factionalization within the traditional parties, the evolution of the political system
suggests otherwise. While it is certainly the case that factionalism within the
parties has dramatically increased—evident, as noted earlier, in the large increase in electoral lists presented—this seems to be more the result of an increase in particularistic demands than a result of institutional changes introduced by the 1991 constitution (a contentious issue that is still to be
resolved). The growth of these particularistic demands has made it much
more difficult for the parties to speak with one voice and develop an integrated and macrolevel program for the country. With legislatures increasingly
dominated by the competition among particularistic demands, independent

third parties and even "modernizing" factions within the traditional parties have seen only modest increases in their representation in Congress and city councils. While there was a slight closure to these forces in the 1980s, as institutional reforms were just beginning to take hold, the 1990s witnessed a greater opening to these forces, no doubt a result of changes introduced by the 1991 constitution, which provided more opportunities for third parties to achieve representation in legislatures. Assemblies, by contrast, continued to be dominated by the traditional parties, with usually just one of the two parties exercising control.

The traditional parties continue to win legislative elections with regularity. If instead of using the indicator of party representation we were to use another way of indicating the real power of parties, such as voting power within legislative organs, the magnitude of bipartisan hegemony within legislatures would become even more apparent. In order to show this more clearly, we measured the evolution of voting power between 1972 and 1998 in two arenas: (a) a sample of 210 of the 1,050 municipal councils in Colombia; and (b) the councils of the twelve largest cities in the country, according to the National Department of Statistics.[6] This permits the contrast between "urban" (big-city) and "nonurban" voting.

The Colombian legislative system, including Congress, assemblies, and councils, has remained relatively stable since the early 1970s. The ability of traditional forces to maintain their power is observed in the index of rotation in power of the parties.[7] As figure 11.2 suggests, we find some movement upward in the early 1990s, which then quickly froze. Of the 210 municipalities considered, 49, or a little over 20 percent, lived under "local hegemonies"

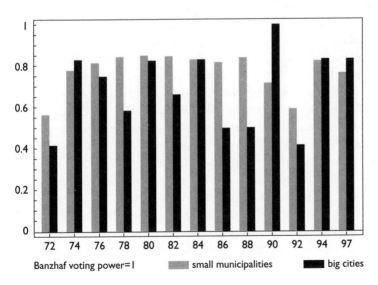

Figure 11.2. Proportion of councils in which one of the traditional parties (Liberal or Conservative) was absolutely dominant. Measured in terms of voting power by year of election.

where one party dominated and could count on having absolute voting power in the council (an analogous phenomenon had already been noted for previous periods by Pinzón 1989). There was a clear analogy with what was occurring in Congress: an evolution from a two-party system to a dominant party system, with the Liberals emerging as a dominant force, the Conservative Party losing ground, and a heterogeneous mass of independent parties attempting to break through. The voting power of Liberals in Congress since 1986 has also approached 1.0 for qualified votes (two-thirds majorities), which in theory would give the party the power to unilaterally change the constitution. This power might have become a destabilizing factor, insofar as the adversaries of the Liberal Party began to sense that the dominant party could change the rules of the game to its own advantage.

While the executive-legislative relation and its tensions have been the focus of much analysis, it is important to also note the division between the "modern city" and the "rest of the country" and its impact on the political system. Much of the emphasis in the 1991 constitution appeared to focus on the cities as sources of modernity and political openness. Some authors suggest that this gave rise to a majoritarian urban bloc that was a stabilizing factor, insofar as it was "a median in all directions" (Nielson and Shugart 1999). This new bloc supposedly was responsible for institutional changes that together were both modernizing and democratizing the country. According to this interpretation, the 1991 constitution has fulfilled its promise of fundamentally reshaping the political system. Nonetheless, the evidence behind this interpretation is at best contradictory. For example, as was noted earlier, independent parties have achieved notable successes in some large cities such as Bogotá and Barranquilla. But the reality in other big cities (e.g., Cali and Medellín) is different, with the traditional parties continuing to dominate political preferences. In several cities where Liberals have traditionally been strongest, they have remained strong. In the four mayoral elections realized between 1988 and 2000, the Liberals have had an acceptable performance, obtaining between 35 and 55 percent of the mayoralties of the country. Independent candidates did well, but basically at the expense of Conservatives (Querubín, Sánchez, and Kure 1998). The situation of municipal councils is even more clouded. If we contrast the situation of the 210 small municipalities and the twelve cities in our sample, we find that the large cities have a higher degree of electoral volatility and rotation in power and that no political force has the sufficient durability or power to install a local hegemony. On the other hand, in terms of traditional dominance, the Liberal presence and effective number of parties are similar to other municipalities.

Are these differences significant? Although there are similarities, as noted above, in terms of effective competition there is a significant difference: independent third parties have a real possibility of winning mayoral elections. In other words, third parties have a chance in urban executive elections, not in the legislative arena. This situation explains the strong antiparliamentary position of most independent parties. At the same time it suggests that the "modernizing" bloc in Colombia and other Andean countries may have a strong built-in antidemocratic tendency. In other words, the nontraditional parties are a "hope" insofar as they present themselves as *the* inclusionary force in the system, both in terms of incorporating new social sectors and being the standard-bearer of political modernization. At the same time, they are all set, strategically and morally, against the legislative system, including Congress. The independents represent both an opportunity for change and a danger for the political system. While modernizing and inclusionary in their attempt to open up the system, they may also foster authoritarian antisystem tendencies. In this sense, Colombia may follow the path of other countries of the Andean region.

Violence and Corruption in Traditional Politics?

The tendencies analyzed above illustrate how the Colombian system has evolved since the 1970s. Independent parties have grown, especially for executive offices. The Conservative Party has shrunk. The Liberals have maintained, and in some cases increased, their power in several institutions, although this has been accompanied by a loss of prestige in the Congress and other legislatures. The two traditional parties are no longer united, as in the "good old days" of the National Front, and must compete for the preferences not only of the general public but also of a skeptical socioeconomic elite. Nonetheless, the traditional parties maintain their dominance. This is especially surprising given the high degree of dissatisfaction among the public with politicians, parties, and the state of the country.

One possible hypothesis to explain the continued dominance of the traditional parties is that the institutional limitations in place until the 1970s were replaced by a series of extrainstitutional limitations developed during the 1980s and 1990s. The analysis here would focus on violence and corruption in particular. Colombia has a very high rate of political murders, and although there are no quantitative studies of this phenomenon, it appears that the probability that a leader or activist of the political left or of a social movement will be assassinated is higher than that of a leader or activist of one of the traditional parties. This fact is critical to any understanding of the Colombian political system. Brute force has been used to eliminate political options through the physical extermination of party leaders and members (as in the cases of UP and EPL). As a result of violence, the social base of these political options is dispersed and may adopt completely different political preferences, even once intimidation has come to an end. As an extensive empirical record in comparative politics suggests, countries with a high level of political violence are also "semirepressive." That is, faced with repression, political violence behaves like an inverted U, with closed regimes or relatively democratic regimes least vulnerable. Colombia is a good example of a semirepressive system (terror against the opposition and humanitarian tragedies, but at the same time relatively competitive elections and a legal system that is more than merely cosmetic), with the caveat that repression is exercised haphazardly and in a decentralized fashion. As a result, violence is combined with a high level of generalized uncertainty. This uncertainty generates distinct effects on different actors, depending on their levels of risk—a theme worthy of its own analysis—but there is some evidence that voters from upper-class sectors have become more averse to risk than in the past. Put more directly, the most educated and powerful groups in society would have more quickly abandoned the traditional parties if they were not as affected by the fear generated by internal war and organized crime. All of this has come to have a prejudicial impact on nontraditional parties, which see their ability to attract potential voters limited by a fear of political change.

In an environment of violence, uncertainty, and impunity, political groups and their leaders who are critical of the traditional parties and the existing social structure create mechanisms to adapt their preferences (Elster 1988), essentially becoming minimalists in order to avoid becoming military targets. There is sufficient evidence to suggest that this is the case in Colombia. In the wake of the assassination of the leader of the AD-M-19, Carlos Pizarro, the new leader of this group, Antonio Navarro Wolf, declared that his top priority was to avoid being killed (Peñaranda and Guerrero 1999). If this is in fact the case, then the Colombian political system has been artificially narrowed, with new political groups adopting centrist and moderate policies and behaviors they would most likely not have put forward if the political situation were less violent and more predictable. Following this line of reasoning, the artificial narrowing of choices in Colombia's political system creates an additional, and very significant, advantage for the traditional parties. Insofar as all the candidates look and sound alike in their proposals, voters will most likely lean toward the "brand" that is best known, that is, one of the traditional parties.

These are just some of the ways repression and violence distort the political system. Nonetheless, they do not automatically explain the majorities that traditional parties continue to obtain. In this sense, there are as many vacuums as there are inconsistencies in our understanding of this phenomenon. For example, it is not at all clear that paramilitary violence leads to more two-party dominance in regions than guerrilla violence. In some regions and periods it has; in others it is not clear. A good example of the former is the case of Puerto Boyacá, where paramilitary groups and the Liberal Party eliminated the presence of the Communist Party, which in turn had been based on support of the FARC during its heyday in the region (Medina Gallego 1990). On the other hand, in the last few years paramilitaries have adopted a strong "antipolitical" stance that is already showing very concrete consequences. We still lack a broader understanding of the phenomenon. It is unknown, for example, what sort of regional correlation might exist between the violence of one group—the FARC, the National Liberation Army (ELN), the paramilitary umbrella organization, the United Self-Defense Forces of Colombia (AUC), or the state—and two-party dominance, and without this information it is difficult to arrive at definitive conclusions. In fact, it is not even apparent that there is a significant correlation at a national level between amount of repression and votes for independent parties. Moreover, there are clear anomalies in the explanation. In the majority of territories with a strong guerrilla influence, traditional parties are quite healthy and enjoy sufficient political space to the point of even using the guerrillas as allies in their factional disputes.[8] In several regions, there is also a notable insensitivity on the part of the traditional parties toward the direct influence of armed groups of different tendencies. This is partly explained by the fact that the parties preceded the arrival of armed groups in these zones and/or have become accustomed to living with them. It is important not to forget that armed groups are not omnipotent and often are electorally defeated in zones under their military control (Gutiérrez 2000a), an event that is not as rare as is often believed and that requires further study. Once again we return to a phenomenon noted earlier: the results of a consultation are not proportionally and directly related to the levels of protection, and vice versa.

Studying the evolution of corruption is even more difficult than studying that of violence, among other reasons because it is far less visible than violence. Investigations and studies of the phenomenon have only uncovered a fraction of the existing levels of corruption. During the period under consideration, the most important form of corruption, although most certainly not the only one, was related to drug trafficking, and even though it affected all political forces, its epicenter was the Liberal Party. Once again, it is not at all clear whether drug trafficking has helped Liberals maintain their ample majorities, although we can find arguments both for and against this position. On the one hand, drug trafficking introduced enormous new resources, both monetary and violent, into the party; converted it into an icon and mechanism of social mobility and acceptability; and, finally, made it a champion of illegal incorporations without having to develop reformist policies. Thus, while the party distanced itself from a program of social change, it also became a vehicle for one of the most antioligarchic experiences of the 1980s and 1990s. This relationship also permitted the party to foster more potent and pernicious forms of clientelism.

On the other hand, "narco-politics" generated a significant degree of dein-stitutionalization within the party, giving regional and local forces greater power at the expense of the national leadership and thus contributing to the destabilization of the party. This is not to mention the extraordinary exhaustion caused by the almost daily eruption of scandals that helped create an enormous disillusionment among the middle classes, especially in Bogotá, which had been a bastion of Liberal strength. Bringing to the fore political personalities with practices and clear links to criminal organizations, socioeconomic elites were also scandalized. When the Samper administration appeared to endanger Colombia's relationship with the United States as a result of the drug scandal mentioned earlier, the conflict with these sectors broke into the open. The divorce between the wealthy and the Liberal Party promises to be long and lasting and, coupled with the reforms introduced in the 1991 constitution, damaging to the party's long-term interests. Institutional rules such as the "ballotage" for presidential elections and even the introduction of the vice-presidency have facilitated the formation of heterogeneous and negative anti-Liberal coalitions, with the vigorous participation of the media, opinion makers, those in favor of further political reforms, conservatives, and *gentes de bien* (decent people). While perhaps divided in the first round of voting, they have tended to unite in the second round against the Liberal candidate. This is largely why in 1998, for the first time in the twentieth-century history of the Liberal Party, the party lost a presidential election despite being united behind its candidate (and also despite the fact that the candidate, Horacio Serpa, won the largest number of votes in the party's history).

Certainly the political system and clientelism in Colombia are difficult to separate, although one is not simply reducible to the other. New entrants into the political system have had to adapt to existing clientelist networks (Leal Buitrago and Dávila 1991), and that has not necessarily benefited them. On the contrary, this has tended to factionalize these parties and convert them into targets of corruption investigations or violence from one of the armed groups (or political adversaries). If all of the above demonstrates the difficulty the current system would have functioning without a certain level of corruption, it also underlines that the development of the system is not functionally dependent merely upon corruption.

Our answer to the question of whether Colombia has been undergoing democratization appears to remain ambiguous. But at the very least our analysis has hopefully allowed a more nuanced characterization of the evolution of Colombia's political system.

12   State Making against Democracy

The Case of Fujimori's Peru

⁊⁊   In Peru, the process of state breakdown and the disruption of organized politics in the 1980s gave way to the emergence of an authoritarian and personalistic leader, Alberto Fujimori (1990–2000), who rebuilt state institutions and forged new modes of state-society relations, but did so in a way that was antithetical to the affirmation of democratic principles and procedures. The process of rebuilding state institutions in the 1990s became inimical to the imperative of building democracy. Thus the social conflicts that came to a head in the 1980s—manifested by a deep-seated economic crisis, widespread political violence, and an exacerbated alienation of social groups from organized politics—created a set of conditions that favored an authoritarian model of state-building and worked against the affirmation of democratic governance.

Scholars writing on state making have tended to focus on the process, often bloody and violent, of creating and supporting centralized state institutions (Tilly 1975). Yet state making is a continuous, ongoing process; the affirmation of central state institutions is one outcome, but other outcomes are also possible (Bright and Harding 1984). Processes that seem to be leading toward the centralization of power may be blocked or stalled; in other cases, relatively stable state institutions may, for different reasons, be dismantled or destroyed. In this sense, the Peruvian case is highly suggestive, as it is a case in which state institutions, though never fully centralized, collapsed in the 1980s and, after a period of intense social conflict, were rebuilt along authoritarian lines in the 1990s. The weakening and partial collapse of state institutions in the late 1980s, coupled with the debilitation of political and civil society, created the conditions for the reaffirmation of state power by an extremely personalistic and anti-institutionalist leadership. The result was an inherently unstable process that, by 2000, also collapsed as evidence of mafia-like behavior and extreme corruption emerged. Shifts in the composition and power correlations between elite groups leading the state-building process during the 1990s led to two distinct phases of state building: in the early period (1990–97), elites focused on reasserting state power by reorganizing the economy, subduing guerrilla movements, and reordering social relations; by the late 1990s, however, a small clique had assumed near total control of the state apparatus, using it for personal enrichment and to assure, in mafialike fashion, their continued power and impunity until the regime's collapse in late 2000. This chapter attempts to explain this process and to highlight why analyses focusing on regime type alone are inadequate to explain the nature of political change in Peru over the past two decades and the ambiguous regime that was constructed over the course of the decade of the 1990s under Fujimori's rule.

State Making against Democracy

Constructing a democratic regime means more than free and fair elections; it implies building a democratic state in which leaders have the capacity to exert authority over society and economy but in which there are mechanisms of accountability at different levels that protect citizens and the market against arbitrary action by state makers. In this sense, state making and democracy building can be mutually reinforcing processes, but they are not necessarily so. As those who write about processes of state building would suggest, it has often been a nondemocratic and bloody process concerned with concentrating state power rather than building norms and mechanisms of democratic accountability.[1] Indeed, some authors have defined state building as "organized crime" (Tilly 1985) and a "protection racket" (Stanley 1996). Later processes of social mobilization and protest demanding rights and inclusion in the polity helped broaden definitions of citizenship and redefine the terms of democratic accountability to make states more democratic. In examining state making in Peru in the 1990s, this analysis concentrates on the way in which reaffirming state power in the context of state breakdown, economic crisis, and political violence worked against the affirmation of democratic institutions.

Despite the proliferation of scholarly work on democratization in the wake of the so-called third-wave transitions, the realm of the state and its relationship to democracy has been largely neglected. More recently, scholars have begun to address this theoretical lacunae. A seminal piece by Guillermo O'Donnell (1993) highlighted the problematic nature of democracy in societies in which states do not exercise full control over their national territory and/or perform expected functions, such as policing and rule adjudication. The presence of nondemocratic, nonstate actors in areas of low state presence/functionality may limit the state's operative capacity, and such actors (such as regional party bosses who use state resources for private gain or to oil their patronage networks) may privatize state functions, thereby undermining democracy. Such actors may also fundamentally challenge the legitimacy of the state itself, a contingency O'Donnell does not envision. If we accept the notion that a functioning state ("stateness") is a basic condition for democratic governance (Linz and Stepan 1996), then it behooves us to understand what happens when states lose their ability to function qua states. In this chapter, I examine a case study in which "stateness" is disintegrating and suggest that the consequences for democracy are nefarious.

In the Peruvian case, nonstate actors—specifically, the Shining Path—operated in areas of low state presence/functionality in such a way as to fundamentally challenge the legitimacy of the state. Numerous anthropologists and political scientists have written about the "political vacuums" evident in the Peruvian countryside in the aftermath of the 1969 land reform and the ability of the Shining Path guerrilla movement to operate in these vacuums in such a way as to build its own support networks and expand its operating capacity (Degregori 1986; Manrique 1989; Isbell 1992; Berg 1992). While the Shining Path was not a mass-based peasant movement, as most scholars agree, it nevertheless was able to establish a presence and operate in vast regions of the country, particularly where the state was absent or largely ineffective, building alternative structures of authority (but not mass-based support networks) that sometimes challenged, sometimes replaced, the state itself. In these spaces, the Shining Path contested state authority and contributed to the erosion of the state's legitimacy in the late 1980s, particularly after the onset of hyperinflation in 1988. The state's use of indiscriminate violence and terror against the rural population, its inability to stop the growing violence, and the downward spiral of the economy contributed, in a recursive process, to further delegitimizing the state and opening up the field of contestation of the very nature of the state. Understanding this process is crucial to understanding the posterior process of the formation of new alliances among state elites, the armed forces, and the domestic business elite (with the implicit support of transnational capital) to reconstitute the state along authoritarian and neoliberal lines in the 1990s. In the context of severe state breakdown, the authoritarian dimension of the reconsolidation of state power will be very high, while the ability of political and civil society to organize will be very low, limiting the possibilities of establishing mechanisms of control and accountability over state elites and institutions. State building in such a context, in other words, is likely to be antithetical to democracy building.

The Breakdown of the State and the Failure of Democratic Governance

On March 27, 1989, a group of some three hundred Shining Path guerrillas attacked a police post in Uchiza, a small town located in the northeastern province of San Martín on the edge of the Peruvian jungle. Most of the residents in the surrounding areas were small-scale peasants who had turned to the illegal cultivation of coca, the primary ingredient in cocaine, as the country's economy took a nosedive after mid-1987. The Shining Path, a Maoist organization that took up arms against the Peruvian state in 1980, had established a presence in coca-growing areas by providing protection to coca growers from Colombian drug lords and the Peruvian police.

After several hours of exchanging fire with the guerrillas, the police were overwhelmed when their munitions ran out; ten policemen, including three high-ranking officials, were killed. In the following days, it became public knowledge that Prime Minister Armando Villanueva had personally promised reinforcements by radio to the police commanders, but military troops at a nearby base had refused to assist their besieged comrades.[2] The Uchiza debacle, which opposition leaders criticized as evidence of the regime's lack of a coherent counterinsurgency policy, forced Villanueva to resign his post, provoking a severe political crisis for the reformist government of Alan García (1985–90).

Growing political violence, the government's inability to provide protection to citizens or even state agents, and the ensuing vacuum of power in many parts of the country indicated a breakdown in state authority and capacity throughout the country. The number of politically motivated deaths increased dramatically in the second half of the García administration, from 2.0 per day in 1987 to 8.8 and 9.4 per day in 1989 and 1990 respectively.[3] Despite the fact that by the late 1980s emergency zones had been established in over one-third of the national territory, giving the armed forces control over half the Peruvian population, increasing swaths of territory were no longer controlled by the government—a situation that grew worse as Shining Path launched an all-out campaign to boycott the municipal elections scheduled for November 1989. In the weeks before the elections, Shining Path assassinated dozens of local elected officials, and each killing prompted waves of resignations by officials and candidates in surrounding areas. In Huancayo, an area technically under the control of the armed forces, Shining Path declared fifteen of thirty-six districts "liberated zones," prompting mayors from twenty-six districts to resign their posts.[4] By early July, 656 mayors and town council members had been killed or had resigned or abandoned their posts throughout the country.[5]

The incapacity of the Peruvian state to provide basic levels of order and security reflected more than the ineffectiveness of state agencies like the police and the military, or the lack of coordination—and sometimes the open conflict—between these agencies; it reflected a larger problem of declining state capacity and legitimacy in Peru. The Peruvian state has historically been weak and ineffectual, despite reformist efforts to strengthen the state apparatus in the 1960s and 1970s, but this was a deeper, more entrenched crisis.[6] In 1988, a combination of political and economic mismanagement, government corruption, and external constraints brought an end to the heterodox economic experiment being implemented by then-president Alan García. The economic gains of the first years of the García regime—including both gross domestic product (GDP) growth and rising income levels—were quickly swept away, as the government proved incapable of sustaining a coherent policy coalition to support its reformist measures.[7] Political miscalculations also alienated business elites from García's reformist program, in particular the failed attempt to nationalize the country's banking system in 1987. As the country's economic elite withdrew their support from the regime and their capital from the country, GDP fell, hyperinflation soared, and income levels declined dramatically. As the formal economy declined, the informal economy expanded, depriving the state of crucial fiscal resources, particularly after the cutoff of international assistance by multilateral financial institutions in response to García's unilateral decision to reduce debt payments to 10 percent of export earnings. The resulting fiscal crisis, coupled with repeated corruption scandals, severely undermined state capacity to perform basic administrative functions and weakened its institutional, administrative, and coercive presence in society, which was already under siege in more remote regions of the country due to the expansion of guerrilla violence and drug trafficking.

If we accept a Weberian definition of the state as the apparatus that maintains a legitimate monopoly of violence over a defined territory, the Peruvian state by the late 1980s ceased, in many respects, to be a functioning state. Inability to manage the country's economic crisis and rising labor conflict, the growing disengagement of the state from society, pervasive government corruption, and government paralysis in the face of a dramatic expansion of political violence undermined public confidence in the state's authority and in the government's ability to govern the country. Taken together, these elements constituted a growing crisis of legitimacy that seemed to undermine the very belief in the state as an institution that sets the rules of the game for political and economic interaction. In other words, what began as a fiscal crisis of the state (the inability of the state to assure capitalist accumulation) soon ballooned into a crisis of the state of far greater dimensions, encompassing an institutional crisis of the state and the erosion of state authority (the inability of the state to assure legitimacy).

There were structural problems as well, of course, that contributed to state breakdown in Peru. Peru has been widely characterized as a weak state in which private elites tended to dominate policy-making and structures of racial and socioeconomic exclusion left the vast majority of the population on the margins of politics and society (Cotler 1978). While the reformist experiment under General Juan Velasco sought to strengthen the state and to forge a more inclusionary model of state-society relations, it ultimately failed to substantially alter weak state capacities or bridge the gap between state and society.[8] When Peru made the transition to democracy in 1980, the state remained very weak, despite its growing interventionism in the economy and society.[9] While the transition process put in place a democratic regime, with regular elections, a free press, and other civil liberties, few reforms were undertaken to democratize the state, create mechanisms of horizontal and vertical accountability, and assure universal citizenship.[10]

The government's inability to expand state services to poor urban and rural areas, assure basic conditions of government accountability and citizenship, and democratize social relations provided political space for Shining Path guerrillas to organize and build local support in remote areas of the countryside in the early 1980s.[11] As the guerrillas' local power grew stronger, the state sought to quash their influence through massive repression; this only exacerbated the extraordinary gap between state and society and was completely ineffective at controlling the insurgency; on the contrary, it fueled grassroots support for the Maoists during the early phase of the insurgency. While the García government attempted initially to develop new methods to deal with the insurgency by reaching out to poor citizens in urban and especially rural areas, this effort collapsed under the weight of the fiscal crisis that set in after 1988. The regime's efforts to impose more stringent human rights standards in the counterinsurgency war was also met with resistance by the armed forces and eventually was abandoned in favor of earlier patterns of indiscriminate repression.

The fiscal crisis, growing bureaucratic incompetence, corruption, and the breakdown of state authority evident by the late 1980s contributed to a process of disengagement of the state from society. While the state in Peru had never fully engaged society in many regions of the country, in the period after 1980, when the country transitioned from military rule to a new elected civilian government, there were efforts, particularly during the García government, to bridge the state-society gap through a plethora of social programs in urban and rural areas. The floundering of such efforts after the onset of the fiscal crisis in 1988 led to a retrenchment of the state from social programs in urban and rural areas, opening up new breaches in state-society relations. For example, the Temporary Income Support Program (PAIT), a temporary employment program that ensured wages to the urban poor, especially women, and the Direct Aid Program (PAD), a program providing material assistance to communal soup kitchens, were scuttled as state funds dried up, leaving the urban poor vulnerable just as hyperinflation hit.[12] Traditional state services, such as health and education, suffered drastic budget cutbacks. Spending in the education sector, for example, decreased by nearly 75 percent between 1986 and 1990 (Ministry of the Presidency 1993). Other state institutions mediating relations with society, such as the national police and the judicial system—the basic institutions guaranteeing justice and equal treatment before the law—were hobbled by the fiscal crisis. While they were traditionally seen as ineffective and corrupt, popular confidence in these institutions eroded still further, as the state's incapacity to ensure public order added to the erosion of public confidence in public authority.

The crisis also affected the ability of political parties to mediate state-society relations. Peru's party system had always been weak, but there was great hope that the transition to democracy in 1980 would give rise to more modern forms of political representation and participation. The mass-based parties that came to dominate politics in the mid-1980s—the historic mass-based party American Popular Revolutionary Alliance (APRA) and the newer left-wing coalition United Left (IU)—held out the promise of more democratic and participatory forms of channeling popular demands while forging a more responsive, less distant state at the national, regional, and local levels.[13] But the spiraling economic and political crisis after 1988 began to erode these linkages between state and society, as citizens became increasingly disillusioned with the inability of the political parties and their representatives in power at the local and national levels to alleviate the worst effects of the economic crisis and the growing political violence.

In other words, the state's ability to engage society as it had in the early years of the García administration through social programs and state services began to wither. The fiscal crisis of the state forced the government to shut down social programs such as PAD and PAIT that had served as crucial linking (if clientelistic) mechanisms between state and society. This withdrawal of state support left social groups without state subsidies, employment, and other benefits. Coupled with the growing revelations of government corruption, this severely eroded popular confidence in APRA. But as suggested earlier, the impact was more widespread, as blame for the economic and political crisis was directed at all political parties. In the eyes of the public, the parties represented in Congress, which seemed oddly aloof to the mounting problems facing ordinary Peruvians, were as much to blame as the executive branch for the state's inability to ensure basic living standards and basic levels of security. The crisis of the state translated directly into a crisis of representation.

In addition, APRA and the IU began to suffer internal crises that fueled popular disillusionment. This was particularly the case with APRA, because of the situation described above, and the United Left, as it fell victim to its own internal contradictions and the petty personal rivalries of its top leaders.

The IU—at that time the most significant left-wing force in South America and top contender for the 1990 presidential elections—came under fire for its inability to develop concrete policy alternatives to the crisis and for the inability of its leadership to overcome personal and programmatic conflicts. Differences in how to respond to Shining Path violence further divided the IU and led to a formal split in the coalition in 1989.[14] The division of the left and the popular disillusionment that followed eroded one of the key mediating linkages between the urban and rural poor and the political system. The result was the undermining of the ability of state actors and political society to articulate the demands of societal groups and mediate their access to the larger political system.

Several analysts have noted how the erosion of popular confidence in "traditional" political parties as effective representatives of societal interests created political space for the emergence of an amorphous set of "independent" candidates who ironically had even more questionable links to broader social groups outside their immediate circles of influence.[15] The election of Ricardo Belmont as mayor of Lima in 1989 was the first sign of this trend, followed in 1990 by the election of political outsider Alberto Fujimori to the presidency. But this vacuum of representation and concrete service delivery also created the conditions for a dramatic expansion of the Shining Path. The movement's leadership interpreted the situation after 1988 as a looming crisis of the state and the prelude to its revolutionary triumph.[16] The weakening and disengagement of the state created opportunities for Shining Path to develop their presence in the shantytowns that ringed the capital city, which it saw as key strategic sites for the launching of the "final offensive" against the "bureaucratic-capitalist state."[17] Analyses of Shining Path have tended to focus on the group's brutal and unflinching use of violence against its enemies, which it defined broadly to include not only agents of the state but anyone, including left-wing social activists, who opposed or did not support its "popular war." Nevertheless, it is important to analyze the political strategies and tactics Shining Path deployed in its efforts to build popular support for or neutralize resistance to its "revolutionary" war.[18] Specifically, Shining Path sought to exploit—and often exacerbate or deepen through assassinations and intimidation—the dramatic gaps in state-society relations to advance its presence and gain popular support. It did this in rural areas, for example, by seeking to "punish" local state authorities and landowners who were perceived as corrupt by local peasants (Isbell 1992; Berg 1986–87, 1992). It repeated this tactic in Lima after the onset of the crisis in 1988, under the logic that this was not a short-term crisis but rather a structural crisis of the state. At the microlevel, the gaps left by a state in retreat opened opportunities for Shining Path to provide key public goods to shantytown residents, facilitating the Maoists' penetration of these strategic areas. Security was one of the most basic "public goods" Shining Path provided; the Maoists also sought to provide some semblance of "justice" and "order" by punishing alleged "wrongdoers" such as thieves, drug dealers, and corrupt authorities, first by warning them to cease their ungainly ways and then by meting out "exemplary punishments"—sometimes beatings but often cold-blooded assassinations. Notwithstanding the premodern nature of these tactics, they were often quite effective in marshalling local support for Shining Path, given growing physical and economic insecurity in these poor neighborhoods and the inability (or unwillingness) of the state to protect citizens in these areas. In recursive fashion, the expansion of Shining Path and the state's inability to stop it further eroded popular confidence in the political class and in the state itself, creating a dramatic crisis of state legitimacy.

Shining Path's growing presence in the poor shantytowns of Lima, coupled with the launching of dramatic offensives in the capital city through the use of car bombs and selective assassinations, led to growing fear of a Shining Path victory. By the early 1990s, the expansion of Shining Path and the seeming inability of state elites to halt its advance heightened the threat perception of Peru's ruling elites, leading to the creation of an alliance between political and social forces interested in reverting the decline of the Peruvian state. These forces—including an important sector of the armed forces in alliance with state managers and segments of the domestic bourgeoisie (with the support of key international actors, primarily the U.S. government and multilateral financial institutions)—congealed under the regime of Alberto Fujimori, who came to power in 1990, in an attempt to thwart a Shining Path victory and reconstitute the Peruvian state.

The reconstitution of the Peruvian state under Fujimori was impressive and dramatic in many respects, making the policies and actions undertaken between 1990 and 1995 a compelling case study of the dynamics of state reconstitution. It also raises a number of disturbing questions, especially for those concerned not just with the reestablishment of order but also with the democratic process. The remaking of the state in Peru, it will be argued here, took place along authoritarian lines, leading to the creation of a regime that, while it retained some semblance of a democracy (e.g., elections), was in fact authoritarian. In other words, Peru is an illustrative case of how the decimation of social and political life, which is a constituent element of state breakdown, creates the conditions for the establishment of arbitrary, authoritarian, and often personalistic forms of rule. On the one hand, extreme social conflict creates the conditions for a high degree of state autonomy. Distinct social groups—from the bourgeoisie to the professional middle classes to poor rural and urban voters—demonstrated their willingness to cede broad powers to

Fujimori and his allies in a desperate search for a return to normalcy after several years of economic and political upheaval under the previous two democratic governments. On the other hand, the weakness of political and civil society undermined the possibility of forging a more democratic model of state reconstitution. The weakness of organized political actors meant that there were few checks on newly assertive state elites who, under the increasingly authoritarian and personalistic leadership of Fujimori and his entourage, sought to centralize state power, reassert state control over society, and refashion state-society relations with little regard for democratic norms and procedures.

The Authoritarian Reconstitution of the State

By the time of the April 1990 presidential elections, the depth of the political and economic crisis undermined popular support not only for the APRA regime but for political parties in general. The erosion of support for what came to be known as the "traditional" political parties and how this opened political space for the emergence of so-called independent candidates have been analyzed extensively. Several authors have noted the importance of the breakdown of the party system for the emergence of "outsider" candidates in general and of Fujimori specifically.[19] Here, I would like to suggest that while this is indeed a crucial variable in understanding the rise of Fujimori, it is insufficient. We must consider a prior variable—the breakdown of state authority—and how this contributed to (1) increasing the autonomy of a group of elites within the state apparatus; and (2) the weakening of political and civil society, which in turn set the conditions for the affirmation of power of an outsider candidate who lacked a party apparatus as well as a coherent political platform and who quickly sought to centralize power and establish an authoritarian and personalistic style of leadership. Understanding the relationship between state breakdown and the consolidation of power under Fujimori during his first administration is also important in helping us better understand the ambiguous nature of the regime type that evolved during his decade in power. First, let us examine the process of state making as it evolved under the Fujimori regime.

The Three Dimensions of State Reconstitution

There were three key dimensions to state reconstitution under Fujimori. First, the Fujimori regime laid the foundation for state reconstitution by marshaling international financial support to stabilize the economy and thereby gain domestic support for the state and for a new social and political project, neoliberalism, among both the business class and average citizens. This so-called reinsertion of Peru into the international financial community permitted international loans and foreign capital to enter the country, funds that were desperately needed given the deep fiscal crisis and administrative disarray that characterized Peru in the late 1980s. This flow of international funds helped curb inflation and stabilize the economy, while providing crucial resources to reorganize key state agencies such as the tax agency, SUNAT, and the customs agency, SUNAD, which permitted the state to more effectively extract resources from citizens, businesses, and travelers. It also helped the state to rebuild clientelistic links with society by helping to finance massive public works programs through institutions like the Social Compensation and Development Fund (FONCODES) and thereby obtain a modicum of support and legitimacy. At the same time it consolidated the support of the bourgeoisie, which at the beginning of Fujimori's term was very wary of this political unknown.[20]

The second dimension of state reconstitution was the centralization of power in the hands of the executive. This process culminated in the *autogolpe* of April 5, 1992, in which Fujimori dissolved the parliament and the judiciary and suspended the constitution with the backing of the armed forces. This reorganization of state power and the removal of democratic checks and balances in Congress and the judiciary permitted the regime to pursue a radically militarized counterinsurgency policy as well as to implement a full-blown neoliberal program. Despite the fact that Congress was reinstated in November 1992 and a new constitution was written a year later, power dynamics remained centralized in the executive branch for the rest of Fujimori's period in power. Those democratic institutions that remained in place were systematically subverted to the regime's political will, including the judiciary and independent agencies like the Constitutional Tribunal.

The third dimension of state reconstitution was the containment of the Shining Path, which began with the capture of the insurgency's top leader, Abimael Guzmán, in September 1992, just six months after the *autogolpe*. While it may reasonably be argued that the *autogolpe* and the subsequent hardening of the regime's policies had little if anything to do with Guzmán's arrest (the arrest was made by intelligence police and did not involve the use of repression, but of careful surveillance and intelligence measures that in fact highlight the achievements of democratic forms in dealing with insurgents), the regime adeptly manipulated public opinion to credit the arrest to the new efficacy in governing since the *autogolpe*. The arrest of Guzmán was crucial in rebuilding public confidence in the Peruvian state and its ability to restore order and some modicum of normalcy to daily life. It provided the Fujimori regime with crucial political capital to pursue a wide range of policies aimed at reconstituting the Peruvian state along neoliberal and authoritarian lines.

Of the three dimensions of state reconstitution discussed above, it is important to briefly analyze the 1992 *autogolpe*. The power that accrued to the executive and the military after the coup—which continued in place despite the reinstatement of Congress and the writing of a new constitution—was the basis for the authoritarian centralization of power that came to define state building in Fujimori's Peru throughout the 1990s.

Establishing the Authoritarian Bases of the Fujimori Regime

The debacle in Uchiza was one of a series of dramatic state failures in the war against Shining Path that prompted rethinking of the state's role on the part of a group of strategic elites within the state apparatus—more specifically, within the armed forces.[21] This group began to define the need to unify the military command structure in order to devise a coherent counterinsurgency policy and overcome the debilitating interinstitutional rivalries that were hampering the state's actions vis-à-vis Shining Path. The military's growing frustration over its failures in the war against Shining Path and the limitations placed upon its counterinsurgency operations by democratic institutions (as limited as these were), coupled with the growing inability of civilian politicians to deal with the spiraling economic crisis and the expansion of the Shining Path, prompted a group of military officers to devise a coup plan in the late 1980s known as "Plan Verde."[22] Building on traditional notions of national security, which portray civilian politicians as weak and democracy as ineffectual and claim that the armed forces are the only institution capable of protecting and strengthening the nation-state, Plan Verde called for the dissolution of Peru's civilian government, military control over the state, and total elimination of armed opposition groups. This would be achieved through a military coup in which the armed forces would govern for fifteen to twenty years and radically restructure state-society relations along neoliberal lines.

It was not until the election of Fujimori and the consolidation of an alliance between the new president and the armed forces that this group was able to deploy this plan, however. The international community no longer favored military governments (Washington was now in the business of promoting "free elections and free markets"), making a traditional military coup problematic. The election of political neophyte Fujimori offered the coup mongers a unique opportunity. Fujimori's lack of a political party made him extremely vulnerable, and persistent coup rumors immediately before the second-round election against Mario Vargas Llosa made it imperative for him to seek out allies within the armed forces. This was facilitated by Vladimiro Montesinos, a former army captain who was cashiered from the army in 1976 for reportedly selling state secrets to the Central Intelligence Agency (CIA) (for which he spent a year in jail) but who had retained close ties to the army and had since become a lawyer and was closely associated with leading drug traffickers and influence-peddling within the judiciary. During the runoff campaign, Montesinos offered to help Fujimori by using his connections in the judiciary to get charges of fraudulent real-estate dealings against him dropped. He did so, and Montesinos gained Fujimori's confidence and soon became his principal adviser and main link to the armed forces.[23]

The *autogolpe* made it evident that Fujimori had adopted the military's twenty-year coup plan as his own, making the dissolution of the executive branch (as in a traditional coup) unnecessary. The *autogolpe* was designed to concentrate power in the hands of the president and his allies so that the executive would have a free hand to dictate wide-ranging economic reforms as well as political measures granting full power to the armed forces in the counterinsurgency war and in its effort to reassert state control over society. It marked the consolidation of a civil-military alliance that radically militarized political and social life in Peru.

The authoritarian intentions of the strategic elites united behind Fujimori were evident even before the *autogolpe*. Shortly after assuming office, under the guidance of Montesinos, Fujimori carried out massive purges within the police and armed forces, allowing them to place sympathetic officers in high posts and remove those who might oppose their plans. Fujimori named an active army general minister of the interior, placing the police under direct control of the armed forces. Again with Montesinos's help, Fujimori secured the personal loyalty of the military high command by getting legislation approved that gave the president control over promotions and retirements within the armed forces. Previously, promotions and retirements had been decided by the high command itself, and this law was pegged as establishing civilian control over the military. In fact, it permitted Fujimori and Montesinos to promote loyal officers to high-ranking positions while forcing suspect officers into early retirement (Obando 1998). In December 1991, on Montesinos's suggestion, Fujimori named Nicolás Bari de Hermoza head of the army and commander in chief of the armed forces, a position he retained until August 1998. This broke all precedents: commanders in chief normally held their post for one year and then retired, allowing other generals a shot at the supreme military command post.[24] This early program of purges and promotions suggests, as Gustavo Gorriti (1994) and Fernando Rospigliosi (1996) have argued, that the coup plan was in the works long before April 1992. By dismissing uncooperative officers as well as institutionalists within the armed forces and promoting more sympathetic officials, Fujimori and his allies were laying the groundwork for institutional military support for a coup.

This is further supported by an examination of the situation immediately preceding the *autogolpe*. Some have argued that the *autogolpe* was the result of an institutional deadlock between the executive and legislative branches.[25]

Fujimori did not have a working majority in Congress, and Peru's presidential system does not promote legislative cooperation among different parties. Yet Fujimori had been granted special-decree powers by Congress to implement reform measures, giving the president a great deal of freedom to legislate economic as well as internal security policies without the noted congressional interference. At the end of the 150-day period in which these decree powers were effective, Fujimori emitted an avalanche of 126 decree laws aimed at a rapid liberalization of the economy and granting total control over counterinsurgency policy, without congressional oversight, to the armed forces. Opposition groups in Congress argued that Fujimori had overstepped the boundaries of his decree powers, and in a special session in early 1992 they joined forces to modify or overturn decree laws they considered egregious violations of the constitution (Vidal 1993). Congress was scheduled to reconvene on April 6, and the opposition was planning to continue its review of Fujimori's decree laws. But that possibility was cut short with the announcement of the *autogolpe* on the evening of April 5. This suggests more than just a legislative impasse; it suggests an authoritarian intention on the part of Fujimori and his allies to remove all constraints inherent within a democratic system of checks and balances in order to permit the centralization of power and decision-making in the hands of the executive.[26]

Peru's political class opposed the *autogolpe,* but their criticism found little echo in society. Many Peruvian citizens, weary of economic and political chaos, supported Fujimori's "get tough" stance. But conditions were not so favorable on the external front; Fujimori and his allies faced unexpected criticism from Washington and the Organization of American States (OAS). Most significantly, Washington announced it would cut assistance to Peru until it returned to constitutional government. To appease his international critics— and assure the inflow of much-needed external funds—Fujimori declared that new congressional elections would take place in November 1992.

Despite this setback, little in terms of real power relations changed. Fujimori and his military allies—with the firm support of the Peruvian bourgeoisie—took every precaution to maintain power in the hands of the executive and limit the powers of other agencies and branches of government. While Fujimori was forced to hold new congressional elections in late 1992, by eliminating the two-chamber Congress and replacing it with a small unicameral assembly (eighty members), he established a body that was easily coopted. The following year, this body wrote a new constitution, which was approved by a slim majority in a referendum on October 31, 1993. The new document eliminated many of the social protections for workers and peasants enshrined in the 1979 constitution and set the stage for the expansion of neoliberal reforms. It also expanded the power of the military and, contrary to the 1979 constitution, allowed a sitting president to run for reelection. The international community accepted congressional elections and the approval of a new constitution as sufficient evidence of Peru's return to the democratic fold.

This institutional reordering did not reinstate democratic governance in Peru, however. Each of the democratic institutions that were reinstated, such as Congress, was stripped of its democratic content and became a virtual appendage of the executive branch. While the reinstatement of Congress resolved Peru's problems in terms of the international community, it did not alter the fact that Fujimori and his allies continued to rule the country in near-dictatorial fashion. When other democratic institutions attempted to carry out their functions, the executive or Congress intervened, often violating the constitution the regime itself had put in place in 1993 to stop them. A few examples will illustrate the way power operated in Fujimori's Peru.

Perhaps the most notorious case of the Fujimori regime's evisceration of democratic institutions is that of La Cantuta, which involved the disappearance and murder of nine university students and a professor in July 1992 by a death squad known as the Colina Group, made up of members of the Peruvian National Intelligence Service (SIN) and army intelligence (SIE). When opposition leaders in Congress sought to open an investigation in April 1993, after evidence emerged implicating members of the armed forces, the military high command refused to cooperate, and the commander in chief of the armed forces, General Nicolás Bari de Hermoza, accused the investigating legislators of acting "in collusion with the homicidal terrorists."[27] The following day, Lima awoke to a parade of army tanks, while the army accused Congress of engaging in a "systematic campaign orchestrated with the sinister objective of undermining the prestige of the armed forces."[28] Two months later, after the charred bodies of the students had been found, the case was brought before a civilian court. The progovernment majority in Congress maneuvered first to have the case heard by a military court—a clear violation of the autonomy of the judicial branch. After a handful of officers were convicted by the military court of the Cantuta murders, the ruling majority in Congress then engineered an amnesty law to free them. When a judge investigating another massacre in which the Colina Group was also implicated sought to continue her investigation, Congress passed a second law obligating the courts to obey the amnesty law, again violating the autonomy of the judicial branch.

Another case illustrating the way democratic institutions were routinely eviscerated in Peru surrounds the so-called Law of Authentic Interpretation. While the 1993 constitution clearly states that a president may be reelected one time to a consecutive term, the same progovernment majority in Congress passed a law in 1996 establishing that President Fujimori was eligible to run for a third term, arguing that since the new constitution had not been in force when he was first elected in 1990, his first term did not count. When the Constitutional Tribunal ruled that the law was unconstitutional, the dissenting judges were unceremoniously removed by majority vote of Congress. Efforts by opposition groups to hold a referendum on the Law of Authentic Interpretation—a right granted by the 1993 constitution—were also thwarted by the ruling majority in Congress, which passed another law clearly contrary to the mandate of the constitution stipulating that forty-eight members of Congress must approve a referendum vote for it to proceed. Despite the fact that opposition leaders had collected 1.4 million signatures in favor of the referendum on the reelection law, they fell three votes short of the required forty-eight, effectively killing the referendum.

This case in particular is illustrative of the weakness of civil and political society in the face of a regime with a high degree of autonomy and a seemingly limitless willingness to engage in authoritarian and illegal methods in order to maintain its power and disarticulate any challenges to that power. This was seen time and time again, as democratic forces failed consistently in their efforts to oppose authoritarian solutions to different political situations and crises. And, as will be discussed further below, the regime became adept at exacerbating the disarticulation of political and civil society through the selective use of co-optation and repression.

Finally, if we consider citizenship a key element of democracy, the protection of civil and political liberties must be considered in our discussion. The antiterrorism laws established in the wake of the *autogolpe,* and that remained on the books until well after the end of the Fujimori regime, systematically undermined freedom of expression and the right to due process. While some justified the harsh laws as necessary to deal with the threat of terrorism, in fact these laws were so broadly defined as to be easily misused by the regime to intimidate opponents operating within the boundaries of the political system. For example, Decree Law 25475, on the crime of terrorism and related acts, defines terrorism broadly to include not only those responsible for carrying out acts of violence, as was the case in the previous legislation, but those who "create a state of anxiety" by any means, including nonviolent ones—a clear violation of civil rights. The law also established prison sentences of six to twelve years for the crime of "apology for terrorism," which is not defined—a clear threat to freedom of expression and to the ongoing work of human rights groups, whom Fujimori frequently accused of being "apologists" for terrorism. Other changes virtually eliminated the democratic principles of due process and the presumption of innocence. The new laws made it nearly impossible for defendants to obtain adequate representation: defense attorneys were restricted to representing one client at a time nationwide, and suspects could be held for fifteen days incommunicado, during which time they were not allowed to see a lawyer.[29] Perhaps most alarmingly, a system of faceless military courts to try terrorism cases removed accountability from the entire trial process.[30] Military trials are in effect summary trials, in which one of the parties to the conflict—the military—is judge and jury, meaning that defendants do not receive an impartial trial. Hundreds of people who had no connection to guerrilla movements, or who may have collaborated unwittingly with guerrilla groups or under coercion, were arrested and sentenced to long prison terms under this legal regime (Burt 1994). In most instances the defendant is presumed guilty and must prove his or her innocence. In practice, these laws resulted in massive arbitrary arrests, and thousands of individuals were incarcerated who were in fact innocent of any wrongdoing. This created a climate of fear and effectively undermined the exercise of citizenship in Peru.

Refashioning State-Society Relations

A key problem for authoritarian rulers is how to maintain legitimacy. In the case of Fujimori, some semblance of legitimacy was derived from the reinstatement of electoral processes in November 1992. However, the regime's legitimacy was primarily derived from its policy successes. The social disarticulation resulting from the process of state breakdown exacerbated the tendency of average citizens to value concrete policy successes as opposed to more abstract principles of democratic rule and procedures. Each policy success strengthened the authoritarian coalition—and the public's tendency to measure political performance according to concrete outcomes. One of the key policy successes of the Fujimori regime was on the economic front: hyperinflation decreased from over 7,000 percent in 1990 to under 10 percent in 1995, while GDP improved dramatically after years of negative growth rates to 7 percent in 1993 and 13 percent in 1994. Another was the arrest of the top Shining Path leadership. While the state did not completely regain its monopoly over the use of violence, the economic reprieve and the decline in political violence gave Peruvians a new sense of hope and confidence, bestowing the regime with newfound legitimacy and substantial political capital. Clearly this played a significant role in Fujimori's reelection in 1995. It also made it possible for Fujimori and his military allies to consolidate a highly authoritarian and personalistic form of rule in postwar Peru, despite the electoral processes held in the aftermath of the 1992 *autogolpe.*

Another key factor was weakness of political and civil society, as noted above. Democratic theorists have long noted that in the context of authoritarian regimes, transitions to democratic forms of governance are impossible until there is a viable alternative that has won credibility and support from a substantial sector of the population (Przeworski 1986). Fujimori and his allies were keenly aware of this fact and sought deliberately and systematically to weaken political and civil society so that no effective opposition to their rule could emerge. The social and political fragmentation and deinstitutionalization that contributed to the rise of Fujimori and his authoritarian government became the conditions for sustaining its power over the long term.

Attacks against organized politics were directed at three levels. Fujimori attacked the "traditional" political parties and the "party-ocracy" that he claimed had failed Peru in the past. He often railed against the traditional parties, contrasting the efficacy of his government and the armed forces with the "incompetence" of civilian politicians. Employing language strikingly similar to that of national security doctrine—which views civilian politicians as corrupt and weak and holds that their elimination is necessary to allow the armed forces to reestablish order—he attacked Peru's politicians and parties, reinforcing popular sentiment against the predominantly white and Lima-based political class. Fujimori also routinely lambasted democratic institutions like Congress and the judiciary, exacerbating popular disdain for these institutions and reinforcing support for his authoritarian model.

The Fujimori regime also sought to undermine civil society by bypassing established social movements and grassroots organizations, many of which had grown dependent on government aid in the context of the economic crisis. Instead, the Fujimori government began a program of direct government handouts and subsidies to individuals and new groups that had organized for precisely this purpose. Preexisting grassroots organizations, already weakened by the economic crisis, which had sapped their resource base, and political violence, were further hobbled by this practice. While during its first two years the Fujimori regime lacked a coherent set of social policies, by 1993 it began to establish a variety of new government agencies, which began a slow process of co-optation of existing social organizations. This was the case, for example, with the community soup kitchens, or *comedores populares,* which were so frequently cited in the 1980s as independent locally initiated solutions to the very real problem of hunger and malnutrition in Lima's shantytowns. Denied government support in the early period of the Fujimori regime, the *comedores* lost a crucial resource base, eroding much of their organizational capacity. When government officials later approached *comedor* organizers with offers of government assistance, they often felt obliged to accept in order to continue functioning. Through its control of resources, the regime was then able to co-opt support by guaranteeing assistance to progovernment organizations. Where it could not co-opt, it imposed political conditions, obliging members to participate in pro-Fujimori rallies and the like.[31]

Repression and the manipulation of fear was a third tactic, and one that is not broadly discussed in analyses of the Fujimori regime. With the arrest of

Shining Path leaders in 1992 and the subsequent decline in violence, many analysts ceased to pay attention to the way fear continued to operate in Peruvian society and how it was manipulated by the Fujimori regime to keep its opponents disorganized. In the context of the regime's "triumph" against Shining Path, it articulated a discourse in which all opponents were terrorists, making it extremely risky for grassroots activists to attempt to articulate an opposition discourse. One social activist in the popular district of Villa El Salvador replied, when I asked her why she and those like her who opposed the Fujimori regime did not organize or mobilize to demonstrate their concerns: "He who speaks out is [considered] a terrorist." Fear was clearly part of her calculus when deciding whether to publicly express her opposition to the Fujimori regime (Burt 2002).

Fujimori and his allies not only repressed organized politics. They also sought to replace it by reordering state-society relations along clientelistic lines. With power centralized in the hands of the executive and Shining Path under control, the state had both the means and the ability to reestablish its presence throughout the country. Establishing vertical and clientelistic linkages with society was key to building legitimacy for the Fujimori regime and to crowding out other independent organizing initiatives. Fujimori himself led the drive to build clientelistic relations with society by traveling widely throughout the country to deliver immediate benefits to poor rural communities. The state ministries that normally directed state social policy were eviscerated, and the newly created Ministry of the Presidency directed nearly all social projects and public works, including the building of schools and clinics; the development of infrastructure such as electricity and potable water; and the bestowing of gifts, such as computers and school supplies. The army, meanwhile, through civic-action campaigns, became the main distributor of other state benefits such as foodstuffs and medicine, which it handed out directly to the poor, bypassing local forms of organization and reinforcing the direct link between the state and social groups.

This type of direct, unmediated relationship between the leader and the masses has led several analysts to adopt the term "neopopulist" to describe the approach of Fujimori and other leaders in the region such as Hugo Chávez.[32] The usage of this concept is misleading, however. In contrast to historic populism, which while often nondemocratic was nonetheless characterized by inclusionary policies toward the popular sectors, Fujimori's project was radically exclusionary. Reducing populism to the direct relationship between leader and masses strips the concept of all historic content, when it is much more useful analytically to retain its usage to describe a specific historical phenomenon: the redistributionist state-led regimes of the 1940s and 1950s, such as that of Perón in Argentina, Vargas in Brazil, and Cárdenas in Mexico.[33] Moreover, those using the term "neopopulism" fail to explain why Fujimori's social policies could not be described as clientelism and co-optation, which seem to more effectively capture the nature of the state's interactions with popular sectors in rural and urban areas. The state provided government handouts in exchange for concrete political support (political clientelism) and sought to control and manipulate formerly independent groups in support of its programs and policies (co-optation).

As the regime's policy successes became fewer and further between—particularly after 1997, when economic growth slowed and there were no improvements in unemployment and underemployment—the bases of its legitimacy began to weaken. This is evident in public-opinion polls, which show a declining trend of support for Fujimori and his regime from 1997 onward. The return of outright repression—now linked not to the counterinsurgency war but directly to the regime's need to silence opponents in order to assure its continuity in power—also began to harm its legitimacy, though there was still a significant segment of the population willing to counter such abuses given that they perceived there to be few alternatives. Nonetheless, domestic opposition to the regime began to build in the context of the regime's efforts to assure a third term for Fujimori at any cost. The regime's blatant power grabbing also contributed to growing international criticism of the regime, especially surrounding the irregularities of the 2000 electoral process. There is not sufficient space to examine this process in detail here, but it is important to note the growing shift in domestic and international support for the regime. Most important, however, were the changes within the regime itself. A small band of mafialike leaders had assumed control over the state by 1998 (the year that Bari de Hermoza was forced out as commander in chief of the armed forces, allowing Montesinos to assume virtually complete control of the military). This was facilitated, as suggested above, by the extreme personalism and anti-institutionalism of the Fujimori regime and the debilitation of civil and political society. By 1997, the regime's emphasis on rebuilding the state, albeit in authoritarian fashion, had shifted radically to simply maintaining power and assuring its continued impunity. The vast networks of corruption that continue to be discovered bear witness to this fact. But this mafialike behavior became the predominant characteristic of the regime only in the late 1990s, when state building was abandoned in favor of outright corruption and cynicism. While the state enjoyed great autonomy in the early 1990s in its efforts to rebuild the state, the inability of civil and political society to exercise democratic controls on this process allowed for the establishment of an extremely personalistic and anti-institutional regime that by the end of the decade had degenerated into a state of mafialike predation.

The State, Democracy, and Civil Society

The scholarship on the Fujimori regime reveals conceptual confusion about how to categorize the regime: most analysts refer to it as a democracy, though its circumscribed nature is customarily noted with the addition of some adjective—delegative democracy, semidemocracy, authoritarian democracy, neopopulism.[34] The 1995 reelection of Fujimori in particular was pointed out by some scholars (and policy makers as well) as evidence of Peru's full return to the democratic fold after the authoritarian hiatus represented by the 1992 *autogolpe*. Such a reading of Peruvian politics under Fujimori fails, however, to grasp the underlying power dimensions of the regime, focusing too much on formal political arrangements and not examining the everyday political practices of the regime. It also represents a very limited definition of democracy as coterminous with free and fair elections, rather than adopting a broader definition that examines other institutional bases of democracy, such as civilian control over the armed forces and dimensions of representation and citizenship. This narrow focus on formal institutions has also led scholars to reread the Fujimori regime after its demise as one in which authoritarian tendencies were evident *after* the 1995 elections, as the regime sought by any means to ensure a third term in office for Fujimori. Again, this negates the continuity between the 1992 *autogolpe* and the post-coup reordering of power.

The Peruvian case offers an important lesson for scholars and policy makers concerned with democratic governance. Weak states provide a weak institutional basis for the affirmation of democratic institutions. Without a strong state that guarantees the rule of law and universal citizenship, civil society cannot exist; as John Keane (1988) suggests, civil society cannot remain civil unless it is ordered politically. Without political society, there is no mediation between the leader and the masses. And without limits on state rule (asserted primarily by actors in civil and political society), accountability is undermined and democracy eviscerated: "State power without social obstacles is always hazardous and undesirable, a license for despotism" (Keane 1988, 51). Peru under Fujimori represented just that, state power without social obstacles, and it undoubtedly gave him and his regime "a license for despotism."

This analysis also offers broader theoretical lessons for students of weak states that, like Peru in the 1980s, begin to break down or disintegrate: the imperative of rebuilding state institutions in such a context is likely to trump democracy building. The case of Colombia today is a case in point: like Peru in the late 1980s, massive political violence, a declining economy, and disintegrating state institutions have created a groundswell of support for authoritarian solutions, be they societally based, as in support for the paramilitary groups that are leading a violent and brutal counterinsurgency war against guerrilla groups, or state-based, as in the massive support for hard-liner Alvaro Uribe Vélez, Colombia's new president, who has promised to mobilize a million civilians to combat the insurgents and bring Colombia's conflict to an end not through peace negotiations but through warfare. Unless actors in civil and political society are well organized and able to assert alternative models of rebuilding the state, democracy will surely be a casualty.

The collapse of the Fujimori regime in 2000 has opened new possibilities for Peru to reconstruct democratic governance. However, the above analysis suggests that the problem is deeper than simply the nature of the elites who held power between 1990 and 2000 (though the gangsterlike quality of some of those elites did imprint their own characteristics on the regime). The weakness of the state and its nondemocratic nature are clearly one dimension of the problem that must be addressed through a series of state reforms to re-order the relationship among the branches of government to ensure that checks and balances operate properly (horizontal accountability); to guarantee that the military remains a nondeliberative body subject to democratic civilian control; to ensure a fair justice system based on the rule of law and (vertical) accountability; and to develop adequate forms of political representation and mediation between state and society. Just as important as these state-based reforms is overcoming the persistent weakness of political and civil society. While some state reforms may help establish a stronger foundation for the development of political and civil society (e.g., a law requiring all political parties to hold internal primaries might be a way of helping to democratize political representation; guaranteeing civil liberties through a nonpartisan judiciary may facilitate organization within civil society), the extreme weakness of political and social actors is a long-term problem that works against the consolidation of democratic governance, for it is organized political and civil society that is most likely to press for democratic reforms and institutions in the first instance. These remain very weak in post-Fujimori Peru, making it tempting for new rulers to employ similar tactics—co-optation, clientelism, repression—to control opposition movements and maintain power. Democracy building in such a context is likely to remain an elusive objective.

Jo-Marie Burt and Philip Mauceri

Conclusion

We began this book by noting the high degree of instability that has affected the Andean region in the last decades. At the same time, we have been sensitive to the significant policy and political differences among the Andean nations. It has been our intention to flesh out some of the common historical and social experiences of the region that could help us understand the sources of this instability, while being attuned to the different political and policy responses adopted in this very diverse region. Three specific issues are increasingly of concern to social scientists looking at Latin America: the state, social control, and conflict; globalization and transnational actors; and democracy and political change.

The State, Social Control, and Conflict

Social conflict can be an effective indicator of the social control—that is, the level of compliance, participation, and legitimation—available to the state (Migdal 1988, 33). Extensive or continuous social conflict suggests that states have failed to gain or perhaps lost the ability to achieve social control within their territory. In turn, the ways in which social control is exercised (or not) by the state reflect patterns of state formation and how these historical processes shape state institutions and state-society relations. The mechanisms of social control adopted—whether coercion, charismatic leadership, clientelism, or repression—are likely to have arisen from specific patterns of state formation. Although the literature does not identify the full range of state formation "pathways," it is clear that there are many processes integral to state building that are relevant for an understanding of social control, including the creation of a common national discourse (Anderson 1991), the experiences of external or internal warfare (Tilly 1975; López-Alves 2000), and the types of class alliances favoring/disfavoring centralizing power for economic modernization (Mann 1986; Tilly 1995).

Throughout the Andean countries, levels of social conflict, both violent and nonviolent, remain high. In examining social conflict, however, it is necessary to keep in mind the links among such conflict, social control, and state building processes. Both state development and social organization in this region have been shaped by shared, historically persistent factors, although each country has responded to the challenges and opportunities presented in different ways.

As the institutions and state-society relations resulting from the exclusionary and highly authoritarian state formation experiences of the nineteenth and twentieth centuries are challenged in the Andean region, it is not surprising that social conflict has increased. Yet this should not be seen as necessarily threatening or dangerous, as those who frame such issues from a "crisis of governability" perspective suggest. Social conflict has enormous potential to democratize state structures, as well as to make them less susceptible to corruption and clientelism—as has been the case, for example, in such countries as Bolivia and Venezuela (Grindle 2000). As voices that have been excluded or repressed are increasingly making themselves heard, the ways state institutions deal with society are being radically altered in the region.

Yet not all the challenges to state structures and the relations they are built upon have resulted in greater democracy or peaceful reform. Many of those challenging the state, as well as the state actors responding to challengers, have engaged in violence, political repression, and gross violations of human rights. It is clear that the choices these actors make are at least in part shaped by historic patterns of state-society relations. The rapid disintegration of democratic institutions in Venezuela during the 1990s, for example, cannot be understood outside of this country's historic context.

Globalization and the Influence of International Actors

The peoples, products, and cultures of the Andean region are still marked by the first wave of globalization, namely the so-called encounters of the sixteenth and seventeenth centuries among the Americas, Europe, and Africa. Where conquest, resource extraction, and the violent subjugation of peoples were characteristic of that initial wave of globalization, the current wave finds the region's countries better able to take advantage of opportunities to advance economic and political interests, although they are clearly still at a disadvantage in the distribution of international power. The process and history of globalization is a complex subject (Hirst and Thompson 1996; Berger and Dore 1996), but at least two themes point to some of the most important debates regarding the impact of globalization.

In the economic arena, the promise of stable export markets and investments along with rising growth has been displaced by intense competition in commodity markets, capital flows that shift rapidly in search of short-term profits, and rapidly changing production structures that are linked to regional and global trade networks through a complex array of regional integration pacts and the global structures of multinational corporations. Underdeveloped economies, particularly those heavily reliant on primary-product exports with only limited industrial capacity, as in the Andean region, face a particular challenge, especially in the political realm. In Ecuador, for example, not only have economic changes altered the political landscape, but some historic patterns, many of which are detrimental to both democratization and economic development, have also been reinforced by global economic trends. Specifically, the "Washington Consensus" has helped "rentier elites" improve their ability to pursue short-term gains and increased their access to the state, while the state's autonomy and regulatory capacity have significantly deteriorated.

Challenges to traditional parties and systems of representation may also be linked to the increased strains on the economic models that sustained them. Venezuela's oil exports, for example, financed import-substitution industrialization, vast structural improvements, and growing political clientelism. Nonetheless, the global economic changes in the 1980s involving declining oil prices and open markets undermined these traditional political institutions. After several unsuccessful efforts to adapt through neoliberal restructuring, which left a growing population impoverished, traditional political elites found themselves displaced, and Venezuela confronted an unprecedented degree of political uncertainty. Although the economic challenge is less dramatic in Colombia, the country's traditionally stable economic strategy has been shaken. Facing increased competition in commodity markets, especially in coffee, and pressures to "open" its markets during the 1990s, Colombia's political elites have been hard-pressed to maintain the system of clientelism that has long sustained them in power. Yet Colombia's ongoing internal war and the continued presence of drug-trafficking activities may have ironically alleviated pressures on the formal political system. Insurgents provide an "extrasystemic" outlet for those disenchanted with the traditional system, while drug money allows local politicians to find "informal" means to finance their clienteles. As a result violence and democracy coexist, albeit in tension.

In attempting to manage the global changes brought about by new technologies and the restructuring of production, investment, and trade, political actors in the Andes are presented with new opportunities as well as dangers to democracy and economic development. Integrated global transportation networks along with new communication networks reliant on satellite and Internet technologies have broken down administrative and organizational barriers, allowing previously isolated social groups to transcend national and cultural boundaries. Still, there remains much disagreement in the literature between those who believe that many of these trends are fostering privatization and individualism, both of which threaten democratic values (Putnam 1995), and those who argue that new forms of community and self-definition are reshaping the conceptualization and practice of democracy (Norris 1999). The impact that these processes are having on societies and regimes is clearly far from uniform; rather, the effects of these processes are multifaceted and even contradictory. On the one hand, globalization appears to be helping to foster social resistance to the dominant discourses of traditional elite structures as well as to promote organizational support and political relationships across existing boundaries, that is, moving to develop a regional and, in some instances, a global civil society. This can be seen in the transnational reach of women's groups, the indigenous movement, and human rights organizations.

Yet the same processes that have promoted increased connections among the indigenous and women in the region have also presented new challenges for social and political actors. The global reach of drug trafficking, for example, has been facilitated by the globalization of finance, communications, and transportation and has made the trade in drugs far more lucrative than at any other time.

A final element to consider is the impact of globalization on the state. While there appears to be a growing consensus that the concept of "state sovereignty" is undergoing serious revision, few predict its imminent demise, and it is far from apparent what the new bounds of sovereignty will be (Sassen 1996; Spybey 1996; Strange 1998). As new identities emerge that transcend national boundaries, what will this mean for the loyalties upon which state authority and legitimacy rest? Can the growing body of international human rights law and associated institutions finally help restrain state actors from engaging in the sorts of abuses that have for too long been considered the norm? With underdeveloped states increasingly competing for investments and markets, will they be forced to reduce their regulatory functions to merely providing physical security? From the uncertainty that these questions suggest it should be clear that the nature of state power is undergoing a radical shift, and with it the relations between states and societies and between states and markets. Ultimately, the impact of these changes will depend not only on the transformations wrought by globalization but also on the ways in which political leaders and social groups respond to the opportunities and dangers they present.

Political Change and Democracy in the Andes

Over the past two decades, there have been remarkable shifts in the politics in each of the five countries examined in this book, posing deep challenges to democratic forms of governance. What is most striking, however, is that within the region, two countries—Colombia and Venezuela—were considered long-standing and stable democracies, while the other three countries—Peru, Bolivia, and Ecuador—were classic praetorian societies that experienced seemingly endless cycles of military and/or authoritarian rule, and civilian democratic rule. Yet despite these different political histories, today each of these countries is facing deep social conflict that is straining even the most long-standing democratic arrangements.

These crises have manifested themselves in different ways: coups and attempted coups (Venezuela, Peru, and Ecuador); creeping authoritarianism (Peru under Fujimori and Venezuela under Chávez); authoritarian practices in the context of formal democratic arrangements (military tribunals, police brutality against social protests, gross human rights violations); and civil conflict. Yet underlying these different manifestations of democratic instability are remarkably similar problems linked to the exclusionary nature of the region's democratic systems. Despite some efforts to open political systems (witness the important constitutional changes throughout the region in the past decade), decision-making remains an elite affair, with little input from citizens. The much-discussed crisis of representation, a circumscribed understanding of citizenship, low levels of democratic accountability, and weak state institutions have all affected democratic governance in Latin America and the Andean region. While these crises clearly take on different forms and have distinct causes, some commonalities can be drawn out for comparative purposes.

Over the course of the past two decades, with the emergence of the so-called third wave of democracy, social scientists have extensively examined the question of democratization in Latin America and beyond. The focus has shifted from the question of the process of transition from authoritarian regimes to more open, democratic systems (O'Donnell and Schmitter 1986), to issues of democratic consolidation (Linz and Stepan 1996), to approaches that analyze the "quality" and "depth" of democracy. Those writing from the latter perspective have suggested that the paths to transition seem less determinate than they did a decade or more ago and question the concept of consolidation for mistakenly setting up a teleological endgame for new democracies and for missing the fact that many Latin American democracies, while not in danger of immediate collapse, are far from meeting the criteria for "democratic consolidation" (Hagopian 1993; O'Donnell 1996). As a result, increasingly greater emphasis has been placed on examining questions of accountability, rule of law, representation, and citizenship under the rubric of the "quality of democracy" and democratic governance (Agüero and Stark 1998; Méndez, O'Donnell, and Pinheiro 1999; Touraine 1997).

The framework outlined by Felipe Agüero and Jeffrey Stark is particularly useful in this regard. While recognizing the importance of competitive elections and other procedural aspects of democracy that largely evaded the region only a couple of decades ago, its metaphor of the "fault lines" of democracy in post-transition Latin America opens new lines of inquiry, permitting a critical analysis of "really existing democracies" in the region. In the Andean region in particular, such an approach is most useful, as it allows analysts to examine the complexity of the region's politics by taking seriously the existence of democratic institutions in countries like Colombia and Venezuela, as well as the important political liberalization that has taken place in Bolivia, Ecuador, and Peru since the late 1970s and early 1980s, while at the same time recognizing the severe limitations and challenges each of these democracies, new and old, confronts. In the Andean region, democratic institutions and procedures including competitive elections, citizen participation, a free press, and so on, coexist with practices that are far from democratic—ranging from those that may, over time, erode the notion of democratic citizenship, such as persistent clientelism and bossism, to those that fundamentally challenge the civil and political liberties that underpin democratic governance, including intimidation of the press, repression, and outright murder of political opponents. The empirical evidence discussed in much of this book vividly illustrates the dramatic gap in the Andes (evident throughout much of Latin America as well) between formal democratic institutions and everyday politics and practices.

Representation and Citizenship

Perhaps the most dramatic gap is evident in the chasm between formal institutional politics, including the state and political parties, and society. This has been conceptualized primarily as a crisis of representation, and while clearly evident throughout Latin America, it is particularly acute in the Andean region. Presumably linked to declining voter identification with political parties and in some cases, such as Peru and Venezuela, the complete collapse of existing party systems, this crisis of representation has been identified as a serious problem for democratic governance. While some authors have suggested that democratic politics is possible without strong political parties (Levitsky 1999), others have argued that parties are the sine qua non of democratic governance (Hagopian 1998; Roberts 2002). While other organizations may emerge that are able to channel voter preferences (as has been the case in much of the Andean region, particularly Peru, with the rise of independent candidates and candidate-specific electoral vehicles that often disappear after the election itself), political parties are the actors that historically have best been able to ensure accountability to citizens. Still, as Frances Hagopian

(1998) has argued, there is evidence to suggest that the crisis of representation is more than just a temporary phenomenon, as traditional parties in some countries have had a difficult time reorganizing themselves and as party systems weaken under the combined challenges of economic dislocation, corruption scandals, declining ideologies, and cultural shifts that undermine clientelist or patronage relationships.

In Peru, for example, following the dramatic crises of the 1980s, traditional political parties faded from political view in the 1990s, eclipsed by "outsider" and "independent" candidates who went out of their way to distance themselves from traditional parties. The party system in Venezuela also collapsed in the face of corruption and citizen discontent, paving the way for the election of a former paratrooper who had once tried to overthrow democracy via a military coup. The Venezuelan case is perhaps more dramatic than the Peruvian case, as parties in Peru were always weak and unstable and the period during which they became more vigorous—the decade of the 1980s—was not propitious for their consolidation, as political violence and economic crisis undermined their ability to organize coherently. In Venezuela, however, the traditional parties—Democratic Action and the Social Christian COPEI—had dominated politics since 1958, and their demise marked a dramatic deterioration of organized politics. The rise of "outsider" politicians with marked authoritarian tendencies in each case seems indelibly linked with this decline in organized political parties.

Parties in Ecuador and Bolivia were, as in the Peruvian case, always weak and unable to maintain consistent voter loyalty. In these countries, however, actors in civil society have to some extent been able to bridge the crisis of representation by organizing and mobilizing their constituents and effectively projecting their demands into the political system. In Ecuador, for example, the indigenous movement moved with much success into electoral politics at the local level, although it faces greater difficulty at the national level. In Bolivia, groups based in civil society have also seriously challenged the traditional party system. This was most recently demonstrated in the 2002 presidential elections, in which indigenous leader and relentless critic of neoliberalism and coca-eradication programs Evo Morales closely contested the election, garnering 21 percent of the vote, just behind frontrunner and former president Gonzalo Sánchez de Lozada.

In Ecuador, parties have always been weak and inchoate; Catherine M. Conaghan (1995) describes its political system as being populated with "floating politicians and floating voters." In the face of weak representative institutions, the military and economic elites have been the principal actors in Ecuadorian politics. These elites have been short-sighted in their failure to develop a national project and have consistently vetoed efforts to develop a more broad-based understanding of national interests (as pursued, e.g., by inclusionary military regimes during the 1920s and again in the 1960s). This myopia of the elites has undermined democratic governance in Ecuador, as it has undercut the formation of a broadly based set of identities and has favored private interests over national interests. There are encouraging signs that this may be changing as new groups mobilize in Ecuador. Pachakutik, for example, is clearly bridging a gap in representation by linking a long-excluded segment of the population, the indigenous, to the political system, and it appears to be doing so by practicing good governance in terms of internal democratic practices. Still, support by some of the more radical factions of the party for the January 2000 military coup highlights the fact that even democratic social movements may engage in practices that undermine, rather than fortify, democracy.

Peru bears some similarity to the Ecuadorian case in the weakness of its political parties, the predominance of the military in political life, and the inability of elites to conceive of a broad-based national project that incorporates a diverse and heterogeneous population (Cotler 1978; McClintock and Lowenthal 1983). And, like Ecuador, its experience with democracy was tenuous at best. The collapse of the democratic experiment in 1992 was not preordained, but it was not surprising either, given the failure of elites to address the deepening economic crisis that had set in by the late 1980s; the dramatic expansion of political violence, which revealed the state's tenuous hold on authority in vast swaths of the countryside; and the abdication of democratic authority by governing elites, who handed control over counterinsurgency and nearly two-thirds of the national territory to the military. But neoliberalism cannot be construed as the cause of economic collapse in Peru; on the contrary, it was the failure of the heterodox experiment implemented by Alan García (1985–90) and Shining Path violence that sparked a dramatic weakening of the state and the collapse of representative institutions. In this vacuum, Peruvians placed their faith instead in a political unknown, Alberto Fujimori (1990–2000), who promised to restore order and stability—though at the cost of civil and political liberties. Expediency and the dramatic desire for security led many Peruvians to tolerate human rights abuses, authoritarian leadership, and the evisceration of democratic institutions. With the dramatic collapse of the Fujimori regime in late 2000, many observers were optimistic about the possibility of reinstating democratic rule in Peru, but the persistence of the very factors that made Fujimori possible— the undemocratic nature of the Peruvian state and the weakness of political parties and of civil society—means that securing democracy is a far more daunting challenge than it might seem at first glance.

Colombia is perhaps the most anomalous case of all, given the long-standing nature of its party system and the durability of its "traditional" parties. Highlighted as a "first-wave democracy" and long praised in the literature as an example of democratic governance, Colombia displays perhaps the most dramatic fault line of all: a huge gap between democratic procedures and norms and the fact of systematic political exclusion, first by political arrangement (the National Front agreement, which limited participation to two parties, the Liberals and Conservatives) and later by political repression (both state-sponsored and privatized violence, through paramilitary groups).

Despite the real limitations facing the regions' democracies, it is important not to minimize the significance of a democratic political climate. Democracy opens political space for groups in civil society to organize, mobilize, and press their demands at the level of the state—as indigenous groups have done in Bolivia, Ecuador, and Colombia. While these movements may effectively contest citizenship, however, they are also under assault from neoliberal state policies, which often seek to turn their members not into citizens with full rights and responsibilities but into clients or consumers of targeted social programs. Neoliberalism implies a deliberate decoupling of social and political citizenship (Lechner and Calderon 1998), seeking to reduce the notion of citizenship to mere political rights while robbing it of the crucial dimension of social and economic rights. This raises issues of the substantive aspects of democracy that are increasingly difficult to ignore. The problem is not only one of inequality and poverty, which clearly undercut the ability of individuals to be effective and informed citizens. It is also related to the way citizenship is being redefined in the neoliberal mold to exclude social and economic rights, which historically have been a defining element of citizenship in a democratic polity.

The State and Democratic Governance

When the state is "captured" by shortsighted elites, or when it is so weak that it fails to perform the basic functions of a state, democracy is not easily sustained. Without a clearly defined public sphere where the rule of law and public accountability is assured, where citizenship is broadly defined, and where public security is guaranteed to all members of the polity, democratic governance is at risk. And while this relationship is evident in many parts of Latin America, it is perhaps most acute in the Andean region, where the inability to forge a broad public sphere has seriously curbed the possibilities of democratic governance.

Ecuador is a case in point. Patterns of state building there, in which regional elites pursued private interests over national interests and sought to maintain a weak state that they could easily manipulate to their advantage, undermined more inclusive forms of participation and hence created the bases for a weak, even dysfunctional, democracy. In the context of neoliberal reforms, coastal elites used financial reforms, particularly the deregulation of the banking system (which led to a massive collapse of the economy and eventually to dollarization), to shift blame from their own corrupt practices to the central government and to advocate decentralizing changes that further weakened the central state and its capacity to regulate the economy. The inability of state elites to manage the economic crisis further deinstitutionalized the political sphere, which ultimately benefits coastal elites as it makes it even easier for them to secure their own interests and extract resources from a weak state. This, in turn, undermines the very notion of a public sphere; accountability and citizenship—the cornerstones of democratic governance—are eviscerated as elites "capture" the state and pursue their own interests to the detriment of the national good.

In Peru in the 1980s and Colombia in the 1990s, the absence or weakening of central state power undermined democratic accountability and citizenship, even as state repression increased. The abandonment of entire areas of the country by the state contributed to the exacerbation of social conflict and privatized violence, as well as to new forms of illegal activity, particularly the drug trade. In the Colombian case, in the void left by an absent state, drug traffickers and guerrillas engaged in local dispute resolution, building local power bases and extracting needed resources to finance their wars. A similar situation was evident in Peru in the 1980s and early 1990s, as the fiscal crisis of the state led to its retreat in areas where it had been previously engaged; there and elsewhere, where the state's absence had long been evident, Shining Path guerrillas also became involved in local dispute resolution (Manrique 1989; Burt 1997). This privatization of violence and dispute resolution—clear evidence of a weakening or collapsing state—is antithetical to democracy, as it removes such issues from public debate, deepens the tradition of exclusion of the poor from the public arena, and undermines the adopting of public policies to improve the social and economic conditions of the poor. Unlike the Peruvian case, which represented an effort on the part of the state to reimpose legitimacy (though this ultimately degenerated into a mafialike regime under Alberto Fujimori and Vladimiro Montesinos), in Colombia the state has delegated its authority to private actors. The bulk of the counterinsurgency effort in that country is carried out by paramilitary groups, who, during the late 1990s, were responsible for over 75 percent of the acts of violence committed there. In both cases, democratic governance was eviscerated in the context of expanding political violence, the incapacity of state elites to establish legitimate authority, and the growing weariness of the local population, which led to growing support for heavy-handed solutions.

The chapters in this volume represent just a small sample of the ongoing research by the authors and others into the politics, economics, and societies of the Andean region. We believe that they highlight what will be the continuing challenges for the region in the coming decades: building and deepening democratic institutions and practices; ending structures of social exclusion and reevaluating social policies and practices that have perpetuated poverty, inequality, and racism; balancing the need for macroeconomic stability while pursuing a development model that addresses the needs of ordinary citizens; and managing demands from international actors while defending national and regional interests. Clearly, these are challenges that many of the other regions of Latin America will also share in the coming decades. It has not been our purpose to offer policy prescriptions for addressing these challenges. Nor have we been focused on providing either overly pessimistic scenarios based on some of the real problems that continue to plague the region or overly optimistic scenarios based on some very tangible positive trends. Rather we hope to have provided a realistic assessment of the challenges and prospects facing one of the most analytically neglected but fascinating regions of Latin America.

No volume on a region as large and diverse as the Andes can hope to answer all the outstanding questions that affect its politics, society, and economy. Our hope here is that we have provided a road map, with some notable highlights, through the difficult terrain of the Andes that may entice and encourage further comparative research in and reflection on the region. Many of the questions we have raised in this volume may provide the basis for future research agendas, particularly as the impact and evolution of some of the changes analyzed here become clearer. For example, much work still needs to be done on the long-term impact of neoliberal policies in the region, from the implications of privatization and the insertion of international actors in the economies of the countries, to the social and political transformations wrought by these policies. While all of the chapters in this volume have struggled with assessing the torrent of political changes that took place during the 1990s, the task of analyzing specific elements of these changes remains. New institutional structures, including new constitutions, new roles for the military, and new identity-based parties, all provide areas where future research needs to be directed. At the same time, the region is not isolated from the rest of Latin America or the world, and many trends noted here are global. Research that compares indigenous movements in light of ethnic conflict globally, for example, may help us understand these trends better. In short, we have seen this volume as a beginning and hope that it will be merely one of many attempts to reassess the politics of the Andes.

↶ Notes

Notes to Introduction
1. See in particular, Conaghan and Malloy 1994; Thorp 1991; and Stern 1987.

Notes to Chapter 1
Translation from the Spanish by Philip Mauceri.

1. It is difficult to provide precise figures on the number of indigenous peoples, particularly given that acceptance of indigenous identity still carries a social stigma in the region. Bolivia is perhaps the most advanced of the countries, insofar as its Rural Indigenous Census of the Lowlands, done in 1994, provided an accurate and sensitive count of the rural indigenous. See Albó 1995 and Pozzi-Escot 1998. For Peru see Chirinos and Schwager 1997 and Chirinos 1998; on Ecuador see Knapp 1987.

2. With few exceptions, modern historians have tended to analyze these rebellions separately, heavily influenced by geographic divisions that were defined after independence. In reality, these divisions obscure the fact that the rebellions were merely two phases of a single movement.

3. Cited in de la Peña 1998, 41.

4. De la Peña 1998, 46.

5. On Peru see Carlos Franco 1991 and Nugent 1992; on Bolivia see Toranzo 1991.

6. Of the rebellions, the 1990 protests have been the most studied. See, among others, Ileana Almeida et al. 1992 and León 1994. On the 1992 protests, see Whitthen, Whitthen, and Chango 1997; on the 1994 protests see Pacari 1996.

7. Jorge Flores Ochoa, personal communication with the author, June 2000.

Notes to Chapter 2
1. Pachakutik also ran candidates on the coast but did not win any seats there.

2. These figures were reported to the author by Pachakutik staff people, Quito, August 24, 2000.

3. Because past national censuses did not contain questions pertaining to ethnicity, as of the time of this writing there are no reliable statistics on the size of the indigenous population in Ecuador.

4. Under Spanish colonial rule, Quichua, a derivation of Quechua, the language of the Inca Empire, became the lingua franca among all highland indigenous groups. Today highland indigenous peoples consider it their native language.

5. Whereas Quichua is the only remaining indigenous language spoken among highland groups, there are eight distinct Amazonian nationalities, each with its own language (CONAIE 1999).

6. In 1954 approximately one-fourth of the peasant population, probably almost completely indigenous, was subordinated to large haciendas through the debt-bondage system known as *huasipungo* (Zamosc 1989).

7. Two other national-level indigenous organizations, the Ecuadorian Federation of Evangelical Indians (FEINE) and the National Federation of Campesino, Indigenous, and Black Organizations (FENOCIN), have historically had competitive and at times conflictive relations with each other and CONAIE, but neither of them can match the organizational strength of CONAIE.

8. For an analysis of the indigenous movement's participation in the National Assembly, see Andolina 1999 and Endara Osejo 2000.

9. Previous to the formation of CONAIE, a number of indigenous leaders in small rural provinces helped launch local chapters of political parties and ran for office on various left and center-left tickets (Pallares 1997, 457).

10. For more detailed analyses of MUPP-NP see Andolina 1999 and Mijeski and Beck 1998.

11. District magnitude refers to the number of seats assigned to a given district. As a general rule, the greater the number of seats, the more proportional the system, whereas fewer seats result in more majoritarian outcomes.

12. See Beck and Mijeski 2001 for a detailed analysis that challenges the contention that Pachakutik has succeeded in capturing the votes of the indigenous poor.

13. See CEPLAES 1996.

14. See Moreno Yánez 1989.

15. See Iturralbe 1995.

16. See, for example, Selverston-Scher 2001; CEDIME 1993; and León 1994.

17. Auki Tituaña, interview with the author, Cotacachi, April 14, 2000.

18. To read about the experiences of some of these municipalities, see Grupo Democracia y Desarrollo Local 1999 and Cameron 2001.

19. Patriarchal structures are still prevalent in many indigenous communities and families, which often impedes female leadership in decision-making.

20. Congressman Gilberto Talahua, interview with the author, Quito, March 14, 2000.

21. *El Comercio,* "Gobierno-CONAIE: La firma no se dio," April 25, 2000.

22. Until 1998 members of Congress had direct access to patronage appointments and resources to distribute in their provinces, but these privileges were done away with by the 1998 constitution.

23. These comments are based on the author's interviews with three of the six Pachakutik congressional representatives serving from 1998 to 2002: Nina Pacari, Quito, February 3, 2000; Miguel Pérez, Quito, February 3, 2000; and Antonio Posso, Quito, February 1, 2000.

Notes to Chapter 3

I conducted research in Ecuador for this chapter during April 1998 and August 2001, and in Bolivia during October–November 1995, February–May 1999, and August 2001. In addition, my research was conducted through ongoing e-mail correspondence, telephone conversations, and analysis of media coverage in both countries throughout the past five years. This project is an extension of my earlier research on women's organizations and neoliberal politics in Ecuador, which I began in 1988 with the support of dissertation grants from Fulbright-Hayes and the Inter-American Foundation. I thank the Women's Studies Program and the Latin American Studies Center at Arizona State University for their summer support in 1998, 1999, and 2001. For the Ecuador study, I thank Gioconda Herrera, Rocío Rosero, Susana Wappenstein, Maruja Barrig, Virginia Vargas, and Sonia Alvarez for their input on earlier drafts. I also thank Silvia Vega and Patricia Palacios for information on the Coordinadora Política de Mujeres Ecuatorianas. In Bolivia, I warmly thank Vivian Arteaga. I also thank María Esther Pozo, Pamela Calla, Tom Kruze, María Lourdes Zabala, Diana Urioste, Wendy McFarren, Juan Arbona, and several others for their generosity, input, and support. Finally, many thanks to Jo-Marie Burt and Philip Mauceri for their comments and suggestions. While many people have provided their insight, all opinions expressed in this chapter are my own.

1. In this chapter I use "engender" in two senses: first, in the sense of "giving rise to" or "creating"; second, in the sense of illuminating the gender aspects of the process. To my knowledge, Sonia Alvarez (1990) was the first to systematically apply a feminist definition of "engendering" to research on Latin American women's movements.

2. For a historical analysis of Latin American women's movements, see Jelin 1990 and Jaquette 1994.

3. The Ecuador case study included in this chapter is based in part on an earlier study I conducted on the political responses of women's organizations to Ecuadorian nationalism in the late 1990s (see Lind 2003a).

4. Neoliberal reforms were put into place by the governments of President Victor Paz Estenssoro (1989–93) and President Gonzalo Sánchez de Lozada (1993–97), Decentralization policies shaped contemporary Bolivian politics through the current period of President Jorge Quiroga (August 2001–present). (After President Hugo Banzer resigned due to illness, Jorge Quiroga, the vice-president, became president.)

5. By "institutionalization" I am referring to the ways in which structural adjustment policies and other types of International Monetary Fund (IMF) and World Bank–inspired neoliberal reforms have become viewed as the norm in Latin American countries—and indeed throughout the world (Benería 1996). See also Lind 2002.

6. On February 6, 1997, Congress voted forty-four to thirty-four to remove Bucaram. This followed a nationwide strike in which two million people marched through the streets of cities, towns, and villages in Ecuador. For a comprehensive discussion of the events surrounding Bucaram's ousting, see Báez et al. 1997.

7. This resonates with other research conducted on this topic. See especially Verónica Schild's (1998) study on Chilean women's movements, in which she draws similar conclusions about the contradictory and increasingly unequal relationships between community-based women's organizations and the state, and between working-class and middle-class feminists, in the context of neoliberal reform. Also see Ríos 1998.

8. Directors of state women's agencies are appointed. Thus many come from the government's political party, rather than from civic women's organizations, although there have always been important exceptions.

9. Martha Ordoñez, interview with the author, April 1998.

10. For example, the state women's agency, which changes leadership with each new administration, determines which women to target, how to distribute funds, and where to implement projects.

11. María Lourdes Zabala, interview with the author, Cochabamba, April 15, 1999.

12. Diana Urioste, interview with the author, Coordinadora de la Mujer, April 20, 1998.

13. President Bucaram decorated Ecuadorian-born Lorena Bobbitt as a national hero following her trial in the United States for severing the penis of her husband, John Wayne Bobbitt. Like millions of Ecuadorians, President Bucaram viewed Bobbitt as a victim of U.S. imperialism and racism, as well as a victim of domestic violence, and honored her for "having cut off neocolonial relations." Bobbitt was officially acknowledged by the president in front of the Ecuadorian National Senate.

14. By this time, both the indigenous movement and the women's movement had acquired official political party status within the state. See Rosero, Vega, and Ávila 2000.

15. Vivian Arteaga, personal communication with the author, La Paz, July 22, 2001.

16. This is evident in the number of women's marches, protests, and public events focusing on this issue in all three countries, as well as in women's articulated political perspectives on issues of gender in Andean societies. See, for example, Abya-Yala n.d.

17. Many Latin American governments have relied upon women's unpaid and/or underpaid labor for social welfare distributive projects. Food-for-work programs, communal kitchens, daycare centers, cooperative stores, and local markets have all been developed by governments with the assumption that women have time to participate, often for free. For research on this topic in Ecuador, see Delgado Ribadeneira 1992b; Ojeda Segovia 1992; and Lind 2001. In Bolivia, see Salinas Mulder 1994 and Zabala 1995.

Notes to Chapter 4

This essay is a revised and abridged version of "Dismembering and Remembering the Nation: The Semantics of Political Violence in Venezuela," *Comparative Studies in Society and History,* 33.2 (1991):288–337. Included with the permission of Cambridge University Press.

1. The authors acknowledge research support by the Michigan Society of Fellows and the Spencer Foundation and institutional support by the Centro de Estudios Latinoamericanos Rómulo Gallegos.

2. See Coronil 1989.

3. The term "pueblo" (people) has a dual set of meanings: it encompasses the entire citizenry of Venezuela, and it refers to people who have lower-class (popular) origins.

4. Leftist guerrillas were active in the 1960s and "pacified" in 1970; the barrios remained the base for small radical groups. See Ellner 1980.

5. World oil prices quadrupled in late 1973 and remained high until the close of the decade, when they doubled. Government income from oil (which constitutes 60–75 percent of its total income and over 90 percent of export earnings) quadrupled just before Pérez took office. See Walton 1989.

6. The currency, stable since the 1920s, was drastically devalued in 1983.

7. The CEJAP combined members of the army, the Policia Técnica Judicial (PTJ), and the Dirección de los Servicios de Inteligencia y Prevención (DISIP), a paramilitary intelligence police agency.

8. A Colombian participant in the attack confessed it was an ambush (*El Nacional,* "La confesión de Yaruro," April 10, 1989).

9. These death factories were documented by Ralph Schusler in *El Diario de Caracas,* December 22–23, 1988, and *El Nacional,* May 1–3, 1989.

10. The line "A canoe travels up the Arauca River" opens the novel *Doña Bárbara,* written by Rómulo Gallegos during the dictatorial regime of Juan Vicente Gómez (1908–35). Gallegos became the nation's first freely elected president (1947), and this work was canonized as the national novel. An allegorical tale of national, class, and family foundations set in the *llanos* of Apure, it brings Bolívar back to earth in the form of a modernizing leader who courts the untutored pueblo. For the emerging middle-class leadership it became a template for action. This hopeful view of national transformation became imaginable with the growth of the oil industry (Skurski 1996).

11. See Amnesty International 1987, 1988.

12. See *Veneconomia,* March 1989, and *SIC,* April 1989.

13. The U.S. Department of State Report (1990) acknowledges this estimate.

14. Venezuelan legislation continued the Spanish colonial legal definition of the subsoil, and thus of petroleum, as the property of the estate. In 1976 President Pérez nationalized the oil industry with generous compensation.

15. On February 28 the debt negotiating commission signed a letter of intent with the IMF.

16. This tactic was used in Chile against President Salvador Allende; see *PROVEA* (1989).

17. Fear of police retaliation prevented many from denouncing their relatives' deaths.

18. Among government forces, one policemen and two members of the army were killed.

19. The rumor circulated that Fidel Castro had left three hundred trained agents who organized the riots.

20. See Coronil and Skurski 1991a on the double discourse of postcolonial nationalism.

21. A dramatic decomposition of the party system and reorganization of the political system have since occurred. The removal of President Pérez on charges of corruption, followed by two attempted military coups in 1992, culminated in the rise to the presidency in 1998 of Hugo Chávez, a military officer from the *llanos.* He marked the 1989 *disturbios* as the beginning of his political movement, for the military was forced to fire on the defenseless pueblo; he gained massive popular support for a policy newly divided along class and racial lines on a platform of Bolivarian peaceful revolution.

22. This draws on Anderson's discussion of nationalism as a modular "cultural artifact" (1991).

Notes to Chapter 5

Translation from the Spanish by Philip Mauceri. The author wishes to thank Dr. Elmar Rompczyk, primary advisor to the GTZ Group, for his assistance in the research for this project, although the author bears sole responsibility for the analysis offered here.

1. Matard-Bonucci 1994, 30.

2. Romano 1970, 180.

3. Matard-Bonucci 1994, 27.

4. Matard-Bonucci 1994, 150.

5. Romano 1970, 69.

6. Leopoldo Franchetti, cited in Matard-Bonucci 1994, 26.

7. Matard-Bonucci 1994, 122.

8. Matard-Bonucci 1994, 130.

9. IGAC 1993, 22–23.

10. Raffestin 1993.

11. See, for example, Romero 1997.

12. Romero 1997, 240.

13. Misión Rural 1998.

14. Misión Rural 1998, 6–7.

15. IGAC 1993, 104.

16. Díaz Sierra 1988.

17. For security reasons, the names of individuals have been changed.

18. When Cuesta was arrested in Santa Marta he was released due to the intervention of the senator from Magdalena.

19. *Informe de la comisión de organismos de derechos humanos sobre la masacre en la Ciénaga Grande de Santa Marta* (report of a commission of human rights NGOs, including the Colectivo de Abogados José Alvear Restrepo, the Asociación para la Promoción Social Alternativa MINGA, and the Centro de Investigación y Educación Popular [CINEP]), presented to Ciénaga Grande de Santa Marta, December 5–7, 2000; available at <http://www.derechos.org/nizkor/colombia/doc/cienaga.html>.

20. A historical overview is found in Acosta 1999.

21. Field research for this section was carried out in mid-February 2001.

22. See the "conversation" with Jorge Visbal in *El Espectador,* February 25, 2001.

23. In Puerto Asis alone, it is estimated that there are fifteen hundred intermediaries involved in the commercialization of coca paste, providing a clear idea of the potential role such a group can play in local conflicts.

24. Stone 1990, 77–78.

25. For an overview see Melo 1990 and Palacios 2001.

Notes to Chapter 6

1.Thomas Kahn, "Bolivians Fear a U.S.-Led War on Drugs," *Wall Street Journal,* June 24, 1991.

2. "The Drug Trade," *Fortune,* June 20, 1998.

3. This funding was included in both the FY2002 foreign operations request and the Pentagon's defense budget.

4. In January 2001, it was renamed the Western Hemisphere Institute for Security Cooperation.

5. Isacson 2001, 2.

6. Scott Wilson, "Colombia Increases Military's Power," *Washington Post,* August 17, 2001.

7. Anthony Fiaola, "In Venezuela, a Revolution from the Top," *Washington Post,* July 27, 1999.

8. See, for example, Samuel Doria Medina, Embassy of Bolivia, "Hearings before the Senate Committee on the Judiciary and the Senate Caucus on International Narcotics Control," March 27, 1990, 7.

9. Quoted in Andreas et al. 1991–92, 116.

10. "Drug Funds Termed Source for Terrorists," *Washington Post,* August 3, 1984.

11. "El Doctor" 1998.

12. Loayza 1998, 36.

13. Karen DeYoung, "'The Doctor' Divided U.S. Officials," *Washington Post,* September 22, 2000.

14. "U.S. Shrugged Off Corruption, Abuse in Service of Drug War," Center for Public Integrity, July 12, 2001, 1.

15. Coletta A. Youngers, "U.S. Policy toward Peru as the Elections Near," Washington Office on Latin America, March 29, 2001, 2–3.

16. Memorandum on Bolivia, Washington Office on Latin America, June 3, 1997, 1–2.

17. "Bolivia under Pressure: Human Rights and Coca Eradication," Human Rights Watch/Americas, May 1996, 2.

18. See Andean Information Network 2000.

19. See Ledebur 2002.
20. Human Rights Watch 2001, 13.
21. Human Rights Watch 2001, 13.
22. Human Rights Watch 2001, 1.
23. Diana Jean Schemo and Tim Golden, "Bogotá Aid: To Fight Drugs or Rebels?" *New York Times,* June 2, 1998.
24. "U.S. Wields Carrot and Stick in Colombia," *Reuters,* December 3, 1998.
25. Isacson 1998, 15; Schemo and Golden, "Bogotá Aid."
26. See Tate 2001, 9.
27. Bishop Belarmino Corea, interview with the author, San José del Guaviare, May 6, 1997.
28. Lesley MacKay, "The Coca Wars," *Ms. Magazine,* August–September 2001, 16.

Notes to Chapter 7
1. The conceptual framework as outlined here and most of the discussion regarding Peru are based on Mauceri 1996.
2. An overview of the literature and current debates is found in Migdal 1997.
3. On social relations before the 1960s, see especially Cotler 1978 and Klarén 2000.
4. On the military government see Lowenthal 1975 and McClintock and Lowenthal 1981.
5. See Crabtree 1991 and Maxwell Cameron 1993.
6. See Leal Buitrago 1989 and Palacios 1995.
7. Palacios 2001, 62.
8. The best overview of Colombia's economic history is found in Salomón Kalmanovitz 1994. On the post-1960 period, see Berry, Hellman, and Solaún 1980.
9. For a theoretical elaboration of this approach see Migdal 1988.
10. Hartlyn 1988.
11. Leal Buitrago and Zamosc 1990 and Leal Buitrago 1994b.
12. See for example, Peñate 1999, 55–98. Peñate notes that over two hundred municipalities in Colombia are controlled by armed groups.
13. On social relations in the Andean highlands and the impact of the War of the Pacific, see Manrique 1985. On the link between the open-market economy and state development, see Thorp and Bertram 1978.
14. On corporatism and its impact, see Stepan 1978; Nieto 1983; and Tovar 1985.
15. See Tilly 1975.
16. See Tokatlian 1998 and Shifter 2000.
17. One of the few comparative analyses of Peru and Colombia concerns their economic development (Thorp 1991).
18. See Ahumada 2000.
19. See DESCO 1989.
20. Figures for 2000 are from Ministerio de Defensa Nacional 2001, 15–16. Figures for the mid-1990s are from Alfredo Rangel 1998, 12.
21. Although not all self-defense groups evolved into paramilitary organizations, and indeed many of the first *autodefensas* were formed by peasants against large landowners, they represent the same process of privatized violence. Moreover, since the late 1970s, they have overwhelmingly become linked to the paramilitary phenomenon.
22. Melo 1990, 489.
23. See Medina Gallego 1990.
24. Melo 1990, 500.
25. See Bowden 2000.
26. Vicepresidencia de la República de Colombia 2000.
27. Rospigliosi 2000, 201. Budget figures for 2000 are cited in *Caretas* (May 12, 2001), 12.
28. These links are detailed by former army general Rodolfo Robles in Robles 1996.
29. Unlike Colombia's paramilitaries, or *autodefensas,* the *rondas* were made up exclusively of peasants, operated only at a local level, and maintained very close ties both to local military com-

manders and to pro-Fujimori politicians (with the exception of the *rondas* in Cajamarca, who maintained their operational and political autonomy).

30. Starn 1998, 224–57.

31. On the Fujimori regime's antidemocratic character, see especially Cotler and Grompone 2000; Tuesta Soldevilla 1999; and Bowden 2000.

32. See Silva Colmenares 1977 and Palacios 1986.

33. Palacios 1986, 91.

34. Leal Buitrago 1998, 15–21.

35. The best history of the Colombian armed forces is found in Leal Buitrago 1994a.

36. See Dávila 1998.

Notes to Chapter 8

1. Other Latin American countries that formed national *defensorías* include Puerto Rico (1977), Guatemala (1985), Mexico (1990), El Salvador (1991), Costa Rica (1992), Paraguay (1992), Honduras (1992), Argentina (1993), and Nicaragua (1995). Some countries, like Argentina, Brazil, and Mexico, also have state *defensorías*.

2. Oficio No. 95-6737-DAJ-T.1444-C.2, March 10, 1995, 34.

3. One of the agencies most vocal opponents, Congressman Enrique Chirinos Soto, laid out his objections in an opinion piece in *El Comercio,* July 21, 1994.

4. *El Defensor,* February–April 1999, 5.

5. Oscar Crespo Soliz, attorney general, interview with the author, Sucre, July 24, 2000.

6. See <http://www.diario-expreso.com>.

7. Carolina Oliva, MP liaison to Congress, interview with the author, Caracas, April 6, 1995.

8. Human Rights Watch/Americas 1993, 16.

9. Alicia Marquez, director of the Citizen Defense Office, Fiscalía General, interview with the author, Caracas, March 27, 1995.

10. Dirección de Planificación, Consejo de la Judicatura, *Memoria y cuenta del Consejo de la Judicatura,* internal report (1996).

11. Torres 1987, 90.

12. Statistics are from reports by the National Penitentiary and Jail Institute, which runs Colombia's prison system.

13. Anna María Romero de Campero, interview with the author, La Paz, July 12, 2000.

14. *El Defensor,* January 1999, 12.

15. *Revista El Defensor,* February–April 1999, 7.

16. *El Nacional,* September 9, 1988, 12; *El Diario de Caracas,* June 21, 1989, 18.

17. Saúl Ron Brasch, Superior Court criminal judge; interview with the author, Caracas, March 22, 1995.

18. Santos Alvins 1992, 86.

19. Búvinic and Morrison 1999.

20. Oficina Central de Estadística y Información, Presidencia de la República (Venezuela) 1993, 799–800.

21. Instituto Nacional de Estadística e Informática, Gobierno de Perú.

22. Samual Abad Yupanqui, interview with the author, Lima, June 20, 2001.

23. Luis Enrique Oberto, president of the Legislative Commission, Chamber of Deputies, interview with the author, Caracas, June 29, 1998.

24. *Revista de la Facultad de Ciencias Jurídicas y Políticas,* no. 68 (Caracas: Universidad Central de Venezuela, 1987).

25. Laserna 1994.

26. The amnesty law was overturned shortly after the collapse of the Fujimori government.

27. Defensor del Pueblo de Colombia 1995b, 23; Defensor del Pueblo de Colombia 1996, 18.

28. Defensor del Pueblo de Colombia 1995a.

29. Matt Moffett, "The Go-Between: Peru's Ombudsman Takes On Fujimori," *Wall Street Journal,* March 9, 2000.

30. See <http://www.larepublica.com.pe>.

31. Ana María Romero de Campero, Defensor del Pueblo of Bolivia, interview with the author, La Paz, July 12, 2000.

32. Van Cott 2000, 215.

33. See <http://www.elespectador.com>, accessed May 13, 2000; Defensor del Pueblo 1998.

Notes to Chapter 9

This chapter was developed from a larger project on grassroots-based development programs and neoliberal adjustment policies in Ecuador supported by the Social Sciences and Humanities Research Council of Canada (SSHRCC). That project has been jointly conducted with Louis Lefeber, who provided helpful comments on an earlier version of this chapter.

1. A third regionally based elite finds its seat in Cuenca, in the southern highlands. However, due to space limitations, I will limit my discussion here to the two principal elite clusters.

2. For studies on the contemporary manifestations of the racist legacy, see Cervone and Rivera 1999.

3. Don't steal, don't lie, and don't be lazy.

4. El Oro was outranked only by the two provinces in which the country's principal cities— Quito and Guayaquil—are located and by the Galápagos Islands, whose population is very small and benefits from tourist revenue.

5. Anonymous, interview with the author, Quito, April 1999.

6. For an account of the many aspects of the crisis, see, for example, Guzmán 2000.

Notes to Chapter 10

Translation from the Spanish by Jo-Marie Burt.

1. Several authors characterize the model of Venezuelan development as a "rentier state" because of its dependence on petrol rents, which distinguishes its economy from other countries in the region. See Karl 1997.

2. Measured in 1984 *bolívares*.

3. We define confrontational protests as those that create tension and a sense of danger in the opponent or the public in general, but without causing damage to persons or property. Violent protests are those in which there is damage to persons or property, whether due to the direct action of protesters or the action of others (Lander, López Maya, and Salamca 2000).

4. Numerous opinions on diverse aspects of the constitution have been published by politicians, political analysts, and constitutional experts. See, among others: Allan Brewer Carias (*El Nacional,* October 28, 1999, November 17, 1999); Molina (*El Nacional,* December 11, 1999); Alberto Quiróz Corradi (*El Nacional,* December 12, 1999); and BCV (*El Nacional,* November 4, 1999)

5. Former minister of energy and mines Alí Rodríguez and present minister Álvaro Silva Calderón are both well-known experts on the petrol industry, and both are opponents of the oil-liberalization policy.

6. *El Nacional,* January 1, 2000; *El Nacional,* June 18, 2000.

7. BCV, *El Universal,* December 29, 2001, 1–2.

8. "Internationalization" refers to the investment policies carried out by PDVSA abroad in order to acquire refineries that represent a significant source of revenue for the country.

9. The unemployment figure is for November 2001 and was taken from the Web site of the Oficina Nacional de Estadística e Informática (OCEI); available at <http://www.ocei.gov.ve/estadistica>. The figure for informal-sector employment is from *El Universal,* December 20, 2001.

Notes to Chapter 11

Translation from the Spanish by Philip Mauceri.

1. Members of other political groups could participate in elections, but in the event that they won, they would have to declare an affiliation with one of the traditional parties.

2. This does not necessarily mean that Front elites were never able to make these distinctions, but simply that in several critical cases they were unable to make them.

3. Many of the key ideas in this section are elaborated in Gutiérrez 2001a.

4. This section draws on Gutiérrez 2001a.

5. Galán and Sanín were very different leaders, acting in different institutional settings (before and after the 1991 constitution). The election of a Liberal dissident (Alvaro Uribe Vélez) to the presidency in 2002 departs from this tendency. Still, Uribe has the support of a broad section of the most traditional politicians, an advantage inaccessible to previous dissidents.

6. A more detailed technical explanation of the methodology used and the results are found in Gutiérrez 2001a.

7. By rotation in a legislature, we mean the number of times the dominant party has changed, according to the voting power exercised from one election to another. It is possible to measure the total rotations in municipalities and thus obtain an indicator of system stability, which would be between 0 and 1.

8. For example, the assassination of Rodrigo Turbay Cote by the FARC appears to have been the product of manipulation by a faction within the Liberal Party against the so-called hyenas. See *Semana,* July 7, 1997, 38. Two excellent works that examine the fluid relations between guerrillas and clientelism are Peñate 1991 and Palacios 1999.

Notes to Chapter 12

1. See the classic work Tilly 1975.

2. This description is based on newspaper articles reviewed during the days following the attack, as well as IDL 1990 and *Resumen Semanal* 512 (March 24–30, 1989) and 514 (April 7–13, 1989).

3. Comisión Especial de Investigación y Estudio sobre la Violencia 1989, 1992.

4. *Resumen Semanal* 542 (October 20–26, 1989).

5. Jurado Nacional de Elecciones, Oficio No. 819-89-P, July 11, 1989.

6. On the historic weakness of the Peruvian state, see Cotler 1978 and Mauceri 1996.

7. On García's economic policy, see Pastor and Wise 1992.

8. For an analysis of the Velasco years, see Stepan 1978 and McClintock and Lowenthal 1981.

9. For an analysis of the "conservative" transition, see Lynch 1992 and Mauceri 1996, 1997.

10. For a discussion of horizontal and vertical accountability, see O'Donnell 1999.

11. For an analysis of the social bases of Shining Path support, see Degregori 1986; Berg 1986–87, 1992; Isbell 1992; and Burt 1997, 1998.

12. See Graham 1992 on the APRA government's social programs.

13. APRA ruled at the national level from 1985 to 1990; between 1983 and 1989, first the IU then APRA ran the important municipal government of Lima, and both led a plurality of local municipalities throughout the country. The APRA government launched a decentralization process in which both parties were also key actors.

14. For an excellent study of the crisis of political parties in the late 1980s, see Grompone 1991.

15. See, for example, Tanaka 1998 and Lynch 2000.

16. See statements by the Shining Path leadership published in the organization's newspaper, *El Diario,* on July 24, 1988, and September 21, 1988.

17. I examine this process in greater detail in the case of Lima in Burt 1997, and in a case study of Villa El Salvador in Burt 1998a.

18. The most extensive analysis of Shining Path's political strategies can be found in Palmer 1992. See also Tapia 1997.

19. See, for example, Degregori and Grompone 1991; Cameron 1997; Panfichi 1997; and Tanaka 1998.

20. The Peruvian elite supported the candidacy of novelist Mario Vargas Llosa, who entered politics in 1987 to protest García's nationalization of the banking system. His political movement, FREDEMO (Democratic Front), joined forces with the two main conservative parties, Popular Action (AP) and the Popular Christian Party (PPC). There were virulent protests against Fujimori's election, some with racist overtones, by middle- and upper-class groups in the immediate aftermath of the second-round runoff. Once Fujimori demonstrated that he would pursue similar economic

policies to those proposed by Vargas Llosa, upper-class support for his regime became evident. See Degregori and Grompone 1991. On elite and business support for the Fujimori regime, see Durand 1997.

21. On the notion of strategic elites, see Stepan 1978.

22. For an excellent discussion of Plan Verde, see Rospigliosi 1996.

23. For a fascinating account of the evolution of Montesinos's career as army captain, spy, drug-lord lawyer, and shady advisor to President Fujimori, see Gorriti 1994.

24. For Hermoza to be promoted, several prestigious generals ahead of him in seniority were forced into retirement, generating serious discontent within significant sectors of the armed forces. See Obando 1998.

25. See Kenney 1995 for an argument along these lines.

26. See Rospigliosi 1996 and Gorriti 1994.

27. As cited in APRODEH 1994.

28. APRODEH 1994.

29. This was later expanded to thirty days (Human Rights Watch/Americas 1993).

30. Human Rights Watch/Americas 1992, 1993.

31. This discussion is based on my long-term observation of the evolution of the *comedores populares* in Peru since 1986 and specifically on interviews with organizers done during fieldwork in 1992–94 and during follow-up visits in 1995, 1998, and 1999.

32. See, for example, Roberts 1995 and Weyland 1996.

33. For a more elaborate critique of the term "neopopulism," see Lynch 1999.

34. See Collier and Levitsky 1997. In one interesting paper, Cynthia McClintock (1998) asks if the "authoritarian regime" label should be revived in reference to the Fujimori regime. Her analysis, however, centers on whether the 1995 electoral process was fully democratic or not and as such remains focused on formal institutional politics rather than the broader dimensions of power that I argue here are important to examine.

෴ Bibliography

Abecia, Valentín. 1979. *Las relaciones internacionales en la historia de Bolivia*. La Paz: Amigos del Libro y Academia Nacional de Ciencias de Bolivia.

Abya-Yala. N.d. Alicia Canaviri habla con SAIIC sobre la mujer, los jovenes, y la globalización en lad comunidades indígenas de Bolivia. *Abya-Yala* 10.4: 22–24.

Acosta, Alberto. 1994. *La deuda eterna: Una historia de la deuda externa ecuatoriana*. Quito: Libresa.

————. 1999. Proceso de reordenamiento pesquero ecosistema Ciénaga Grande de Santa Marta. Santa Marta: CORPAMAG. Mimeograph.

————. 2002. *Ecuador: Un modelo para América Latina?* N.p.

Acosta, Alberto, and José E. Juncosa, eds. 2000. *Dolarización: Informe urgente*. Quito: ILDIS and Abya-Yala/UPS.

Agüero, Felipe, and Jeffrey Stark. 1998. *Fault lines of democracy in post-transition Latin America*. Miami: North-South Center Press.

Ahumada, Consuelo. 2000. Una década en reves. In *Que está pasando en Colombia*, ed. Consuelo Ahumada, 15–55. Bogotá: El Ancora.

ALAI (Agencia Latinoamericana de Información), ed. 1996. *Por el camino del arcoiris*. Quito: Asociación Cristiana de Jóvenes del Ecuador, ALAI, and Fundación "José Peralta."

Albán Peralta, Walter, ed. 2001. *Debate defensorial*. Lima: Defensoría del Pueblo.

Albó, Xavier. 1987a. De MNRistas a kataristas: Campesinado, estado, y partidos 1953–1983. *Historia Boliviana Cochabamba* 5.1–2 (1985): 87–127. Reprinted in *Resistance, rebellion, and consciousness in the Andean peasant world: Eighteenth to Twentieth Centuries,* ed. Steve Stern, 379–419. Madison: University of Wisconsin Press.

————. 1987b. Formación y evolución de lo aymara en el espacio y el tiempo. In *Estado y región en los Andes,* 29–44. Cusco: Centro Las Casas.

————. 1991a. Bolivia: La Paz/Chukiyawu: Las dos caras de una ciudad. *América Indígena México* 4:107–58.

————. 1991b. El retorno del indio. *Revista Andina* 9.2: 299–366.

————. 1993. *¿ . . . Y de kataristas a MNRistas? La sorprendente y audaz alianza entre aymaras y neoliberales*. La Paz: CEDOIN and UNITAS.

————. 1995. *Bolivia plurilingüe: Guía para planificadores y educadores*. La Paz: CIPCA and UNICEF.

————. 1996. Making the leap from local mobilization to national politics. *NACLA Report on the Americas* 29.5:15–20.

————. 1997. El resurgir indígena en un mundo excluyente. In *Identidades étnicas,* ed. Manuel Gutiérrez Estévez, Manuel, 31–41. Madrid: Casa de América, Diálogos Amerindios.

————. 1999a. Andean people in the twentieth century. In *Cambridge history of the native peoples of the Americas,* vol. 3, *South America,* ed. Frank Salomon and Stuart Schwartz. 765–871. New York: Cambridge University Press.

————. 1999b. Etnias y pueblos originarios: Diversidad étnica, cultural y lingüística. In *Bolivia en el siglo XX: La formación de la Bolivia contemporánea,* ed. Fernando Campero, 451–82. La Paz: Harvard Club de Bolivia.

————. 1999c. *Ojotas en el poder local, cuatro años después*. La Paz: CIPCA and PADER.

————. 2000. Aymaras divididos por fronteras. *Cuarto Intermedio* 54:62–93.

————. 2002. Bolivia: From Indian and campesino leaders to councillors and parliamentary leaders. In *Multiculturalism in Latin America: Indigenous rights, diversity and democracy,* ed. Rachel Sieder, 74–102. London: Palgrave Macmillan and Institute of Latin American Studies.

Albó, Xavier, and Josep M. Barnadas. 1995. *La cara india y campesina de nuestra historia.* 4th ed. La Paz: CIPCA and Ministerio de Educación.

Almeida, Ileana, et al. 1991. *Indios: una reflexión sobre el levantamiento indígena de 1990.* Quito: ILDIS and Abya-Yala.

Almeida, Ileana, and Nidia Arrobo, eds. 1998. *En defensa del pluralismo y la igualdad: Los derechos de los pueblos indios y el Estado.* Quito: Fundación Pueblo Indio del Ecuador and Abya-Yala.

Almeida, José, Hernán Carrasco, Luz María de la Torre, Andrés Guerrero, et al. 1993. *Sismo étnico en el Ecuador: Varias perspectivas.* Quito: CEDIME and Abya-Yala.

Almeida, Rebecca. 1994. *Kemmerer en el Ecuador.* Quito: FLACSO.

Alvarez, Sonia. 1990. *Engendering democracy in Brazil: Women's movements in transition politics.* Princeton: Princeton University Press.

———. 1998. Latin American feminisms "go global": Trends of the 1990s and challenges for the new millennium. In *Cultures of politics/politics of cultures: Revisioning Latin American social movements,* ed. Sonia Alvarez, Evelina Dagnino, and Arturo Escobar, 293–324. Boulder: Westview Press.

Alvarez, Sonia, Evelina Dagnino, and Arturo Escobar, eds. 1998. *Cultures of politics/politics of cultures: Revisioning Latin American social movements.* Boulder: Westview Press.

Amnesty International. 1987. *Political prisoners in Venezuela.* London: Amnesty International Publications.

———. 1988. Memorandum al gobierno de Venezuela. London: Amnesty International Publications.

Andean Information Network. 2000. El costo de la dignidad. November. Memorandum.

Anderson, Benedict. 1991. *Imagined communities: Reflections on the origin and spread of nationalism.* London: Verso.

Andolina, Robert. 1999. Colonial legacies and plurinational imaginaries: Indigenous movement politics in Ecuador and Bolivia. Ph.D. diss., University of Minnesota.

Andreas, Peter R., Eva C. Bertram, Morris J. Blackman, and Kenneth E. Sharpe. 1991–92. Dead-end drug wars. *Foreign Policy* 85 (winter): 106–29.

APRODEH (Asociación Pro-Derechos Humanos). 1994. *De la tierra brotó la verdad: Crimen e impunidad en el caso Cantuta.* Lima: APRODEH.

Arboleda, María. 1994. Mujeres en el poder local en el Ecuador. In *Jaque al Rey: Memorias del taller "participación política de la mujer,"* ed. REPEM (Red de Educación Popular entre Mujeres). Quito: REPEM/CIUDAD.

Aroca, Javier. 1996. Los derechos humanos de los pueblos indígenas en la legislación peruana. In *Derechos humanos y pueblos indígenas de la Amazonía peruana: Realidad, normativa y perspectivas.* Lima: APEP and CAAAP.

Baptista, Asdrúbal. 1997. *Bases cuantitativas de la economía venezolana, 1830–1995.* Caracas: Fundación Polar.

Baretta, Silvio, R. Duncan, and John Markoff. 1978. Civilization and barbarism: Cattle frontiers in Latin America. *Comparative Studies in Society and History* 20.4: 587–605.

Barragan, Valeria, and José L. Levasquz. 2000. Continúa el drama migratorio. *Tiempos del Mundo.*

Barrig, Maruja. 1996. Women, collective kitchens, and the crisis of the state in Peru. In *Emergences: Women's struggles for livelihood in Latin America,* ed. John Friedmann, Rebecca Abers, and Lilian Autler, 59–77. Los Angeles: UCLA Latin American Center.

———. 1998. Los malestares del feminismo: Una nueva lectura. Paper presented at the twenty-first International Congress of the Latin American Studies Association, Chicago, September 24–26.

Baud, Michiel, Kees Koonings, Geert Oostindie, Arij Ouweneel, and Patricio Silva. 1996. *Etnicidad como estrategia en América Latina y el Caribe.* Quito: Abya-Yala.

BCV (Banco Central de Venezuela). 2000. *Anuario de cuentas nacionales.* Caracas: BCV.

———. 2001. *Anuario de cuentas nacionales.* Caracas: BCV.

———. 2002. Economic indicators accessed in February 2002 at <www.bcv.org.ve/indices.htm>.

Beck, Scott, and Kenneth Mijeski. 2001. The Pachakutik political movement and the 1996 and 1998 elections: A closer examination of the effects of regionalism and ethnicity. Paper presented at the twenty-third International Congress of the Latin American Studies Association, Washington, D.C., September 6–8.

Benería, Lourdes. 1992. The Mexican debt crisis: Restructuring the household and the economy. In *Unequal burden: Economic crisis, persistent poverty, and women's work*, ed. L. Benería and S. Feldman, 83–104. Boulder: Westview Press.

———. 1996. Globalization, gender, and the Davos man. *Feminist Economics* 5.3: 61–84.

Benería, Lourdes, and Shelley Feldman, eds. 1992. *Unequal burden: Economic crisis, persistent poverty, and women's work.* Boulder: Westview Press.

Benjamin, Walter. 1969. *Illuminations.* New York: Schocken Books.

Berg, Ronald. 1986–87. Sendero Luminoso and the peasantry of Andahuaylas. *Journal of Inter-American Studies and World Affairs* 28.4: 164–96.

———. 1992. Peasant responses to Shining Path in Andahuaylas. In *The Shining Path of Peru*, ed. David Palmer, 83–104. New York: St. Martin's Press.

Berger, Suzanne, and Michael Dore, eds. 1996. *National diversity and global capitalism.* Ithaca: Cornell University Press.

Berlant, Lauren. 1988. Race, gender, and nation in *The Color Purple. Critical Inquiry* 14 (summer): 831–59.

———. 1991. *The anatomy of national fantasy: Hawthorne, utopia, and everyday life.* Chicago: University of Chicago Press.

Beroes, Agustín. 1990. *RECADI: La gran estafa.* Caracas: Universidad Central de Venezuela.

Berry, Albert R., Ronald Hellman, and Mauricio Solaún, eds. 1980. *Politics of compromise: Coalition government in Colombia.* New Brunswick: Transaction Press.

Bertram, Eva, Morris Blachman, Kenneth Sharpe, and Peter Andreas. *Drug war politics: The price of denial.* Berkeley and Los Angeles: University of California Press, 1996.

Blanes, José. 2000. *Mallkus y alcaldes.* La Paz: CEBEM and PIEB.

Blank, David Eugene. 1973. *Politics in Venezuela.* Boston: Little, Brown and Co.

Block, David. 1997. *La cultura reduccional de los llanos de Mojos.* Sucre: Historia Boliviana.

Boserup, Ester. 1970. *Woman's role in economic development.* New York: St. Martin's Press.

Bouysse-Cassagne, Therese. 1999. *Identidad aymara: aproximación historica (siglo XV, siglo XVI).* La Paz: Hisbol-IFEA.

Bowden, Sally. 2000. *The Fujimori file: Peru and its president, 1990–2000.* Lima: Peru Monitor.

Bravo, Agustín E. 1998. La iglesia india, sueño profético de Monseñor Proaño. In *En defensa del pluralismo y la igualdad: Los derechos de los pueblos indios y el Estado*, ed. Almeida, Ileana, and Nidia Arrobo, 229–53. Quito: Fundación Pueblo Indio del Ecuador and Abya-Yala.

Briceño León, Roberto. 1999. La violencia en Venezuela. In *Venezuela en Oxford*, 287–312. Caracas: Fundación la Casa de Bello.

Briceño-León, Roberto, Alberto Camardiel, Olga Avila, Edoardo de Armas y Verónica Zubillaga. 1997. La cultura emergente de la violencia en Caracas. *Revista Venezolana de Economía y Ciencias Sociales*, 3.2–3.

Briceño Vivas, Gustavo, ed. 1993. *El Defensor del Pueblo en Venezuela: La figura del ombudsman.* Caracas: Editorial Kinesis.

Bright, Charles, and Susan Harding. 1984. *State-making and social movements.* Ann Arbor: University of Michigan Press.

Brodie, Janine. 1994. Shifting the boundaries: Gender and the politics of restructuring. In *The strategic silence: Gender and economic policy*, ed. Isabella Bakker, 46–60. London: Zed Books.

Brysk, Alison. 2000. *From tribal village to global village.* Stanford: Stanford University Press.

Bubba, Cristina. 1993. Nos querían robar el alma. *Cuarto Intermedio* 23:34–55.

Burt, Jo-Marie. 1994. La inquisición pos-senderista. *Que Hacer* 92:30–35.

———. 1997. Political violence and the grassroots in Lima, Peru. In *The new politics of inequality in Latin America: Rethinking participation and representation*, ed. Douglas Chalmers, Carlos Vilas, Katherine Hite, Scott Martin, Kerianne Piester, and Monique Segarra, 281–309. London and New York: Oxford University Press.

—————. 1998a. Shining Path and the "decisive battle" for Lima's barriadas: The case of Villa El Salvador. In *Shining and other paths: War and society in Peru, 1980–1995*, ed. Steve Stern, 267–306. Durham: Duke University Press.

—————. 1998b. Unsettled accounts: Militarization and memory in postwar Peru. *NACLA Report on the Americas* 32.2: 35–40.

—————. 2002. "Quien habla es terrorista": Fear and loathing in Fujimori's Peru. Paper presented at the conference The Fujimori Legacy and Its Impact on Public Policy in Latin America, the Dante B. Fascell North-South Center, University of Miami, and the University of Delaware, March 14, 2002.

Búvinic, M., and A. Morrison. 1999. Notas técnics sobre la violencia. Washington, D.C.: Inter-American Development Bank.

CAJ (Comisión Andina de Juristas), ed. 2001. *Acceso a la justicia y Defensoría del Pueblo.* Lima: CAJ.

—————. 1996. *Foro internacional: Defensoría del Pueblo.* Lima: CAJ.

Call, Charles. 1991. *Clear and present dangers: The U.S. military and the war on drugs in the Andes.* Washington D.C.: Washington Office on Latin America.

Cameron, John. 2001. Local democracy in rural Latin America: Lessons from Ecuador. Paper presented at the twenty-third International Congress of the Latin American Studies Association, Washington, D.C., September 6–8.

Cameron, Maxwell A. 1993. *Democracy and authoritarianism in Peru.* New York: St. Martins Press.

—————. 1997. Political and economic origins of regime change in Peru: The eighteenth brumaire of Alberto Fujimori. In *The Peruvian labyrinth: Polity, society, economics,* ed. Maxwell A. Cameron and Philip Mauceri, 37–69. University Park: Pennsylvania State University Press

Cameron, Maxwell A., and Philip Mauceri, eds. 1997. *The Peruvian labyrinth: Polity, society, economics.* University Park: Pennsylvania State University Press.

Canessa Oneto, Mario. 1999. *La Banca del Ecuador: Una explicación histórica.* Guayaquil: Escuela Superior Politécnica del Litoral.

Carrera Damas, Germán. 1972. *El culto a Bolívar.* Caracas: Universidad Central de Venezuela.

—————. 1996. *La era de la información: Economía sociedad y cultura,* vol. 1. Madrid: Alianza Editorial.

Castro, Milka, ed. 2000. *Derecho consuetudinario y pluralismo legal: Desafíos en el tercer milenio.* Acts of the twenty-second International Congress of the Commission on Folk Law and Legal Pluralism, Arica/Santiago, Universidad de Chile and Universidad de Tarapacá, March 13–17, 2000.

Catalá, José Agustín. 1989. *El estallido de febrero.* Caracas: Ediciones Centauro.

Catanzaro, Raimondo. 1992. *El delito como empresa: Historia social de la mafia.* Madrid: Taurus.

CEDIB (Centro de Documentación e Investigación Bolivia). 1993. *Catálogo coca-cocaína.* 3 vols. Cochabamba: CEDIB.

CEDIME (Centro de Investigacion de los Movimientos Sociales del Ecuador). 1993. *Sismo étnico en el Ecuador.* Quito: Abya-Yala.

Centro de Estudios Para la Paz. 2002. Base de datos. Caracas: Universidad Central de Venezuela.

Centro María Quilla/CEAAL (Centro de Educación de Adultos para América Latina). 1990. *Mujeres, educación, y conciencia de género en Ecuador.* Quito: Centro María Quilla.

CEPAL (Comisión Económica Para América Latina). 2002. Indicadores de pobreza tomados en febrero. Available at <http://www.eclac.cl>.

CEPLAES (Centro de Planificación y Estudios Sociales). 1996. Informe final, proyecto de investigación: Pueblos indígenas y participación electoral. Quito: n.p.

Cervone, Emma, and Freddy Rivera, eds. 1999. *Ecuador racista: Imágenes e identidades.* Quito: FLACSO.

Chalmers, Douglas, Carlos Vilas, Katherine Hite, Scott Martin, Kerianne Piester, and Monique Segarra, eds. 1997. *The new politics of inequality in Latin America: Rethinking participation and representation.* London and New York: Oxford University Press.

Chevigny, Paul. 1995. *The edge of the knife.* New York: New Press.

Chirinos, Andrés. 1998. Las lenguas indígenas peruanas más allá del 2000. *Revista Andina* 12.2: 453–79.

Chirinos, Andrés, and Christoph Schwager. 1997. Mapas lingüísticos del Perú. Cusco: GTZ, CADEP, and DED.

Chua, Peter, Kum-Kum Bhavani, and John Foran. 2000. Women, culture, development: A new paradigm for development studies? *Ethnic and Racial Studies* 23.5: 820–41.

CISA (Consejo Indio de Sudamérica). 1980. *Primer congreso de movimientos indios de Sudamérica.* París: Ediciones MITKA.

Clavero, Bartolomé. 1994. *Derecho indígena y cultura constitucional en América.* México: Siglo XXI.

———. 1997. Multiculturalismo y monoconstitucionalismo de lengua castellana en América. In *Derecho indígena,* ed. Magdalena Gómez, 65–112. Mexico D.F.: Instituto Nacional Indigenista and Asociación Mexicana para las Naciones Unidas.

Clawson, Patrick L., and Rensselaer W. Lee III. 1996. *The Andean cocaine industry.* New York: St. Martin's Press.

Colegio de Abogados del Distrito Federal. 1987. Análisis del impacto de algunos de los aspectos preventivos en la ley orgánica sobre sustancias, estupefacientes, y psicotrópicas. In *Revista de la facultad de ciencias jurídicas y políticas,* no. 68. Caracas: Universidad Central de Venezuela.

Collier, David, and Steven Levitsky. 1997. Democracy with adjectives: Conceptual innovation in comparative research. *World Politics* 49.3: 430–51.

Collins, Jennifer. 2000a. Gains for campesinos, stalemate for cocaleros. *NACLA Report on the Americas* 34.3.

———. 2000b. A sense of possibility: Ecuador's indigenous movement takes center stage. *NACLA Report on the Americas* 33.5: 40–46.

Comaroff, John L. 1989. Images of empire, contests of conscience: Models of colonial domination in South Africa. *American Ethnologist* 16.4: 661–83.

Comisión Especial de Investigación y Estudio sobre la Violencia y Alternatives de Pacificación. 1989. *Violencia y Pacificación.* Lima: DESCO/Comisión Andina de Juristas.

———. 1992. *Violencia y pacificación en 1991.* Lima: Senate of the Republic.

Conaghan, Catherine M. 1988. *Restructuring domination: Industrialists and the state in Ecuador.* Pittsburgh: University of Pittsburgh Press.

———. 1995. Politicians against parties: Discord and disconnection in Ecuador's party system. In *Building democratic institutions: Party systems in Latin America,* ed. Scott Mainwaring and Timothy R. Scully, 434–58. Stanford: Stanford University Press.

Conaghan, Catherine M., and James Malloy, eds. 1994. *Unsettling statecraft: Democracy and neoliberalism in the central Andes.* Pittsburgh: University of Pittsburgh Press.

CONAIE (Confederación de Nacionalidades Indigenos del Ecuador). 1989. *Las nacionalidades indígenas en el Ecuador: Nuestro proceso organizativo.* Quito: CONAIE.

———. 1994. *Proyecto político de la CONAIE.* Quito: CONAIE.

———. 1999. *Las nacionalidades indígenas y sus derechos colectivos en la constitución.* Quito: CONAIE.

Consejo de la Judicatura, Dirección de Planificación. 1994. *Memoria y cuenta del consejo de la judicatura.* Caracas: Consejo de la Judicatura.

Coppedge, Michael. 1994. *Strong parties, lame ducks: Presidential partyarchy and factionalism in Venezuela.* Stanford: Stanford University Press.

Coronil, Fernando. 1989. Discovering America again: The politics of selfhood in the age of postcolonial empires. In *Discourses on colonialism,* ed. Rolena Adorno and Walter Mignolo, *Dispositio* 14: 36–39.

———. 1997. *The magical state: Nature, money, and modernity in Venezuela.* Chicago: University of Chicago Press.

———. 2000. Magical illusions or revolutionary magic? Chávez in historical context. *NACLA Report on the Americas* 33.6: 34–41.

Coronil, Fernando, and Julie Skurski. 1982. Reproducing dependency: Auto industry policy and petrodollar circulation in Venezuela. *International Organization* 36.1: 61–94.

———. 1991a. Country and city in a colonial landscape: Double discourse and the geopolitics of truth in Latin America. In *View from the border: Essays in honor of Raymond Williams,* ed. Dennis Swordin, and Leslie Roman. New York: Routledge.

———. 1991b. Dismembering and remembering the nation: The semantics of political violence in Venezuela. *Comparative Studies in Society and History* 33.2: 288–335.

Cotler, Julio. 1978. *Clases, estado, y nación en el Perú.* Lima: IEP.

Cotler, Julio, and Romeo Grompone. 2000. *El fujimorismo: Ascenso y caída de un regimen autoritario.* Lima: IEP.

Crabtree, John. 1991. *Peru under Garcia: An opportunity lost.* Pittsburgh: University of Pittsburgh Press.

CSUTCB (Confederación Sindical Unica de Trabajadores Campesinos de Bolivia). 1994. *Anteproyecto de ley agraria fundamental.* La Paz: CSUTCB.

Cubides, Fernando. 1999. Los paramilitares y su estrategia. In *Reconocer la guerra para construir la paz,* ed. Malcolm Deas and Maria Victoria Llorente, 153–99. Bogotá: Editorial Norma/Universidad de los Andes.

Cueva, Agustín. 1990. El Ecuador de 1925 a 1960. In *Epoca républicana IV: El Ecuador entre los años veinte y los sesenta,* ed. Jaime Durán Barba, vol. 10 of *Nueva historia del Ecuador,* ed. Enrique Ayala Mora. Quito: Corporación Editora Nacional.

———. 1991. El Ecuador de 1960 a 1979. In *Epoca républicana V: El Ecuador en el último período,* ed. Fernando Tinajero and José Moncada, vol. 11 of *Nueva historia del Ecuador,* ed. Enrique Ayala Mora. Quito: Corporación Editora Nacional.

Dávila, Andres. 1998. *El juego del poder: Historia, armas, y votos.* Bogotá: Universidad de los Andes.

———. 1999. Ejército regular, guerra irregular: La institución militar en los últimos quince años. In *Reconocer la guerra para construir la paz,* ed. Malcolm Deas and Maria Victoria Llorente, 283–345. Bogotá: Editorial Norma/Universidad de los Andes. Bogotá: Editorial Norma/Universidad de los Andes.

de Certeau, Michel. 1984. *The practice of everyday life.* Translated by Steven Rendell. Berkeley: University of California Press.

Deas, Malcolm, and Maria Victoria Llorente, eds. 1999. *Reconocer la guerra para construir la paz.* Bogotá: Editorial Norma/Universidad de los Andes.

Deere, Carmen Diana, and Magdalena León de Leal. 2001. Institutional reform of agriculture under neoliberalism: The impact of women's and indigineous movements." 36.2: 31–63.

Defensor del Pueblo de Colombia. 1995a. *Segundo informe anual del Defensoría del Pueblo al Congreso de Colombia 1995.* Bogotá: Defensor del Pueblo.

———. 1995b. *Situación de mujeres en centros de reclusión para mujeres.* Bogotá: Defensor del Pueblo.

———. 1996. *Tercer informe anual del Defensoría del Pueblo al Congreso de Colombia 1996,* vol. 1. Bogotá; Defensor del Pueblo.

———. 1997. *Impacto de la violencia de oleoductos en Colombia.* Bogotá Defensor del Pueblo.

Defensor del Pueblo del Perú. 1998. *Primer informe del Defensor del Pueblo al Congreso de la República.* Lima.

———. 2000. *Institucionalidad democrática y ética: Tareas pendientes: Tercer informe del Defensor del Pueblo al Congreso de la República.* Lima.

Degregori, Carlos Iván. 1986. *Sendero Luminoso.* 2 vols. Lima: Instituto de Estudios Peruanos.

———. 1989. *Qué difícil es ser Dios: Ideología y violencia política en Sendero Luminoso.* Lima: El Zorro de Abajo Ediciones.

———. 1990. *Ayacucho, 1969–1979: El Surgimiento de Sendero Luminoso.* Lima: Instituto de Estudios Peruanos.

———. 1998. Movimientos étnicos, democracia, y nación en Perú y Bolivia. In *La construcción de la nación y la representación ciudadana en México, Guatemala, Perú, Ecuador, y Bolivia,* ed. Claudia Dary, 159–225. Guatemala: FLACSO.

Degregori, Carlos Iván, and Romeo Grompone. 1991. *Elecciones 1990: Demonios y redentores en el nuevo Perú.* Lima: Instituto de Estudios Peruanos.

de la Cadena, Marisol. 1995. Race, ethnicity, and the struggle for indigenous self-representation: De-indianization in Cusco, Peru, 1919–1992. Ph.D. diss., University of Wisconsin, Madison.

———. 2000. *Indigenous mestizos: The politics of race and culture in Cuzco, Peru, 1919–1991.* Durham: Duke University Press.

———. 2001. Culture as race and the denial of racism: From liberal to neoliberal Peru. Paper presented at the twenty-third International Congress of the Latin American Studies Association, Washington, D.C., September 6–8.

de la Paz Vela, María. 2000. El peligro de una dolarización a la ecuatoriana. *Gestión* 68 (February).

de la Peña, Guillermo. 1998. Etnicidad, ciudadanía, y cambio agrario: Apuntes comparativos de tres países latinoamericanos. In *La construcción de la nación y la representación ciudadana en México, Guatemala, Perú, Ecuador, y Bolivia,* ed. Claudia Dary, 27–86. Guatemala: FLACSO.

Delgado Ribadeneira, Ernesto. 1992a. Ecuador: Balance de las políticas para pagar la deuda social, 1987–1990: Programa red comunitaria para el desarrollo infantil. N.p.

———. 1992b. Programa red comunitaria para el desarrollo infantil, 1987–1990. In *Ecuador: Los costos sociales del ajuste, 1980–1990,* vol. 2. Santiago de Chile: PREALC.

Delpino, Nena. 1991. Las organizaciones femeninas por la alimentación: un menú sazonado. In *La otra cara de la luna: Nuevos actores sociales en el Perú,* ed. Luís Pásara et al., 29–72. Buenos Aires: CEDYS.

Departamento Nacional de Planeación. 1998. *La Paz: Un desafío para el desarrollo.* Bogotá.

DESCO (Centro de Estudicos y Promoción de Dessarollo). 1989. *Violencia política en el Perú, 1980–88.* Lima: DESCO.

Díaz Sierra, Guillermo José. 1988. Marihuana, sociedad, y estado en la Guajira. Sociology Department, Universidad Nacional de Colombia, Bogotá.

Dobyns, Henry, and Paul Doughty. 1975. *Peru: A cultural history.* New York: Oxford University Press.

Drake, Paul W. 1989. *The money doctor in the Andes: The Kemmerer missions.* Durham: Duke University Press.

Dresser, Denise. 1994. Bringing the poor back in: National solidarity as a strategy of regime legitimation. In *Transforming state-society relations in Mexico,* ed. Wayne A. Cornelius, Ann L. Craig, and Jonathan Fox, 143–64. San Diego: Center for U.S.-Mexican Studies.

Durand, Francisco. 1997. The growth and limitations of the Peruvian right. In *The Peruvian labyrinth: Polity, society, economics,* ed. Maxwell A. Cameron and Philip Mauceri, 152–75. University Park: Pennsylvania State University Press.

Dwyer, Daisy, and Judith Bruce, eds. 1988. *A home divided: Women and income in the Third World.* Stanford: Stanford University Press.

Economist Intelligence Unit. 2001. *Country Forecast: Ecuador.* June.

El Doctor: Vladimiro Montesinos. 1998. *Debate* 20.103 (November/December): 24–36.

Ellner, Steven. 1980. Political party dynamics in Venezuela and the outbreak of guerrilla warfare. *Inter-American Economic Affairs* 34.2: 3–24.

———. 1982. Populism in Venezuela, 1935–48: Betancourt and "Acción Democrática." In *Latin American populism in comparative perspective,* ed. Michael L. Coniff. Albuquerque: University of New Mexico Press.

El Nacional. 1989. *El día que bajaron los cerros.* Caracas: Editorial Ateneo de Caracas.

———. 1990. *27 de Febrero: Cuando la muerte tomó las calles.* Caracas: Editorial Ateneo de Caracas.

Elson, Diane. 1992. From survival strategies to transformation strategies: Women's needs and structural adjustment. In *Unequal burden: economic crisis, persistent poverty, and women's work,* ed. Lourdes Benería and Shelley Feldman eds., 26–48. Boulder: Westview Press.

———. 1998. Talking to the boys: Gender and economic growth models. In *Feminist visions of development: Gender analysis and policy,* ed. Cecile Jackson and Ruth Pearson, 155–70. London: Routledge.

———, ed. 1991. *Male bias in the development process.* Manchester: Manchester University Press.

Elster, Jon. 1988. *Uvas amargas: Sobre la subversión de la racionalidad.* Barcelona: Ediciones Península.

Endara, Lourdes. 1998. *El marciano de la esquina: Imagen del indio en la prensa durante el levantamiento de 1990.* Quito: Abya-Yala.

Endara Osejo, Ximena. 2000. Debate y adopción de los derechos colectivos de los pueblos indígenas en la Constitución Ecuatoriana. In *De la exclusión a la participación: Pueblos indígenas y sus derechos colectivos en el Ecuador,* ed. Angélica Bernal. Quito: Ediciones Abya-Yala.

Escobar, Arturo. 1995. *Encountering development.* Princeton: Princeton University Press.

Escobar, Arturo, and Sonia Alvarez, eds. 1992. *The making of social movements in Latin America.* Boulder: Westview Press.

España, Luis Pedro. 1994. Introduction to *La violencia en Venezuela,* ed. Luis Ugalde et al., 11–20. Caracas, Monte Ávila Editores Latinoamericana-UCAB.

Esté, Raúl. 1987. *La masacre de Yumare.* Caracas: Fondo Editorial "Carlos Aponte."

Estupiñan de Burbano, Patricia. 1991. Recuento del período 1979–1990. In *Epoca republicana V: El Ecuador en el último período,* ed. Fernando Tinajero and José Moncada volume coordinators, vol. 11 of *Nueva Historia del Ecuador,* ed. Enrique Ayala Mora. Quito: Corporación Editora Nacional.

Esvertit Cobes, Natalia. 1995. Caminos al oriente: Estado y proyectos regionales en los proyectos de vías de comunicación con la Amazonía ecuatoriana, 1890–1930. In *La construcción de la Amazonía andina siglos XIX–XX,* ed. Pilar García, 287–356. Quito: Abya-Yala.

Fitch, J. Samuel. 1998. *The armed forces and democracy in Latin America.* Baltimore: Johns Hopkins University Press.

Foucault, Michel. 1979. *Discipline and punish: Birth of the prison.* New York: Vintage Books.

Foweraker, Joe. 1990. Popular movements and political change in Mexico. In *Popular movements and political change in Mexico,* ed. Joe Foweraker and Ann Craig, 3–20. Boulder: Lynne Rienner Publishers.

Fox, Jonathan, ed. 1990. *The challenge of rural democratization: Perspectives from Latin America and the Philippines.* London and Portland: Frank Cass.

Franco, Carlos. 1991. *La otra modernidad.* Lima: Centro de Estudios para el Desarrollo y la Participación.

Franco, Jean. 1989. *Plotting women: Gender and representation in Mexico.* New York: Columbia University Press.

———. 1996. The gender wars. *NACLA Report on the Americas* 29.4: 6–9.

Fuentealba, Gerardo. 1983. La sociedad indigena en las primeras decadas de la Republica: continuidades colonials y cambios republicanos. In *La nueva historia del Ecuador,* ed. Enrique Ayala Mora, 45–77. Quito: Abya-Yala.

Gallegos, Rómulo. 1954. *Una posición en la vida.* Mexico: Ediciones Humanoismo.

———. 1959. *Doña Bárbara,* in *Obras Completas,* vol. 1. Madrid: Aguilar.

García, Miguel. 2000. Elección popular de alcaldes y terceras fuerzas: El sistema de partidos en el ámbito municipal, 1988–1997. *Análisis Político* 41:84–98.

García, Pilar, ed. 1995. *La construcción de la Amazonía andina siglos XIX–XX.* Quito: Abya-Yala.

———. 1998. *Fronteras, colonización, y mano de obra indígena en la Amazonía Andina siglos XIX–XX.* Lima: Pontificia Universidad Católica del Perú.

García Canclini, Néstor. 1999. *La globalización imaginada.* Barcelona: Paidós.

García-Sayán, Diego, ed. 1989. *Coca, cocaina, y narcotrafico: Laberinto en los Andes.* Lima: Comision Andina de Juristas.

Gilmore, Robert . 1964. *Caudillism and militarism in Venezuela, 1810–1910.* Athens: Ohio University Press.

Gómez, Magdalena, ed. 1997. *Derecho indígena.* Mexico D.F.: Instituto Nacional Indigenista y Asociación Mexicana para las Naciones Unidas.

González de Olarte, Efraín. 1991. *El péndulo peruano: Políticas económicas, gobernabilidad, y subdesarollo, 1963–1991.* Lima: Instituto de Estudios Peruanos.

Gorriti, Gustavo. 1994. The betrayal of Peru's democracy: Montesinos as Fujimori's Svengali. *Covert Action Quarterly* 49 (summer): 4–12, 54–59

Graham, Carol. 1992. *Peru's APRA: Parties, politics, and the elusive quest for democracy.* Boulder: Lynne Rienner Publishers.

Grindle, Merilee. 2000. *Audacious reforms: Institutional invention and democracy in Latin America.* Baltimore: Johns Hopkins University Press.

Grompone, Romeo. 1991. *El velero en el viento: Política y sociedad en Lima.* Lima: Instituto de Estudios Peruanos.

Grupo Democracia y Desarrollo Local, ed. 1999. *Ciudadanías emergentes: Experiencias democráticas de desarrollo local.* Quito: Abya-Yala.

Guerrero, Andrés. 1993. La disintegración de la administración étnica en el Ecuador. In *Sismo étnico en el Ecuador: Varias perspectivas,* ed. José Almeida, Hernán Carrasco, Luz María de la Torre, Andrés Guerrero, et al. Quito: CEDIME and Abya-Yala.

Guerrero, Fernando. 1999. La experienca de participacion y gestion local en Cotacachi. In *Ciudadanias emergentes: Experiencias democraticas de desarollo local,* 113–28. Quito: Abya-Yala.

Gutiérrez Estévez, Manuel, ed. 1997. *Identidades étnicas.* Madrid: Casa de América, Diálogos Amerindios.

Gutiérrez, Francisco. 1995. Tendencias de cambio en el sistema de partidos: el caso de Bogotá. *Análisis Político* 24:73–83.

———. 1996. Dilemas y paradojas de la transición participativa, *Análisis Político* 29:35–53.

———. 2001a. Agregando votos en un sistema altamente desinstitucionalizado. In *Archivos de Macroeconomía,* Departamento Nacional de Planificación, no. 157.

———. 2001b. ¿Se ha abierto el sistema político colombiano? Una evaluación de los procesos de cambio 1970–1998. *América Latina Hoy* 27: 189–215.

Gutiérrez, Francisco, and Dávila Andrés. 2000. Paleontólogos o politólogos: ¿Qué podemos decir hoy sobre los dinosaurios? *Revista de Estudios Sociales* 6:39–50.

Guzmán, Marco Antonio. 2000. *Ecuador: La hora trágica: Los diferentes rostros de la crisis actual.* Quito: Corporación Editora Nacional.

Hagopian, Frances. 1993. After regime change: Authoritarian legacies, political representation, and the democratic future of South America. *World Politics* 45.3: 464–500.

———. 1998. Democracy and political representation in Latin America in the 1990s: Pause, reorganization, or decline? In *Fault lines of democracy in post-transition Latin America,* ed. Felipe Agüero and Jeffrey Stark, 99–144. Miami: North-South Center Press.

Hanson, David P. 1971. Political decision making in Ecuador: The influence of business groups. Ph.D. diss., University of Florida.

Hargreaves, Clare. 1992. *Snow fields: The war on cocaine in the Andes.* New York: Holmes and Meier Publishers.

Hartlyn, Jonathan. 1988. *The politics of coalition rule in Colombia.* New York: Cambridge University Press.

Hellinger, Daniel. 1991. *Venezuela: Tarnished democracy.* Boulder: Westview Press

Hirst, Paul, and Graham Thompson. 1996. *Globalization in question.* Cambridge: Polity Press.

Holston, James, and Teresa P. R. Caldeira. 1998. Democracy, law, and violence: Disjunctions of Brazilian citizenship. In *Fault lines of democracy in post-transition Latin America,* ed. Felipe Agüero and Jeffrey Stark, 268–89. Miami: North-South Center Press.

Human Rights Watch. 2001. *The "sixth division": Military-paramilitary ties and U.S. policy in Colombia.* Washington, D.C.: Human Rights Watch.

Human Rights Watch/Americas. 1992. *Peru under fire: Human rights since the return to democracy.* New York: Human Rights Watch.

———. 1993. *Human rights in Venezuela.* New York: Human Rights Watch.

Huntington, Samuel. 1991. *The third wave: Democratization in the late twentieth century.* Norman: University of Oklahoma Press.

Hurtado, Javier. 1986. *El katarismo.* La Paz: Hisbol.

———. 1999. Interview. *Vistazo* 758 (March 31).

IDEAM (Instituto de Hidrología, Meteorología y Estudios Ambientales Diagonal). 1998. *El medio ambiente en Colombia.* Bogotá: IDEAM.

IDL (Instituto de Defensa Legal). 1990. *Peru 1989: En la espiral de la violencia.* Lima: IDL.

IESA (Instituto de Estudios Superiores de Administración de Venezuela). 2000. <http://www.iesa.edu.ve>.

IGAC (Instituto Geográfico Agustín Codazzi). 1993. *Magdalena: Características geográficas.* Bogotá: IGAC.

INEC (Instituto Nacional de Estadísticas y Censos). 1998. *Encuesta de condiciones de vida.* Quito: INEC.

Isaacs, Anita. 1993. *Military rule and transition in Ecuador, 1972–92.* Pittsburgh: University of Pittsburgh Press.

Isacson, Adam. 1998. U.S. drug war and military aid to Colombia: An overview. *Colombia Update* (spring/summer): 15.

———. 2001. Militarizing Latin America policy. *Foreign Policy in Focus* 6.21: 2.

Isacson, Adam, and Joy Olson. 1999. *Just the facts.* Washington, D.C.: Latin America Working Group and the Center for International Policy.

Isbell, Billie Jean. 1992. Shining Path and peasant responses in rural Ayacucho. In *The Shining Path of Peru,* ed. David Palmer, 59–82. New York: St. Martin's Press.

Iturralbe, Diego. 1995. Nacionalidades indígenas y estado nacional en Ecuador. In *Nueva Historia del Ecuador,* vol. 13, ed. Enrique Ayala Mora, 9–58. Quito: Corporacion Editora Nacional.

IULA (International Union of Local Authorities), CELCADEL (Centro Latinoamericano de Capacitación y Desarrollo de los Gobiernos Locales), and USAID (United States Agency for International Development). 1992. *De la mujer al género: democratización municipal y nuevas perspectivas de desarrollo local.* Quito: USAID.

———. 1997. *Los procesos de reforma del estado a la luz de las teorías de género.* Quito: IULA.

Izard, Miguel. 1991. *El poder, la mentira, y la muerte: De el Amparo al Caracazo.* Caracas: Fondo Editorial Tropykos.

Jackson, Cecile, and Ruth Pearson, eds. 1998. *Feminist visions of development: Gender analysis and policy.* New York: Routledge.

Jácome, Luis I. 1994. La experiencia de estabilización en el Ecuador. *Apunte Técnico* 28.

Jaquette, Jane, 2001. Paper presented at the twenty-third International Congress of the Latin American Studies Association. Washington, D.C., September 6–8.

———, ed. 1994. *The women's movement in Latin America: Participation and democracy.* 2d ed. Boulder: Westview Press.

Jelin, Elizabeth, ed. 1990. *Women and social change in Latin America.* London: Zed Books/UNRISD.

Jiménez, Atenea, and Katiuska Maestre. 1998. *Factores que inciden en el aumento de la violencia en Caracas: Años 1989–1997.* Caracas: Escuela de Sociología, FACES-UCV.

Jones, Mark P. 1995. A guide to the electoral systems of the Americas. *Electoral Studies* 14.1: 5–21.

Kalmanovitz, Salomon. 1994. *Economia y nación: Una breve historia de Colombia.* Bogotá: Tercer Mundo.

Karl, Terry Lynn. 1997. *The paradox of plenty: Oil booms and petro-states.* Berkeley: University of California Press.

Keane, John. 1988. *Democracy and civil society.* London: Verso Press.

Kenney, Charles. 1995. The politics of Fujimori's self-coup and implications for democracy in Peru. Paper presented at the nineteenth International Congress of the Latin American Studies Association, Washington, D.C., September 28–30.

Klarén, Peter. 2000. *Peru: Society and nationhood in the Andes.* New York: Oxford University Press.

Knapp, Gregory. 1987. *Geografía quichua de la Sierra del Ecuador.* Quito: Abya-Yala.

Kruse, Thomas 1999. Mujeres Creando paints Bolivia. Available at <http://www.americas.org>.

Laclau, Ernest. 1977. *Nationalism, populism, and ideology.* London: Verso Books.

Lander, Luis E. 1998. La apertura petrolera en Venezuela: De la nacionalización a la privatización. *Revista Venezolana de Economía y Ciencias Sociales* 4.1.

———. 2001. *Gobierno de Chávez: ¿Nuevos rumbos en la política petrolera?* Paper presented at the twenty-third Congress of the Asociación Latinoamericana de Sociolgia (ALAS), Antigua, Guatemala, October 29–November 2.

Lander, Luis E., Margarita López Maya, and Luis Salamanca. 2000. *Manual de uso y glosario de descriptores de la base de datos el Bravo Pueblo.* Mimeograph. Caracas.

Larrea Maldonado, Carlos. 1992. The mirage of development: Oil, employment, and poverty in Ecuador (1970–1990). Ph.D. diss., York University.

———. 1998. Structural adjustment, income distribution, and employment in Ecuador. In *Poverty, economic reform, and income distribution in Latin America,* ed. Albert Berry. Boulder: Lynne Rienner Publishers.

Larrea Maldonado, Carlos, and Liisa L. North. 1991. La estructura social ecuatoriana entre 1960 y 1979. In *Epoca Repúblicana V: El Ecuador en el último período,* ed. Fernando Tinajero and José Moncada, vol. 11 of *Nueva historia del Ecuador,* ed. Enrique Ayala Mora. Quito: Corporación Editora Nacional.

———. 1997. Ecuador: Adjustment policy impacts on truncated development and democratization. *Third World Quarterly* 18.5: 913–34.

———, eds. 1987. *El banano en el Ecuador: Transnacionales, modernización, y subdesarrollo.* Quito: Corporación Editora Nacional.

Laserna, Roberto. 1994. Las drogas y la justicia en Cochabamba: Los narocos en el país de Culpables. Paper presented at the eighteenth International Congress of the Latin American Studies Association, Atlanta, March 10–12.

Laserna, Roberto, Natalia Camacho, and Eduardo Córdova. 1999. *Empujando la concertación: Marchas campesinas, opinión pública, y coca.* La Paz: CERES and PIEB.

Leal Buitrago, Francisco. 1989. *Estado y política en Colombia.* 2d ed. Bogotá: Siglo XXI.

———. 1994a. *El oficio de la guerra: La seguridad nacional en Colombia.* Bogotá: Tercer Mundo.

———. 1994b. *En busca de la estabilidad perdida: Actores políticos y sociales en los años noventa.* Bogotá: Tercer Mundo.

———. 1998. Prologo. In *El juego del poder: Historia armas y votos,* by Andrés Dávila Ladrón de Guevara, 15–21. Bogota: Uninandes.

———. 2002. *La seguridad nacional a la deriva: Del Frente Nacional a la postguerra fría.* Bogotá: Alfa-Omega, Ceso-Universidad de los Andes, FLACSO-Sede Ecuador.

Leal Buitrago, Francisco, and Andrés Dávila. 1991. *Clientelismo: El sistema político y su expresión regional.* Bogotá: IEPRI-UN.

Leal Buitrago, Francisco, and Leon Zamosc, eds. 1990. *Al filo del caos: Crisis política en la Colombia de los años 80.* Bogotá: IEPRI/Tercer Mundo.

Lechner, Norbert and Fernando Calderon. 1998. *Mas allá del estado, mas allá del Mercado, la democracia.* La Paz: Plural Editores.

Ledebur, Kathryn. 2002. Coca and conflict in the Chapare. Washington Office on Latin America, July.

Lee, Rensselaer W., III. 1989. *The white labyrinth: Cocaine and political power.* New Brunswick: Transaction Publishers.

León, Jorge. 1994. *De campesinos a ciudadanos diferentes.* Quito: CEDIME.

Leons, Madeleine, and Harry Sanabria, eds. 1997. *Coca, cocaine, and the Bolivian reality.* Albany: State University of New York Press.

Levitsky, Steven. 1999. Fujimori and post-party politics in Peru. *Journal of Democracy* 10.3: 78–92.

La ley de tierras y su reglamento. 1997. Cusco: Arariwa, CBC, CEPES, and SER.

Lichbach, Mark, and Allen Zuckerman, eds. 1997. *Comparative politics: Rationality, Culture, and Structure.* Cambridge: Cambridge University Press.

Lind, Amy. 1992. Gender, power, and development: Popular women's organizations and the politics of needs in Ecuador. In *The making of social movements in Latin America,* ed. Arturo Escobar and Sonia Alvarez, 134–49. Boulder: Westview Press

———. 1997. Gender, development, and urban social change: Women's community action in global cities. *World Development* 25.8: 1205–24.

———. 2000. Negotiating boundaries: Women's organizations and the politics of development in Ecuador. In *Gender and global restructuring,* ed. Maríanne Marchand and Anne Sisson Runyan, 161–75. New York: Routledge.

———. 2001. *Development engendered: Women's movements and the cultural politics of neoliberalism in the Andes.* N.p.

———. 2002. Making feminist sense of neoliberalism: The institutionalization of Women's struggles for Survival in Ecuador and Bolivia. *Journal of Developing Societies* 18.2–3: 181–207.

———. 2003a. Gender and neoliberal states: Feminists remake the nation in Ecuador. *Latin American Perspectives* 30.1: 181–207.

———. 2003b. The paradoxes of survival and struggle: Women's organizations and the cultural politics of neoliberalism in Ecuador. N.p.

Linz, Juan J., and Alfred Stepan. 1996. *Problems of democratic transition and consolidation: Southern Europe, South America, and post-communist Europe.* Baltimore: Johns Hopkins University Press.

Loayza, Francisco. 1998. Formé un Frankenstein. *Debate* 20.3: 36.

Lombardi, John V. 1971. *The decline and abolition of Negro slavery in Venezuela, 1820–1854.* Westport: Greenwood Press.

López-Alves, Fernando. 2000. *State formation and democracy in Latin America, 1810–1900.* Durham: Duke University Press.

López Maya, Margarita. 1997. The rise of Causa R in Venezuela. In *The new politics of inequality in*

Latin America: Rethinking participation and representation, ed. Douglas Chalmers, Carlos Vilas, Katherine Hite, Scott Martin, Kerianne Piester, and Monique Segarra, 117–43. London and New York: Oxford University Press.

———. 1999a. Venezuela: Formas de la protesta popular entre 1989 y 1994. *Revista Venezolana de Economía y Ciencias Sociales* 5.4: 11–42.

———. 1999b. Venezuela: La rebelión popular del 27 de febrero de 1989: ¿Resistencia a la modernidad? *Revista Venezolana de Economía y Ciencias Sociales* 5.2–3: 177–200.

López Maya, Margarita, and Luis E. Lander. 1999. Triunfos en tiempos de transición: Actores de vocación popular en las elecciones venezolanas de 1998. *América Latina Hoy* 21.

Loveman, Brian. 1998. When you wish upon the stars: Why the generals (and admirals) say yes to Latin American transitions to civilian government. In *The origins of liberty: Political and economic modernization in the modern world,* ed. Paul Drake and Matthew McCubbins. Princeton: Princeton University Press.

Lowenthal, Abraham, ed. 1975. *The Peruvian experiment.* Princeton: Princeton University Press.

Lubrano, Aldo, and Rosa Haydee Sánchez. 1987. *Del hombre completo a Jaime es como tú: Recuento de un proceso electoral venezolano.* Caracas: Vadell Hermanos.

Luengo, Néstor Luis. 1994. Estado, sistema político, y violencia en Venezuela. In *La violencia en Venezuela,* ed. Luis Ugalde et al., 126–60. Caracas: Monte Ávila Editores Latinoamericana-UCAB.

Luque, Alberto. 2000. Dolarización: El salto al vacío. In *Dolarización: Informe urgente,* ed. Alberto Acosta and José E. Juncosa. Quito: ILDIS and Abya-Yala/UPS.

Lynch, Nicolás. 1992. *La transición conservadora: Movimiento social y democracia en el Perú, 1974–78.* Lima: El Zorro de Abajo Ediciones.

———. 1999. Neopopulismo: Un concepto vacío. *Socialismo y participación* 86.

———. 2000. *Política y antipolítica en el Perú.* Lima: DESCO.

MacCoun, Robert J., and Peter Reuter. 2001. *Drug war heresies: Learning from other vices, times, and places.* Cambridge: Cambridge University Press.

Mader, Elke. 1999. *Metamorfosis del poder: Persona, mito, y visión en la sociedad Shuar y Achuar.* Quito: Abya-Yala.

Maiguashca, Juan, and Liisa L. North. 1991. Orígenes y significado del velasquismo: Lucha de clases y participación política en el Ecuador, 1920–1972. In *La cuestión regional y el poder,* ed. Rafael Quintero, 89–159. Quito: Corporación Editora Nacional/FLACSO/CERLAC.

Mainwaring, Scott. 1999. *Rethinking party systems in the third wave of democratization: The case of Brazil.* Stanford: Stanford University Press.

Malavé Mata, Héctor. 1987. *Los extravíos del poder: euforia y crisis del populismo en Venezuela.* Caracas: Universidad Central de Venezuela.

Manifiesto de Tiahuanacu. 1986, Mimeograph. La Paz: 1973. Reprinted in *El katarismo,* by Javier Hurtado. La Paz: Hisbol.

Mann, Michael. 1986. *The sources of political power: A history of power from the beginning to a.d. 1760.* New York: Cambridge University Press.

Manrique, Nelson. 1985. *Yawar Mayu.* Lima: DESCO.

———. 1989. La década de la violencia. *Márgenes* 5:137–82.

Maravall, José Antonio. 1989. *Culture of the baroque: Analysis of a historical structure.* Trans. Terry Cochran. Minneapolis: University of Minnesota Press.

Marta Sosa, Joaquín. 1984. *Venezuela: Elecciones y transformación social.* Caracas: Ediciones Centauro.

Martz, John. *Acción democrática: Evolution of a modern political party in Venezuela.* Princeton: Princeton University Press, 1966.

Martz, John, and Enrique Baloyra. 1979. *Electoral mobilization and public opinion: The Venezuelan campaign of 1973.* Chapel Hill: University of North Carolina Press.

Martz, John, and David J. Myers, eds. *Venezuela: The Democratic Experience.* New York: Praeger Publishers, 1977.

Matard-Bonucci, M. A. 1994. *Histoire de la mafia.* Brussels: Éditions Complexe.

Matos Mar, José. 1968. *Desborde popular y crisis del estado.* 4th ed. Lima: Institute de Estudios Peruanos.

Matthews, Robert D., Jr. 1977. *Violencia rural en Venezuela, 1840–1858*. Caracas: Editorial Ateneo de Caracas.

Mauceri, Philip. 1996. *State under siege: Development and policy making in Peru*. Boulder: Westview Press.

———. 1997. The transition to democracy and the failure of institution building. In *The Peruvian labyrinth: Polity, society, economics*, ed. Maxwell A. Cameron and Philip Mauceri, 13–36. University Park: Pennsylvania State University Press.

McAdam, Doug, Sidney Tarrow, and Charles Tilly. 2000. *Dynamics of contention*. London: Cambridge University Press.

McAdam, Doug, John D. McCarthy, and Mayer N. Zald. Introduction: Opportunities, mobilizing structures and framing processes: Toward a synthetic, comparative perspective on social movements. In *Comparative perspectives on social movements: Political opportunities, mobilizing structures, and cultural framings*, 1–20. Cambridge: Cambridge University Press.

McClintock, Cynthia. 1998. Should the authoritarian regime label be revived? Paper presented at the twenty-first International Congress of the Latin American Studies Association, Chicago, September 24–26.

McClintock, Cynthia, and Abraham Lowenthal, eds. 1983. *The Peruvian experiment revisited*. Princeton: Princeton University Press.

McFarren, W. 1992. The politics of Bolivia's economic crisis: Survival strategies of displaced tin-mining households. In *Unequal burden: Economic crisis, persistent poverty, and women's work*, ed. Lourdes Benería and Shelley Feldman, 131–58. Boulder: Westview Press.

Medina Gallego, Carlos. 1990. *Autodefensas, paramilitares, y narcotrafico en Colombia: El caso Puerto Boyacá*. Bogotá: Editorial Documentos Periodisticos.

Meisel Roca, Adolfo, ed. 1994. *Historia económica y social del Caribe Colombiano*. Bogotá: Ediciones Uninorte–Ecoe Ediciones.

Melo, Jorge Orlando. 1990. Los paramilitares y su impacto en la política. In *Al filo del caos: Crisis política en la Colombia de los años 80*, ed. Francisco Leal Buitrago and Leon Zamosc, 475–514. Bogotá: IEPRI/Tercer Mundo.

Méndez, Cecilia. 1995. *Incas sí, indios no: Apuntes para el estudio del nacionalismo criollo en el Perú*. Lima: Instituto de Estudios Peruanos.

Méndez, Juan E., Guillermo O'Donnell, and Paulo Sérgio Pinheiro, eds. 1999. *The (un)rule of law and the underprivileged in Latin America*. Notre Dame: University of Notre Dame Press.

Migdal, Joel. 1988. *Strong societies, weak states: State-society relations and state capabilities in the Third World*. Princeton: Princeton University Press.

———. 1997. Studying the state. In *Comparative politics: Rationality, culture, and structure*, ed. Mark Lichbach and Allen Zuckerman, 208–35. Cambridge: Cambridge University Press.

———. 2001. *State in society: Studying how states and societies transform and constitute one another*. New York: Cambridge University Press.

Migdal, Joel, Atul Kohli, and Vivien Shue. 1994. *State power and social forces: Domination and transformation in the Third World*. Princeton: Princeton University Press.

Mijeski, Kenneth, and Scott Beck. 1998. Mainstreaming the indigenous movement in Ecuador: The electoral strategy. Paper presented at the twenty-first International Congress of the Latin American Studies Association, Chicago, September 24–26.

Mills, Nick D. 1991. Sector privado y estado nacional en el Ecuador democrático, 1979–1984. In *La cuestión regional y el poder*, ed. Rafael Quintero, 207–45. Quito: Corporación Editora Nacional/FLACSO/CERLAC.

Ministerio de Defensa Nacional. 2001. *Informe anual de derechos humanos y DH 2000*. Bogotá: República de Colombia.

Ministerio de Economía. 1960. *Primer censo de población del Ecuador—1950, resumén de características*. Quito.

Ministry of the Presidency. 1993. Lineamientos básicos de la política social. November 1993. Lima. Mimeograph.

Misión Rural. 1998. Misión Rural: Una perspectiva regional. In *Misión Rural: Convivencia y sostenibilidad*, vol. 9. Bogotá.

Moleiro, Moisés. 1978. *El partido del pueblo.* Valencia: Vadell Hermanos.

Mommer, Bernard. 1983. *Petroleo, renta del suelo, e historia.* Mérida: Universidad de los Andes.

———. 1988. *La cuestión petrolera.* Caracas: Fondo Editorial Trópikos.

Montaño, Sonia. 1996. La construcción de una agenda de género en el gobierno de Bolivia de 1989–1995. La Paz: Proyecto de Recursos Humanos para el Desarrollo.

———. 1997. Género, cultura, y poder local. In *Los procesos de reforma del estado a la luz de las teorías de género,* ed. IULA, CELCADEL, and USAID, cuaderno 26: 55–68. Quito: IULA.

Moreano, Alejandro. 1991. El sistema político en el Ecuador contemporáneo. In *Epoca republicana V: El Ecuador en el último período,* ed. Fernando Tinajero and José Moncada, vol. 11 of *Nueva historia del Ecuador,* 1818–19, ed. Enrique Ayala Mora. Quito: Corporación Editora Nacional.

Moreno Yánez, Segundo. 1989. La sociedad indígena y su articulación a la formación socioeconómica colonial en la Audiencia de Quito. In *Nueva historia del Ecuador,* vol. 5, ed. Enrique Ayala Mora. Quito: Corporacion Editora Nacional.

Morin, Françoise. 1983. L'indianité comme nation contre l'état. In *L'indianité au Pérou: Mythe ou réalité?* Toulouse: GRAL/CNRS.

Moscarella, Javier V., and Carlos G. Pinilla. 2000. *La revolución azul: Una salida cultural para la ciénaga grande de Santa Marta.* Barranquilla: CERES-CIDHUM/Universidad del Norte.

Moser, Caroline. 1989. The impact of recession and structural adjustment policies at the microlevel: Low-income women and their households in Guayaquil, Ecuador. Paper prepared for UNICEF-Ecuador.

Moya, Alba. 1998. *Ethnos: Atlas etnográfico del Ecuador.* Quito: Proyecto EBI GTZ.

Mueller, Adele. 1985. The bureaucratization of feminist knowledge: The case of women and development. *Resources for Feminist Research/Documentation sur la Recherche Feministe* 15.1: 49–51.

Nairn, Tom. 1977. *The break-up of Britain.* London: Verso Editions.

Navarro, Guillermo J. 1976. *La concentración de capitales en el Ecuador.* Quito: Ediciones Soltierra.

Navarro, Wilson, Alonso Vallejo, and Xabier Villaverde. 1996. *Tierra para la vida: Acceso de los campesinos ecuatorianos a la tierra: Opción y experiencias del FEPP.* Quito: Fondo Ecuatoriano Populorum Progressio.

Neruda, Pablo. 1978. *Canto general.* Caracas: Biblioteca Ayacucho.

Nielson, Daniel, and Matthew Shugart. 1999. Constitutional change in Colombia: Policy adjustment through institutional reform. *Comparative Political Studies* 32.3: 313–42.

Nieto, Jorge. 1983. *Izquierda y democracia en el Perú.* Lima: DESCO.

Norris, Pippa, ed. 1999. *Critical citizens: Global support for democratic governance.* Oxford: Oxford University Press.

North, Liisa L. 1985. Implementación de la política económica y la estructura de poder político en el Ecuador. In *Economía política del Ecuador: Campo, región, nación,* ed. Louis Lefeber, 425–57. Quito: Corporación Editora Nacional/FLACSO/CERLAC.

———. 1999. Austerity and disorder in the Andes. *NACLA Report on the Americas* 33.1: 6–9.

Nugent, Guillermo. 1992. *El laberinto de la choledad.* Lima: Fundación Friedrich Ebert.

Obando, Enrique. 1998. Civil-military relations in Peru, 1980–1996: How to control and coopt the military (and the consequences of doing so). In *Shining and other paths: War and society in Peru, 1980–1995,* ed. Steve Stern, 385–410. Durham: Duke University Press.

Oberto, Luis Enrique. 1998. *El código orgánico procesal penal.* Washington, D.C.: Inter-American Development Bank.

OCEI (Oficina Central de Estadística y Información, Presidencia de la República). 1993. *Anuario Estadístico de Venezuela, 1993.* Caracas: OCEI.

———. 2002. Indicadores sociales tomados en febrero. <http://www.ocei.gov.ve/estadistica>.

Ochsendorf, A. 1998. *Constructing power through food-for-work projects in El Alto, Bolivia.* Undergraduate honors thesis, Wellesley College.

O'Donnell, Guillermo. 1993. On the state, democratization, and some conceptual problems: A Latin American view with glances at some postcommunist countries. *World Development* 21.8: 1355–69.

———. 1996. Illusions about consolidation. *Journal of Democracy* 7.2: 34–51.

————. 1999. Horizontal accountability in new democracies. In *The self-restraining state: Power and accountability in new democracies,* ed. Andres Schedler, Larry Diamond, and Mark Plattner, 29–51. Boulder: Lynne Reinner.

O'Donnell, Guillermo, and Philippe C. Schmitter. 1986. *Transitions from authoritarian rule: Tentative conclusions about uncertain democracies.* Baltimore: Johns Hopkins University Press.

Ojeda Segovia, Lautaro. 1993. *El descrédito de lo social: Las políticas sociales en el Ecuador.* Quito: Centro para el Desarrollo Social CDS.

Olea, Raquel. 1995. Feminism: Modern or postmodern? In *The postmodernism debate in Latin America,* ed. John Beverley, José Oviedo and Michael Aronna, 195–200. Durham: Duke University Press.

Ortiz Crespo, Gonzalo. 2000a. Elecciones seccionales confirman la regionalización partidaria. *Gestión* 72 (June).

————. 2000b. Esquema de la historia económica del Ecuador en el siglo XX. *Gestión* 68 (February).

————. 2000c. Reportaje a los tres golpes de Estado. *Gestión* 68 (February).

Oviedo y Baños. José. 1987. *The conquest and settlement of Venezuela.* Berkeley: University of California Press.

Pacari, Nina. 1996. Ecuador: Taking on the neoliberal agenda. *NACLA Report on the Americas* 29.5: 22–30.

Painter, James. *Bolivia and coca: A study in dependency.* Boulder: Lynne Rienner Publishers, 1994.

Palacios, Marco. 1986. *Estado y clases sociales en Colombia.* Bogotá: Procultura.

————. 1995. *Entre la legitimidad y la violencia: Colobia, 1875–1994.* Bogota: Editorial Norma.

————. 1999a. *De populistas, mandarines, y violencias: Luchas por el poder.* Bogotá: Planeta.

————. 1999b. *Parábola del liberalismo.* Bogotá: Norma Editorial.

Pallares, Amalia. 1997. From peasant struggles to Indian resistance: Political identity in highland Ecuador, 1964–1992. Ph.D. diss., University of Texas at Austin.

Palmer, David Scott, ed. 1992. *Shining Path of Peru.* New York: St. Martin's Press.

Panfichi, Aldo. 1997. The authoritarian alternative. In *The new politics of inequality in Latin America: Rethinking participation and representation,* ed. Douglas Chalmers, Carlos Vilas, Katherine Hite, Scott Martin, Kerianne Piester, and Monique Segarra. London and New York: Oxford University Press.

Pastor, Manuel, Jr., and Carol Wise. 1992. Peruvian economic policy in the 1980s: From orthodoxy to heterodoxy and back. *Latin American Research Review* 27.2: 83–117.

Paulson, Susan, and Pamela Calla. 2000. Gender and ethnicity in Bolivian politics: Transformation or paternalism? *Journal of Latin American Anthropology* 5.2: 112–49.

Paz y Miño Cepeda, Juan J. 1993. Fuerzas armadas, sociedad, y cuestión nacional. *Laboratorio de Economía de la Facultad de Economía de la Pontificia Universidad Católica del Ecuador* 2.3.

————. 2000. *Revolución Juliana: Nación, ejército, y bancocracia.* Quito: Abya-Yala.

Peñaranda, Ricardo, and Javier Guerrero, eds. 1999. *De las armas a la política.* Bogotá: TM-Iepri-UN.

Peñate, Andres. 1991. Arauca, politics, and oil in a Colombia province. Master's thesis, Oxford University.

————. 1999. El sendero estrategico del ELN: Del idealismo guevarista al clientelismo armado. In *Reconocer la guerra para construir la paz,* ed. Malcolm Deas and Maria Victoria Llorente, 55–98. Bogotá: Editorial Norma/Universidad de los Andes.

Phillips, Lynne, ed. 1998. *The third wave of modernization in Latin America: Cultural perspectives on neoliberalism.* Wilmington, Dela.: Scholarly Resources Books.

Piñerúa, Luis. 1988. *Enfrentamiento con el poder.* Caracas: Ediciones Centauro.

Pinheiro, Paul Sergio. 1996. Prefacio: O passado esta moro, nem passado e ainda. In *Democracia em pedacos: Direitos humanos no Brasil,* ed. Gilberto Dimenstein, 7–45. Sao Paul: Companhia das Letras.

Pinzón de Lewin, Patricia. 1989. *Pueblos, regiones, y partidos: La regionalización electoral: Atlas electoral colombiano.* Bogotá: Ediciones Uniandes, CIDER, CEREC.

Piven, Frances Fox, and Richard A. Cloward. 1977. *Poor people's movements: Why they succeed, how they fail.* New York: Pantheon Books.

Placencia, Mercedes, and Elvia Caro. 1998. Institucionalidad para mujer y género en América Latina y el Caribe. Regional report prepared for the Inter-American Development Bank, Quito.

PNUD (Programa de Naciones Unidas para el Desarrollo). 1999. *Informe sobre desarrollo humano, Ecuador 1999.* Quito: PNUD.

Pozzi-Escot, Inés. 1998. *El multilingüismo en el Perú.* Cusco and Cochabamba: Centro Bartolomé Las Casas/PROEIB.

Proceso Político. 1978. *CAP: 5 Años.* Caracas: Equipo Proceso Político.

PROVEA (Programa Venezolano de Educación-Acción en Derechos Humanos). 1996. *Situación de los derechos humnanos en Venezuela: Informe annual.* Caracas: PROVEA.

———. 1999. *Situación de los derechos humanos en Venezuela: Informe annual.* Caracas: Edisil Impresos.

———. 2001. *Situación de los derechos humanos en Venezuela: Informe annual.* Caracas: Edisil Impresos.

Pueblo Indio. 1981. Vocero del Consejo Indio de Sudamérica, no. 1. Lima.

Putnam, Robert. 1995. Bowling alone: America's declining social capital. *Journal of Democracy* 6: 65–78.

Przeworski, Adam. 1986. Some problems in the study of the transition to democracy. In *Transitions from authoritarian rule: Comparative perspectives,* ed. Guillermo O'Donnell, Philippe C. Schmitter, and Laurence Whitehead, 47–63. Baltimore: Johns Hopkins University Press.

———. 1991. *Democracy and the market: Political and economic reform in Eastern Europe and Latin America.* Cambridge: Cambridge University Press.

Querubín, Cristina, María Fernanda Sánchez, and Ileana Kure. 1998. Dinámica de las elecciones populares de alcaldes, 1988–1997. In *Elecciones y democracia, 1997–1998,* ed. Ana María Bejarano and Andrés Dávila, 141–91. Bogotá: Fundación Social/Universidad de los Andes/Veeduría Ciudadana.

Quijano, Aníbal. 1980. *Dominación y cultura: Lo cholo y el conflicto cultural en el Perú.* Lima: Mosca Azul.

Quintero, Rafael, and Erika Silva. 1991. Región y representación política en el Ecuador contemporáneo 1939–1959. In *La cuestión regional y el poder,* 29–87. Quito: Corporación Editora Nacional/FLACSO/CERLAC.

Radcliffe, Sarah, and Sallie Westwood. 1999. *Rehaciendo la nación: Lugar, identidad, y política en América Latina.* Quito: Abya-Yala.

Raffestin, Claude. 1993. *Por uma geografia do poder.* São Paulo: Editora Ática.

Ramos, Alicia Rita. 1998. *Indigenism: Ethnic politics in Brazil.* Madison: University of Wisconsin Press.

———. 1999. Ethnic politics home and abroad. Paper presented at the conference Estado, Clase, Género, y Etnicidad, Cochabamba, June.

Rangel, Alfredo. 1998. *Colombia: Guerra en el fin del siglo.* Bogotá: Tercer Mundo.

Rangel, Domingo Alberto. 1973. *Los mercaderes del voto.* Valencia: Vadell Hermanos.

———. 1982. *Fin de fiesta.* Valencia: Vadell Hermanos.

Rangel, Domingo Alberto, and Pedro Duno. 1979. *La pipa rota: Las elecciones de 1978.* Caracas: Vadell Hermanos.

Redclift, Michael R. 1978. *Agrarian reform and peasant organization on the Ecuadorean coast.* London: Athlone Press.

Reinaga, Fausto. 1969. *La revolución india.* La Paz: Partido Indio de Bolivia.

República de Venezuela. *Gaceta del Congreso* 28.1. March 1988–January 1989.

Richani, Nazih. 1997. The political economy of violence: The war system in Colombia. *Journal of Interamerican Studies and World Affairs* 39.2: 37–82.

Riley, Kevin Jack. 1996. *Snow job? The war against international cocaine trafficking.* New Brunswick: Transaction Publishers.

Ríos, Marcela, ed. 1998. *Reflexiones teóricas y comparativas sobre los feminismos en Chile y America Latina.* Santiago: Universidad de Chile.

Roberts, Kenneth. 1995. Neoliberalism and the transformation of populism in Latin America: The Peruvian case. *World Politics* 48.1: 82–116.

———. 2002. Do parties matter? Lessons from the Fujimori experience. Paper presented at the conference The Fujimori Legacy and Its Impact on Public Policy in Latin America, the Dante B.

Fascell North-South Center, University of Miami, and the University of Delaware, March 14, 2002.

Robles, Rodolfo. *Crimen y impunidad: El "gropo Colina" y el poder.* Lima: APRODEH.

Rodríguez, R. Juan Carlos. 1998. Participación, sistema de partidos, y sistema electoral: Posibilidades de ingeniería electoral. *Análisis Político* 33:94–109.

Rodríguez, Lilia. 1994. Barrio women: Between the urban and the feminist movement. *Latin American Perspectives* 21.3: 32–48.

———, ed. 1996. *Mujeres del barrio.* Quito: CEPAM.

Roldós Aguilera, León. 1991. La administración de Febres Cordero y el sector público. In *Epoca repúblicana V: El Ecuador en el último período,* ed. Fernando Tinajero and José Moncada, vol. 11 of *Nueva historia del Ecuador,* ed. Enrique Ayala Mora, 343–45. Quito: Corporación Editora Nacional.

Romano, Salvatore Francesco. 1970. *Historia de la mafia.* Madrid: Alianza Editorial.

Romero, Dolcey. 1997. Esclavitud en la provincia de Santa Marta, 1791–1851. Santa Marta: Fondo de Publicaciones de Autores Magdalenenses-Instituto de Cultura y Turismo del Magdalena.

Roper, J. Montgomery, Thomas Perreault, and Patrick Wilson. 2003. Introduction: New indigenous transformational movements in Latin America. *Latin American Perspectives* 30.1: 5–22.

Roseberry, William. 1986. Images of the peasant in the consciousness of the Venezuelan proletariat. In *Proletarians and protest,* ed. Michael Hanagan and Charles Stephenson. Westport: Greenwood Press.

Rosero, Rocío. 1988. Balance y perspectiva del movimiento de mujeres. In *Mujeres, crisis y movimiento: America Latina y el Caribe.* Santiago de Chile: ISIS International.

Rosero, Rocío, María Pilar Vega, and Ariadna Reyes Ávila. 2000. *De las demandas a los derechos: Las mujeres en la constitución de 1998.* Quito: Foro Nacional Permanente de la Mujer Ecuatoriana/Consejo Nacional de las Mujeres/Embajada Real de los Países Bajos.

Rospigliosi, Fernando. 1996. *Las fuerzas armadas y el 5 de abril: La percepción de la amenaza subversiva como una motivación golpista.* Working paper, no. 73. Lima: Instituto de Estudios Peruanos.

———. 1998. *La Operación Chavín de Huántar: Un caso ilustrativo de cómo funcionan las relaciones cívico militares en el Perú a las puertas del siglo XXI.* Lima: Instituto de Defensa Legal.

———. 2000. *Montesinos y las fuerzas armadas.* Lima: Instituto de Estudios Peruanos.

Saad Herrería, Pedro. 2000. *La caída de Mahuad.* Quito: Editorial El Conejo.

Sachs, Jeffrey, and Felipe Larrain. 2000. Por qué la dolarización es más una camisa de fuerza que una salvación? In *Dolarización: Informe urgente,* ed. Alberto Acosta and José E. Juncosa, 229–41. Quito: ILDIS and Abya-Yala/UPS.

Salazar, Ernesto. 1981. The Federation Schuar and the colonization frontier. In *Cultural transformations and ethnicity in modern Ecuador,* ed. Norman Whitten, 589–613. Urbana: University of Illinois Press.

Salinas Mulder, Silvia. 1994. *Una protesta sin propuesta: Situación de la mujer en Bolivia: 1976–1994.* La Paz: Centro de Desarrollo y Fomento a la Auto-Aguda (CEDEFOA).

Sanjuán, Ana María. 1997. La criminalidad en Caracas: percepciones y realidades. *Revista Venezolana de Economía y Ciencias Sociales* 3.2–3: 215–54.

Santos Alvins, Thamara. 1992. *Violencia criminal y violencia policial en Venezuela.* Maracaibo: Instituto de Criminologia de la Universidad de Zulia.

Sassen, Saskia. 1996. *Losing control? Sovereignty in an age of globalization.* New York: Columbia University Press.

———. 1998. *Globalization and its discontents.* New York: New Press.

Scharer-Nussberger, Maya. 1979. *Romúlo Gallegos: El mundo inconcluso.* Caracas: Monte Avila Editores.

Schild, Verónica. 1998. New subjects of rights? Women's movements and the construction of citizenship in the "new democracies." In *Cultures of politics/politics of cultures: Revisioning Latin American social movements,* ed. Sonia Alvarez, Evelina Dagnino, and Arturo Escobar, 93–117. Boulder: Westview Press.

———. 2000. Neo-liberalism's new gendered market citizens: The "civilizing" dimension of social programmes in Chile. *Citizenship Studies* 4.3: 275–305.

Scotto, Carmen, and Anabel Castillo. 1994. La violencia cotidiana en Venezuela: El caso de un barrio. In *La violencia en Venezuela,* ed. Luis Ugalde et. al. Caracas: Monte Ávila Editores Latinoamericana-UCAB.

Secretaría Nacional de Asuntos Etnicos, de Género, y Generacionales et al. 1994. *Primer censo indígena rural de tierras bajas, Bolivia.* La Paz: Secretaría Nacional de Asuntos Etnicos.

Segarra, Monique. 1996. Redefining the public/private mix: NGOs and the emergency social investment fund in Ecuador. In *The new politics of inequality in Latin America: Rethinking participation and representation,* ed. Douglas Chalmers, Carlos Vilas, Katherine Hite, Scott Martin, Kerianne Piester, and Monique Segarra, 489–515. London and New York: Oxford University Press.

Selverston-Scher, Melina. 1997. The politics of identity reconstruction: Indians and democracy in Ecuador. In *The new politics of inequality in Latin America: Rethinking participation and representation,* ed. Douglas Chalmers, Carlos Vilas, Katherine Hite, Scott Martin, Kerianne Piester, and Monique Segarra, 170–91. London and New York: Oxford University Press.

———. 2001. *Ethnopolitics in Ecuador: Indigenous rights and the strengthening of democracy.* Miami: North-South Center Press.

Shifter, Michael. 2000. The United States and Colombia: Partners in ambiguity. *Current History* 99.634: 51–56.

SIISE (Sistema Integrado de Indicadores Sociales del Ecuador). 2000a. Censo de población y vivienda de 1990 (based on figures from INEC). Quito: SIISE.

———. 2000b. Estimación de la población indígena y negra (based on figures from CODENPE). Quito: SIISE.

Silva Colmenares, Julio. 1977. *Los verdaderos dueños del país.* Bogotá: Fondo Editorial Suramerica.

Silva Michelena, José Agustín, and Heinz Rudolf Sonntag. 1979. *El proceso electoral de 1978.* Caracas: Editorial Ateneo de Caracas.

Simmons, Pam. 1997. Women in development: A threat to liberation. In *The post-development reader,* ed. Majid Rahnema, 244–55. Atlantic Highlands, N.J.: Zed Press.

Skocpol, Theda, 1979. *States and social revolutions: A comparative analysis of France, Russia, and China.* Cambridge: Cambridge University Press.

Skurski, Julie. 1996. The ambiguities of authenticity in Latin America: *Doña Bárbara* and the construction of national identity. In *Becoming national: A reader,* ed. Geoff Eley and Ronald G. Suny, 371–402. New York: Oxford University Press.

———. N.d. Representing "the people" in Venezuelan nationalism discourse. Ph.D. diss., University of Chicago.

Sommer, Doris. 1991. *Foundational fictions: When history was romance.* Berkeley: University of California Press.

Spybey, Tony. 1996. *Globalization and world society.* Cambridge: Polity Press.

Stanley, William. 1996. *The protection racket state: Elite politics, military extortion, and civil war in El Salvador.* Philadelphia: Temple University Press.

Starn, Orin. 1998. Villagers at arms: War and counterrevolution in the Central-South Andes. In *Shining and other paths: War and society in Peru, 1980–1995,* ed. Steve J. Stern, 224–57. Durham: Duke University Press.

Stavenhagen, Rodolfo. 1997. Las organizaciones indígenas: Actores emergentes en América Latina. In *Identidades étnicas,* ed. Manuel Gutiérrez Estévez, 13–30. Madrid: Casa de América, Diálogos Amerindios.

———. 2002. Indigenous peoples and the state in Latin America: An ongoing debate. In *Multiculturalism in Latin America: Indigenous rights, diversity and democracy,* ed. Rachel Sieder. London: Palgrave Macmillan and Institute of Latin American Studies.

Stepan, Alfred. 1978. *State and society: Peru in comparative perspective.* Princeton: Princeton University Press.

Stern, Steven, ed.1987. *Resistance, rebellion, and consciousness in the Andean peasant world: 18th to 20th centuries.* Madison: University of Wisconsin Press.

———. 1998. *Shining and other paths: War and society in Peru, 1980–1995.* Durham: Duke University Press.

Stone, Lawrence. 1990. *Familia, sexo, y matrimonio en Inglaterra, 1500–1800.* Mexico: Fondo de Cultura Económica.

Stotzky, Irwin P. 1993. *Transitions to democracy in Latin America: The role of the judiciary.* Boulder: Westview Press.

Strange, Susan. 1998. *Mad money: When markets outgrow governments.* Ann Arbor: University of Michigan Press.

Tamayo Herrera, José. 1980. *Historia del indigenismo cuzqueño, siglos XVI–XX.* Lima: INC.

Tanaka, Martín. 1998. *Los espejismos de la democracia: El colapso del sistema de partidos en el Perú.* Lima: Instituto de Estudios Peruanos.

Tapia, Carlos. 1997. *Las fuerzas armadas y Sendero Luminoso: Dos estrategias y un final.* Lima: Instituto de Estudios Peruanos.

Tarre Murzi, Alfredo. 1989. *Los muertos de la deuda.* Caracas: Ediciones Centauro.

Tarrow, Sydney. 1994. *Power in movement: Social movements, collective action, and politics.* Cambridge and New York: Cambridge University Press.

Tate, Winifred. 2001. Bush announces "Andean counterdrug initiative." *Cross Currents* 3.2: 9.

Taussig, Michael. 1987. *Shamanism, colonialism, and the wild man.* Chicago: University of Chicago Press.

Thompson, E. P. 1971. The moral economy of the English crowd in the eighteenth century. *Past and Present* 50:76–136.

Thorp, Rosemary. 1991. *Economic management and economic development in Peru and Colombia.* Pittsburgh: University of Pittsburgh Press.

Thorp, Rosemary, and Geoffrey Bertram. 1978. *Peru 1870–1977: History of an open market economy.* New York: Oxford University Press.

Ticona, Esteban. 2000. Organización y liderazgo aymara: La experiencia indígena en la política boliviana, 1979–1996. La Paz: Universidad de la Cordillera/AGRUCO.

Ticona, Esteban, Gonzalo Rojas, and Xavier Albó. 1995. *Votos y wiphalas: Campesinos y pueblos originarios en democracia.* La Paz: CIPCA/Fundación Milenio.

Tilly, Charles. 1985. War making and state making as organized crime. In *Bringing the state back in,* ed. Peter B. Evans, Dietrich Rueschemeyer, and Theda Skocpol. New York: Cambridge University Press.

———. 1990. *Coercion, capital, and European States: A.D. 990–1990.* Cambridge: Basil Blackwell.

———. 1995. *Popular contention in Great Britain, 1758–1834.* Cambridge, Mass.: Harvard University Press.

———, ed. 1975. *The formation of national states in Western Europe.* Princeton: Princeton University Press.

Tokatlian, Juan, ed. 1998. *Colombia y Estados Unidos: Problemas y perspectivas.* Bogotá: Tercer Mundo.

Toranzo, Carlos. 1991. A manera de prólogo: Burguesía chola y señorialismo conflictuado. In *Max Fernández, la política del silencio,* ed. Fernando Mayorga, 13–29. La Paz: ILDIS/UMSS.

Torres, Aristedes. 1987. Los pobres y la justicia penal. In *Justicia y pobreza en Venezuela,* ed. Rogelio Pérez Perdomo. Caracas: Monte Avila Editores.

Touraine, Alain. 1993. *Crítica de la modernidad.* Madrid: Ediciones Temas de Hoy.

———. 1997. *What is democracy?* Boulder: Westview Press.

Tovar, Teresa. 1985. *Velasquismo y movimiento popular: Otra historia prohibida.* Lima: DESCO.

Tuesta Soldevilla. 1999. *El juego político: Fujimori, la oposición, y las reglas.* Lima: Friedrich Ebert.

Ugalde, Luis, et al. 1994. *La violencia en Venezuela.* Caracas: Monte Ávila Editores Latinoamericana-UCAB.

Uggen, John Forrest. 1975. Peasant mobilization in Ecuador: A case study of Guayas Province. Ph.D. diss., University of Miami.

UNICEF (United Nations Children's Fund). 1987. *The invisible adjustment: Poor women and the economic crisis.* Santiago: The Americas and the Caribbean Regional Office.

United States Department of State. 1990. Report to Congress on principal human rights concerns in Venezuela. Washington, D.C.: Department of State.

Valecillos, Héctor. 1992. *El reajuste neoliberal en Venezuela.* Caracas: Monte Ávila Editores.

Valenzuela, María Elena. 1998. Las mujeres y el poder: La acción estatal desde una perspectiva de género en Chile. In *Reflexiones teóricas y comparativas sobre los feminismos en Chile y América Latina,* ed. Marcela Ríus. Santiago: Corporación Editora Nacional/FLACSO/CERLAC.

Van Cott, Donna Lee. 2000. A political analysis of legal pluralism in Bolivia and Colombia. *Journal of Latin American Studies* 32.1: 207–34.

———, ed. 1994. *Indigenous peoples and democracy in Latin America.* New York: St. Martin's Press and Inter-American Dialogue.

Vargas, Virginia. 1992. *Cómo cambiar el mundo sin perdernos: El movimiento de mujeres en el Perú y America Latina.* Lima: Centro Flora Tristan.

Vega, Silvia. 1998. Asamblea nacional: Balance de la participacion de las mujeres y reflexiones para el futuro. Quito: Coordinadora Política de Mujeres Ecuatorianas/UNDP.

Vicepresidencia de la República de Colombia. 2000. *Panorama de los grupos de autodefensas.* Bogotá: Observatorio de DH and DIH.

Vidal, Ana María. 1993. *Los decretos de la guerra: Dos años de políticas antisubersivas y una propuesta de paz.* Lima: IDS.

Wade, Peter. 1997. *Race and ethnicity in Latin America.* Chicago: Pluto Press.

Walicki, Andrzej. 1969. Russia. In *Populism: Its meaning and national characteristics,* ed. Ghita Ionescu and Ernst Gellner. London: MacMillan.

Walker, William O., III. 1989. *Drug control in the Americas.* 2d ed. Albuquerque: University of New Mexico Press.

Walton, John. 1989. Debt, protest, and the state in Latin America. In *Power and popular protest in Latin America,* ed. Susan Eckstein. Berkeley: University of California Press.

Wankar, Ramiro Reynaga B. 1978. *Tawantinsuyu: Cinco siglos de guerra qheswaymara contra España.* La Paz: Centro de Coordinación and Promoción Campesina Mink'a.

Weyland, Kurt. 1996. Neopopulism and neoliberalism in Latin America: Unexpected affinities. *Studies in Comparative International Development* 31.3: 3–31.

Witthen, Norman, ed. 1981. *Cultural transformation and ethnicity in modern Ecuador.* Chicago: University of Illinois Press.

Witthen, Norman, Dorothea S. Whitten, and Alfonso Chango. 1997. Return of the Yumbos: The indigenous caminata from the Amazon to Andean Quito. *American Ethnologist* 24.2: 355–91.

World Bank. 1999. Ecuador at a glance. Available at <http://wbln0018.worldbank.org/external/lac/lac.nsf>.

Yampara, Simón, ed. 1993. *Naciones autóctona originarias: Vivir—convivir en tolerancia y diferencia.* La Paz: Centro Andino de Desarrollo Agropecuario.

Yashar, Deborah. 1999. Democracy, indigenous movements, and the postliberal challenge in Latin America. *World Politics* 52.1: 76–104.

Youngers, Coletta A. 2000. *Deconstructing democracy in Peru.* Washington, D.C.: Washington Office on Latin America.

Zabala, María Lourdes. 1995. *Nos/otras en democracia: Mineras, cholas, y feministas, 1976–1994.* La Paz: ILDIS.

———. 1999. *Mujeres, cuotas, y ciudadania en Bolivia.* La Paz: Coordinadora de la Mujer and UNICEF.

Zakaria, Fareed. 1997. The rise of illiberal democracy. *Foreign Affairs* 76.6: 22–44.

Zamosc, Leon. 1986. *The agrarian question and the peasant movement in Colombia.* Cambridge: Cambridge University Press.

———. 1989. *Peasant struggles and agrarian reform: The Ecuadorian sierra and the Colombian Atlantic coast in comparative perspective.* Meadville, Pa.: Allegheny College and the Department of History of the University of Akron.

———. 1993. Protesta agraria y movimiento indígena en la sierra ecuatoriana. In *Sismo étnico en el Ecuador: Varias perspectivas,* ed. José Almeida, Hernán Carrasco, Luz María de la Torre, Andrés Guerrero, et al. Quito: CEDIME and Abya-Yala.

———. 1994. Agrarian protest and the Indian movement in the Ecuadorian highlands. *Latin American Research Review* 29.3: 37–68.

———. 1995. *Estadística de las áreas de predominio étnico de la sierra ecuatoriana.* Quito: Abya-Yala.

Zirnite, Peter. 1997. *Reluctant recruits: The U.S. military and the war on drugs.* Washington, D.C.: The Washington Office on Latin America.

ᔔ Contributors

Xavier Albó is a native of Catalonia Spain who has resided in Bolivia since 1952. A Jesuit priest, Albó is cofounder and first director of the Centro de Investigación y Promoción del Campesinado (CIPCA), where he works as a researcher. He is the author of numerous books and articles, primarily on social, political, cultural, and linguistic issues of rural Bolivia and the Andean region. Some of his recent publications include "Andean People in the Twentieth Century," in *South America*, vol. 3 of *Cambridge History of the Native Peoples of the Americas*, ed. Frank Salomon and Stuart Schwartz (1999); and "Bolivia: From Indian and Campesino Leaders to Councillors and Parliamentary Leaders," in *Multiculturalism in Latin America: Indigenous Rights, Diversity and Democracy*, ed. Rachel Sieder (2002).

Jo-Marie Burt is assistant professor of government and politics at George Mason University. She was formerly editor of the North American Congress on Latin America's *NACLA Report on the Americas*, a bimonthly journal, and has published numerous journalistic and academic articles on Latin American politics, particularly on issues of political violence, democracy, and social movements. She is currently completing a manuscript entitled *Reform, Revolution, Reaction: Power and Politics in Peru, 1980–2000*.

Jennifer Collins is a doctoral candidate in political science at the University of California, San Diego. Her dissertation is on indigenous electoral participation in Ecuador and Bolivia.

Fernando Coronil, a Venezuelan citizen, teaches in the Departments of Anthropology and History at the University of Michigan. His research focuses on contemporary historical transformations in Latin America, and he has written extensively on theoretical issues concerning the state, modernity, and postcoloniality. His recent publications include *The Magical State: Nature, Money, and Modernity in Venezuela* (1997); the introduction to *Cuban Counterpoint: Tobacco and Sugar*, by Fernando Ortiz; "Beyond Occidentalism: Towards Non-Imperial Geohistorical Categories," *Cultural Anthropology* 11.1; and "Toward a Critique of Globalcentrism: Speculations on Capitalism's Nature," *Public Culture* 12.2. He is coeditor, with Julie Skurski, of *States of Violence* (in press).

Francisco Gutiérrez Sanin is a researcher at the Instituto de Estudios Políticos y Relaciones Internacionales at the Universidad Nacional de Colombia. He has written extensively on Colombia's political system. Recent publications include "¿Se ha abierto el sistema político colombiano? Una evaluación de los procesos de cambio (1970–1998)," *América Latina Hoy* 27; "Imitation Games and Political Discourse," *Forum: Qualitative Social Research* 2.1; and "Politicians and Criminals: Two Decades of Turbulence, 1978–98," *International Journal of Politics, Culture, and Society* 14.1.

Luis E. Lander teaches in the Department of Economic and Social Sciences at the Universidad Central de Venezuela, where he is also a doctoral candidate in the social sciences. He has written numerous articles on social and political issues in contemporary Venezuela, with a particular emphasis on the issue of oil policy. His most recent articles include "La apertura petrolera en Venezuela: De la nacionalización a la privatización," *Revista Venezolana de Economía y Ciencias Sociales* 4.1; "Globalización y mercado interno de los hidrocarburos en Venezuela," *Revista Venezolana de Economía y Ciencias Sociales* 4.2–3; and (with Margarita López Maya and Mark Ungar) "Economics, Violence, and Protest in Venezuela: A Preview of the Global Future?" in *Violence and Politics: Globalization's Paradox,* ed. Kenton Worcester, Sally Avery Bermanzohn, and Mark Ungar (2002).

Margarita López Maya is a professor and researcher at the Center for the Study of Development at Universidad Central de Venezuela. She is currently director of *Revista Venezolana de Economía y Ciencias Sociales.* Her research focuses on popular protest and new political actors in Venezuela. She is editor of *Lucha popular, democracia, y neoliberalismo: Protesta popular en América Latina en los años de ajuste* (1999) and author of several articles, including "Venezuela: Entre protestas y contraprotestas: El gobierno de Chávez se endurece y debilita," *Observatorio Social de América Latina* 4. She is coauthor, with Luis E. Lander and Mark Ungar, of "Economics, Violence, and Protest: A Preview of the Global Future?" in *Violence and Politics: Globalization's Paradox,* ed. Kenton Worcester, Sally Avery Bermanzohn, and Mark Ungar (2002).

Philip Mauceri is associate professor of political science at the University of Northern Iowa. He has been Fulbright Senior Specialist at the Pontificia Universidad Católica Madre y Maestra in the Dominican Republic (summer 2002); Fulbright Scholar at the Universidad de los Andes and Universidad Javeriana in Bogotá (spring 2001); Visiting Professor at the Universidad Simón Bolívar in Caracas (summer 1993); and a Visiting Scholar at the Instituto de Estudios Peruanos in Lima, Peru (1988–90). Among his publications are *State under Siege: Policy-Making and Development in Peru* (1996); *The Peruvian Labyrinth: Polity, Economy, and Society* (coedited with Max Cameron; 1997); and articles in *Latin American Research Review, Journal of Third World Studies,* and *Journal of Inter-American Studies.*

Liisa L. North is a professor of political science at York University and a Fellow of York's Centre for Research on Latin American and the Caribbean (CERLAC), where she has headed several international cooperation programs organized with the Quito-Ecuador campus of the Latin American Faculty of Social Sciences (FLACSO) and various Andean nongovernmental organizations. She has published work on party politics, civil-military relations, and development processes in Chile, Peru, and Ecuador; on the civil wars, United Nations peacekeeping missions, and human rights and refugee crises in El Salvador and Guatemala; and on Canadian–Latin American relations. Her articles have appeared in *Studies in Political Economy, Latin American Perspectives, Third World Quarterly, Ecuador Debate,* and *World Development,* among other journals.

Luisa Ramírez Rueda is a doctoral candidate in political psychology at the State University of New York–Stonybrook. She is trained as a psychologist and holds a master's degree in political science from the Universidad de los Andes.

Amy Lind is assistant professor of women's studies at Arizona State University. She has published articles and book chapters on gender, development, and women's movements in Latin America and globally. Currently she is completing a book manuscript entitled *Development Engendered: Women's Organizations and the Cultural Politics of Development in the Andes.*

Julie Skurski teaches in the Departments of Anthropology and History at the University of Michigan. Her research concerns the intersections of national, racial, and gender relations in Latin America and issues of global feminism. Her publications include "The Ambiguities of Authenticity in Latin America: *Doña Bárbara* and the Construction of National Identity," in *Becoming National,* ed. Geoffrey Eley and Ronald G. Suny (1996); and the coedited volume, with Fernando Coronil, *States of Violence* (in press). She is currently completing a book on gender and the state in Venezuela, *Civilizing Barbarism.*

Mark Ungar is associate professor of political science at Brooklyn College of the City University of New York. He is the author of *Elusive Reform: Democracy and the Rule of Law in Latin America* (2002) and coeditor and author of *Violence and Politics* (2001).

Ricardo Vargas is Associate Fellow for the Transnational Institute of Amsterdam. He also represents the regional organization Andean Action in Colombia. He is author of several articles on political violence and drug policy, including "The Anti-Drug Policy: Aerial Spraying of Illicit Crops and Their Social, Environmental, and Political Impacts in Colombia," *Journal of Drug Issues* 32.1; and "Illicit Crops,

Conflict, and the Peace Process," in *Plan Colombia: Critical Essays,* ed. Jairo Estrada (2001).

Coletta A. Youngers is a senior associate with the Washington Office on Latin America (WOLA), a nonprofit research and advocacy organization. She has written widely on human rights in the Andean region of Latin America and on U.S. international drug control policy. Her recent publications include *Violencia política y sociedad civil: La historia de la Coordinadora Nacional de Derechos Humanos* (2003); "U.S. Policy in Latin America and the Caribbean: Problems, Opportunities, and Recommendations," in *Global Focus: U.S. Foreign Policy at the Turn of the Millennium,* ed. Martha Honey and Tom Barry (2000); and *Deconstructing Democracy: Peru under President Alberto Fujimori* (2000).

Index